# PLAYWRITING

# Writing

## THE FIRST WORKSHOP

# Kathleen E. George

**Focal Press**
**Boston    London**

Focal Press is an imprint of Butterworth-Heinemann.

Library of Congress Cataloging-in-Publication Data

George, Kathleen
    Playwriting: the first workshop / Kathleen E. George.
      p.  cm.
    ISBN 0-240-80190-3
    1. Playwriting.  I. Title.
    PN1661.G45   1994
    808.2—dc20               93-34618
                         CIP

Butterworth-Heinemann
313 Washington Street
Newton, MA 02158

10  9  8  7  6  5  4  3  2  1

Printed in the United States of America

*For Hilary*

*I would like to thank all the students in the playwriting classes who have made my work so interesting. And I would like to especially thank those whose work is included here for sharing it with others. My gratitude goes to Jeff Bridge, Stan Denman, Lauri James Bolland, Karl Hendricks, Erin Flynn, Dave Drayer, Marcy Peterkofsky, Rick Van Noy, Judy Woodside, Megan Graham, Pamela G. McCready, Kirsta Bleyle, Punnasak Sukee, Min-Jiuan Wang Chen, Scott Sickles, Mary Hof, Sarabeth Sclove, and Gary Landis.*

—K.G.

# Contents

# Preface

## TO WRITERS WHO WILL USE THIS BOOK

Blossoming playwrights learn best by doing. All aspects of theatre are practical, and the first step, writing the play, is too. When you sit down and put on paper a title (e.g., *Autumn Sale*); a scene description (e.g., The living room of a dilapidated western Pennsylvania farmhouse); and a list of characters (e.g., Evan, 40, single; Louise, his mother); you are learning about plays and how they work.

In this book, I assume that 1) most writers would like to be comfortable with conventional form even if they eventually break with it, and 2) writers learn about writing by writing. Therefore this is an exercise book with sample exercises and text relating to those exercises. I've tried to make it as much as possible like a workshop on paper. I think the most natural way to learn about writing is this—examining what others, professional and non-professional, do, determining what you find successful, examining what you do, asking questions, noticing.

The book addresses people who are just beginning to write for the stage. It is intended for 1) people taking a first class in playwriting, 2) teachers interested in a new approach to courses in introduction to drama, 3) groups of people who want to form their own playwriting workshops, 4) individuals who want to write plays, and 5) people who are simply curious about how plays work. The writing exercises break down plays into basic elements: dialogue, monologue, pantomime.

We will study eight established plays, make our way through seven writing exercises, and analyze examples of the exercises written by others. The workshop experience—on paper, here, and hopefully in your life—is important because discussion, controversy, and disagreement about what works and what doesn't is crucial to developing your opinions. If you are not already a part of a class or a group, make efforts in that direction. In the meantime, I hope the workshop experience of the text will sustain you.

I will ask you to begin with short exercises. In all there are seven exercises, each with a different focus. The exercises get longer as you progress. They are

1. A scene with two characters and an object
2. A monologue
3. A pantomime sequence
4. A scene in which pantomime and dialogue are integrated
5. A scene in which conflict leads to a moment or moments of decision
6. A finished short script, or "playlet"
7. A one-act play or part of a longer play

The first few chapters are preparation for these exercises. The remaining chapters use sample exercises and established plays to call up subjects for discussion.

The greatest ingredient in writing cannot be taught. That is the uniqueness of the individual writer, the voice that is unlike any other voice.

You are about to begin. How will you begin to find your unique voice? There is no magic formula, but it helps to first ask yourself what you care about, what your values are. You must find your own voice and determine your own concerns. Asking yourself a few key questions will help you identify your feelings. What makes you angriest? What makes you happiest? What is your definition of a good life? What is your concept of a spiritual dilemma? What do you care about? What would you risk your life for? What makes you laugh? If you will take the time to seriously answer these questions, you will have many ideas for things you might want to write about, ideas with emotions behind them. To give yourself a good start, sit down and devote a section of your journal to each of the questions above. You may not write about the most powerful of these subjects in your first exercise. You may want to get used to the form of drama first—stretching your muscles, so to speak, getting ready to play. But writing about what matters to you most is the way to find your voice, the way to write what others pay attention to.

## TO TEACHERS WHO CONSIDER THIS BOOK FOR CLASSROOM USE

This book is conversational, discursive, and highly personal. My intention is to help aspiring playwrights begin writing and reflecting on what they are writing by fostering an awareness of traditional devices and their uses. I recognize that there are many other methods of beginning. This is mine. If you are *primarily* interested in *avant garde* drama and in redefining the limits of drama, this book may not serve your needs. Although several writers who begin with the following exercises in conventional playwriting eventually write in unconventional forms (and I use some of those exercises as text material here), over half of my examples are fairly traditional.

If, however, you would like to give your students exercises in conventional playwriting—always with an eye to the ways old devices may be used by individuals in new ways—this book will hopefully be helpful. Its main premise is that writers develop by writing and by talking about writing. To that end, it is as much as possible a workshop on paper, intended to get another workshop, a living one, started.

Secondary premises are: 1) Writers may not be able to tap what they want to write about, to identify what matters most to them, when they are worried about the historical characteristics of the form; therefore to know those characteristics is empowering. 2) Often the deepest feelings have to be coaxed out or nudged out and this is more possible when writers feel confident with some of the mechanics of the form in which they wish to write. (I remember with pleasure the exercises in fiction that John Gardner put to the developing writer of fiction. How consistently people surprised themselves with what they knew! How

often whole stories sprang from small exercises in point of view or description!) 3) Learning by writing exercises and by becoming aware of traditional form does not necessarily keep people from writing in innovative ways, but only makes them more sure, if they choose to construct something unconventional, that they *could* have approached the material in other ways, that they had a choice.

My own bias is evident in the established plays I've chosen to use as examples. Most are departures from realism and from logical progression, but they are plays with a foot or a toe in realism. Most are odd and have something complex to say, and yet for the most part they have been successful in critical and commercial terms—and they continue to be done. I am most attracted to plays that maintain a tension between traditional and non-traditional form. The contemporary plays I deal with are the offspring (it seems to me, on reflection) of Chekhov's plays. For Chekhov is *my* ideal playwright for many reasons, all of which are essentially personal.

So, is my bias "conventional" or "unconventional"? I'm inclined to agree with Michael Vanden Heuvel that polarizing often gets in the way of meaning. And progress. He writes, "Among a small but growing faction of theatre artists, in fact, there is evident an emerging, very self-conscious awareness that polarizing the epistemes of text and performance, and the theatrical practices they designate, is ultimately unproductive ... Instead today's artists often seek the means to break down and dissolve the two categories, and to investigate new relations between them." ("Complementary Spaces: Realism, Performance and a New Dialogics of Theatre," *Theatre Journal* [March 1992]: 52)

It is my hope that the exercises in this book will help the developing writer (whether "modernist/postmodernist, traditional/experimental, representational/nonrepresentational, realist/nonrealist" [Vanden Heuvel, 51–2] at heart) find confidence and sources of material she perhaps did not even know she possessed.

# Introduction

## WHO SAYS WHAT TO WHOM AND WHY?

Because drama so often depicts people talking to other people, it seems easy to understand, and it looks simple to write. Drama is, in fact, not so easy to write. Even though there are situations, even other art forms, which are *like* theatre, nothing at all makes the vigorous demands on *dialogue* that drama does. Why? Because the dialogue is not just talk, not conversation as we know it in our lives, but is the action of the play. Syd Field defines a film as "a story told with pictures." (*Screenplay* [New York: Dell, 1982], 7) Of course he knows it's more than that. How many films depend upon brilliant dialogue? How many films have narrators who in voice-overs add a perspective to what you are seeing? But with his notion of film as a series of pictures, he startles us into understanding that no matter how many other elements contribute to the overall effect of a film, it has to be renderable in pictures.

In much the same way, drama—writing for the stage—is limited too. No matter how visual your script, no matter how many exceptions to the rule come to mind (Beckett's pantomime dramas do, here), no matter how visually splendid the story is, the bulk of drama in the Western world is this: a story told in terms of who says what to whom. Dialogue. And the dialogue is the action. If we think of a play as a story told in terms of who tries to change the status quo by talking to whom, it becomes clear why scenes in plays are most often built of characters urging, persuading, manipulating others. If we notice that in plays the status quo is not easy to change, it gives us some idea of why most plays are about lying or pretending.

And in most plays, much of the urging, persuading, and manipulating of one character by another has financial consequences. A great deal of Western drama amounts to a treasure hunt *for* something that has monetary value (many comedies of marriage fall into this category) or a battle *over* something with monetary value (certainly many tragedies and serious dramas depict this lust for the finite pleasures of ownership, of power).

Drama, for the most part, is built on who says what to whom, and usually something changes ownership in the process. Whether it's the bank loan of David Hare's *A Map of the World* or the cherry orchard of Chekhov's *The Cherry Orchard*, something changes hands. In a complex play, this exchange of something with monetary value signals other, more important human conflicts and values.

These simple characteristics describe most of the drama we know. We could throw away what is old, as Treplev tried to do in the early acts of *The Sea Gull*, because all that is old or standard seems to go against the very nature of the artistic impulse. But we can also study standard practice, learn its virtues, and figure out how to breathe new life into it.

# First Words

## OVERVIEW

This chapter will prepare you to begin writing. We will raise and reflect upon the following questions: What makes drama unique? How do plays work? How is theatre like and unlike film? We will look further into three ideas: that in plays dialogue *is* the action; that almost all plays are about some form of lying and pretending; and that most plays amount to a treasure hunt for something with monetary value or a war over something with monetary value. Are there advantages to the playwright in using these patterns?

We will look at the basics of formatting drama on the page; explore ways of visualizing the stage when you write; and take a look at a first try at dialogue to determine what helps give it tension. At the end of the chapter are twenty principles, or characteristics, of play construction that you can use as a checklist for problem solving.

## OBJECTIVES

At the end of this chapter you should be able to

- Describe how plays are similar to and different from other story forms
- Begin to visualize the stage you will write for
- Write some exploratory dialogue and scene descriptions

### The Playwright as Magician

Theatre has enormous power. You buy a ticket and go to see a play. There you are—your concentration is scattered, you're full from dinner or hungry and looking forward to an after-theatre supper. You've got a program in your hand that you try to read, but the people sliding into your row keep interrupting you. The program lists the characters who will appear in this drama, and tells you what the setting (place or places of the action) will be. You look toward the stage. There are lights on the set, not bright, but intriguing, enough for you to be able to examine the place. Suddenly, the atmosphere fills with music or some other organized sound, the lights dim, the people around you begin to get quiet, stage lights fade to black and then come up, and boom! People begin to talk as if what is happening on the stage is much more important than anything in your life. Far more important than your dinner plans. Or your personal life. Or your own history. And you forget all those things about yourself and give yourself to the events on stage, only to know more about yourself and your own personal history at the end, only—if the play and the production are really good—to have forgotten whether you are hungry or full. Theatre has often been compared to magic, and the playwright to a magician . . . hypnotist . . . wizard . . . dream maker.

### Society's Mirror

Playwrights tend to be watchful people. They have an eye upon the society of their day. They absorb its problems, its political and human rights struggles, its personality. But good playwrights are not just news reporters. They are also critics and philosophers who examine a society with an eye to what makes current struggles like the struggles that have always faced human beings, as well as what makes them different. Many people believe that an effective playwright is less likely to preach than lead, less likely to tell than show. For me, personally, this is true. Holding a mirror up to nature, a mirror that allows people to see and understand, is, I believe, a great accomplishment.

1

## The Play: What Plays Are Like

As I've said before, a play is not a particularly easy thing to write, but most people feel comfortable talking about plays they have seen. Even first-time playgoers have strong opinions. Why is it that plays are so hard to create and so easy to criticize? Because they are familiar to us in deep ways. They are *like* life—like what happens to us in the kitchen, in the living room, in the classroom. People talking to people. And they are also like dreams, the stirrings and imaginings of nighttime, when the subconscious weaves strange tales, comes up with strange images, when characters—the dreamer and the dreamer's cast of characters—are striving to do something that is difficult to do. For isn't that striving the basis of most dreams? And of most plays?

Plays are also *like* worship services—with many watching and a few people in symbolic clothing chanting or speaking. Plays are *like* classrooms—someone moving, gesturing, persuading; a group watching, wondering, judging. And they are like competitive sports in which players, like Montagues and Capulets, wear color-coded costumes, wage a contest between two sides, strain under a set of rules and limitations. I can't go to a baseball game without seeing the drama of it. I sit, as if at a Greek amphitheatre, watching the tight focus on the diamond, the larger picture on the whole field. A good game, is, after all, one that maintains tension—whether it is the quiet tension of a pitching duel or the noisier tension of a high-score game with its many ups and downs and reversals.

Plays are stories—and as such hold some ground in common with television plays, movies, novels, and short stories. Why then are good plays for the legitimate theatre so rare? Why are they so challenging to write? Why do successful novelists and short-story writers, poets and screenwriters, often feel like novices when they try to write plays?

Because effective plays are also *unlike* most lessons of the classroom, most rituals of the church, and most other storytelling forms.

## How Plays Differ from Other Forms They Resemble

In most classrooms the teacher stands alone, not in conflict, unless it is with the class or with some abstract concept. And in church, the clergyman relates to others at the altar in nonconflictive ways. There is no argument between clergyman and altar boys (at least there isn't supposed to be), no final end to the conflict expected by all who watch. On the sports field, if there is dialogue, it's at a minimum, it isn't written, and it's usually not meant to be overheard. The contest is physical. Plays differ from these other formal settings in significant ways. They are sometimes most like the most heightened incidents of our lives—the ones in which we and others have battled over something or for something. The *seeds* of plays can be found in our lives and in our dreams. And yet plays are not transcriptions of life. They are written, organized, given a style and rhythm. We *expect* them to be more heightened, more interesting than life, more meaningful.

Plays differ too from television plays, movies, novels, and short stories. They are written for a stage. To be performed by live actors in a fixed space before an audience.

There are many kinds of stages. Some resemble churches, classrooms, football fields. Most are indoor spaces and follow one of three arrangements: proscenium, thrust, or arena (Figure 1.1).

Most everybody has been in a big old proscenium theatre—in high school or at the ballet. There is a spacial division between the audience and the stage. The whole audience looks at the stage from one direction. In a thrust, a portion of the audience looks at the stage and the rest of the audience as well. The performing space thrusts out into the audience. In an arena, the audience surrounds or nearly surrounds the stage.

## Visualizing a Stage

Perhaps the greatest single problem among those beginning to write for the stage is forgetting the stage itself. Forgetting to see it. Try to imagine yourself in a theatre looking at a stage. Ask yourself, "What can happen in that stage space?"

When Susan Glaspell's husband insisted she write a play for the Provincetown Players, she told him she did not know how to write a play because she had never studied playwriting. And yet she had two summers at Provincetown behind her and had just brought Eugene O'Neill and his work to the theatre. She says that her husband told her, "Nonsense.... You've got a stage, haven't you?" This was her beginning. "I went out on the wharf, sat alone on one of our wooden benches without a back, and looked a long time at that bare little stage. After a time, the stage became a kitchen—a kitchen there all by itself.... Then the door at the back opened, and people all bundled up came in—two or three men, I wasn't sure which, but sure enough about the two women who hung back, reluctant to enter that kitchen." (Susan Glaspell, *The Road to the Temple* [New York: Frederick Stokes, 1927], 255–56. Cited in Linda Ben-Zvi, " 'Murder She Wrote': The Genesis of Susan Glaspell's *Trifles*," *Theatre Journal* 44 (May 1992): 142–143.)

And thus, in 1916, Glaspell wrote *Trifles*, a play based on a murder case she covered when she was a reporter in Iowa years earlier. Certain details of the case stuck in her memory. One was the kitchen of the woman who was held prisoner. When Glaspell became stuck in her writing, she would walk over to the theatre and let the stage space conjure for her. (Ben-Zvi, 143)

To illustrate what can happen when a writer doesn't see the stage clearly, let me tell you about a conversation I had. I'll tell it in play form to get you started thinking about characters, setting, dialogue. As I've said, many things are *play-like*. Just as we've all seen labels that say "peanut-butter-like flavor" or "strawberry-like jam," and found that the product was a little off, not quite full-bodied, we might very well find that many dialogues seem like drama, but don't have the bite we associate with it.

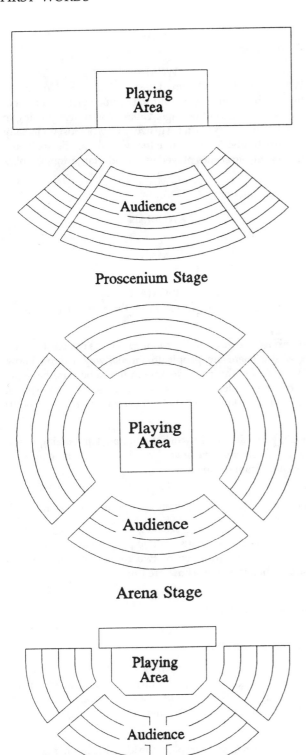

**Figure 1.1** Reprinted from Milly S. Barranger, *Theatre Past and Present* (Wadsworth Publishing Company, Belmont, CA, 1984), p. 5.

## The Repairman

CHARACTERS

MAN, a computer repairman

WOMAN, a teacher

*(Lights up on basement room with desk. On desk is a computer. WOMAN is sitting at the desk chair, but a little to the side. MAN is bending over the desk fiddling with computer parts.)*

MAN
*(putting bolts, covers, clamps, back on, back together)* I took a drama course in school where we read a whole bunch of plays. I like plays. I even have a great idea for one. I mean a *great* idea.

WOMAN
*(handing him the mouse to a Macintosh)* Terrific! There's nothing like live theatre, is there?

MAN
No. It's a fun thing. I wrote a play too. My play was really good. Really good. My teacher really liked it.

WOMAN
Oh, tell me about it! You actually wrote a play for your drama class? An intro to drama class? *(He nods.)* That's a wonderful assignment.

MAN
Yeah. Well, it was this saloon, western, you know. And in the upstairs of it there was a guy in one room and a woman in the other room, and she looked into a mirror—she felt real bad about herself—but she fixed up her hair and tried to keep going. You know, cheerful.

WOMAN
Yes. *(a pause)*

MAN
That's about it.

WOMAN
Ah. What did she say?

MAN
She didn't say anything. And the man in the next room looked right through the wall, right through the mirror and it's as if she could feel him looking. She got more confident, started to feel better about herself.... *(He presses several buttons. The computer sings its familiar notes.)* Here, this is going now.

WOMAN
Wonderful. And then what? Listen, can you make out a bill for me?

MAN
*(crossing to a briefcase, getting out papers and pen)* Well, he loved her. And she really changed ... Hey, I don't know. Are you trying to steal this from me?

WOMAN
(*laughing*) No. If you want to copyright it, I can give you the address. No. I'm just curious.

MAN
Really?

WOMAN
Yes, really. I want to know how he changes her life, what happens when they meet.

MAN
I don't know. I mean, what do you want to know? Are you sure you're not trying to steal this?

WOMAN
(*nods*) Sure. All I meant was, does he come to her *knowing* she's a prostitute and falling in love with her anyway? Or does he meet her some other way?

MAN
They don't meet.

WOMAN
How do they speak to each other?

MAN
They don't. What's the address here?

WOMAN
822 Summerlea. (*confused*) Whom do they speak to then?

MAN
(*thinking*) The guy orders a drink from a waitress. The woman gets a visit from a john.

WOMAN
Well, that could be interesting. You mean the whole thing moves by simultaneous actions. Um-hum. Does the waitress stay on? Is there an extended scene?

MAN
No, she just takes his drink order.

WOMAN
(*trying to get his attention*) Does anybody have a conversation of any length?

MAN
No. . . . What do you mean?

WOMAN
Sounds kind of quiet for a play.

MAN
Well, no, there's a lot of stuff going on in the saloon.

WOMAN
The saloon is on stage?

MAN
Yeah, it's the first floor.

WOMAN
(*warming to her task*) But why do you have to show it? What does it have to do with the cowboy and the prostitute?

MAN
It's the atmosphere.

WOMAN
Why not do that with crowd noises? And music? You really have to think twice before putting a saloon or a restaurant or a crowded bus on the stage. Unless you're really going to use it. You see, it's wasteful in every way, not just financially, but artistically. A big set like that would only be justified if there were big scenes played in it. And a large, longish play.

MAN
You owe me $47.12.

WOMAN
Check okay?

MAN
Yeah.

WOMAN
Tell me again what you see. From the beginning.

MAN
(*thinking*) The guy gets his room. He cleans up. Sits there for a while. There are people in the hallway. I don't know. Waitresses with drinks. People in the saloon are having a good time. Ordering drinks. Then there's the woman in her room. I don't know. What else do you want to know about?

WOMAN
Well, your idea might work if you had some dialogue and some . . . (*becomes caught up in writing check*) help, maybe, to put it in dramatic form.

MAN
(*joking weakly*) You just want a cut of it, don't you? Huh?

WOMAN
No, no. Just a scene between two people somewhere along the way. I like the idea of two rooms on stage. And a simultaneous action. Those are fun.

MAN
It's been done before?

WOMAN
Just about everything has.

MAN
Not mine. The woman looks into the mirror. And the mirror is the guy. And they don't need a scene because it turns out it's a dream. He's dreaming her. And he changes her.

WOMAN
(*showing man to the door*) Now the idea that he changes her I like. You're closer to a play when you talk about feeling and change. But I don't think you need the dream effect. I don't have much time to explain this, but it's one of those easy outs. And besides, a play is like a dream. Look, I promise I won't steal it. Thanks for telling me about your idea. And thanks for fixing my computer. I can't live for too long without it. Thanks. Bye.

MAN

So I should send it to you?

WOMAN

If you want. I think it needs work. I'd have to read it to be *sure. . . .*

MAN

I'll send it. I've got your address right here. *(thinking)* I hope I can *find* it. Bye. Take care.

WOMAN

Bye now. *(Leans against door, looks at computer, worries.)*

It's not that the computer repairman's idea could never work. But it is in the early stages—just a germ of an idea. And somehow not an idea in which the stage was taken very much into account. Why? This writer is not alone.

Sometimes the contemporary playwright has in mind (in the vision of the inner eye) something that is much more suited to film than to the stage. This is a malady only sixty or seventy years old, but it is almost epidemic. Without quite realizing it, a writer meaning to write for the stage is hearing film underscoring and seeing changes of camera angles. Sometimes the camera pans in to a closeup of one of his characters; at other times, the camera takes in the whole room; sometimes the camera stops to catch a tiny gesture or reaction. When the focus of a scene continues to shift, I suspect the writer has forgotten the stage.

Another indicator is lack of dialogue. A film can go on for long periods of time without dialogue. Most films do— because the story is being told in pictures. But most plays are stories told in dialogue. Long periods of silence on stage are hard to pull off. We'll discuss sustained pantomimic actions in a later chapter—and they're fun to do—but it's pretty much the human voice that drives most plays.

The computer repairman was seeing a film. His camera swept over the men in the bar and dismissed them. Then another camera caught a cowboy on the stairs going to his room. Then another camera showed a silent sequence in a woman's bedroom. Maybe the cowboy (camera now on him) hears a sound from the room next door, looks alert, thinks about who might be there. Then the shot changes back to the woman in the room next door. She is taking money from a john. The john leaves. She looks into the mirror. There is a sound from next door. She looks alert. Next we go back to the man's room where we see him order a bottle of whiskey from a waitress, all the while looking distracted as he thinks about and wonders about the imaginary woman (imaginary to him) in the next room. The camera probably focuses on his face in order to report his inner life of imagination. And what we've got is under a minute of film.

If we tried to put this on stage (cut the saloon and replaced it with sound effects, showed two rooms at once with an invisible wall between, the man paying for a drink, saying "Thanks" to the waitress, and the john paying the woman, saying "See you, Rosie"), we'd have geared the

action to a stage instead of a screen, but we'd still have only a minute's worth of drama. Suppose the man fell in love with an image of the woman on the other side of the room, and while he did, she "felt" it, combed her hair and looked into the mirror and felt loved. Another minute maybe.

## Sustained Dialogue

A play will generally tell its story with dialogue based on the interaction between characters—interaction of substantial length. It's very tempting to change the place (or the camera angle) after a few exchanges. But plays depend on extended interaction through words. Pick up a copy of Ibsen's collected works and notice how long he keeps the drama going in one room. Or take a look at the plays of Chekhov, Tennessee Williams, Harold Pinter, Sam Shepard, David Hare. Notice the particular pressure of keeping an action in only one place, as Shepard does in *True West* or as Williams does in *A Streetcar Named Desire*. The fact that people *can't* move is one of the most used pressures of drama.

Not all story ideas are right for the stage. Almost anything is possible with imagination, but the challenges of putting an internal and highly cerebral action on stage are advanced ones. Most ideas for the stage are ideas in which conflict is externalized and in which dialogue contains dramatic tension.

## Indirection in Dramatic Dialogue

When a story idea is suited to conventional dramatic action, the words will be the means by which tension is maintained because in what is spoken is hidden something unspoken. The words will not tell the story directly. The situation will likely be one in which someone is lying or pretending—to others and maybe to himself too. Theatre has been made for many centuries from stories based on lies and hidden meanings. Why has this been so consistent? Perhaps one answer is that pretense is at the core of drama.

## *Pretense as an Element of Drama*

Any art form is a combination of its subject and its materials. The sculptor makes a flying bird or a reclining man of iron or stone. The materials are part of the image, part of the irony.

What are the materials of theatre? What impels people to make walls of canvas and wood, rocks of Styrofoam, snow of paper—or snow that is a trick of lighting? The scene designer makes cloth look like trees; the costume designer distresses new shirts to make them look like old, worn woolens; the lighting designer makes the lights (seen on a person's face) look like the setting sun streaming through the window. The actor makes a nervous breakdown look real and goes off ten minutes later for a few beers with his pals. The materials of theatre are the materials of pretense. The whole art form has been a "let's pretend" game and the form itself is reflected in the subject. Characters pretend. They lie about something.

In most productions, in most aspects of production, some things are real and some are make-believe. Furniture, weapons, bits of jewelry *may* be quite real. But something will probably be false. In fact, what interests the theatre practitioner—this includes playwrights—is the combination of the real and the fake, the combination of reality and fantasy. It would be difficult to find many plays of any consequence that don't resonate with these questions: Does the character mean what she is saying? Is the situation, gesture, line, "the truth or a lie"? If character A said one thing to character B and another to character C, which is true?

## Lying and Pretending

In other words, plays are not only done in a pretend setting, but they tend to be about pretending. About lies. About deceptions—self-deceptions as well as intentional deceptions of all sorts.

I'll name a few plays as they come to mind and let's see if lying and pretending aren't at the center. *Othello, Hamlet, The Playboy of the Western World, Ghosts, Six Characters in Search of an Author, Oedipus, Waiting for Godot, Glengarry Glen Ross, The Sea Gull, The Homecoming.* Name as many others as you like and I think you will see the pattern.

Some more recent plays that come to mind are *American Buffalo, Speed the Plow, Bent, Aunt Dan and Lemon, Coastal Disturbances,* and *Prelude to a Kiss.* Many plays are driven by questions of truth and falseness, appearance and reality, deception. Why do people pretend? Why do they lie to themselves and others, and become mired in situations of great complexity? Simply, in most cases, because something is at stake. Something matters. A lot. And it can't be dealt with easily or directly.

The "something at stake" should reflect values. And yet, for the purpose of focusing action, it is often a concrete thing to be fought over, gained, won. That prize is of great importance to the characters. We will refer to it as *the treasure.* In Western drama, it almost invariably has financial value.

## *The Treasure*

There is a treasure in most plays—a thing valued— something to be fought over—a prize worth the struggle. Often, almost always, it has a physical manifestation on stage. And some issue of money surrounds it. While at first it seems shallow to build plays on financial decisions, it turns out that many plays of great power get at other values by showing decisions that have to do with money, the value of worldly goods (*King Lear, Hedda Gabler, Uncle Vanya, Cat on a Hot Tin Roof, The Piano Lesson*). Ask yourself what has financial value in your life. Other values will come into play in your answer.

In A. R. Gurney's play *The Dining Room,* scene after scene takes place around the dining room table, which rep-resents the whole dining room (not seen), and that single room represents family, tradition, a whole way of life. Characters argue over the value of the room, and specifically of the table; some want to get rid of it, some want to buy it, some want to keep it, some want to ease painful thoughts or terrible memories by sitting there, in the dining room, where they feel safe and happy. The dining room table is the focus of most scenes and is the treasure at the center of the play. It can be bought or sold or lost. It costs something.

In *Table Manners,* by Alan Ayckbourn, food is the treasure at the center of the play. Characters argue about the food, of which there is not enough, and of which the quality is poor, while they also try to pursue other comforts (sexual pleasure, vacations, a rest in the country, a good sleep). The food stands for everything else, all the other things that they can't seem to get. Who was responsible for bringing food, buying food? Why does no one actually provide it? The play is about the promise of sustenance of all sorts that doesn't materialize.

In *Home,* by David Storey, the four main characters take positions at an outdoor metalwork table and chairs while a fifth character tries to take the chairs away. How can it be so hard to find a place to sit, to gain the comfort of a seat at the table? The table and chairs represent "home," or a place of rest. The characters, all deeply troubled, cannot rest, cannot keep a sustained place in society. They vie for the table and chairs. The table and chairs are the treasure—representing much larger values.

In David Mamet's *American Buffalo,* the characters fight over a nickel that is possibly a collector's item and may be worth a lot more than a nickel. All of the actions of the play revolve around the possession of, sale of, search for, and pursuit of that nickel. What the play is really about is the value of human relationships and the value of trust— much bigger issues than coin-collecting!—but the play is accomplished by the use of the nickel as a symbol, a treasure. The treasure in a successful play represents something else. But it focuses the action. Plays can become "talky" (the opposite of action-filled) and they nearly always fall into vagueness when there aren't decisions to be made that cost something.

## *What's at Stake?*

One way to get at the question "what's at stake?" in a play is to ask what has monetary value and then ask what that represents.

Where would the action of *Hamlet* be without the throne of Denmark at stake? In most productions of *Hamlet,* the throne, a piece of furniture, appears on stage and has great symbolic significance: Claudius sits on the throne when the courtroom is full and the elders of Denmark accept his sovereignty; Hamlet sits on the throne when he is alone. Hamlet curses at the empty throne but does not confront Claudius. At the end of the play, when Hamlet is dying, many an actor playing him has climbed up onto the throne to die. The throne symbolizes not only personal power, revenge, the truth revealed, but also political power and ownership.

Where would Christy Mahon be without believing in the pub (or shebeen) as a possible future life for him, away from the toil of the farmland? Yes, of course, he wants Pegeen, the pub-keeper's daughter—and a marriage to Pegeen will signify to the world that he is a successful man, no longer a foolish boy. But, for the purposes of the action, the pub equals Pegeen. If he wins the girl, he wins the place, and vice versa. It's the right to be in that space—the pub—that governs the scenes of the play. It is important and symbolic that Pegeen's intended, Shawn Keogh, is afraid to stay alone in the pub with her. In the case of **Playboy of the Western World**, the setting itself is the treasure, and a terrific metaphor for the sexual politics of the play.

Ibsen's *Ghosts* depends on the Alving inheritance, Chekhov's *The Cherry Orchard* depends upon the value of the cherry orchard. And so on.

Sometimes there are scenes in which it is appropriate to have characters discuss the object itself (the treasure) and sometimes the treasure exists on stage, governing the action, without being mentioned by the characters. Sometimes the treasure is talked about without being seen. All of these ways of dealing with what's at stake are possible. A director will invariably ask, "What is being hunted, fought over, valued by the characters of this play?"

Sometimes the hint for *what's at stake* will come through in your setting. It doesn't have to. But it might.

Before we go on, let's take a moment to evaluate the dramatic qualities of the script I'm calling **The Repairman**. The incident it dramatizes is play-like in that characters are trying to affect each other through dialogue. The dialogue is not quite direct; there are hidden motives and hidden meanings. The woman (based on me, but because she's a character, not me) is at first curious about the man's interest in drama, then subsequently curious about his notion of a romantic story in which a man's love changes a woman. But eventually she is caught up in the fact that what he's calling a play would be very difficult to produce. She wants to point this out to him. At first, the man wants to impress the woman; then he wants to get a good contact for his script— a person who will read it and maybe produce it.

But this real-life situation lacks dramatic tension for several reasons. In both characters, the motivation is weak: what they want comes about accidentally as a reaction to what just happened (the repair of the computer). There is not a great deal at stake. The man has no real drive to get his play produced. (He doesn't even know where he put it!) The meeting between these two is happenstance. The characters have no history and no future of note. Whatever actions either character takes, there will be no serious repercussions. What passes between them is not special—not, in workshop terms, enough of an "occasion" or an "event" to set this day apart from any other day. Another way to think about this is that there is not enough at stake.

## Settings

In your first assignment, and all the others, you will have to specify a setting for your action. This is the beginning step in your visualizing a stage and what it holds. You might want to leaf through books of plays and see what other playwrights do to describe settings. Here are a few examples.

From A. R. Gurney's *The Dining Room*:
*The play takes place in a dining room—or rather, many dining rooms. The same dining room furniture serves for all: a lovely, burnished, shining dining room table; two chairs, with arms, at either end; two more, armless, along each side; several additional matching chairs, placed so as to define the walls of the room. Upstage somewhere, a sideboard, with a mirror over it . . . [The lack of detail and the wall-lessness of the room should] suggest a limbo outside the dining room.* (New York: Dramatists Play Service, 1982, 5)

From *Home* by David Storey:
*The stage is bare but for a round metalwork table, set slightly off-center, L., and two metalwork chairs.* (New York: Samuel French, Inc., 1971, 5)

From *Happy Days* by Samuel Beckett:
*Expanse of scorched grass rising center to low mound. Gentle slopes down to front and either side of stage. Back an abrupter fall to stage level. Maximum of simplicity and symmetry.*
*Blazing light.*
*Very pompier trompe-l'oeil backcloth to represent unbroken plain and sky receding to meet in far distance.*
*Imbedded up to above her waist in exact center of mound, WINNIE.* (New York: Grove Press, 1961, 7)

From *Old Times* by Harold Pinter:
*A converted farmhouse.*
*A long window up center. Bedroom door up left. Front door up right.*
*Spare modern furniture. Two sofas. An armchair.*
*Autumn. Night.*
*Light dim. Three figures discerned.*
*Deeley slumped in armchair, still.*
*Kate curled on a sofa, still.*
*Anna standing at the window, looking out.* (New York: Grove Press, 1971, 6–7)

From *Glengarry Glen Ross* by David Mamet:
*A booth at a Chinese restaurant. Williamson and Levene are seated at the booth.* (New York: Grove Press, 1983, 1)

You have probably noticed that experienced playwrights do not design the whole setting. They sketch it. They sketch it powerfully with words, letting the designer do the rest. If the correct few words are used to describe a setting, the designer will know what to do. Notice the formality *in the description* of the dining room for **The Dining Room**. Notice the relationship of people to furniture in **Old Times**. Notice the way Winnie is swallowed up in the description of the set, much as she is swallowed up *in* the set, for **Happy Days**.

Think about setting your own stage briefly, cogently. Here are some possibilities for sets for imaginary plays:

*An ordinary living room.* The playwright who goes on to describe an ordinary living room is in danger of boring his reader and potential producer before the action of the play even gets started. If it's ordinary, it's ordinary. There is *no* need to say: *couch and two matching chairs in green and gold striped upholstery. Coffee table of walnut. Two end tables. Some lamps. A bookcase with a few books.*

However, if you want an ordinary living room with a special feature, say a large upstage window (and if you want a large upstage window you should want it for some reason to do with the action, not just because your own home had one!), you are already suggesting that the house is not an old house because they don't come with single large windows unless they've been remodelled. Are you picturing a thirty-year-old house? You should say

*An ordinary living room in a split-level house. Large window upstage.*

Here is another example. Imagine your play is set in a restaurant kitchen. You must let us know what kind of restaurant it serves:

*A restaurant kitchen: three old kitchen stoves, a counter for preparations.* Or

*A restaurant kitchen: a wall of gleaming state-of-the-art ovens and other equipment.*

If you set a play in the kitchen of a home, tell us only what's important about this kitchen:

*A kitchen. It is dirty. Dishes on the table, in the sink, on the counter. Chaos. Notes on the refrigerator, a broom propped against the table.*

Be sure to choose details that you will *use* in your play. This set description suggests there will be action regarding the notes on the refrigerator, action with the broom. When you put things on stage, they beg to be used. What the playwright describes of the setting should be useful, not decorative.

If you don't want small details, if you are writing something which requires broad strokes, you might ask for an almost bare stage with a few memorable props. Imagine, for instance, a political play set in an unspecified locale, because your focus is the debate between characters. Perhaps you see the following:

*Stage bare except for three colorful, but unidentifiable, flags on stands. In front of them, two ordinary ladder-back chairs.*

You can suggest the focus of your play with your set description. For instance:

*A college classroom. Six chairs represent many more. The lectern is old, good solid oak, and it shines.*

This tells me a great deal. The play will not show a realistic number of students: there will be a strong focus on the teacher, a romanticized or ideal focus, it appears, from the gleaming podium.

Perhaps you want to write *Lectern usr (upstage right) and six chairs dsl (downstage left)*. Be sure to be careful with stage directions about the *placement* of objects. Don't go too far in specifying arrangements on stage unless you have a really good reason for your design. And make sure, if you do have a good reason, that you use terms accurately. For instance, don't say *backstage* when you mean *upstage*. Remember that *upstage* is the part of the stage away from the audience and *downstage* is the part of the stage nearest the audience. We're talking here about a standard proscenium or thrust arrangement. *Stage right* is the *actor's* right and *stage left* is the *actor's* left. So that looking at the stage from the point of view of the audience, which is what you will do if you are visualizing a stage, you have right and left reversed (Figure 1.2).

| upstage right (UR) | upstage center (UC) | upstage left (UL) |
|---|---|---|
| right (R) | center (C) | left (L) |
| downstage right (DR) | downstage center (DC) | downstage left (DL) |

**Figure 1.2** When using stage directions, be certain that you have the areas of the stage correct.

As for backstage, that means behind the scenery, where the actors wait to make entrances and where the props crew hands out props, etc.

The setting is important to your work, no doubt about it. And you may want to control every inch of it. But practice suggesting the setting with as few words as possible. Make your set description work for you. The character of your language will suggest the character of your set.

## Imagining Characters

Now for your characters: the people of your play. Your characters—who will inhabit the set and engage in a treasure-hunt or treasure-war through dialogue—should be your main inspiration. If you don't care about your characters, the audience won't. And if you don't care about your characters, you won't get very interested in the play you're writing. There is a great deal to say about characters and characterization. Throughout this whole book we will be talking about characters, what makes them tick, what makes them interesting, what makes them dramatic. But here are the first few general notes on that subject.

1. Your characters should be recognizable as human beings. Even if you write robots (**R.U.R.**) or animals (**Story Theatre**), your characters should be in some ways like the people you know and the people your audience knows. This does not mean to say you can't draw an eccentric person. But that eccentric person has to be recognizable as human, with wants and needs and feelings that we can identify with, no matter how strange or buried those feelings are.

2. Your characters must want something. They must want to *do* something. And they must want to *change* something. However their world appears to them at the start of the play is not how they believe it will be or should be when they get through with it. This is the basis of dramatic action—the wish for change.

3. Your characters must be differentiated. They have to be different from each other in some significant ways. You might want to draw two old men with a lot of similarities. Fine. But no matter how similar they are, we should know which one is speaking without having to look at the name over the line. Ah, but, you say, the salesmen in **Glengarry Glen Ross** speak alike. That's part of the idea of the play. Yes, they speak alike, but they don't have the same agenda. Moss is not Aaronow. They don't know the same information, nor do they have the same opinions about what they know. If you block the names out, I still know which is Moss and which is Aaronow.

Later we will do exercises regarding characters—ways of understanding and drawing characters. But for now, in your early assignments, make your characters as real as possible. The way you list your characters will tell a great deal about them too. If you say

MAN
WOMAN

we should expect the characters not to know each other or your action to be quite unrealistic and stylized. If you say

PEG
JOE, her husband

we have certain expectations from the start as to the level of familiarity between the characters.

You will write a description of a setting. Into this setting you will put two characters. Those characters will pursue a treasure of some sort that is important in their lives. They will want something. They will try to do something. What they will try to do will be done primarily with dialogue. The dialogue is the action.

## Dialogue

In your work, it is important to be highly economical with your dialogue. Dramatic dialogue is not lazy. It does a lot of work. It is not like life dialogue even though it imitates the ways we speak to each other. Dramatic dialogue is loaded with energy, conflict, meaning, and possibility. It's almost a rule to avoid lines like "Hi, how are you?" "Oh, I'm fine."

Dramatic dialogue should be more interesting than that. Why? Because when the lights come up on stage, they come up on trouble. Lights up. Trouble. Something is wrong. Otherwise you don't have a play.

Start to make yourself aware of dialogue that is doing no work. The following exchange is not dramatic and the dialogue is lazy.

NELL

Hi, how are you?

PHIL

Fine. You?

NELL

Good. I was wondering if I could ask you something. . . .

PHIL

Sure. Go ahead.

NELL

Okay. It's about Mike.

PHIL

Mike? What about him?

NELL

I think he's on drugs.

PHIL

Oh, no!

NELL

Yes, I'm very worried. I'm tempted to spy, you know, look through his things.

PHIL

What kind of things? What do you expect to find?

Boring! Why? Because Phil is not a character. Phil is an instrument for furthering Nell's lines. That's *all* he is. He does nothing but respond. He offers no resistance, he doesn't move the scene himself, he doesn't divert Nell, or stop her, or egg her on. He might as well not be there. Or she might as well come in and say, "Look, I'm worried about Mike. I think he's doing drugs. I've been thinking of looking through his things to find out." Because that's all that's happened in this exchange—which is not a dramatic exchange even though two people bat the words around. Dramatic dialogue is dialogue with a constant tension. Something is going to happen. Something might happen at any time. Something is stirring inside not one person, more than one person.

There are other problems with the example above. It isn't clear who Nell and Phil (and Mike) are. Are they brother and sister worried about a younger brother? Roommates with a third roommate? Parents of Mike? Friends? Is Mike a contender for Nell's affections? All of the above are possibilities. It's possible to learn a lot more about characters, if not everything about them, from what they do and what they say within a very few lines.

This is more dramatic:

*(Sound of door slamming)*

NELL

*(entering)* I'm home . . . Phil?

PHIL

*(entering from kitchen, towel in hand)* Good thing. I made a meatloaf and it's almost done.

NELL

You did supper? Great. Listen, is Mike home?

PHIL

Same old thing. Not even a note to tell us when to expect him in. I've set the table for two. Candles, wine. There are some advantages to growing old—

NELL

Listen. Since he's not here—look, I want us to search his room. I think I can make a good guess what's the matter with him lately.

PHIL

Nell. I swore I'd never touch his things. Don't try to—. Look, it's an issue of respect.

NELL

All right, I'll do it. And if I turn up something? If he's not just an irresponsible kid? If he's in trouble, do we keep our hands off?

PHIL

I'll ask him then. I'll talk to him about it.

NELL

When will you ask him, Phil? When he sits down to dinner with us? Over a cozy supper of meatloaf?

This time, Phil has a life of his own. He has opinions and even wishes. He hopes for a calm life with Nell, supper on the table, no trouble. And there are hints that he wants renewed romance. Nell can't think about Phil when she's worried about their son. She knows she doesn't have Phil's cooperation, but she pursues the issue anyway. The dialogue is more dramatic than the first exchange because it suggests that something is about to happen. And the people who have to deal with the events of the play are not in agreement about *how* to act. The not-yet-found drugs are a "negative treasure" in the play. The thing that must be hunted out and gotten rid of. The dinner, the calm life, nourishment, is the positive treasure, the thing sought and hoped for.

Keep in mind that dramatic dialogue promises future action. We know that something *must* happen.

For right now, experiment. Write some exploratory scene descriptions, choices of characters, and beginnings of dialogue. Just allow yourself to see a stage, put people on it, and then allow yourself to hear them talk. This is just practice. Just a way of getting the feel of dramatic form.

## Twenty Principles

There are certain characteristics that seem to me to recur in the bulk of plays that are produced. I think of them as principles of playwriting because they are so common. I'm going to list those principles here. You will not be asked to use them as a formula! In fact, I hope that while you're writing you will forget them, and that only after you've written and thought about what you've written, you will read over them. I find them best used as a critical tool when *you* feel something is not working in a scene, but you can't figure out what to do with it to make it go better. Perhaps then a reminder about keeping characters differentiated, or making sure a scene builds, or employing dramatic irony, or resolving things on an ironic note might help.

Following are the principles of play construction that I suggest as a guide to dialoguing with yourself as you revise. Toss them out if they don't help you. But consider them first.

1. The characters of a play are significantly different from each other. Action comes from the dynamic of character interaction.
2. The setting of a play is a metaphor for the action of a play. Settings must be carefully chosen to pressure the dramatic action.
3. In a play something is at stake for more than one of the characters. Action is only possible when more than one person has a stake in what happens.
4. Dramatic characters want something. To get it, they want to do something, and they want to change something. The attempt to change the status quo is a necessary part of dramatic action.
5. At the center of the play is a treasure of some sort, something of value that is fought over, struggled over. It almost always has a financial aspect.
6. There are many obstacles to the pursuit of the treasure and to each character's pursuit of his or her goal. Obstacles are absolutely necessary factors in dramatic action.
7. Characters must try to get what they want more than once. Otherwise the situation is a single incident, not a drama. Drama consists of multiple attempts and multiple strategies to solve the problems confronting the characters.
8. Most plays are built on pretense. Most theatre is about theatre: about acting, about lying, about pretending.
9. A play's story or dramatic action is accomplished by dialogue. The dialogue is the action. Dramatic dialogue is dialogue in which characters try to do something and try to change something, in which characters seek to have effects on other characters.
10. A play also has physical action, but the physical action should accompany and underline the dialogue, not substitute for it. The physical action is a pattern in itself, dance-like, the play stated in movement terms.
11. Plays are heavily dependent on the device known as *dramatic irony*. Dramatic irony keeps the audience en-

gaged in the action. Dramatic irony is distinct from simple irony because it is a device for plotting.

12. Plays are also dependent upon the device known as *peripety*. The idea of drama—what a drama is—is almost synonymous with peripety, or reversal of intention.

13. The best dramatic characters are complex. The more human they are, the more faults they have, the more contradictions in their characters, the more interesting they are.

14. Style is partly a matter of establishing a convention and using it more than once. Devices used only once are almost always unsatisfying.

15. The language of a play may mimic realistic language or not, but it should be consistent with the style and meaning of the play and it should be language that an actor would like to speak.

16. Everything must be "set up" or "framed" in a play. This includes actors' entrances and exits, the use of props, jokes, important pieces of information. Plays require preparation, execution, and follow-through for each of their elements.

17. The scenes of a play must build. The tension of the overall play must increase from beginning to end, but individual scenes require mounting tension and release as well.

18. The end result, feeling, of a play is irony.

19. Plays gather meaning and significance by the use of analogy.

20. Whole plays and individual scenes operate on three structural points: the inciting incident, the crisis, the climax. Sometimes these points are subtle and almost buried, but they are almost invariably there.

When you read and study established plays, focus on their craft in the use of these twenty principles. Of course there are exceptions! If a writer writes a one-character play, number 3, for instance, won't always make sense. And yet there are times, even in a one-character play, that two sides of a character are in conflict, each wanting something. Before you think of all the possible exceptions, give the rule a chance.

In summary, traditional plays tend to tell a story in dialogue. People persuade and manipulate others toward decisions of importance. Dialogue drives the drama. Something is at stake. The dialogue reflects the difficulty of dealing with the conflict directly. The tension of dialogue, in fact, comes of its indirection in dealing with difficulty. Characters pretend something. This pretense includes small lies, self-deceptions, plots to delude.

---

### Study Questions and Exercises

1. Write another set of lines for Nell and Phil, keeping the same basic situation.
2. Describe a scene between the cowboy and the prostitute in which words are used to further the action.
3. Write three descriptions of a bedroom set, making each one different. In all cases, be economical in your sketch and make sure you choose details that will set up expectations for a drama.

# TWO

# Beginnings: Two Characters and a Prop

## OVERVIEW

After you read this chapter, you will do Exercise 1, which is to write a short two-character scene. Since you will learn by doing—by writing—you will find this book full of assignments and exercises. In order to prepare you for this assignment, I've already given you notes on writing descriptions of settings and on beginning to pressure dramatic dialogue. In this chapter, I will ask you to think about framing character entrances and will give you a few notes on basic ways to do that. Then I will include two humorous pieces that illustrate roads not to take. These are "A Note from the Playwright" by Ian Frazier and "Summer Session" by Veronica Geng. Finally, I will ask you to read, before you write your first script, *The Dining Room* by A. R. Gurney, and I'll provide extended notes on *The Dining Room*.

## OBJECTIVES

At the end of this chapter you should be able to

- Frame the entrance of a character
- Describe the playwriting problems spoofed in the Frazier and Geng pieces reprinted in this chapter
- Discuss the craftsmanship of two scenes from *The Dining Room*
- Do your first exercise, which is to write a two-character scene about the length of the one given between the computer repairman and the woman in Chapter 1 and about the length of the scene between the client and the agent in *The Dining Room*

If you are working alone, choose from among the following possibilities:

a. Two old men, a tree
b. An old woman, a young man, a deck of cards
c. An old man, a young woman, a suitcase
d. A rich woman, a poor woman, a photograph
e. An ill man, a healthy man, a book
f. An old man, a young man, a pair of binoculars

If you are working in a group, get the group to agree on one of the assignments above. Or have the group come up with another combination in which there are two characters clearly different from each other and an object around which their conflict can be shaped.

### Beginning

Where should you begin?

By writing. And follow that with talking about writing. There is no substitute for these two acts—writing and talking about writing. To this end, I've included in the next chapter some examples of "first tries" by developing playwrights. The exercises were turned in as class assignments by people who, in most cases, were absolutely new to writing drama. I hope reading their work will be like having your own workshop group at home with you in your study. You can look at their exercises and your own, see if there are moments that you think work especially well, see if there are things that everybody has difficulty with at first. You can begin to answer the question, "What makes characters, dialogue, scenes satisfying?" It's often what we also say makes them "dramatic"—and by this I don't mean overblown in any of the senses of that expression. You don't have to tear a passion to tatters, or ask your characters do that, to maintain tension in the story line, or to make us care about your characters.

Getting us to care about your characters and their story is

your task as a playwright. All of the pleasures of drama go back to that. No matter how many theories we study or how academic our concerns, the simple fact is that plays succeed or fail, live or die, on the basis of that one very complex and challenging task. Do we care? Are we interested? Do we believe it?

## Entrances

When you write your assignment you may have both characters already on stage, engaged in an action. Or you may have one or both characters enter. If you choose to have one or both characters enter, you will begin to work on *framing entrances*. Here are some things to think about.

Let's look, first of all, at the actor's problem. If you remember you are writing for people who must play these roles, you will have an easier time knowing what to do. Actors always have to come up with a way to "frame" their entrances, that is, to make the moment of entrance noticeable and important. Actors can't do miracles; they need the cooperation of the playwright. Actors, directors, and designers will collaborate on entrances and other effects by placement of doorways and timing of movement, but they will be grateful for plays in which the playwright has thought much of this out for them. Here are some classic ways to prepare an entrance:

1. Stage bare of actors, lights up, silence, character enters *doing something that will be significant*: eating thoughtfully, reading the cover of a record album, scratching himself. We ask, what is he thinking? What record does he have? What skin disease or nervous condition? We wait to learn more.
2. Stage bare of actors, lights up, a *sound* prepares the entrance: keys falling, or keys fumbling in lock, or singing off stage, or talking off stage, or the sound of a car approaching, the engine off, silence; the character enters.
3. Stage bare of actors, lights up, character exhibits extreme behavior upon entrance: runs into the room, hides; or character slams into the room, plops down; or character tiptoes into the room, looks at letter, etc. These are attention-getting by their startling nature.

If you already have a character (or characters) on stage, one of the following methods is likely to be useful.

1. Person on stage hears noise or speech, reacts, preps in some way for entering character—stands up, sits down, looks in mirror, goes toward door, etc.
2. Person on stage is fully occupied, doesn't see entering character. Entering character stops and regards first character. First character senses the presence of entering character, turns, moment of recognition.
3. Person on stage is fully occupied, doesn't see entering character. Entering character says or does something to get attention of first person.
4. Character or characters on stage talk about another. The

person being talked about enters. Preparation has been made by expectation.

If you remember that an entrance is an important point in a character's development, you will remember to frame entrances and give them meaning.

As you begin your first assignment, you will do well to be simple and to go straight for the dialogue between the two people in your script. There are a thousand temptations to get off the track. Amazing when it seems so simple to write a play, right? Following are two humorous pieces that will warn you of some of those temptations. Both of these pieces are excellent examples of some things not to do when writing a play.

## Two Lessons by Parody

Two parodies of drama, one of which appeared in *The Atlantic Monthly* and the other which appeared in *The New Yorker*, point out some things not to do when writing a play. The first, by Ian Frazier, supposes a playwright who did not imagine the stage and did not move his play with dialogue. This imagined writer is, after the disaster of production, in a fury about the way his work was misunderstood. The piece is very broad, and, I think, hilarious. At the same time it drives home several of the points I've been making.

### Ian Frazier: "A Note from the Playwright"

Frazier's "A Note from the Playwright" may seem far-fetched. But in fact, not long ago, I attended a play for which the playwright wrote an answer to critics who had reviewed his production. Since the newspaper didn't publish his response, he handed copies out to each member of the audience. He wasn't complaining about the production itself (as the fictional playwright in the Frazier piece does) because he had directed it and starred in it. He was complaining, however, as the fictional playwright does, about how it was received.

It is always a jolt for the playwright when others take over and *produce* the work. One of the best defenses against a wrong-headed production is a well-written play. One that can be produced! One that does not depend on the audience's reading notes and stage directions to understand what the playwright intended. A playwright who has been working in the theatre, then sitting and staring at an empty stage, as Glaspell did, is not likely to ask for underwater scenes, buses or decorative crowds and choruses. Read and enjoy.

---

### A Note from the Playwright*

To the theatergoer: The performance of *Songs for a Conquered Moon* that you are about to see differs so com-

* From *Dating Your Mom* by Ian Frazier. Copyright © 1986 by Ian Frazier. First appeared in *The Atlantic Monthly*, July 1985. Reprinted by permission of Farrar, Straus & Giroux, Inc.

pletely from the spirit of the play as I wrote it that I wish hereby to disavow any and all association between myself and this production. If I could, I would remove my name from the marquee and from the program you hold in your hands; unfortunately, I am informed by my lawyers that contractual considerations render this impossible. When I wrote *Songs*, I set out to weave a net of speech, action, and mood with which to ensnare certain moments in human existence that are as fleeting and evanescent as a dream. Seeing my lovely net filled instead with the unappetizing aesthetic baggage of one particular director and set of actors makes me wonder briefly why I ever chose this regrettable profession in the first place.

My carefully crafted stage directions, absolutely essential to any understanding of the play, have been discarded from this production with a thoroughness that suggests the hired vandal. The freeway pile-up in the middle of Act II has mysteriously disappeared, without an explanation; the chorus of forty Greek sailors commenting on the action has been replaced by two town criers (obviously not Greek); the underwater sequences have been crudely faked; and the marvelous moment at the climax of Act III, when Lord Hargreaves draws his breath to sneeze and his starched shirtfront rolls up under his nose like a window shade, has been so toned down as to lose all its impact. I could continue this list almost endlessly . . . But really, why bother?

Now, as per the agreement between my attorney and the attorneys for the Top Contemporary Theatre Company, I include here the first few pages of *Songs for a Conquered Moon*, exactly as they were written. I hope that they will give some idea of the very great distance between my play as it was originally intended and the shabby counterfeit you see on the stage before you.

## Songs for a Conquered Moon
### *A Play in Three Acts*

CAST OF CHARACTERS

MARCELLINE, a woman so beautiful it is impossible to look at her without a sharp intake of breath. A strong woman whose looks are a form of disguise; beneath those high-fashion dresses hides an adventurous tomboy with many of the same traits as her father, a billionaire.

JOHN VANDERJOHN, a third-generation brain surgeon and outsider. Wears his hair a bit overlong, down to and beyond his short collar. The echo of an Old World patronymic in his name is intentional; he should suggest the epic proportions of a Tolstoy, wandering lost in this shopkeepers' century.

RAILROAD TOM STEVENS, a poet, a prophet, a preacher, a liar. A man as full of contradictions as the nightly news. He'd give his last quarter to a little boy

and then change his mind. Also, he is able to "shapeshift"—change from human form to that of any other species—in a matter of seconds. Lover to Pamella.

ONE STAB, a full-blooded Indian. Silent, laconic, terse, and as violent as the occasion requires. Well over seven feet tall. Mr. Earl's factotum.

MARK BRAINARD, a young writer and critic with the most brilliant mind of his generation.

BOB, a neighbor from downstairs.

FIVE CLAIMS ADJUSTERS

THE "SOLID GOLD" DANCERS

ASSORTED MESSENGERS AND PASSERS-BY

SOME OTHER PEOPLE

### Act I
*The time is the present, approximately.*

*The setting is anywhere along the Pacific rim; state or country need not be made explicit. Set designers are referred to postcards of the region, Kabuki drawings, and the imitation–French Regency landscaping favored by gangsters and the newly famous. A western pine perhaps, stunted bonsai-style, clinging to a coastal rock. Stage right, there is a fifty-foot waterfall, and at stage left we see an eight-lane suspension bridge of reinforced concrete. In the background is an active volcano, with molten lava coming down the sides and slowly making its way to the footlights. Overhead a real airport control tower broods above the scene.*

*The lighting should try for an effect both spare and lush, if possible. It should change almost continually, as the moment dictates. For the second act the light panel must be equipped with at least four state-of-the-art military lasers. Interacting with the cast members and the scenery, the lighting will become practically like another character in the drama, as palpable as the charmed radiance in a painting by Raphael or Giotto or someone of equal stature.*

*JOHN is seated in a chair downstage right. The residue of a black mood can still be seen around the corners of his eyes. Occasionally he knits his brow and shakes his head. Close at hand is a fresh cup of imported coffee, which he sips from time to time. MARCELLINE enters stage left.*

MARCELLINE
*[hauntingly]* Oh, hi, John.

JOHN
*[in an upsetting tone]* Oh, hi, Marcelline. How come you're right here?

MARCELLINE
*[movingly]* I just came in from over where I was.

JOHN
*[no longer depressed]* Oh, that's great.

MARCELLINE

*[affectingly]* So, what if we—

JOHN

*[expressing the audience's hidden fears]* Wait, wait no—

MARCELLINE

*[with perfect timing]* Hear me out.

JOHN

*[in his regular voice]* Okay.

MARCELLINE

*[compellingly]* What if we went to a store and bought some things?

JOHN

*[after a pause of twenty-four seconds]* Oh, okay.

*The scene then shifts to Tibet. MARCELLINE and JOHN come in. TOM is already there.*

TOM

*[instantly commanding attention]* Hi, you guys.

MARCELLINE

*[responding to what TOM has said]* Hi.

JOHN

Hi, Tom.

TOM

*[memorably]* What do you say we go and get something to eat?

MARCELLINE

*[with a touching expression]* Thanks. I'd like that.

JOHN

*[this is a great line]* Count me in.

TOM

*[excitingly]* Okay, let's go!

I am sorry that, owing to limitations of space, this excerpt cannot be longer. I would suggest that those of you as yet unfamiliar with my work go out and buy copies of all my plays, the better to judge future productions for yourselves. And I would also ask that the next time you want to see a play by me, you call me first to ask whether the production is good or not. (I am home most evenings, and if I'm out, someone can take a message.) I know full well that a writer's relationship with his audience is the most important one he has. After all, without you, where would I be? I would even go to your houses, no matter how long it would take to see everybody. If you have any questions, I would welcome the opportunity to sit down with each of you on an individual basis to discuss just how great my play could have been.

Hilarious. Hard as we look, we cannot find a play here. The fictional playwright's fancy has not limited itself with the limits of the stage.

**Other Concerns**

A few serious or almost serious notes:

1. No audience would know if a cup of coffee were fresh or imported without a making-coffee scene or dialogue about it. And what's the point? What does it show? Props should be chosen for their significance.
2. A great actress could say, "Oh, hi, John," hauntingly, but I guarantee she wouldn't. She could get into plays with sustained dialogue—good lines, lines that pay off by having a consequence in subsequent lines and subsequent scenes.
3. A pause of three seconds on stage is long. Everything on stage is magnified. So a pause of twenty-four seconds would seem like a lifetime.

And so the only resort of this fictional playwright is to exist in libraries, bookstores, program notes, and visits to his audience's houses . . . anywhere but on stage. He has given his enormous energies to everything but action through dialogue.

**Veronica Geng: "Summer Session"**

The second humorous piece, this one by Veronica Geng, is much more like an actual play. In fact, it is very conventional, and is spoofed for its conventionality. It takes place in a fixed space. The characters have a sustained dialogue of sorts. But the dialogue does not contribute to a credible action. There is tension, but it's false tension.

I sat in my living room, mentally directing this piece, and I wondered if it wouldn't actually be pretty funny in production. But it is comic because it is a critique, a lesson in what not to do. Because it gets closer to the form of a play, its lesson is perhaps a little more subtle. Did Geng come from the theatre, having seen a character like Dad—who is drawn in one dimension? Notice how all of Dad's lines are negative response-questions to the previous line. He has no real life of his own. Notice how the characters repeat dull wishes over and over again. Notice how lazily they pursue what they want, and how difficult it is to identify with or care about their concerns. Geng has written a humorous piece based on the failure to write differentiated, human characters with something at stake that they seek to control through words. Again, enjoy.

---

**Summer Session***

THE TIME: *July, 1962.*
THE SCENE: *A screened porch, evening. Sound of crickets.*

* Originally appeared in *The New Yorker*, February 12, 1990. Reprinted by permission.

THE CHARACTERS:
STEVE (*just returned from high school*)
RONNIE (*his sister, home from her senior year in college*)
DAD

STEVE
Hey, Dad, didn't we use to have a couple bowling balls?

DAD
What do you want with bowling balls in this heat?

RONNIE
Maybe they're in the garage.

DAD
Don't be silly.

STEVE
Come on, Dad, where are they?

DAD
Don't go in the garage now. What do you want bowling balls for at this time of night?

STEVE
Ronnie has to bowl.

DAD
Aw, what are you talking about?

RONNIE
We're just going bowling.

DAD
What do you mean, bowling? Do you know what time it is?

STEVE
It's only nine o'clock.

DAD
Nine o'—Jesus, what's the matter with you? Your mother's already asleep.

RONNIE
Gee, then I guess we can't bowl in the house. We'll have to go to the bowling alley.

DAD
Nine o'clock at night people don't go bowling. Look at it, it's dark out.

RONNIE
I thought the car had headlights.

DAD
You don't even have bowling shoes. What are you gonna do, bowl in those? You can't bowl in sneakers, you gotta have shoes.

STEVE
Look, Dad, they rent the shoes.

DAD
*Rent?* What, you're gonna wear somebody else's shoes?

STEVE
Everybody does that. They put powder in them.

DAD
What do you know about powder? You're a powder expert now.

RONNIE
Fine, then we'll buy some shoes.

DAD
Oh, you're gonna buy a pair of shoes now for one game.

STEVE
Listen, you rent the shoes, they put powder in them, and you wear them. And you bowl with them. They have these nifty little—

DAD
"Nifty"? "Nifty"? Where the hell did you learn to talk, anyway?

RONNIE
Dad, leave him alone. This is getting to be a hassle.

STEVE
It's no hassle, Ron.

DAD
"Hassle." What is it with you two? You got a hassle, nifty, go bowling.

STEVE
Dad—

DAD
What do you want to go bowling for? All of a sudden you've got this big interest in bowling now all of a sudden.

STEVE
Dad, look—Ronnie couldn't pass her grades in college because of her phys-ed credit, so now she has to bowl because she didn't want to go in the water and swim.

DAD
What do you mean, she didn't want to—

RONNIE
Look, Steve, just forget about it.

STEVE
Ron, are you jumping on *me* now?

DAD
How are you two going bowling? What are you gonna use for money?

STEVE
Ronnie, you have money, don't you?

RONNIE

Let's just forget it.

STEVE

No, now I'm getting interested. Come on, Dad, want to go bowling with us?

DAD

What, *now*?

RONNIE

Forget about it.

DAD

Aw, for Christ's sake, you don't go bowling at this hour.

STEVE

Come on, Dad, just bowl a few frames with us. You and Mommy used to bowl all the time, remember?

DAD

You don't know what you're talking about. Your mother doesn't bowl at midnight.

RONNIE

Come on, Steve, I can't stand here all night arguing about the proper times to bowl.

STEVE

Dad, come on. You can wolf down an order of French fries.

DAD

I'm not hungry.

RONNIE

You're sitting there with candy bars.

STEVE

So he eats candy bars—so what? Leave him alone.

RONNIE

It's not healthy.

STEVE

Yeah, Dad, come on over to the alley and work up an appetite for some fries.

DAD

Jesus Christ, do you know how much a bowling ball weighs? How is Ronnie gonna go bowling? She looks like a good meal of corned beef and cabbage would stand her on her feet.

RONNIE

Look, all I want to do is graduate from college.

STEVE

Dad, leave her alone. She's upset enough that she doesn't want to put her head under water.

DAD

What's that got to do with anything?

STEVE

You know, it's a swimming credit she couldn't get.

DAD

Swimming. You know what it is swimming?

RONNIE

No, Dad, what is it?

DAD

Swimming—all swimming is is relaxing. In the water. That's all it is. Swimming is a relaxing. You put your head in, you relax, that's it. Otherwise you sink like a stone. Tense up in the water and you can forget about it.

RONNIE

Oh, so, Dad, wait a minute, when's the last time I saw *you* swimming? You go out there and wade.

STEVE

Come on, Ronnie, don't pick on him.

RONNIE

You *wade* in there, in your shorts—

DAD

Get out of here. You're gonna tell me about swimming? You've been in college too long, that's what your problem is. Then you come here and tell me about bowling and swimming.

RONNIE

This is just really upsetting me. If I don't fulfill this credit—Oh, forget it. Forget about it. I'm not graduating from college. Just forget about it. We're not going bowling.

DAD

Oh, you're not graduating from college now, huh? Now it's my fault you're not graduating from college because you don't have bowling shoes.

STEVE

Dad, forget the bowling shoes. They have millions of 'em in the alley.

DAD

So you know all about bowling. Where's your bowling ball?

STEVE

They have balls all over the place.

DAD

What, at this time of night?

RONNIE

They don't take the balls away just because it gets dark outside.

STEVE

Really, she has to bowl to graduate from Penn. She was supposed to pass her swimming test, but she can't swim.

DAD

Of course she can swim.

STEVE
She can't swim. She's afraid to swim.

DAD
Where in the world did you get that idea?

STEVE
Dad, look, have you ever once seen her swim?

DAD
You're crazy.

STEVE
You know how she just stands there in the shallow end and then comes out and lounges around on a towel.

DAD
She could swim fine if she wasn't too goddam hoity-toity to swim.

STEVE
Dad, I'm telling you, she had a traumatic experience in Atlantic City that time when we were kids. She got knocked down by a wave. So now she won't put her head under water.

DAD
Where the hell do you kids get this stuff?

RONNIE
Forget about all that. They said I could graduate without swimming. All I have to do is bowl a certain number of frames over the summer and send them the score sheets.

DAD
That's the silliest thing yet. They're gonna let you go bowling when you're supposed to swim?

RONNIE
They couldn't care less what I do. So I'm not swimming.

DAD
You better start swimming in a hurry, because you're not gonna be able to bowl. You couldn't bowl if your life depended on it.

STEVE
Dad, anybody can bowl.

DAD
And that's where you're wrong. Swimming, yes. As long as you don't tense up. But with bowling it's a horse of a different color.

STEVE
Dad, if she can't bowl I'll teach her. It's no big thing. All she has to do is keep hurling the ball down the alley and boom!—sooner or later she'll hit something.

DAD
She'll hit something, all right.

RONNIE
They didn't say I had to bowl *well.*

DAD
What, now you want to have a traumatic bowling experience? You have to prepare for these things, you can't just get up there and—

STEVE
Bowling is a Zen thing. It's all in the—not actually in the mind but in the non-mind. Like an animal, or a fish.

DAD
Fish breathe in the water.

STEVE
That's what I'm saying.

DAD
Look, people cannot breathe water. People and animals—they have lungs, not gills.

STEVE
Will you stop? Of course people don't have gills. Of course they don't. Do you think I'm stupid?

DAD
Are you calling me stupid?

RONNIE
Steve, look, leave him alone. Forget about it.

DAD
'Cause if you're calling me stupid, you can forget about the bowling.

RONNIE
I don't care. This is upsetting me now.

DAD
*You're* upset?

RONNIE
Yes. This is just upsetting me. Forget the whole thing. Forget college. I'll go to the Sorbonne.

DAD
She'll go to the Sorbonne. Listen to this. What are you gonna study there, French water sports?

STEVE
Dad, are you coming bowling with us or not? That's all we want to know.

DAD
If you're so smart, what are you planning to do for money? You know how much it costs to go bowling?

RONNIE
It's only a couple of dollars. Just give Steve a couple of dollars and we'll go. I don't need anything.

DAD
Give *Steve* a couple of—Jesus Christ, you want me to give him money to go bowling? He's only a kid! It's

dark out there. You're being silly now. You want to go bowling, first of all you need *shoes*, and then you need money. And you're gonna take this kid in the middle of the night—

RONNIE
It's not the middle of the night at nine-thirty.

DAD
You don't listen to reason. You know how hard your mother and I worked to send you to college, and now all it comes down to is bowling in the middle of the night?

RONNIE
Look, it's not—

STEVE
Ronnie, let me tell him. All you're doing is pissing him off.

RONNIE
What are you, my lawyer now?

DAD
All this happens because you don't want to put your head under water? That's what this is all about? I thought I told you about swimming.

STEVE
Dad, will you back off the swimming thing?

DAD
No, wait a minute, let me tell her about swimming. You reach down to the bottom of the pool, and you keep your head straight, and you breathe. When you're in the water, you breathe. That's it.

RONNIE
That sounds terrific on paper—

DAD
What do you mean,"on paper"? What are you talking about? Where does this kid get this from? I'm talking about swimming, she's talking about paper.

STEVE
Dad, will you—

RONNIE
Steve, no, wait a minute, I want to hear what Daddy has to say about swimming. He's telling us all about swimming now.

DAD
Look, don't get smart.

RONNIE
No, I want to hear this. I want to hear about swimming. *That's why I can't swim! Because you never taught us to swim!*

DAD
Oh, you want to hear *me* now. I thought two minutes ago you wanted to go bowling.

RONNIE
Fine. Forget it, I'm not staying here with this. I'm packing. I'll be upstairs packing.

STEVE
Ron, look, forget about packing, we're going bowling.

DAD
Bowling, packing, swimming . . .

STEVE
Dad, stop.

DAD
All I'm telling you is, you don't fight the water—You never fight the water. Never ever. You let the water support you, because if you're afraid to let it support you, you just go right to the bottom. The bottom will draw you like a magnet. Gravity takes you right to the bottom and you can't breathe and that's it.

STEVE
Dad, this is the same thing I'm saying about bowling. It's a gravity thing. The alley creates its own momentum, and you just go with it. It happens *for* you. And the gutters—the gutters create fear in a bowler. They're there as a fear thing. If you tense up, the ball will leap into the gutter. Whereas the pins actually draw the ball to them. It's an attraction of bodies—like planets. It's perfectly natural. If you relax, the ball goes for a strike.

RONNIE
Yeah, but only in the middle of the night, when it's really dark out. You turn on the car headlights, you breathe, keep your head down, plenty of powder, a few candy bars just to make sure you keep your strength up, and boom!—the next thing you know you're graduating from the Sorbonne with a degree in packing.

DAD
I swear I don't know where you kids learned to talk this way. (*Goes into house, slamming screen door. STEVE and RONNIE look at each other, shrug, and exit toward bowling alley. DAD opens screen door and calls after them.*) You want to go bowling, go bowling. But I'm telling you, they're not gonna let you wear those shoes.

---

One of the tendencies that Geng is spoofing is the tendency in plays by inexperienced playwrights to write only *expressed conflict*. In almost every line the characters are arguing. Everybody is against everybody else, everything comes to disagreement. Plays *do* require conflict, but they require conflict that can't easily be fought out, issues that can't easily be confronted directly, characters who are hiding facts or feelings rather than expressing them. Dramatic dialogue clothes and hides characters, rather than the reverse. In the Geng piece, the people have no serious needs, no serious trouble, and they fight it out all the time, the opposite of what a play generally is. Which, of course, Ms. Geng knows very well.

### The Dining Room

*The Dining Room*, by A. R. Gurney, a deceptively simple play, will be helpful reading at this point in your work for the following reasons:

1. *The Dining Room* is made up of many short scenes that will help you get into the rhythm of dramatic construction. You can see that it is possible to accomplish *a finished action* in a few pages. For instance, notice the scene between the architect and the psychiatrist. It is about the length of what you will write for your first assignment.

2. You can see that character differentiation is possible in a few pages and that resolution of a conflict is also possible. Depth of character is not. That is not to say the characters aren't interesting and accurately drawn, but that the nature of the piece doesn't allow us to know them over time.

3. It will become immediately apparent that the treasure, which is the focus of each scene, is the dining room, and that there are a variety of possible scenes about this one subject. In some ways you might look at this play as a whole series of class assignments put together—as if some teacher had said, "All right, everybody write a play about two characters and a dining room table!" Except of course, that the play is a full play in one voice—A. R. Gurney's voice, which is distinctive. The feeling and rhythm of the voice gives the play its unity and uniqueness.

You will do yourself a service if you get into the habit of writing plot summaries when you read a play. Doing a summary helps you to *notice* construction. What is the pattern of the play? What is the conflict of each scene? What are the intentions of the characters?

### Plot Summary of *The Dining Room* by A. R. Gurney

*The Dining Room* consists of many scenes that are unrelated in terms of plot and character relationships. With the exception of one maid who appears twice, characters don't recur from scene to scene. The time scheme is not logical or chronological. We jump from the sixties to the thirties to the fifties to the forties, etc. In most cases the scenes overlap by five to ten lines; i.e., one scene begins before the other ends. The scenes are as follows:

Act I, Scene i. Early morning. A real estate agent tries to sell a client an old house with an old-fashioned dining room. The dining room makes the client nostalgic about his own childhood, but he can't find a way to make such a house work for him in his adult life.

Scene ii. Unspecified time. A brother and sister come to divide their mother's furniture. Old sibling rivalries surface as they draw lots for the dining room.

Scene iii. Breakfast. A father gives his children conservative American propaganda, controlling their lives and their morning while the children find small ways to question this order. He tells them they will grow up to remember these ordered mornings with fondness when they have forgotten everything else.

Scene iv. Breakfast. A married mother tries to type a research paper at the dining room table inherited by her husband. Her husband tries to get her to move someplace else. She fights him, but after he leaves, she capitulates.

Scene v. Breakfast. A mother tries to manipulate her daughter into rejecting her free-spirited, unmarried aunt. The daughter becomes all the more interested in rejecting her mother and accepting her aunt.

Scene vi. Morning. A boy tries to get the family's maid to stay with them, but she explains that she has decided to go. He tries to understand what he sees as her rejection of him, and, in the end, rejects her because he cannot bear to lose her.

Scene vii. Unspecified time. An architect tries to persuade a psychiatrist to get rid of the dining room of his new old house and to put an office in its place, inadvertently revealing that his own terrible childhood makes him hate dining rooms. The psychiatrist finds himself working in that room, in spite of himself.

Scene viii. An afternoon. At a child's birthday party, a married woman and a married man complain about their spouses and fantasize about running away together. They can't find the energy or conviction to fight their condemning spouses.

Scene ix. Lunchtime. A boy asks his grandfather for money to go to a private school. The grandfather agrees, but only after making the boy question the whole enterprise and beg not to go.

Scene x. Afternoon. A divorced woman hires a carpenter to fix her old dining room table. She can't seem to talk about the table without finding it a metaphor for her ailing love/sex life. The carpenter offers to fix it, suggesting that the work is simple.

Scene xi. Dinnertime. An old woman's senility is traumatizing Thanksgiving dinner. Her sons and their wives try to bring her around, but she wants to go to her childhood home.

Act II, Scene i. Late afternoon. Two teenage girls drink vodka and gin in a formal dining room after school. The girl who lives there hates the room and her parents. Her friend envies her the dining room and the ordered, if oppressive, life.

Scene ii. Late afternoon. A woman serves tea in the dining room to her lover (who happens to be her husband's best friend) in order to get him to stay. Before he can leave what is not a comfortable affair, the woman's son comes home and discovers them.

**Scene iii.** Afternoon. A young man visits his aunt to research her WASP dining ware for his anthropology class. She kicks him out when she understands he's trying to prove she belongs to a dying breed—and that the breed is overly polite and sexually repressed.

**Scene iv.** Cocktail hour. A woman with three children asks her dad if she can move back home after a failed marriage and failed affairs with a man and a woman. He tells her she's not welcome for longer than a visit.

**Scene v.** Dinnertime. A family watches as their father interrupts a great lamb dinner to go to his club and fight the man who intimated that his brother was a homosexual. The children learn that the facts aren't important, only family honor is.

**Scene vi.** Evening. A father goes over his funeral arrangements with his son, not content to leave anything out of his control, including the price of the liquor served.

**Scene vii.** Evening. A woman says goodbye to her retiring maid and fantasizes about having a dinner party at which everyone she ever knew and liked is present, a real gathering of the past.

While you are reading, you might find yourself asking, as many others have, the following questions:

1. Why are scenes overlapped? Why does one scene begin before the other ends?
2. Should there be a relationship between these families?
3. How can the play say something universal if it is all about one class of people in New England?
4. What is the advantage of having six people play all the roles? What is the effect?

I think it is a good idea to live with the questions while you read. The questions are usually stress points between playwright and audience and, as such, hold the power and the value of the play in them. What bothers us is also what thrills us. While you are reading, try to notice how much we learn about the characters from how they speak. My notes on the first scene will appear in bracketed boldface. Pay attention to the craft of the writing. We know much more about the situation in which the agent and the client find themselves (first scene) than we are told directly.

---

| The Scene* | Things to Notice |
|---|---|
| *No one on stage. The dining-room furniture sparkles in the early morning light. Voices from Off R. Then a woman real-estate agent and her male client appear in the doorway. Both wear raincoats.* | A lighting effect focuses our attention on the setting. Voices act as preparation for an entrance. The costumes tell us these are fast moving people. The day is going to be dreary. |
| AGENT<br>. . . and the dining room. | They have already seen the rest of the house. |
| CLIENT<br>Oh boy. | He likes it but he's stuck for words. |
| AGENT<br>You see how these rooms were designed to catch the early morning light? | Past tense: Were designed. This word sets up much of the following dialogue. |
| CLIENT<br>I'll say. | |
| AGENT<br>French doors, lovely garden, flowering plants? Do you like gardening? | Agent is reading client. She wants to *do* something: She wants to sell a house. He likes the room; he perks up when she opens the door to the garden. |
| CLIENT<br>Used to. | Past tense again. |
| AGENT<br>Imagine, imagine having a long leisurely breakfast in here. | |
| CLIENT<br>As opposed to instant coffee on Eastern Airlines. | He tells us, without saying so, that he doesn't have leisurely breakfasts. He has just flown into town this morning. |

\* The first scene from *The Dining Room* by A.R. Gurney. Copyright © 1982 by A.R. Gurney. Reprinted by permission of Dramatists Play Service, Inc., and the William Morris Agency, Inc.

AGENT

Exactly. You know, this is a room after my own heart. I grew up in a dining room like this. Same sort of furniture. Everything.

CLIENT

So did I.

AGENT

Then here we are. Welcome home. *(Pause)*

CLIENT

What are they asking again?

He didn't quite consider it until she said "Welcome home." He has to do something: He has to buy a house. But he allows himself to want something else—change. He wants to change his life back to how it used to be.

AGENT

Make an offer. I think they'll come down. *(Another pause)*

She is pursuing her goal.

CLIENT

Trouble is, we'll never use this room.

He is talking himself out of what he wants.

AGENT

Oh now.

A maternal-sounding response—appropriate because he is remembering childhood.

CLIENT

We won't. The last two houses we lived in, my wife used the dining-room table to sort the laundry.

He is not happy with his present life or his wife. Maybe not with adulthood.

AGENT

Oh dear.

She likes order. She is also always on the customer's side.

CLIENT

Maybe you'd better show me something more contemporary.

He continues to work himself away from the dream.

AGENT

That means something farther out. How long have we got to find you a home?

CLIENT

One day.

His life is not so much fun. He is caught in the worst of corporate life.

AGENT

And how long will the corporation keep you here after you've found it?

She hears what his life is, gives him a chance to complain.

CLIENT

Six months to a year.

AGENT

Oh then definitely we should look farther out. *(She opens the kitchen door.)* You can look at the kitchen as we leave.

CLIENT

You shouldn't have shown me this first.

AGENT

I thought it was something to go by.

CLIENT

You've spoiled everything else.

An image of his past, of his childhood, is going to stick with him now, a reminder of what he doesn't like about the contemporary homes he's forced to live in, the way his life has turned out.

AGENT

Oh no. We'll find you something if we've got all day. But wasn't it a lovely room?

She knows her job. She keeps all lines open. Just in case he changes his mind.

CLIENT

Let's go or I'll buy it.

He jokes, but there is some truth there. He has to leave to pursue his goal, to buy a house in one day.

---

In every play, people try to affect other people through dialogue. Each character *wants* something. Each wants *to do* something. At least somebody in the play wants *to change* something.

*The Dining Room* is a one-of-a-kind play. I don't think anybody else should try to write something like it. Most plays need to be made of fewer characters who have a longer time on stage. This one manages to be successful doing something very different. The characters are almost composites—full of longing for the old life, the old ways, childhood, and full of energy and longing for the future, too. Many of the scenes are touching. The characters, briefly seen, come alive in some ways better than characters with longer stage lives. *The Dining Room* is a play of nostalgia and yet it is not without bite, irony, and wisdom about the impossibility of living in the past. It is more than simply sweet.

It is possible to perform it with twenty-five, thirty-five, or twelve people. But most productions follow the original concept and use only six—three men and three women. The advantage of this is twofold. First, it increases the theatricality. Theatre, remember, is pretense. What better way to engage the audience in the game of pretense than to show them Actress One in her trench coat, as a very modern real-estate agent, and then let them see her in a 1930's dressing gown two scenes later as the spoiled and beautiful mother of the third scene? In other words, we become more aware of the acting as acting, the costuming as costuming. Gurney suggests that costume changes be minimal. When there are only symbolic changes of clothing, we become aware of the theatricality, the pretense.

A second advantage of having only six actors is that each actor has to play children, old people, and middle-aged adults. At the end of *The Dining Room*, you've seen the generations turn over again and again. Someone who was a difficult child is a troubled adult and also a senile older adult. The audience doesn't forget the basic actor under the change. And although the characters are not supposed to be the same person—and are not drawn as such, in type or in the logic of chronology—Gurney makes us think about how lives ripen, mature, and decline just as we see the life of a part of America ripen, mature, and decline. Change is the governing force in this play. And when you watch the same actors playing out the changes, there is a (not-logical) pull on your emotions. The changes in *The Dining Room* get you right in the gut.

I've known actors rehearsing this play to want to go against the stage directions and finish one scene before the other begins. Hopefully, a good director will not allow them to do this. The playwright is right. The play works better with overlapped scenes. The very thing that is frustrating about it is the very thing that is valuable about it. Just when you are getting used to a set of characters and their problems, a stranger walks in and fills the stage with a whole new set of problems, needs, wants. You have to concentrate to hang onto the established characters. You have to live with both for a time. And then the new takes over, before you've been able to catch up with the exit of the old. *And*, isn't this, *in form*, exactly what the play is about? The *form* mirrors the *subject*. For the play is about goodbyes not properly said, about how people who are important to us disappear, never to be included in our lives again, about the new, the modern, the stubborn snuffing out the old. It happens over and over in individual scenes. But it also happens in the form of the play. That's what gives this play broad appeal in spite of the fact that it deals with one group of people at one income level in one part of the country. In fact, the more specific the place and the people, the more exact they are (and you are as a writer), the more likely they are (and you are) to make their situation meaningful to *anybody* who is watching your play. It's one of the truths of all art, evident here, that the specific, carefully handled, signifies the general. Gurney's careful handling is just another of the things that makes *The Dining Room* an extraordinary play, well worth studying.

## Assignment: Exercise 1

You should now write a two-character scene, choosing from among the possibilities given at the beginning of this chapter. There are several restrictions:

1. The scene must be two or three pages long.
2. There are to be no changes of scene.
3. There are to be few stage directions.
4. Your play will be composed of dialogue.
5. There are to be only two characters.

You should try to make the most of the natural differences between the characters as they relate to each other and to the object of the scene, because differences between characters will cause action.

## Study Questions and Exercises

1. Choose a scene from *The Dining Room* (other than the first scene) and describe how much an audience will understand about the characters without being told directly about them.
2. Choose a scene from *The Dining Room* and study how the playwright has one or more characters make an entrance. How is the entrance made memorable? What methods of framing are used?

# THREE

# Playwriting Workshops

## OVERVIEW

This chapter consists mainly of the exercises of other writers. Each exercise is followed by my commentary on the script as well as by simulated workshop reactions. The simulated workshops are intended to show you that disagreement is not only acceptable but desirable and valuable, and that people in the workshop should be free to explore whether a particular drama worked for them. Reactions are often highly individual, but we can always ask whether the characters are interesting, sympathetic, or believable. And we can always try to determine what one playwright is trying to do (as we see it) and whether or not we think that playwright succeeds.

## OBJECTIVES

At the end of this chapter you should be able to

- Give your own reactions to the scripts
- Compare your successes and whatever problems you encountered with those of the writers of the exercises in this chapter

The writing workshop is a current, popular way to study all writing. (Poets and fiction writers use the workshop method too.) Certainly, playwrights benefit from the workshop method because theatre is an active art, meant to be heard, meant to be performed.

Here is your first playwriting workshop. It is your chance to learn from the work of other new writers. Have you made some of the same gains? Some of the same mistakes? There are four examples of Writing Exercise 1—a scene about two people and an object. The first two are scenes using the

assignment to write about a man, a woman, and a book. The second two are scenes using the assignment to write about an old man, a young woman, and a suitcase. Following each of these student scripts is a simulated workshop (based on notes for what actually happened in the workshop in which that student's work was discussed).

### How to Workshop Scripts

There are a few rules for workshopping plays. They are few but they are important.

1. The play should be read aloud whenever possible (given the limits of time). The play may be read aloud by the playwright who reads all the stage directions as well as the character names. The playwright should not try to act the play but should simply read it and let a production form in the minds of all listeners.

2. As the class gets more advanced and comfortable, the plays should be read by members of the class, taking roles. In this case, although the class members do not try to act the plays, there is a little more invention in the reading—as if it's an audition. In this case the play rather than the actors is the object of the audition.

3. After a reading of the play, class members will react to it. All members of the class or group should be active in responding, no matter what the method. If necessary, go around the room, letting each person speak in turn.

4. During this time *the playwright should not speak*. The playwright should listen and take notes, but mainly listen to the reactions. This is not a time to act out "A Note from the Playwright" or to otherwise justify the writing.

5. The comments from the teacher and from the class are meant to be helpful. Discussion should be focused on what the writer was attempting to do and whether the attempt

was successful. If it is not, discuss what things would make it more successful.

The whole idea of a workshop for playwrights is to maximize your experiences, to learn not only from your own work and from the things you've tried to do, but from others. Here is a first scene, which we will call *The Date*. Periodically, throughout this book, I'll give a running commentary on the script. It's probably a good idea to read the script through once and respond to the flow of it, then read it a second time, including the notes.

## The Date
### *by Jeff Bridge*

*(The scene takes place in a large, tastefully decorated living room. An antique couch sits center stage. A chair and table are left of the couch. There is a telephone on the table. An older woman, seated, is talking on the phone.)*

ETHEL

*(holding clip from newspaper)* . . . It says here, Stella, that he's widowed too, is looking for someone who is warm, bright, sensitive . . . and oh, listen to this, not afraid to bake a peach cobbler in the morning and then go dancing at night. *(Laughs. Short pause.)* Oh, I know. He seems charming enough. We talked last night on the phone for a . . . *(Doorbell rings.)* It's him. Okay, remember to call just in case. Bye. *(Primps self, goes to door.)*

The writer has given Ethel conversation that is in a believable phone rhythm. There is a suggestion of Stella's conversation in what Ethel says. He used the phone as a means of exposition—getting across the premise to the audience—and also, along with Ethel's primping, to prepare for, or frame, William's entrance.

WILLIAM

*(standing in doorway, holding flowers in one hand, candy in the other)* Uh, hello. Ethel?

The writer has chosen to characterize William with props.

ETHEL

*(flushed)* William, you shouldn't have. Please, come in. *(Looks down.)* They're . . . dandelions. They're gorgeous. *(to self)* Dandelions?

Is this choice, dandelions, believable or too much of a "signal" as to how we should view William?

WILLIAM

*(Looking around. Sits on couch.)* I picked them myself. There's this yard and . . . You have a beautiful home here, Ethel.

William sits without being asked. Is this a good choice?

ETHEL

*(Puts flowers in vase. They're barely visible. Sits next to him.)* Thank you. It's been a part of my family for six generations. *(Pause. Ethel and William gaze around the room.)* Would you like a cup of coffee? I just put on a fresh pot. It's decaffeinated. *(Short pause.)* But I could grind some beans if you . . .

Although there's barely time to put the flowers in a vase, many established playwrights give no more time than this.

WILLIAM

No. No. Decaffeinated's fine. *(Ethel exits. William quickly pulls a book from his jacket and begins flipping through it. Reading aloud.)* Chapter One. Asking Questions that Promote Conversations. Always try to end the conversation with an open-ended question. Never resort to closed-ended question asking. If impossible to end conversation with an open-ended question employ the Freymann Method, Chapter 7. *(Frantic pause.)* Freymann Method! Chapter 7! *(Glances through book.)*

Would Ethel leave the room without another line after having sat next to him? Do you buy the premise of this scene? That William would carry the book with him and read from it? Or is this action geared for the audience alone? Does the behavior come from character?

ETHEL

*(entering through rear, carrying a tray)* I hope you don't mind milk in your coffee but we're all out of cream.

A good amount of time has elapsed before Ethel's entrance. It is just credible that she has poured coffee.

WILLIAM

*(quickly sitting on book)* No . . . cream's fine.

ETHEL

*(sweet sarcasm)* William, I only have milk.

WILLIAM

*(wiping off brow)* Milk's fine.

ETHEL

Is something wrong, William? You seem to have broken out in an awful sweat. Do you want me to turn down the thermostat?

There are a series of actions that make William very awkward, that point up his insecurity and highlight Ethel's ability to handle social situations. Do you find William's behavior credible? Are you building any expectations as a result of his awkwardness and Ethel's teasing?

WILLIAM

Huh? Oh . . . no. I'm fine.

Our knowing about the book William is using is "dramatic irony." We know something the other character doesn't know. We expect to find out what will happen when he tells Ethel about the book or when she otherwise discovers it.

ETHEL

Maybe you should take off your coat. Hmmm?

WILLIAM

Yes. *(Starts to rise, remembering, sits down quickly.)* Well. *(Pause.)* This sure is a beautiful place. Yes sir. Ma'am. Umm. This coffee is delicious. Colombian?

ETHEL

Sanka.

Is Sanka a good joke or a cheap joke (by which we mean "too easy" a joke)?

WILLIAM

*(not paying attention, searching for a question)* So, what have you been up to lately?

ETHEL

Since I went into the kitchen, William?

WILLIAM

*(shifting in his seat)* Yes. No. I mean . . . *(Pause.)* I'm sorry. It's just that . . . this is . . . well, this is the first date that I've been on in *(counts his fingers)* forty-eight years and . . . well, I'm just a little rusty, that's all.

The writer continues to add expository detail (forty-eight years, Bay Rum) which is generally a good principle in a realistic script such as this.

ETHEL

Oh, William. Here, give me your hand. *(sniffing)* Is that Bay Rum you're wearing?

WILLIAM

The one and only.

ETHEL

Well, I'll be. I haven't smelled that since Peter d- . . . More sugar?

Is Ethel the kind of person who would not be able to speak comfortably of her husband's death? Or is this a "signal" to tell the audience how to feel?

WILLIAM

Please. *(Rises.)*

ETHEL

*(Takes book. Reads aloud.)* Confidence in Communication, Social Anxiety and Self-Evaluation of Interpersonal Performance by Albert Aiken. *(Soft laughter)* Oh, William.

WILLIAM

*(embarrassed)* What? I just . . . I just wanted to . . .

ETHEL

*(Takes book from table drawer. Laughing. Hands it to William.)*

WILLIAM

*(reading aloud)* I Can If I Want To: A Practical Guide to Effective Interpersonal Communication for the New Assertive Woman by Albert Aiken. *(Short pause.)* You mean . . . *(Both start laughing.)*

ETHEL

*(still laughing)* I've read it twice! What do you say we try this again? *(William, laughing, heads for the door.)*

WILLIAM

*(Doorbell rings. Ethel opens the door.)* Hello, Ethel Phillips. *(Takes her hand.)* I'm William Litton. *(Phone rings in the background.)*

Ethel's finding the book is the resolution of dramatic irony. Is the book revealed in a satisfying way? Do you like the idea of her finding the book? And using a similar one? Are there other ways to end the scene?

The conclusion of this scene—the new understanding between the characters—is at a much faster pace than the previous lines. Is there a reason this seems to be rushed over?

Does the scene have a sense of completion? The end of what was begun? Does the re-entrance along with the ringing phone sum up the scene?

---

The following is a reconstructed workshop (from notes) of the session on **The Date**. The first assignment was to write a short scene—in this case between a man and a woman and in which the important object was a book. This student seems to have the form of a play clearly in mind. He hasn't written things that can't be staged or asked for actions that don't flow naturally from the lines. It is performable.

I wondered, upon reading it, if the class would like it. For me—too much television and too little theatre inspired this. It's a very competent first try, but the characters are *cute* in the way that television sit-com characters often are. Their faults, awkwardness, and differences are glossed over; the playwright wants to solve their problems for them and give them a happy life. Even though Ethel does not seem to be the kind of person who would read a book telling her how to be—and read it twice, no less—she does in this play so that we will have a patched-up unity with William. Yet, the writer is definitely learning how plays work. (As the term progressed he relied less and less on television solutions to his characters' problems.)

**Workshop: Discussion of *The Date***

*(Most workshop dialogue, here and later, contributed by Karl Hendricks)*

KG: Catherine, why don't you start the discussion?

CATHY: You can call me Cathy.

KG: Okay. Cathy?

ALICE: Anyway, I liked this a whole lot.

KG: Can you give us any reasons why?

CATHY: Well, it was cute.

KG: Is that a good thing? Cute?

CATHY: I thought it was funny. Like when William sits on the book, that was funny.

DAN: I just thought that was dumb.

KG: Why?

DAN: It just didn't seem realistic. Like when he was reading from the book. First of all, who would go on a date and then read aloud from a book? And what kind of book reads like that? It was obviously contrived. And there were some other mistakes. For example, Ethel said that the house had been in her family for six generations. If I'm counting right, that's going back to the Civil War, maybe earlier. That's an old house!

ALBERT: I think you're being a little too picky, Dan. I think it's important for us to know that she's been in the house for a long time. It tells us a lot about her character. I think it's also important that we know that William is the kind of character who would be reading that kind of book right before a date.

DAN: If those details are so important, they should be more believable.

ALICE: I agree with Dan about the book. What William read from it did seem kind of contrived.

KG: And Cathy?

CATHY: Yes, it's contrived. I'd say re-write that section. At least, maybe William doesn't find a pertinent section right off the bat.

KG: You're suggesting some re-writing to make the book more believable. Anything else?

ALICE: I found it pretty interesting that right from the start Ethel used William's name in the conversation as if they had known each other for a really long time. I mean, if I meet someone for the first time I don't call them by their first name in every other sentence. It made Ethel seem really flirtatious, which is good because that's the kind of character I thought she was. One thing that kind of bothered me though—and I guess this might be a small point—was that what William's singles ad said seemed to be incongruous with what he was really like. In the ad it said that he wanted a woman who wasn't "afraid to bake a peach cobbler in the morning and then go dancing at night," which seemed kind of bold, demanding, yet romantic. But then when he shows up he brings dandelions, which is kind of a bumbling thing to do, and that kind of sets the tone for the way he is for the rest of the scene. Since the ad is the first piece of information we have in the scene, I think it should tell us more about him.

CATHY: I think it's kind of charming that he brings her dandelions. And with those singles ads, nobody ever turns out to be what their ad is like. Everybody lies in those things.

ALICE: But I think if William was clever enough to make his ad sound as smooth as it does then he should be smart enough to bring something a little more romantic, like roses, to a first date.

KG: Did you end up caring about these characters?

DAN: I think the scene tries too hard to get our sympathy. William, the poor sap, hasn't been on a date in 48 years. Talk about a dry spell! Then Ethel starts getting all teary-eyed because William reminds her of her dead husband.

ALBERT: But I liked that part of the scene because Ethel doesn't come right out and say, "You remind me of my dead husband." Instead there's the concrete detail of the Bay Rum that tells us indirectly how she's feeling.

KG: Do you think that Ethel has been out on other dates since her husband died?

ALBERT: Yes, you can tell she's relaxed and, like Alice was saying before, she was flirting with William. But I think that's one of the good things about the scene. If they were both nervous or both relaxed, then the scene wouldn't be as interesting.

KG: Now that we've had a free response time, let us go to our first workshop question. What was the playwright trying to do?

DAN: He was trying to write a funny little play or scene about older people in the dating scene. But it didn't really work all that well—for me. It wasn't funny.

CATHY: He wanted to entertain. That's all. It was entertaining.

ALBERT: He wanted to show that natural is better, that people don't need books to relate to each other.

ALICE: He wanted us to like the characters, to find them sympathetic and charming, and he wanted us to want them to get together, I think. It's geared to finding them some common ground.

KG: Here is an important point: do you agree that what Alice says is true, that the playwright wants us to like these people and to believe that getting them together is a good thing? And that, as some of the rest of you point out, the playwright wants to do this in a light, entertaining way?

ALL: Yes, that's about it. Seems like the intention.

KG: Second workshop question: Did he accomplish these things?

CATHY: More or less.

DAN: He didn't entertain everyone because the characters are not particularly realistic. If we can't believe in them, we're not likely to be charmed by them.

ALICE: But it was clear that it was a good thing to get these people together.

ALBERT: I wanted them to get together.

KG: Let's look at the characters' motivations for a moment. Third workshop question: Is there something they want—that you can believe in? Something they try to do? Is there a way they try to pursue a goal?

CATHY: Yes, they try to please each other.

DAN: They don't try all that hard in a real way.

ALBERT: What do you expect them to do? It's a first date. And the scene is a comedy.

ALICE: Maybe it should be more comic.

KG: That's possible. I need to bring up a concern of mine. That you are not unduly influenced by television sit-com writing. We've all had a lot of exposure to an idea of dramatic writing that glosses over real characterizations and aims to do away with real problems. Sit-coms tend to deal with surface problems—surface, because they're solved quickly by some small misunderstanding being revealed. People think better of whatever they've been doing for twenty-five minutes and in the last five minutes turn over new leaves. I'm going to ask you to not be satisfied with that. If Ethel is more sophisticated than William, let that be a factor in their relationship. Maybe it's hopeless between them. Or maybe the compromises they have to make hurt in some way. But if there's no problem, there's no drama. Try not to make everything easily solvable.

However, the writer has done some things really well. He has prepared for William's entrance, he has used the phone accurately—Ethel says just enough for us to get the drift of the other person's conversation. The lines and the action are smoothly written—he clearly sees these people on a stage. This is performable.

Now let us turn to a script we'll call *Garage Sale*. Notice in this, too, the handling of entrances and exits. This writer also gets one character offstage for a moment to let us see another alone, hiding a book. Like the incident in **The Date**, the secretive action lets the audience know something one of the characters doesn't know. This is the most basic ingredient of playwriting: dramatic irony.

## Garage Sale
*by Stan Denman*

*(The setting is in the living room/den of a modest middle-class home. UC is a dining room table and four chairs complete with a crocheted white tablecloth and a milk glass bowl full of plastic fruit. DSL is a coffee table and a couch covered with a brightly patterned afghan. SR is a recliner, overstuffed rocker, and a foot stool. A large set of windows draws the focus UC. A swinging door UL leads to the kitchen. Immediately DS is a door leading outside, and UR is a hallway leading to the remainder of the house. The house has the look and comfort of old-fashioned, conservative southern living.*

*As the lights rise, Charlotte, 63, is cleaning the house. She is seen on her hands and knees near the front door picking something out of the carpet and putting it in her other hand. Lucas, 68, enters the front door and squeezes by his wife as the scene begins.)*

CHARLOTTE
Take off your shoes.

LUCAS
What?

CHARLOTTE
Take off your shoes. You're tracking grass burrs all through this house.

LUCAS
*(He looks at the bottom of his shoes.)* Oh. *(He takes them off and places them on the welcome mat as she finishes and goes into the kitchen. As he hangs his jacket on the coat rack, he takes a small, tattered black journal from the pocket and hides it under the cushion of the recliner where he sits pretending to read the newspaper. He is obviously up to something. She re-enters from the kitchen.)*

CHARLOTTE
Now, I want you to do that every time you come in with those old work boots. It's getting to where you can't even

walk through the house without shoes on. *(She sees his coat.)* Lucas, I have asked you not to leave your coat in here. . . .

LUCAS
*(He hasn't heard a word she has said.)* I talked to Martha this morning.

CHARLOTTE
*(taking his coat to the bedroom)* You did? How's her knee?

LUCAS
Fine. She gave me the stuff from the garage sale that they couldn't get anybody to take.

CHARLOTTE
How much did we make? *(She removes the tablecloth and begins to wax the table.)*

LUCAS
Almost thirty dollars.

CHARLOTTE
Oh, I was hoping for more than that. What was left?

LUCAS
Just some old clothes and a box of books.

CHARLOTTE
Well, what did you do with it?

LUCAS
I told her to just give it to the Goodwill, or haul it off.

CHARLOTTE
Well, I didn't get to go through half that stuff. I hope there wasn't something I missed.

LUCAS
*(knowingly)* No, nothing you hadn't seen before. *(Pause, then, unable to contain himself any longer)* I found out the derndest thing today.

CHARLOTTE
*(working)* What's that?

LUCAS
I heard that Charlie Hukel was quite a playboy in his day. *(She stops and looks at Lucas, who continues talking while looking through the paper.)* Seems he made a move on every woman in Webster County.

CHARLOTTE
*(tense)* Oh?

LUCAS
Yeah, even the married ones . . . course you wouldn't know about that, would ya? *(With this he looks right at her; she continues polishing even harder, avoiding his eyes. A tense pause.)*

CHARLOTTE
You want leftovers for supper?

LUCAS
*(exploding)* I knew it! I knew you couldn't lie to my face!

CHARLOTTE
Now wait, Lucas. I don't know where you got . . .

LUCAS
(It is now obvious what he has been up to and he intends to play the martyr to the hilt.) It don't matter where! Fifty-one years! Fifty-one years, and I have never looked at another woman, and all this time I have been part of a sordid, seedy love triangle!

CHARLOTTE
Oh, don't be ridiculous, Lucas, it was one innocent encounter nearly 50 years ago.

LUCAS
Innocent! A man grabs your tit behind the barn full of people, and that's innocent?

CHARLOTTE
Lucas, he did not grab my . . . me! It was a fleeting moment. Charlie's brother came in and . . .

LUCAS
Oh, he did, did he? Did good ole Arty try to give you a poke in the woods, too?

CHARLOTTE
(aghast) Lucas!

LUCAS
Or did he just watch?

CHARLOTTE
Lucas Coleman, you are way out of line. I will not take these insults. If fifty-one years of faithfulness doesn't count . . .

LUCAS
Don't you mean forty-nine?

CHARLOTTE
I NEVER HAD RELATIONS WITH CHARLIE HUKEL!

LUCAS
Well . . .

CHARLOTTE
OR ARTHUR! . . . Or anyone else for that matter!

LUCAS
But he did grab your tit.

CHARLOTTE
(trying to regain control) He touched my breast, yes, but . . .

LUCAS
For Christ's sake, you make it sound so clinical! Admit it, you had the hots for him.

CHARLOTTE
I may have been fond of him.

LUCAS
You had the hots for him.

CHARLOTTE
Alright, I had a school girl crush on him, but not more than any . . .

LUCAS
Oh geez, Charlie Hukel. Lottie, that was 1940, we'd been married a year by then. Besides, the guy was a thief. You knew he stole the watch your father gave me.

CHARLOTTE
Now, we don't know that for sure. Nobody ever proved that. We never found the watch.

LUCAS
But everybody knew it was him.

CHARLOTTE
Everyone thought that he . . . What am I doing? Why am I defending the man? He's been dead for nearly ten years.

LUCAS
(ranting) I can't believe it! Charlie Hukel! Of all the . . .

CHARLOTTE
Now, Lucas . . .

LUCAS
Charlie Hukel. You know what the guys at the plant use'ta call him?

CHARLOTTE
I have no idea.

LUCAS
(cutting her off) Wee Willy.

CHARLOTTE
(confused) What?

LUCAS
And do you know why they called him that?

CHARLOTTE
Lucas, really, I don't care.

LUCAS
Well, I'll tell you why. He got that name at the Ni-Pak Company picnic in 1939 when some of the fellas went skinny dippin' in Miller's Creek to cool off. You women were up at the hill fixin' supper and half the men in the company were down at the creek bed, buck nekked, laughin' their butts off at Wee Willy Hukel. That poor guy was worse than a dang cat. You ever seen a Tom cat's hooter?

CHARLOTTE
(shocked and appalled at his whole tirade) I certainly have not!

LUCAS
Well, there you go, then! Wee Willy, the watch thief.

CHARLOTTE
Will you please . . .

LUCAS

And let me tell you somethin', it wasn't on account a the water neither. God in Heaven never made water cold enough to do that to a man.

CHARLOTTE

Alright! That is enough! This is absolutely ridiculous to dig up the past after all these years. For Heaven's sake, Lucas. We were kids then. Since then we've raised children of our own and had a wonderful life together. Don't spoil memories of our marriage by digging up innocent mistakes from the past. *(Pause.)* Don't be silly. You know that I love you. No one else would have put up with you for this long. *(Lucas stands DR facing out away from his wife. As she hugs him from the back we see a slight smile as a new plan of attack strikes him.)*

LUCAS

Well, I guess you're right. It was probably nothing.

CHARLOTTE

Of course it was nothing. We went on to have four children, didn't we? *(She goes back to finish the table.)*

LUCAS

Yeah, you were probably just another innocent victim in a long line of young girls.

CHARLOTTE

Well, thank you, but I wasn't exactly a victim, dear.

LUCAS

Well, I'm sorry for gettin' so mad. I should've known it didn't mean anything. I mean why would he have picked you with so many other attractive, unattached girls around?

CHARLOTTE

*(slightly defensive)* Well, I wasn't entirely without appeal, dear. He was an experienced young man and I was a reasonably attractive young lady, even though I was married.

LUCAS

Yeah, but I'm sure you were right, it was just an unimportant flash in the pan thing.

CHARLOTTE

Well, I don't know . . .

LUCAS

You know, just Wham, Bam, Thank You . . .

CHARLOTTE

*(suddenly)* Lucas Coleman, it was not Wham or Bam! I'll have you know it was a very passionate and moving experience.

LUCAS

No, Lottie, really. it's okay. I'm sure it was nothing. Groping around in the dark behind an old barn, a little kiss. Phffft. *(He waves his hand, dismissing it.)*

CHARLOTTE

*(very defensive)* We didn't grope! It wasn't like that at all. It was a full moon. The stars were out. You were in the barn

cuttin' up with your friends and I met him accidentally out by the well. He began to sweet-talk and I was so flattered . . . well . . . things sort of got out of hand. *(By this point she is sitting on the coffee table facing out, caught up in the memory. Lucas has gone back to reading the paper. She sighs and notices he is not paying attention.)* Lucas Coleman.

LUCAS

What?

CHARLOTTE

You . . . Oh, never mind . . . *(She crosses to the couch and begins to cry.)*

LUCAS

What? *(She turns away.)* What'd I do?

CHARLOTTE

*(She controls her tears, angry with herself.)* I feel so foolish. For a moment there, just for a moment, I thought you really cared. I thought you were jealous and it was almost as if we were young again, . . . well . . . *(she breaks away to herself)* Stupid, stupid.

LUCAS

*(He is now genuinely concerned and realizes he has gone too far.)* Lottie . . .

CHARLOTTE

*(regaining control)* Never you mind. It doesn't matter. I should have known that I could have had a torrid, adulterous affair with a man who had one foot in the penitentiary and you wouldn't have batted an eye. *(She begins to tear up again.)* I only thought that . . . oh . . . *(She cries.)*

LUCAS

*(He crosses back to the chair, takes out the book and solemnly begins to read.)* "Last night at the dance I accidentally met Charlie Hukel behind the Emerson's barn, near the well. He began to talk to me so quietly and sweetly, and he told me how beautiful I looked. Then he put his arm around my waist and pulled me close. I felt his hand on my . . . uh, *(Lucas clears his throat as he is clearly uncomfortable reading these words)* breast as he gave me a long, deep kiss. I know I should have stopped him, but it was so tender and romantic, I couldn't resist. No one ever told me I was actually beautiful. At that moment we heard someone coming down the path, so I ran back to the barn and back to Lucas." *(During the reading Charlotte regains her composure and looks out as she listens. By the end she is looking at Lucas. A bit afraid and confused, she begins to speak.)*

CHARLOTTE

Lucas, please don't think that . . .

LUCAS

*(He holds his hand up to stop her.)* Wait, there's more. *(He turns several more pages and begins to read again.)* "Today the doctor confirmed what I already knew. Lucas and I are going to have a baby. Lucas said that he knew, too, because I had been getting prettier by the day. He said that in 50 years I'll be so

pretty he won't be able to stand it. Won't be able to stand it. Poor Charlie Hukel. That's something he'll never see."

CHARLOTTE

Then you knew it was nothing?

LUCAS

Yeah, I knew.

CHARLOTTE

Then why did you . . . ?

LUCAS:

Because I . . . I just found out this morning. I didn't mean to. I was just going through that box of books and . . . well, it made me jealous, even after all these years. I knew it didn't really mean anything, but I wanted to show you that it still mattered, that you still matter. . . . Oh, I don't know.

CHARLOTTE

Shhhh. It's alright. I understand.

LUCAS

I guess I just went a little too far. You think I went a little too far?

CHARLOTTE

In a word?

BOTH

Yes.

LUCAS

You are a pretty gal, you know that? *(teasing her)* You're getting kind of old . . .

CHARLOTTE

Well, it's no wonder.

LUCAS

Ready for our walk?

CHARLOTTE

I suppose. *(as they move toward the door)* Put your boots on outside, I don't want . . .

LUCAS

Grass burrs, I know.

CHARLOTTE

*(Lucas picks up his boots and goes out the front door. Charlotte follows. Just before she is out of sight she calls to Lucas.)* Wee Willy, huh?
 *(The lights fade as she shuts the door behind them.)*

This writer is having a good time. His pleasure in his script comes through in energy. It has energy. However, I'd like to ask you to keep to page limits for these exercises. It's a very different challenge to develop a situation in eight pages or in three pages. Some of the fullness of character coming through here comes from giving characters enough time to act on contradictions. But this situation could have been developed in fewer pages. The middle section gets very repetitive. This writer, like the last, is eager to *solve*

everything. Lucas may be mean in his teasing of Charlotte, but it feels as if the playwright can't let that be. He wants to wrap it all up and let us know all is forgiven. What if the memory of Charlie Hukel stirs up for Charlotte a memory of what she's missed? That might be interesting.

The class questioned the accuracy of the dialogue in *Garage Sale*. Would Lucas really say "buck nekked"? Isn't he too articulate, one student asked? Or is Lucas actor-like, playing with language? Should language be consistent? Obviously, there are no easy answers to this.

The thing is, you can just feel how much this writer likes language. And that's to the good. Actors are attracted to roles partly because of the passions they get to play, but also for *how* they get to speak. It would be fun to speak this play. Actors like to taste lines that are not ordinary in the same way we like to taste food that isn't bland. The more flavorful, the more we're attracted to it. Mamet and Shepard are too spicy for some people; for others, they create a taste-addiction.

Since, for the first assignment, we are studying entrances, look at *Garage Sale* again. I think the entrance of Lucas in *Garage Sale* is well-handled. Charlotte is on stage, doing something that tells us who she is. When Lucas enters, the expectation is that he'll say something. When he doesn't and when he squeezes past Charlotte, we also learn something about him. Since Charlotte knows him so well, she can tell him, as she obviously usually does, to take off his shoes. This is a reinforcement of who we think she is, a very clean and orderly woman, and a statement about who he is. Here is part of the workshop reaction.

## Workshop: Discussion of *Garage Sale*

KG: How do you want to start talking about the scene?

CATHY: It was really long.

ALICE: I like how we're introduced to Charlotte and Lucas. What they do at the beginning of the scene tells us a lot about their characters. Lucas is kind of this rough guy who doesn't care if he tracks dirt in the house, and Charlotte is kind of reserved and likes to maintain an outward appearance of order and likes to have everything in its proper place. They're different from each other.

KG: So you're saying both Lucas and Charlotte are pretty well established as characters at the beginning of the scene. Did they stay the same throughout the whole scene?

DAN: I thought there were times when they slipped out of character. Lucas is set up as being this red-neck guy in the first two-thirds of the scene, you know, he's saying stuff like "he gave you a poke in the woods" and "he grabbed your tit." But then at the end of the scene he turns out to be Mr. Sensitive. I mean, I'm not saying you can't love your wife just because you have a rural accent, but Lucas just seemed to be a shaky character for me.

ALICE: I agree with Dan. I think the writer goes way too far with Lucas' dialect. One section that I particularly had a problem with was when he's explaining to Charlotte why Charlie Hukel was called Wee Willy. He talks about Charlie running around "buck nekked" and how he was "worse than a dang cat." I think there are two things wrong with Lucas having such a heavy dialect. First of all, he doesn't keep it up all the time. A little earlier he tells Charlotte that she makes her little thing with Charlie "sound so clinical." From the kinds of things he says in other places it's hard for me to believe that he would use a word like *clinical*. And the other thing about Lucas' dialect is that it clashes so much with what Charlotte is like. If they come from the same background, how come Charlotte doesn't sound more like Lucas? I couldn't figure out how these two people ended up together.

CATHY: Me neither. They have so little in common. And why would someone like Charlotte settle for someone like Lucas?

ALBERT: Maybe it just shows that Charlotte has changed over the years, and Lucas hasn't, which I think creates an interesting kind of tension.

ALICE: But there's nothing in the scene to show us that. We shouldn't have to guess at essential knowledge of a character's life. It should be in there somehow.

KG: Well, you've talked about Lucas and his relationship with Charlotte, but what about Charlotte herself? Is she a believable character?

ALBERT: Well, she appears to be more consistent than Lucas. She does change at the end of the scene, but in a more subtle way. She kind of loosens up a little bit when she makes that joke about Wee Willy, although she still bugs Lucas about his boots.

KG: Do you think she and Lucas are too dissimilar for their relationship to be believable?

ALBERT: The way I read it was that Lucas normally doesn't act so rough or talk so vulgar to his wife. I kind of imagined that he had mellowed out over the years, but when he finds Charlotte's old diary the thing about Charlie Hukel causes him to get really upset and revert back to his farmboy roughness or whatever. And that's why Charlotte sort of enjoys it when he's jealous because it reminds her of when they were young.

CATHY: Yeah, I thought it was interesting that Charlotte gets the most upset when Lucas acts like he doesn't care.

DAN: She's the typical woman. No matter what poor Lucas does, he can't please her.

CATHY: Well, I think Lucas pretty much acted like a jerk. He didn't trust his wife at all, and they'd been married for 51 years.

DAN: You know, I just noticed something. It says in the beginning that Charlotte is 63 and yet they've been married for 51 years. That means they got married when she was 12. Man, that was a backwoods wedding.

ALBERT: Dan, always a stickler for detail.

KG: Hmm. One of those numbers should be changed.

Here are two more scripts—these are on the subject of an older man, a young woman, and a suitcase.

## Childish Things
### by Lauri James Bolland

*This scene takes place in a large, dark room. The room is empty, except for a small bed, center stage. The lights are dim, but a young woman can be seen sleeping in the bed. She is wearing a long, child-like nightgown. The bed covers are partially covering her and drape to the floor.*

*An older man (Papa), dressed in white, enters from the right. As he enters, the lights come up. He walks to the bed and touches the girl (Mary) on the shoulder.*

MARY
(*sitting up straight*) Papa! I was sure you'd be back! (*climbing out of bed, kneeling beside bed on floor*)

PAPA
(*stepping back from bed, looking into audience*) Your Papa hasn't come for you.

MARY
(*not hearing, beginning to lift covers and peer under bed*) You've been gone so long.

The setting is not realistic.

The writer sets up a question. The age of the woman and the style of the nightgown don't go together. Why?

The lights reflect the character of Papa. There are no light switches, no dependence on realism.

Many moves right away. Even if we don't know what she's doing, we sense an urgency in her actions.

PAPA

Papa died, little Mary.

MARY

*(still not hearing, reaching under bed)* I waited, and waited, we just . . . *(grunting, as she drags an obviously heavy suitcase from under the bed)* . . . Umpf . . . didn't . . . oh . . . know where you went. *(Kneels beside suitcase, with back to P., stroking it as P. speaks.)*

PAPA

*(to M.)* Mary, you are Papa's dearest child. Your Papa would never have chosen to leave you.

MARY

*(still looking at suitcase)* Isn't it a lovely suitcase, Papa? *(unzipping suitcase)* And so full of memories. I filled it right after you left. *(Opens suitcase, reaches in with both hands, and removes hands as if holding a doll, though holding nothing.)* Just look at this, Papa. My Raggedy Ann Doll. *(Lifts doll's dress, and "reads" heart inscription.)* "Papa loves Mary." This was for my seventh birthday, see— *(She turns, and carefully hands doll to P. After M. turns around, P. tosses "doll" away as if setting a bird free.)*

MARY

*(Removes and examines "something," though nothing is there; smiling)* Your pipe. *(Smells it.)* Mmmm. Black Jack Tobacco. *(She hands "pipe" toward P., but doesn't look back. Papa takes "pipe," and launches it similarly to doll. Mary has removed from the suitcase a "necklace," and is dangling it by the "chain.")*

MARY

*(admiringly)* Grandma Nellie's Cameo. *(She slips "necklace" on, over her head.)* Papa gave this to me on his last Christmas with us. *(Mary quickly reaches into suitcase and removes a large "picture frame" . . . touching the picture)* His last Christmas. So handsome . . . *(Papa unfastens "necklace" from back of Mary's neck, tosses it, then, leaning over M's head, takes "picture" out of her hand, and tosses it, as well.)*

MARY

*(noticing none of this, removes a "book" from suitcase. She caresses the "cover," sniffs the "leather," then opens the "cover" and begins turning "pages.")* Funny, I don't remember this book. *(Turns another "page," then stops.)* Oh . . . *(reading)* "And yet, do not mourn for me . . ."

PAPA

*(interrupting)* "And yet, do not mourn for me with tear, or psalm, or tolling bell. Simply await the dawn, my dear, with anxious heart, avow to make-believe that we do not say Farewell . . ."

Papa speaks almost as if he is a third person telling her this.

Does the writer mean "dearest child" or "dear child"?

Does the writer need "and so full of memories"? Or is that implicit in calling the suitcase, which should certainly be old, "lovely"?

There are some things that theatre alone can do—not the same things that prose fiction and film do. One of those things is *play* (like child's play) with objects. An actor can pantomime objects and we still know what is intended. Playwriting offers a chance to play with the materials of theatre—to play a game with pretense. Audiences tend to be fascinated by actors dealing with things that are not there, for it shows off the actor's art, the actor's skill at pretending. Remember, drama plays with the notion of what is real and what is not real. So I think it's interesting that the playwright tried this in a first assignment.

Is this sentimental? You will see that some of the people in the workshop thought so. i.e., Papa is awfully good, not selfish at all, has no contradictions, is only bent on helping Mary.

The scene is highly symbolic and dance-like. Too much so for a whole play? There was a fashion in plays of this sort, but it was short-lived. If you want to read something that is highly symbolic, take a look at something by Maurice Maeterlinck— **The Intruder** or **Pelleas and Melisande**. These plays are identified as *impressionistic* or *symbolist* plays. The symbolist plays aren't done much today, outside of a few classes in directing style.

MARY
Just "Till we meet again," God's Grace allow . . . (*Exit P. off right. Mary zips suitcase, stands, and lifts case, which is surprisingly light. She sets it at the bottom of the bed, climbs back in, and sleeps.*)

Has there been a change? Does the scene, like a small play, seem to conclude?

---

The scene is *interesting* because it uses the materials of theatre (and I can imagine it performed in quite a moving way).

In the workshop Albert said that the scene seemed like a dance. That was what Dan did not like about it: he found the piece too poetic, yet there tends to be a grace of movement (like dance) suggested by most plays that work well. The brothers in *True West* "dance." So do the characters of *Old Times* and *Home*. Those "dances" will be the subjects of later chapters. In drama, movement, gesture, and the handling of objects take on significance beyond themselves. It is valuable that in *Childish Things* the playwright is beginning to explore the possibilities for movement.

The writer didn't resolve this by waking everyone up and saying in effect that the preceding drama didn't matter, that it was all a dream! Just as you should steer away from lines like "Hi, how are you," because they're too common, too easy, you should also steer away from plays that are resolved with "It was all a dream." Plays *are* dreams. They have the same mixed messages of the real and the unreal combined. You will nearly always negate the experience of a play by announcing that it was a dream. This writer has used the dream *better* than that. She has just used it and let it be the action.

There is a suggestion that Mary almost dies in her sleep and that something—some life force—keeps her alive. People who have the condition known as sleep apnea almost die many times a night because their bodies forget to breathe. In any case, Mary's *danger* is part of the drama here. Whether it's physical or emotional, Mary is in danger of not going on with her life. And there's an element of drama in her saving herself—as if her mind remembered to breathe—just as her body remembered to breathe and get on with it.

## Workshop: Discussion of *Childish Things*

KG:  Now we have *Childish Things* to look at. This time the important object is a suitcase. Start with whatever is first on your mind.

ALBERT:  I really enjoyed this scene. I thought it was really powerful because it was unrealistic, sort of dream-like.

DAN:  Well, Papa does come while Mary's sleeping.

ALBERT:  I liked the action of the scene. Simply throwing away stuff became really significant. It was almost like a dance.

ALICE:  I agree with Albert that the action of the scene could really be dramatic. I liked the idea behind what was going on with Mary taking stuff out of the suitcase. But I don't understand why everything she takes out has to be imaginary. This seems kind of awkward to me; the writer seems to be trying too hard to give the scene a dream-like quality. Couldn't that stuff just as easily have been real? I think it would have more of an impact on the audience if they could see a real pipe and a real doll. And then there's the part where she's reading the inscription on the doll. How will the audience be able to understand that if they don't see it?

CATHY:  I'm not sure whether it matters if we see the objects or not. On the one hand I can see Alice's point that having them be imaginary makes it more confusing, especially when the scene already sort of has an unreal feeling to it. But on the other hand, if the objects were imaginary, that would add to the dream-like feeling in the scene, make it more like a dance, like Albert was saying.

DAN:  My main problem with the scene doesn't have anything to do with the objects. I was just bothered because there didn't seem to be much of a story happening here. I mean, it was poetic and everything, but it seemed like a photograph or painting or something. I guess I can't expect gobs of conflict in a first short assignment, but still, I wish I could feel like I knew more at the end of the scene than I knew at the beginning.

ALBERT:  But, I don't know. I paid attention because I knew something was wrong and I didn't know what was going to happen.

CATHY:  Me, too. I paid attention.

KG:  That's not a small thing. And, at the end, there's a change. Mary is lighter, unburdened. She has failed at her objective—to hold on to Papa—but she has stayed alive.

## Leavetaking
*by Karl Hendricks*

*The scene is set in the living room. There is an old couch in the center with two chairs on each side. There is a fireplace to the left and the mantelpiece and end table next to the couch are cluttered with photographs and knick-knacks. An old man, about 70, is sitting in the chair to the left, and a young woman, about 18, is on the couch. Next to her is an overnight bag.*

GRANDPA
Well, sorry I didn't get you anything for school. Your grandmother usually took care of things like that.

MAUREEN

(brightly) Oh, that's alright, I think I've packed too much already. There's barely room in the car for me and Mom. (Pause.) Is there anything I could get you? I could have gone shopping for you or something. . . .

GRANDPA

No, no, no, I'm okay. Your Uncle Fred stops in once in a while, and I can still get around well enough.

MAUREEN

But your feet still hurt?

GRANDPA

Eh, well . . . I'm okay. (Pause.) You know, you ought to get yourself some snacks for your room. You might get hungry late at night. You ought to take some crackers or something so you don't have to leave your room.

MAUREEN

Oh, I got some stuff to eat. My mom thought of all that.

GRANDPA

Where is your mother anyway? Why didn't she come in?

MAUREEN

(slightly nervous) Um, she went to the store to get some last minute things. She said she would be back in a few minutes. We're going straight to the airport from here. (Pause. He doesn't respond.) But, um, actually, I might stop and say goodbye to a few more people. I really should say goodbye to Sara and Mr. and Mrs. Lloyd. I think we should have time. . . .

GRANDPA

She didn't want to come in.

MAUREEN

Ummm . . .

GRANDPA

(irritated) I want to tell you something and I want you to listen to me. When you get to school, don't be like your mother and start protesting and demonstrating against everything. Don't believe everything that people tell you.

MAUREEN

Oh, I don't . . .

GRANDPA

I'd like to know how many of these people who go out and protest nuclear power actually turn out lights when they're not using them. They go out to protest and all the lights in their houses are on.

MAUREEN

(quickly) I don't know. Listen, Grandpa, I called the hospital about your legs.

GRANDPA

(ignoring her) They're out protesting and then they go home and waste all that energy.

MAUREEN

Grandpa, the doctor told me that you might be a candidate

for a new procedure they have, but you're going to have to go in to have some tests run.

GRANDPA

What?

MAUREEN

They could fix your legs. They have a new instrument that can clear arteries. But you have to have a new angiogram done because your last one was too long ago.

GRANDPA

I'm too old to have any more operations.

MAUREEN

My mom could take you to get the tests done.

GRANDPA

I'll ask Fred if I decide to do it.

MAUREEN

(quietly) Please go, Grandpa. (Pause.)

GRANDPA

(looking at her and the bag) Why'd you haul that big bag in here?

MAUREEN

Oh, I almost forgot. I brought you something. (She searches through the bag, and pushing aside some shirts and towels, she pulls out a framed photograph of them. She gets up and hands it to him.)

GRANDPA

Thank you. (looking at picture) This is nice. (He starts to get up and he groans.)

MAUREEN

Here, let me. (She takes the picture from him and places it on the mantelpiece.)

GRANDPA

No, no. Move it over. Put it next to the picture of me and your mother. (A car horn is heard outside.)

MAUREEN

(slightly startled) That's my mom.

GRANDPA

Don't keep her waiting.

MAUREEN

(kissing him on the cheek) I love you, Grandpa. Promise me you'll make an appointment to get those tests done.

GRANDPA

Okay, okay. Good luck. I'll see you at Thanksgiving.

One of the things I think the playwright has done well in this first assignment is that he gave it a natural consequence, a natural ending. The scene shows the characters trying to be good to each other and it suggests that the separation coming up between Maureen and her grandfather is going to be hard to fight. The mother's effect on both of them is powerful. She's out, she's in the world, she functions, she doesn't want to see her father. What can Maureen do in the face of this when she is young and about to embark upon a new life? There is no attempt to fix it all up at the end. Maureen doesn't call her mother in; the mother doesn't arrive with a change of heart; the grandfather doesn't find a way (magically) to speak to his daughter, letting all old hurts disappear in a line or two. The tendency to fix up the ending—the television tendency—is absent here.

Everything about the grandfather's ailment and Maureen's involvement has to be made more specific to be believable. She could say, "Grandpa, I've done something—I hope you won't be angry with me. But my friend, Angie, remember her? Well, her grandmother's arteries were worse than yours. Well, she had surgery, and you should see what they can do. So—I made an appointment with the same doctor for you." He might say, almost hopefully, "Did your mother put you up to that?" And maybe she says, "No, I never told her I did it. Please go, Grandpa. Please let them take a look." Maybe she hands him an appointment card or a slip of paper. "You'll have to get someone to drive you. It's over on the North Side—what they call the Professional Building, right next to the hospital." If the playwright wants us to believe that Maureen went to the trouble of calling a doctor for her grandfather, he can work out the details that will *make* it believable and that will tell us more about her.

## Workshop: Discussion of *Leavetaking*

KG: Okay, here we are with another from the first batch of assignments. Two people and a suitcase. What did you think?

CATHY: I was pretty touched by it. I thought it was sweet. It seemed to be realistic in the way it portrayed people relating to each other.

DAN: I don't know, I thought it was too sentimental. The writer seems to be trying too hard to tug at our heartstrings. I think an especially good example of this is when Maureen gives him the picture and he tells her to move it next to the one of him and her mother. I could just picture the writer sitting there writing this, thinking, "Now how am I going to make this symbolic?"

KG: I think what you're trying to say is that you feel the playwright's hand at that point. The action is chosen for symbolic meaning and isn't necessarily natural.

ALICE: I agree with Dan that that part is awkward, but that was really the only point where I was bothered. I thought the dialogue was good in other sections. For example, there's the one part where Grandpa says, "I'm too old to have any more operations." And then Maureen says, "My mom could take you to get the tests done," and then he says he'll ask Fred, and she says, "Please go." I just thought that part was great because it's like there's this

negotiation going on, and they're talking about the same thing and yet they're missing each other, which was realistic. The dialogue was really good in that respect.

KG: Do you have any suggestions for the writer on how he could improve this?

ALBERT: Well, one thing I think he needs to work on is making his details more specific. There are a couple of spots where there could be some minor adjustments, like when Maureen says her mother went to the store to get some "last minute things." I think it would be better if she had some specific thing she had to get, like soap or something. A point where lack of specifics is a big problem is when Maureen says that she called the hospital about her grandfather's legs. There are so many important details missing from that section, like: what specifically is wrong with his legs, who did she call at the hospital, what is the new procedure they have, and so on. And wouldn't it be more believable if she said she called his doctor or something, rather than just "the hospital." Also, I feel in this scene that Maureen really does care for her grandfather, but maybe there could be some further details that would make us believe she's the kind of person who would take the initiative to contact someone on her grandfather's behalf.

KG: I'm glad you're noticing details. Being specific is what makes a scene believable.

ALICE: You know what I've discovered about details? This may sound weird, but I think that the more specific you make a character the more it seems that there are things about him or her that are universally true, or at least understandable to all people. If you give very specific details about a character, it makes him or her seem more alive, more vivid, and so people can more easily find something in that character to identify with.

KG: That's a good point, Alice. Well put.

ALICE: We talked about this in one of my other classes.

KG: Back to workshop question one. What is the writer trying to do?

ALICE: A realistic play. Touching. About the loss of family. Loss of communications between generations.

DAN: Trying to show a family falling apart and a girl who tries to fix the problems but it's too much for her.

---

### Study Questions and Exercises

1. What changes could the writer of *Garage Sale* make to shorten the script without losing the intention?
2. What changes could the writer of *Garage Sale* make to unsentimentalize the ending?

# FOUR

# Monologue

## OVERVIEW

This chapter introduces the dramatic monologue as an integral part of drama. After a survey of the kinds of monologues in contemporary drama (and some reasons for them) is a more in-depth look at monologues in the play *Glengarry Glen Ross* by David Mamet. *Glengarry* is then discussed, referring to some of the twenty principles of playwriting as a starting point for noticing patterns in its construction.

There are also, in this chapter, instructions for the second writing exercise—the dramatic monologue. Examples of this exercise written by students are included and workshopped. We'll call the exercises *Sleepover, After the Game, The Room, Group Session, Therapy*.

## OBJECTIVES

At the end of this chapter you should be able to

- Discuss the usage of dramatic monologues in plays
- Determine whether you find the sample monologues believable or not
- Write your second exercise, a dramatic monologue

Most drama is made of people in interaction through dialogue. The best thing about rules is breaking them, or finding a way around them. For the next assignment, you will put two people on stage. One speaks; one doesn't. And yet I'm not sure you'll be ready to say that a dialogue of sorts doesn't exist, even though you find a way to make one person speak, one remain silent. That is the assignment.

If you look through plays, you'll see that sometimes a character speaks a short monologue, not much more than a paragraph, and sometimes a character speaks a long monologue, possibly as much as a few pages. The monologue might slow down the pace of the play, but it also can send the drama to a higher pitch. Why? Because when one person is motivated to go on and on with an idea, there is usually something extraordinary and powerful compelling that person.

To do this assignment, you have to ask yourself, why does a person speak and speak without the verbal response of another person? You've no doubt spoken monologues in real life. People you know have, too. What were the reasons? Here are some possible ones: you were angry and wanted to say what you had to say until you felt better. You spoke to the person who made you angry, and you didn't want to be interrupted by any excuses or reasons. You just wanted to give your end of the deal. Or maybe you were angry with one person, but you told another about it. The difficulty of setting up the situation and explaining to your listener just what happened took all your emotional energies and all of your concentration. You didn't want or need an interruption; you just wanted to vent.

Or you were in love and the overflow of feeling took the form of words and words, lots of them.

Or something very complex had happened to you and you had to fit in all the little qualifications and explanations to describe it—even to explain it to yourself. . . .

Or you felt sad or anxious and searched about, *cast* about, for the cause.

Monologues have been spoken in plays, as in life, when a character attempts to relive or reconstruct the past—or some element of it. Or when one character lectures another character; when one character, either agitated or dim-witted, rambles, oblivious to others. Sometimes characters get caught up in their own language-play—and the language begins to drive *them*. It's got its own energy and force, like a machine that won't stop.

Yet not all monologues are dramatic.

What makes a monologue dramatic? What makes it more than just a long speech in a play? For it must have dramatic motion. One way that a monologue can be very dramatic is if the person who doesn't speak is part of the tension, and if the tension in the speaking character rises because of the silence. Part of the work of writing a good monologue is making it believable that the second character—the other person on stage—does not speak. Some of the reasons for silence in the presence of a monologuer are these: the silent character is stunned by what is being said and is literally speechless. The silent character is interested, has something at stake, and is listening intently. The silent character is afraid—afraid to speak, afraid to interrupt, afraid of the emotional power of the monologue. Or the silent character is listening, planning, learning, saving up for a dandy reply. Or the silent character would like to speak, but can't get a word in. Ideally, the silent character is participating somehow in the speech—wordlessly, but responses are there.

## Chekhov, Albee, Pinter, Williams

Anton Chekhov writes monologues when there are several people on stage. Uncle Vanya in the play of that name is in agony, in love with Elena, and furious at the professor, Elena's husband. Vanya is brimming over with frustration and jealousy. Whenever he can collar a listener, he denounces the professor. But he criticizes Elena as well. This second subject of the monologue is especially interesting—a true reaction because the loved one is often the target when love isn't returned in kind.

At the end of Chekhov's *The Sea Gull*, Nina tells Treplev about her love for Trigorin and about her failures as an actress. Treplev, who is in love with her, is stuck for speech. He cannot respond. Nina's speech becomes more and more hysterical and full of despair.

And there are many other examples from Chekhov. Astrov, Sonia, Treplev, Trigorin, Vershinin, Masha, all speak at length to others who see how painfully self-deceived they are, but can do nothing to help.

Edward Albee has the characters of *A Delicate Balance* engage in monologues—and the silent people stay silent because there is so much tension in the family, so much that is hidden and unspoken, that they can't come up with a safe response. Perhaps Albee's best-known play is still the early one-act, *The Zoo Story*, which is practically known for Jerry's long, crazy monologue spoken in Central Park to Peter, a stranger.

Pinter likes monologues. In fact he is known for writing extended speech that is really silence, speech that is clothing to cover emotional nakedness. Take a look at any of his plays—*Old Times, The Caretaker, The Dumbwaiter, A Slight Ache*. There is no lack of drama when a Pinter character speaks a monologue because there is a battle between the speaking character and the silent character in which the tension is constantly rising.

Tennessee Williams, too, finds his characters speaking monologues. In *A Streetcar Named Desire*, Blanche Dubois fantasizes, weaves spells, relives bad memories, even tells the truth—often in extended speech. Amanda in *The Glass Menagerie* goes into reveries about her fantasized past. Those reveries make her children, Tom and Laura, uncomfortable and drive a wedge between her and them. Their silence in the face of her monologues is eloquent. There are many other monologues in *The Glass Menagerie*, in addition to the well-known ones in which Tom Wingfield addresses the audience. There are monologues *within* scenes, like when Tom finally explodes and drunkenly tells his mother off, or when Jim, the Gentleman Caller, tries to encourage Laura to believe in herself. In these cases, the silent characters are very much a part of the action.

## Glengarry Glen Ross

Your second writing assignment is to put two people on stage and have one of them speaking and one of them silent. But before you work on this monologue, you should read David Mamet's *Glengarry Glen Ross*, and think about—among other things—the source of the monologues in it.

### The Film Version

Mamet's play is known also in its film version, released in the fall of 1992. Although much of the film follows the play, the two forms should not be confused. It is important to read the play as it was written for the stage and to notice how Mamet worked with the limits of the stage. Screenplays almost always, in Hollywood language, "open up" a script. Usually, this means new physical locations, visual variety, changes of place, breakup of scenes into smaller units. In the case of *Glengarry Glen Ross*, Mamet, who adapted his own play for the screen, introduced a new character, who, according to Vincent Canby ("David Mamet's Sharks of Real Estate and Their Prey," *New York Times* (Sept. 30 1992: B1,4) is vital. This new character, Blake, "sets the scene for everything that comes after, . . . is an emissary from 'downtown,' that is, from Mitch and Murray, who run this real estate firm. . . ."

Blake gets the film going by insulting the salesmen. He's not *needed* in the play version, though. The sense of threat hanging over the characters comes through without him. One of Canby's phrases reminds us of the power of the original script: Mamet and director James Foley, he says, have managed to preserve "the claustrophobic nature of the original stage work."

See if you can sense the pressure in your reading of the play and in your study of the plot summary. Here, as in all cases in this book, the plot summary is not a substitute for the play, but an aid. Also, the plot summaries are meant to encourage you to write summaries of the plays you read as well as of your own scripts. The summaries reveal the pattern of *action*, show how the playwright has turned ideas to scenes with events.

## Plot Summary of *Glengarry Glen Ross* by *David Mamet*

**Act I, Scene i.** A booth at a Chinese restaurant. Levene tries to get Williamson to assign him more "leads" so that he can do well in sales once again. Williamson refuses and tells Shelley he blew the last ones he had. Levene promises Williamson a cut. Williamson says yes, but to a much higher take. Levene tries to negotiate, but Williamson is firm. It becomes clear only midway through the scene that they are discussing real estate leads, and at the end of the scene that Levene is totally broke.

**Scene ii.** A booth at the restaurant. Moss complains to Aaronow about the leads, the customers (particularly the non-Americans who don't buy), and the bosses at the real estate office. He suggests someone rob the office of the leads. Aaronow is nervous, but continues to question how it might be done. Moss reveals that he already has a buyer. He tells Aaronow that he, Aaronow, has to do the actual stealing. Aaronow doesn't want to. Moss tells him that he bought the idea, listened to it, which makes him an accessory.

**Scene iii.** Two booths at the restaurant. Roma rambles about life, sex, money, to Lingk, who is at the next booth. He philosophizes about unhappiness. He buys Lingk a drink. He introduces the subject of real estate in Florida.

**Act II.** The real estate office, ransacked. Roma is in a fury to see that the office has been robbed. But he calms down when he is told his contract with Lingk was filed safely. That means, he says, he has won the contest prize, a Cadillac.

Meanwhile, a detective takes people one by one into an inner office for questioning. Aaronow tells Roma he doesn't think he has the ability to sell anymore. Roma boosts his spirits. Williamson has only old leads to give Roma. Roma says they're not worthwhile leads, that he can't close the sales.

Levene, joyful at having closed a sale, comes in, offering to buy everyone lunch. Levene tries to tell the others how he made the sale, how he got his confidence back. He is interrupted when Moss comes out of questioning, furious at the way he got treated. Roma and Moss trade insults about their attitudes, particularly about being first and second on the sales contest board. After Moss leaves, Levene tells Roma about his big sale, about the way he manipulated the customers into signing.

Lingk appears at the office. Roma tells Levene to pretend to be a customer and he'll pretend to be selling him something. Lingk waits for a word with Roma while Roma pretends that Levene is a big shot and that he has to rush him to a plane. Lingk manages to say that his wife insists he cancel the deal. Throughout Roma's maneuverings, Lingk persists. Aaronow comes out of questioning, furious and shaken at the treatment he got.

The detective then calls Levene for questioning, which leaves Lingk with Roma. But Roma manages to press Lingk into seeing his problem as a marriage problem rather than a real estate problem. He tells him there is time to think because his deposit check hasn't been cashed.

Williamson, coming out of the questioning room, misreads the situation and soothes Lingk by telling him his check *has* been cashed. Lingk runs out, upset.

Roma refuses to go in for questioning until he has accused Williamson of ruining a deal. Levene jumps on the bandwagon and tells Williamson he doesn't belong there, that he shouldn't make things up unless they'll help a salesman.

Williamson asks Levene how he knew the story about the check was made up. He forces Levene to admit he knew it because it was he who stole the leads and the contracts from the desk the night before.

Levene tries to buy himself out of trouble, suggesting that his big sale shows he is back on track. Williamson tells Levene that the big sale he thinks he made doesn't exist. The buyers are crazy; their signature is worthless.

Roma comes out of questioning as angry as everyone else has been. He tells Levene that he admires him and that they should work together.

Levene is called back into questioning, but Roma, unaware that Levene is the thief and has been caught, tells Williamson that he wants half of Levene's share of everything.

---

Plot summaries are not substitutes for reading the plays. They are intended as samples of notes you take as you notice and learn about plotting.

In some ways *Glengarry Glen Ross* is a 1980's **Death of a Salesman**. The protagonist, Shelley Levene, is in the last stages of falling apart—a salesman who can't cut the mustard any longer. He exists in a largely inhuman world, one inhospitable to any but the most aggressive of personalities. Levene is a product of this world. He has been an aggressor, but now he's getting older, his luck has run out, and he's being shown up in the competition. It begins to seem that maybe he was never all that good anyway. He has no money. He has very little pride left. But worse, his confidence is shattered. What can he do without confidence? A salesman lives on confidence. Through all of his attempts to sell himself, there is a smell of failure, an animal sign to the predators (his boss and co-workers) that he is afraid, lost. The play is filled with monologues of different lengths. Understanding where they come from will help you understand dramatic monologues. While you read, you might notice the following features in *Glengarry Glen Ross*.

### About *Glengarry Glen Ross*

The set description is brief. *A booth at a Chinese Restaurant.* Why did Mamet set his first three scenes in this place? Why not a burger joint, a fast food restaurant? Why not an office? I suggested you think hard before you set a play in a restaurant and here is one of our most successful playwrights doing just that. But notice that he does not ask for a whole restaurant to be set up. In fact, in the two productions I've seen, what you get is what he asked for, "a booth at a Chinese restaurant." Or several "booths" along a banquette wall. There is no need for other customers, no need for waiters. The characters are in a place without other contacts and the effect is startling. We have all been in empty restaurants and we have all been in Chinese restaurants (which can bear a remarkable similarity to each other). If we notice the world around us, and it's a good idea to do so if we're going to do any of the work of theatre, we've seen that usually there is a staff of family members who live and work in the place. It's hard work to keep any sort of restaurant open. If we've thought about it, we've thought about the Asian-American pursuing the American dream—a place of his own, an income large enough to send a child to school. In the meantime, humble clothes, long working hours, quiet resignation.

What else does the setting suggest? Chinese restaurants that have booths are often a little tacky, a little dirty, in spite of the table cloths and the plastic flowers in the vases on the tables. In other words, the struggle of the Asian-American owner is apparent. It's a struggle to stay in business. How do they keep the right amount of food in stock for those who will order when the number of customers is uneven, and not large?

This is the kind of restaurant real estate salesmen of the sort drawn in Mamet's play might very well frequent. It's not going to be expensive. It's not going to be noisy. It's right down the street from the office. It's like a *part* of the office. Mamet sets the first act of his play in the Chinese restaurant; the second half takes place in the actual office.

The play is a treasure hunt. The treasure is identified in the first speech—"the leads." For a salesman "the leads" are the treasure, the means by which to make a living, by which to get "a name on the board," by which to win a Cadillac. The leads are like money, but better, more desirable, because even though they promise more money than they are likely to deliver, with leads, a salesman can *act* and he can dream.

What are the leads? Pieces of paper in the real estate office. With names on them. Mamet allows the audience to see and understand that the leads are worth little. They are a mere *chance* to possibly make a small amount of money—a reminder of the way we symbolize, of the small things we fight for.

The play is built on *who gets them* and who tries by persuasion, cunning, or theft to control them. The leads are pieces of paper that promise financial success for a real estate salesman. But, it turns out, the leads represent people, with their *own* financial problems and their own lives falling apart. And in this play, they are victims.

Just as with **The Dining Room**, one set of people and circumstances stands for all other sets of people and circumstances. You don't have to be a real estate salesman to identify with the play. Students, actors, university faculty, dentists, doctors, lawyers—you name it—can find themselves in this play, in the fight for something which *in itself* is

so much less valuable than all the symbols around it; but it's all there is, it's the goods, so you fight for it.

The play is a play of competition, of greed, of dog-eat-dog, of strength wiping out weakness without compassion, of youth cheating age, of failure; and everybody identifies with it. It is dark, it is true, and it is very, very funny.

Are there characters who are trying to do something? Is there something at stake? Is there someone who is trying to change something?

Yes, all of the principles of traditional play-making are evident here. The characters are trying *to close*, to finish a deal. They are trying to sell themselves. They are trying to sell real estate that nobody *should* want. The product isn't good, but they've got to sell it. This is an obstacle. They are trying to make a living. What is at stake is their livelihood, their standing in the office, their chance at future deals. All this comes down to the leads. If you get the leads you can change anything—so Shelley Levene thinks. The play opens with his attempt to change something. He tries to get Williamson to give him the leads instead of giving them to Roma. Shelley Levene tries to change his luck and his life.

## Monologues in *Glengarry Glen Ross*

Let us take a look at a couple of monologues. The very first speech of the play is a monologue:

### LEVENE

John . . . John . . . John. Okay. John. John. Look: (*Pause*) The Glengarry Highland's leads, you're sending Roma out. Fine. He's a good man. We know what he is. He's fine. All I'm saying, you look at the *board*, he's throwing . . . wait, wait, wait, he's throwing them *away*, he's throwing the leads away.

And so on—for a long time. Levene keeps talking out of desperation, guessing at what John would say if he gave John a chance to say anything. He *can't* give John a chance to say anything, because what John will say will destroy him. Notice the unusual punctuation of Levene's lines. He can't finish a thought just as he can't finish a deal. He finishes sentences abortively. He's sidetracked and interrupted by his own anxieties.

Because this is a good monologue, the second character, John Williamson, is not a prop. He is not there just to further Levene's lines. He is the instrument of torture, the person to be won over. He is fully necessary.

By the time Levene gets to his third speech he is using four-letter words, and over the next two pages the four-letter words increasingly fill his speech until there is practically nothing else. Mamet offends some people. But he chooses his language; he knows what he is doing. Not only do "people really talk like this," but it is also true that they *don't* really talk like this, that Mamet has done what a playwright must do and has turned real dialogue into something better than real, something with sound and rhythm, and its own drive. Many people have called the result poetic.

The language of four-letter words (which eventually becomes empty from overuse) is a hard-edged way of talking about bodies and sex. People's physical lives *can* be talked about in other terms—loving terms, romantic terms, clinical terms. Mamet's language fits the play. To the salesmen of *Glengarry*, people aren't noticed as people. They are potential victims, to be done out of money, to be screwed over. The salesmanship of *Glengarry* is one step up from street muggings.

Levene is the protagonist. The play hinges on the revelation that Roma is both a present antagonist and a future protagonist. He's at a high now, but he won't be there forever. Roma's language tells us this, even when we don't quite understand yet what we're being told. His monologue in Act I, Scene 3 is worth studying because he winds the audience in while he winds Lingk in. It begins

### ROMA

... all train compartments smell vaguely of shit. It gets so you don't mind it. That's the worst thing that I can confess. You know how long it took me to get there? A long time. When you *die* you're going to regret the things you don't do. You think you're *queer* . . . ?

Roma's monologue is as aggressive as Levene's was, but it's sneakier. It's a comic mind-rape. "Where is he going with all this rambling?" we ask ourselves. "What's it all about?" We see eventually that his talk is an intrusion into another's life, another's privacy. We listen, trying to figure out who Lingk is to Roma—only to find out that they don't know each other, that they didn't come into the restaurant together! We come to understand that Roma, the successful one, is always selling. He can't stop, not even when he's sitting at a restaurant; he's a salesman, he is tired, but he can't stop. It's as if he is on a train that smells bad. Does he need the leads to keep going? He doesn't need them as much as Levene does, but he wants them.

Many of the principles of traditional playwriting are at work here. Characters try to affect each other through dialogue. Something is at stake. There is a treasure to be hunted or found or otherwise manipulated. And people don't go at their intentions directly. (If they did go at their intentions directly, there would be no dramatic tension as we've come to know it—from plays like this one.) In *Glengarry Glen Ross*, Levene goes all around the block trying to get leads from Williamson. Moss implicates Aaronow in his plot to steal the leads from Williamson by seeming to gossip about office politics with him. Roma pretends to strike up a casual (if bizarre) conversation with a stranger, but he's angling the conversation to sell a piece of Florida swampland to this stranger, an unsuspecting, shy, low-key sort of guy, who *looks* unhappy. Dramatic characters do not go about doing what they do directly because there is too much at stake and they are running scared.

## Monologues in Other Plays

Before you write your own monologue exercise, you might want to pick up a few plays and leaf through them, looking at monologues within full plays. You might notice Jean telling Miss Julie (in Strindberg's *Miss Julie*) about how he used to hide in the grounds of her house and watch her when he was a boy. She seemed so far above him, rich and spoiled. He wanted to play with her, to be in her world, and he wanted to bring her down to his. Or you might happen upon Edward talking to the silent Matchseller in Pinter's *A Slight Ache*. Edward's long monologues are filled with many things: he makes guesses at what the Matchseller must be thinking, offers drinks, tells of his accomplishments, in fact, talks about anything to fill the void of the Matchseller's silence. Or you might come across a whole one-act "monologue" by August Strindberg—*The Stronger*. The dramatic action is between two women—Mrs. X and Miss Y, generic types. In the entire play, which takes place at one table in a restaurant (no other tables, no other people except a silent waiter), Miss Y says nothing. Mrs. X goes from treating Miss Y as a friend, to becoming uncomfortable in the silence, to figuring out that Miss Y's superior attitude means that Miss Y is having an affair with Mr. X, to pulling herself together and deciding that she is still better off than Miss Y. All the lines belong to one character, but when the play is performed, Miss Y, the silent one, has just about as much to learn, in terms of reactions and her blocking, as Mrs. X does.

Or look at Norman's breakfast monologue in Alan Ayckbourn's *Table Manners*. Everyone in the family is angry with Norman and that fact comes through by the way *he* speaks a comic monologue. The monologue has tension because Norman is making things worse. We expect that sooner or later somebody will have to speak to him.

Monologues in novels (and they appear frequently enough) are different from monologues in plays. For instance, in the last fourth of Keri Hulme's *The Bone People*, there is a monologue by the character named Joseph Gillalley. Joe tells the story of his life to a strange, mystic old man out on a deserted beach. The old man then tells Joe about his life. Every once in a while actors choose to use novel monologues as audition pieces and quite often they don't work as well as dramatic monologues do. The reason is that, in the novel, monologues are usually informative. They usually fill in a past for a listener in the novel as well as for the reader. They are a way of getting information across without having the narrator simply find a way to narrate it. The information is given personality and feeling by coming from the person who has experienced the events.

However, in plays, even monologues of information about the past tend to have implications for an immediate future. And that's the main difference. In the dramatic monologue, the events are told with an eye to making something happen *in the moment in which the event is being told*. The past pressures the present and the future. There is a promise of action. Something will happen as a result of what is said. Something must happen. When Jean tells Miss Julie about his past, his childhood, how he dreamed of her, he is poised between two situations: they have *just* had a flirtation and they are just about to have a sexual encounter. For her, the encounter will be an unsatisfactory compromise of her position in the household. For him, a triumph. And the aftermath will be questions: Will they go away together? What will they do next? What Jean tells Julie about the past—his past as a boy—pressures the future, the immediate future. His monologue is working on her; it is part of the seduction; therefore it is action through words.

## Your Monologue

Next, *you* will write a dramatic monologue. You should put two people on stage. Your non-speaker should not be dead or unconscious, but alive and capable of responding. Your scene should be about two pages long. You may write, at most, two lines for the other (silent) character—if you must. Try to keep the monologue uninterrupted and try to play

with the tension of a speaking character and a non-speaking character. What makes monologues work?

The goal of this exercise is for you to play with language and with extended speech. All too often, new playwrights cop out with the minimalist line. They fall into a rhythm of having their characters say only half-lines to each other. They don't allow their characters to hold forth because they are afraid of, maybe even unsure of, what the character might do with extended expression. They confuse hiding information from the audience with drama, tension, and mystery. Actually, letting the audience in on things is the better method. Don't put a lid on your characters as a matter of course. Here is a chance to experiment with someone who talks and talks.

Let us look at a few of the monologues students have written for this assignment. You may want to study these before you write. In any case, use them after you have written a monologue to think about your own work. Have you had any of the same problems? Any similar successes?

### Sleepover
*by Erin Flynn*

*A small apartment in the Oakland area of Pittsburgh. PAUL, 19. DANNY, about the same age.*

*PAUL lights up a cigarette and puts his feet up on the old coffee table. DANNY, also smoking, slouches down on the couch next to PAUL.*

#### PAUL

Man, you should've shown up at Jane's last night. Everyone went over after the show—Louis was there. He'd been there all afternoon and was really drunk. I knew he was going to fuck with someone, and he did. He smashed this beer bottle over some kid's head for no reason—he was wasted—and of course, you know, everyone started to jump in . . . *(laughs)* Wendi beat the shit out of that Tracy girl—Mike's girlfriend. Well, you know how she gets when she fights—she fucking freaks out. Well, Jane told me before that I could crash there but she started kicking everyone out. I actually started heading up here, but Wendi came up to me and said she knew somewhere we could stay. I thought we were coming up here, or Krissie's, but we got in her car and she just started driving *(laughs)* and bragging . . . she fucking hates that girl . . . Anyways, we ended up at her parents' house! She just said something about wanting to stay over at her house. I mean I was kind of drunk and tired—so was she—she said her mom and dad wouldn't care. They have a cool relationship I think. Could you see me showing up at home just for the night? *(laughs)* Fuck, it was in this little neighborhood in Bethel Park. All the houses

The writer might want to specify that the Oakland area has some sections with very inexpensive housing. It attracts students and transients alike.

This monologue was performed. Both characters moved in it—to the couch, and in Paul's case, away from the couch and back. Actors often change the playwright's blocking. Don't be too rigidly locked in to an idea of staging. State what you see, as this writer does, but don't make it impossible for actors to try things.

The language and syntax is purposefully chaotic here. It conjures up the scene of chaos the night before—people fighting, getting drunk, beating each other up, not knowing for sure why.

An important subject comes up naturally. Paul didn't know where he was going to sleep. He almost came up to Danny's place.

One of the successful comic aspects of this script is Paul's fascination with the ordinary—a mom, a dad, a suburban street, everything, one assumes, he is trying to escape. Walking quietly, an offer of breakfast—everything seems wonderful, and mature, to Paul as he thinks about the evening's events.

looked alike. Hers was at the end of this street—in one of those circle streets. (Makes diagram with hands) You should have seen me, man, fucking tiptoeing up to the front door. I didn't want to wake her folks up. We walked inside—we were both being so quiet I couldn't believe it—and we were in her kitchen . . . she looked at me and offered me breakfast. She just smiled and said, "You want breakfast?" It was really fucking cool. It was like three in the morning and she made me macaroni and cheese. I mean, you know Wendi, man, you know how she is. But, she was really excited to have me in her kitchen, it seemed. Making me this macaroni and cheese. And later we headed upstairs and went in her room. We both just crashed right on her bed. It was just really cool—we didn't fuck—we both slept. She left the door open—I mean her parents were in the next room and she didn't shut the door. I just didn't expect Wendi to be like that, you know, making me food. Dan, I haven't been in a house—someone's home—for the longest fucking time. I mean, you know how Wendi gets at parties and that shit, but it was just different. Waking up next to her in her bed . . . was great. I woke up before she did, and just being there . . . I mean it was nice to have a real bed, and it wasn't in Oakland. And with Wendi! Man, I never expected to spend last night like that. She fucking made me pancakes when we got up. . . . Her mom was cool—really cool—and kept giving me more and more orange juice. I kept thanking her. (laughs at self.) Then we left—she dropped me off here. I mean, that probably won't happen again—it was just like our only place to go. I'd go there every fucking night if Wendi'd invite me. (DAN merely grins and gets up to flip the record.)

The contradictions in Wendi mirror the contradictions in Paul. Wendi is tough. And yet, she has this conventional side. She walks the line between child and adult. Of course, Paul's feelings for Wendi start to come through. He may find her tough side worth applauding, but he is much more taken by the possibility of her being ordinary, and sweet-tempered.

The feeling the writer decides to leave us with is Paul's loneliness. His language makes it clear that Wendi is not likely to take him home again. He's crashing at Danny's place and Danny is too hung-over and maybe uninterested in Paul's feelings to offer a word.

The punctuation of this monologue—the run-on paragraphing—reflects Paul's thinking. The detail is good. Wendi's mother pouring orange juice is memorable.

---

## Workshop: Discussion of *Sleepover*

KG: What is Paul's story?

ALBERT: He's a guy with no place to go. He's young, a teenager, a runaway, I'd say.

KG: What else do we know about him? What does he look like?

DAN: There's no physical description but I'd guess he wears jeans, maybe torn shoes or boots, probably has a weird hair cut.

KG: Why do you think he looks like that?

DAN: That's how those guys look. It's like a uniform. A homeless teenager's uniform. Oh, and I think he's kind of wimpy. He talks about the fight at the party, but he doesn't seem to want to get into it himself. He's even almost giggly when he discusses Wendi's behavior. She's a fighter. He's a guy who likes a tough woman. Maybe he needs to be dominated or led.

ALBERT: Here we go!

KG: So you seem to know—or at least can make a good guess at things about Paul. Does that suggest the beginning of character?

ALICE: I think so. But it's all stuff he reacts to. We don't actually know what decisions he makes. Well, he probably doesn't make any. He's in bad shape. Really without anything or anybody.

KG: Are there improvements to be made to this monologue? Is it dramatic? Does the character want something and try to get that something?

CATHY: Hmm. He wants Wendi, but he doesn't try to get her. He wants orange juice. A mother, a father. Maybe it would be better if we could see him trying to get what he wants.

DAN: I just thought of something. There's a lot of *past* in this monologue. Not much present or future. Isn't it hard to make the past dramatic? This guy is just telling.

ALICE: I don't know. I found it compelling in some way. He's looking back but he's trying to understand. He's longing.

ALBERT: Maybe it's that he's trying to talk to somebody who doesn't care about him. Danny's practically dead.

KG: Do you believe Danny? His silence?

ALBERT: I have a few friends like that. When they're wasted you might as well be alone.

DAN: That's what I wonder about. These characters are unappealing. Shouldn't we care about them?

CATHY: I sort of did.

ALICE: Me, too.

KG: What was the playwright trying to do?

ALICE: Make us laugh. Make us think about this kid—and his loneliness.

DAN: Point out the irony (see I used that word) of the fact that he wants conventional things. But I couldn't care about this guy. He was a loser. So his situation didn't ring bells for me.

ALBERT: I'm not like him, but it did for me. Everybody goes through phases where they're left out of something. And they're trying to fit in.

DAN: But aren't these guys sort of zeros? Why should we care?

ALBERT: They're not awful guys. Do they have to be nice?

KG: There are very few dramatic characters who are interesting to audiences—I think of some of the characters who've lasted over time: Lear, Hamlet, Treplev, the father in *Six Characters*, Jerry in *The Zoo Story*—and nice is not a characteristic. In fact the faults and flaws of these characters are exciting and tend to be what we remember. This is a big hint about characterization.

DAN: Don't write nice people. But there are nice characters in plays. Or good characters. I think Hamlet's good.

KG: I feel something for Hamlet; I'm fascinated by him; I care about him. But he does make a mess of things. He's terrible to Ophelia, he kills Polonius rashly, he puts his friends to death.

DAN: He had reasons.

KG: Ah!

CATHY: And I read *Table Manners*—which you've mentioned several times. Annie's nice.

KG: Annie is very sympathetic, certainly. But she's comically depressed, isn't she? She doesn't comb her hair, she makes fun of her sister-in-law, she sleeps with her sister's husband, she can't make up her mind about things, she doesn't have enough food around for the guests in the house. You might be kind of irritated with her if you had to tangle with her close up. In the family, maybe. Remember: she sleeps with her sister's husband and she's planning to do it again. And yet we're interested in her, sympathetic to her, and caught up in her decision. She's been made real. Characters should be as complex in their motivations as people are. *Nice* is not dramatic, at least not without complicating circumstances; for instance in Chekhov's hands, nice people are fools, ineffectual, and very destructive because of their ineffectuality. The three sisters are pretty good people—in the play of that name. But they do things that we usually censure. Olga buries herself in loneliness and self-righteousness, Masha gets an affair going with a married man under her husband's nose. Irina is unable to love any of her suitors and she gets Tusenbach killed fighting over her. The sisters are far from perfect. They are unhappy and so they strike out in indirect ways. They are a little like Annie in that they manage to hurt themselves a lot while trying to avoid conflict with others. They don't actually avoid the conflict though. And they're not blameless.

Now let us look at *After the Game*.

---

### After the Game
*by Dave Drayer*

*The stage is set up like a teenage boy's bedroom. It has a bed, a small desk with a lamp on it, and the walls are covered with magazine pictures of girls in bathing suits and rock stars. Fifteen-year-old Rick Norman lies in his bed with the light out. Earlier that evening he had been humiliated by a group of kids his own age on the basketball team he had just joined. Charlie, his father, taps lightly on the door and then enters. He turns on the light. It is very bright so he awkwardly shuts it off and turns on the desk lamp.*

#### CHARLIE

Kinda early for bed, ain't it? At least for you. (*Pause*) Your sister told me about the trouble you had tonight. She said you were talking about quitting the team. (*Rick stares at the ceiling. Charlie sighs, shuts off the light, and opens the door to leave. He stops and turns back toward Rick.*) I don't think quitting is a good idea. At least, not now. (*Pause*) Damn it,

"Earlier that evening . . ." Avoid telling past situations in the stage directions. If the information is not something the audience can see or hear, it doesn't belong. We have to find out about Rick's humiliation through words spoken on stage. Notice how the writer had to change tenses to tell us. The past tense is alien in a stage direction. A play is a story told by what people say and do in the present tense.

The action of the father—changing the lighting in the room—is nice. It tells us who he is, that he's gentle.

Another change of lighting. Is it interesting?

Rick, I ain't good at this. Never have been, but if you quit now then you're giving those smart-assed little bastards control over ya. Hell, I don't care if ya play basketball or not. *(Pause)* I just know that quitting now means giving into that fear. Fear that they'll laugh or pull something again. *(Pause)* I know what it feels like and I'm telling you from experience, ya can't let that kinda fear push ya around. *(Rick looks at his father, but doesn't move. Charlie shuts the door and sits down on the edge of Rick's bed.)* You heard me right . . . experience. Old Ted Kerns, he was a prick back in high school. *(Laughs lightly.)* You'd never know it now, but he was. When I started into ninth grade, I was pretty small compared to the other guys in my class. Well, old Kerns really got a charge out of picking on me. He made me look like an ass every time he got a chance. Course, he thought that made him look tough. I tried to avoid him, but it seemed impossible. It got to the point where I quit going anywhere that I might run into him. There I was finally, in high school, and couldn't go to the games or dances or anything. *(Pause)* I lost out on a lot of things cause of that, and it really didn't matter cause he still caught up with me. One day in the lunch line he started his shit. I was so sick of it I said something to him. I don't remember what it was, just some kinda remark to let him know I was tired of it. He comes right toward me and smacks me right in the mouth. *(Pause)* I'll never forget that moment as long as I live. It hurt . . . but nothing like I thought it would. And by God, I was still standing. That big ape hit me in the mouth and I was still standing. *(Pause)* I could taste my own blood, but I wasn't dead and I wasn't even laying on the floor. I was still standing! Man, I felt something inside of me that was so strong and so sick of cowering that I just . . . I just lit into him with everything I had. *(Pause)* One of the teachers finally pulled us apart. I was more bruised up than he was but I felt a hell of a lot better. *(laughing lightly)* Big Ted Kerns had to walk around with a black eye from the smallest kid in the ninth grade. *(Longer pause)* Ya gotta learn how to fight, Rick. I don't mean with your fists. The world comes chock full of guys like Ted Kerns. When ya get older, you'll put your fists away, but the fighting won't ever stop completely. Every time you take a step forward, you're stepping into someone else's territory. They'll keep pushing until you show them you got as much right to be there as they do. *(Charlie stands up and goes toward the door.)* I didn't plan on telling ya all that, but I'm kinda glad I did. You gotta make your own decision about the team. I promise ya I won't think any less of ya if ya quit. But don't think quitting is gonna make things easier cause it won't. If ya want to talk, I'll be out on the couch watching a little T.V. before I hit the sack. If not, that's okay too. Night. *(He exits and closes the door behind him.)*

It's good to have characters make decisions, even when it's just a matter of leaving the room (quitting), and then coming back. Probably without thinking about it the writer was reflecting what Charlie wants his son to do, go back.

Does Charlie's story have an effect on his son? Does Charlie notice how his son is taking the story? The evidence for Charlie's awareness of the silent listener will be found in his language. There is a possibility (when he laughs about old Ted Kerns and a few lines later when he pauses to let the message about missing games and dances sink in) for Charlie to relate to his son—to interact, or *try* to. But much of the time Charlie is caught up in his story for his own reasons. He still has a strong feeling about those days when he was humiliated.

The audience is put in the position of the son. What happened, we wonder. Did Charlie fight back? How did he get over his fear?

As much as there is truth in what Charlie says—that the world is full of Ted Kernses—the monologue loses tension here. Charlie is wise, he's survived, he's come to terms with his fear, etc. There is a possibility of keeping the tension going if Charlie isn't so perfect. Maybe he's still struggling. Maybe there are always axes to grind.

If you want a character to say "ain't," you've got to write "ain't" so the actor will say it. If your actor is worth anything, the ain't will trigger a lot of other speech adjustment. The many "ya's" in this monologue stick out. Are they accurate? Can the writer get the sense of the character's speech in other ways? The actor will shorten "you" and "got to" if you give enough other hints.

The reason for the monologue, the son who won't talk, is a good one, but it could be developed more. There's no growth to the son's silence. It stays at a level and becomes secondary.

Still, one of the writer's skills (in his acting, too) is access to feeling, free expression of feeling. His ability to put himself out there comes through in this script.

## Workshop: Discussion of *After the Game*

KG: Why does Charlie keep talking with no response from his son?

ALICE: Because he can assume that his son will be too embarrassed to respond, but that he has to keep at him anyway. He has to try to change him with words.

KG: In simple terms, what's it about?

CATHY: This is about a teenage boy who plays on a basketball team, and I guess the other guys on the team did something to humiliate him, so he thinks about quitting. His father then comes to talk to him.

KG: And then we have the father's monologue. What's the father like?

CATHY: Well, he seems to be a really nice guy. He tells Rick that it's okay to quit, but it's not okay to let people bully you. He's very understanding, because he's been through some similar things before.

KG: And how does the writer handle the description of that in this monologue?

ALBERT: I think pretty well. It could have been kind of clichéd but I think it turns out to be insightful. I thought it was interesting that he doesn't think Kerns is a jerk any more. That was an interesting thing about his character. And I really liked the part about how when Kerns hit him, it didn't hurt as much as he thought it would. I think there were a lot of good lines in that part, like how he could taste his own blood but he was still standing, and how he was more bruised up than Kerns, but he felt a hell of a lot better. I thought that section was really powerful because it expressed a feeling that I think a lot of people have. That is, when people are expecting something terrible to happen, and it does, but it's not as bad as they thought it would be, they feel energized or something. I think that's an interesting thing about people and about this scene.

KG: Okay, Albert is saying that section of the monologue really works well. Which part of it could be improved?

DAN: One thing that was missing here for me was more of the kid's story. I mean, supposedly Rick's problem is the whole motivation for the monologue, and we don't really find out anything about it except a vague introduction to what is generally wrong. We find out a whole lot about what the father's past problems have been, but he's already solved them so there's no conflict there. And we don't know what really happened to Rick, or what he thinks about what his dad said, so I don't really feel any conflict there. I think that the central problem gets lost in Charlie's speech, which is the same speech every father has given his son.

ALBERT: I think you're being too hard on it, Dan. I thought this was a pretty moving speech.

DAN: It may be well-written, but there's something about it that seems so . . . pat. At the beginning he says he ain't good at this, but of course he turns out to be good.

ALBERT: You don't think anything is at stake for Charlie here?

DAN: Well, yeah, I guess there is, but it just didn't emerge for me. Charlie just kind of breezes in, makes a great speech, and then breezes out, and we haven't learned anything new about the central conflict, which it seemed to me was in Rick's mind.

ALBERT: That was just a monologue.

DAN: Maybe it should have been Rick's monologue then.

ALICE: I can tell you one thing that I didn't like. I think the writer tries too hard to give Charlie a dialect. I started getting annoyed with all the "ya's" and "ain't's." I think you could take all of those out of there and still have the same flavor to Charlie's speech. And maybe notice more about him.

ALBERT: My fiction writing teacher says that it is unwise to attempt dialects because it usually sounds like you're looking down on your characters.

ALICE: Well, I think that does happen to a certain degree here. I think we get a pretty good understanding of what this guy talks like without needing things like "ya" all the time. I mean, I don't think any actor who might do this would make him sound like Laurence Olivier or anything.

KG: So you got a pretty good idea of what Charlie sounds like?

ALICE: Yes, I could imagine his voice while I was reading this.

DAN: That's just because all the signs are there that he's your stereotypical gruff but wise middle-class dad. You know, he hasn't been to college, but he's been educated by life kind of thing. Just too clichéd for me.

ALBERT: Dan, you're so hard to please.

KG: Let's think about these same things as we go on to look at *The Room*.

### The Room
*by Marcy Peterkofsky*

*Scene—Two young women in a small plain bedroom. One is staring down at the ground, shaking, as the other begins to speak.*

### YOUNG WOMAN #1

Look at me; don't be afraid. Hell, I've been through so much crap in my own life I keep the bathroom door permanently open. Well, it won't shock me. You hate your ma? Is that it? So what? You know what I feel for my parents? Nothing. Not love or hate, just emptiness. I shrug at them, and you know what? Even that takes effort. Label me, why don't you? I'm scum. Maybe. Don't matter no more. People always stick it to you—and they don't know. Like cannibals in painted glass rooms they stick it to you. Shattering the fragments of your soul and then filing you away while you're stinking, numb, and bleeding, spoiling the room. And you just take up no time no more. And they don't hurt no more when they think of you. Why should they? *(Pause)* Why care at all, huh? Can't hold onto nothing anyway, life slips away like a salamander's tail every time you reach to touch it. Who really gives a fuck? I don't care. Why should I? What's it to me if my old man pulls up in a gas station one time as I'm filling my own tank, then blows me off with a stinking nod? Don't matter he hasn't seen me in so many years. Why should I even care that he didn't say hi or bye or eat shit for that matter? Not even eat shit. *(Pause.)* The silence bugs me, that's all. I'm never one for quiet. *(Pause. She chews a fingernail.)* Anyhow, he's already filed me, he won't see the changes. I could be totally different! I could be better . . . I try but, I'm already filed under waste you know? I try to see people now, in this moment and this space, and not recall their yesterdays or hold up their tomorrows. Hard to focus though . . . *(Laughs.)* So you? You got nothing to lose with me. I got worse I'm sure. See? My mind it may be full but those files are on empty. *(Pause.)* Well? Ain't ya gonna talk to me? Go on will ya? *(Pause.)* Don't be afraid.

I don't know anyone who talks like this. But I think some of the energy generated in the discussion of this scene was generated exactly because this girl speaks oddly. Some of the class bought it; some didn't. Are the speeches idiosyncratic like those of the disturbed characters in *The Effect of Gamma Rays on Man in the Moon Marigolds*? Is one girl meant to be comic—darkly comic, I grant—in grasping at poetic images that don't work? Shepard's and Mamet's characters do that. Or, does she know her speech is garbled, as Nina does in *The Sea Gull* when she says, "I am a sea gull, no that's not it, I am an actress . . ."?

Some people wish the writer told us where these people are and why the room is so bare. Would it change your perceptions if the opening stage directions said the following: "*A shelter for runaways, young woman #1 is lying on bed, eyes closed, when second young woman enters room. YW#1 makes a hello sign, YW#2 looks away. YW#1 gets up and touches YW#2 on shoulder; YW#2 moves away. YW#1 walks around to look at #2 who again looks away.*" We'd know much more about the characters. Do you think they should be specific and their situation identified?

## Workshop: Discussion of *The Room*

KG: This is an unusual monologue. Did it work for you? Is there an action? Do you care about the speaker?

CATHY: I know people who talk like this all the time, but they never seem to have any actual problems. They sit

around complaining like this, but they don't really seem to deserve to.

KG: Does the young woman in this monologue deserve to talk like this?

CATHY: I'm not sure. Maybe if we could see more clearly what her problems are.

ALICE: I think her problems are pretty obvious. She's been totally ignored and unloved by her parents and probably misunderstood by just about everybody.

CATHY: But is there anything specific . . .

ALICE: She talks about seeing her father at the gas station, and how he won't say anything to her—not even "eat shit." That's a very specific event that could tear anybody up like this.

ALBERT: I'm not even sure how much the specifics matter, anyway. I just think this is really great writing in and of itself. I think the mystery adds to the intensity, too, like what happened to the other young woman that she has to tell her all this stuff right now, and what is the connection between these two women.

KG: You're saying that you like not knowing those things?

ALBERT: Well, yes. Or at least not knowing them doesn't detract from this monologue for me. There is a lot of interesting stuff here. Like isn't it funny that the speaker's way of trying to get this other woman to open up to her is to give this long speech about how screwed up her own life is. Maybe she's just been waiting for someone to open up to. And I thought it was fascinating that at the beginning of the monologue she's throwing out all this really dramatic stuff—you know, "cannibals in painted rooms," stuff like that—and it's only towards the end of the monologue that she actually talks about something specific—her father not talking to her. It's like it's easier for her to say all this dramatic stuff, until she can work up the courage to talk about reality. And it didn't really matter to me that the reality ends up being not quite the same as the "shattering fragments of your soul." It only shows you how deeply she feels about things.

DAN: I think this could go either way. It could be really powerful, or this woman could end up sounding like those people Cathy knows. One thing that I really liked about this monologue, though, is that the event she talks about isn't her getting beat or anything. It was just that her father only nodded to her. I mean, I don't want to sound like I'm not taking child abuse seriously or anything, but it seems to me that whenever a beginning writer wants to be dramatic he or she immediately reaches for the big guns. You know, like, "my father tied me to the car and then dragged me around the neighborhood, then he threw me in the cellar and didn't feed me for three weeks, and then my mother came and spit on me." It seems to me that often a lot of people think that the more horrific the situation they write about is, the more dramatic their play, or story, or whatever will be.

KG: You're saying extremes are not necessarily better?

DAN: Yeah, I am. When this young woman starts talking about what's really wrong and she's talking about her dad ignoring her at the gas station, I was like, "Finally, somebody understands that being dramatic doesn't always mean be as violent as you possibly can." So I think this writer in some ways understands more about writing than most people, already. Then again, it might take a really great actress to pull off a line like, "Shattering the fragments of your soul and file you away, while you're stinking, numb and bleeding, spoiling the room."

ALICE: I think this monologue is in a lot of ways like a poem. The writer just creates this really strong image of two women sitting in a room, and the one is shaking and the one starts talking. I mean, it might be hard to say what happened before it or what's going to happen next, but it didn't matter to me, because this monologue just captures a really dramatic moment in the way a poem might, and it leaves a really strong impression. At least it did on me.

KG: Yes, on most of us. Now let us go on to *Group Session*.

## Group Session
*by Rick Van Noy*

*A group session at a health clinic—*

### CLAIRE

My turn already? . . . I don't know if I can do this. Let me think a second . . . Do I have to sit here? (*She stands, walks to the window, stares out for a few moments.*) . . . There are some children fighting down in the park . . . They've stopped. Can I have a cigarette? I've read about passive smoke but I really need one. Sorry. (*She lights a cigarette, takes a drag.*) Oh God, don't you hate cigarettes? . . . A girl at work used to say she loved to watch me smoke. You know, like I really enjoy it . . . like Bette Davis. Actually I have quit a couple of times . . . When I smoke, I tend to smoke too fast and too deep. . . . I'm pretty compulsive when it comes to cigarettes. (*Pauses and looks as if she may have said something wrong.*) Is this called avoidance? I think I remember that from Psych 101. Sorry. . . . Anyway, my name is Claire, and I'm a workaholic. (*Giggles nervously.*) I really don't mean to make light of this, but it all seems a bit trivial and I'm kind of embarrassed to be here. . . . I'm just having a hard time getting a grip. . . . Maybe just an attitude adjustment . . . The other night . . . well, I had been working long hours at the office. I mean real long hours. Then, bringing work home. I'd hardly seen Jim for weeks. . . . I would work all day, into the night, go home and sleep for a couple of hours then go back to work. And I still had to take care of the kids. . . . I have twins, two boys, clinically hyperactive: The dynamic duo. Sometimes I'd sleep during the day while the kids were gone, and work all night. It was just what I thought I had to

do to succeed, to get a promotion. . . . I don't know . . . I was starting to get really run down . . . but, I didn't want to see a doctor. Doctors! . . . A couple of years ago I went to one. I mean there I was, trying to finish my degree, I had hyperactive twins, my husband was having an affair, my mother was ill and in the hospital, and he kept writing prescriptions for PMS. . . . So, anyway, I woke up the other night when the alarm went off. The clock by the bed said 6:00. But, I didn't know if it was 6:00 in the morning or 6:00 at night. You know, in the winter it's hard to tell. . . . I tried to think. Is it 6:00 in the morning or 6:00 at night? I couldn't remember. I didn't even know what day it was. The kids were at Mom's so I didn't even have their "body clocks" to go by. . . . So I thought I'd call time and temperature. . . . Did you realize that they don't say AM or PM? . . . I kind of lost it. . . . I pulled the phone out of the wall, started throwing things around the room . . . I just started pounding on the floor and screaming . . . Weird . . . It's just that . . . I feel pressure . . . I want to be good . . . at everything. Other people do it, why can't I. . . . Jane Fonda . . . I know there are worse problems. I could be a drug addict or an alcoholic, or a homicidal maniac. I'm not anorexic or bulemic . . . I just need to get my balance. There is nothing really wrong with me, is there? . . . There is more to deal with, being a successful woman of the 80's, than PMS. . . . My husband is busy too but no one gives him water pills . . . I know you're trying to deal with cancer and you're dealing with a miscarriage . . . and you the death of your husband . . . but, I have to deal with my life on my terms. Is that less important? Is that too trivial? I'm hoping this is just another something I'll get through. I hope I don't have to scream and pound on the floor to get someone to hear me. . . . Can you hear what I'm saying . . .

This scene is more polished than some of the others, in this case because the writer had been acting and directing for years and, I think, easily saw and heard Claire. I believe the monologue would benefit from his imagining the other people in the room. For instance, I wonder to whom Claire says, "Oh, God, don't you hate cigarettes?" And I wonder what kind of response she gets from that person, on stage probably imaginary, but in the actress's mind, real. For your assignment, it is best and easiest to put one silent character on stage with your speaker. That way you can concentrate on the silent character as well as the speaking character. You can probably see that this scene could easily be revised to take place between a patient and a therapist, which happens to be the subject of the scene following it.

## Workshop: Discussion of *Group Session*

KG: There are several effective things in this scene. Who wants to start talking about it?

ALICE: It seems really polished for just a second assignment. The things Claire says are really natural. What I mean is, they sound like real speech.

CATHY: I agree with Alice. This monologue seems to have a lot of, I don't know how to say it . . . texture. The writer really seems to know how to have Claire say these little things that really help to set the scene. Like when she's stalling at the beginning and she walks over to the window and notices the children fighting outside. Or when she mentions Psych 101. And then, when she starts talking about her problem, she doesn't just talk about it as if she's moving in a straight line. She talks about it like I would imagine someone in that situation would. She's kind of confused and nervous.

ALICE: In some of the other scenes we've looked at so far, we talked about how you could "feel the playwright's hand" at certain points. Well, I think this is an example of an assignment where that doesn't happen much at all. This is kind of going along with what Cathy was just saying. I feel Claire's mind at work here much more than I feel the writer's.

KG: What do you think about the unusual punctuation?

ALBERT: In some cases it might be really annoying to have a monologue punctuated like this, but in the case of this particular monologue I think it works because it fits the way I imagine Claire is speaking. It's unusual, but it seems to me that the writer is making it work.

DAN: One thing I want to say about this monologue is that I'm sick of reading about the problems of Yuppies. It's like you turn on the TV, and all you see are people whining about "Oh, I'm such a compulsive worker, and oh, are the kids growing up okay, and oh, my marriage is in trouble, and I'm not fulfilled." I mean, I see enough of that stuff on *thirtysomething*, and now I have to come to class and read it too.

ALICE: Dan, this woman has some real problems. I don't understand how you can't see that. You know, if you wake up and you're not sure whether it's morning or night, I think that's a sign that you are really having a breakdown. This is no small problem like, "Will I be able to get the BMW this year?"—this is serious.

ALBERT: It seems to me that you're not having any sympathy for this woman, Dan, just because she's a Yuppie, or at least she says that's what she is. I think one of the most interesting things about this is that Claire herself is struggling with the fact that her problems seem trivial next to someone who has cancer or someone who has just lost a husband. But I think this adds a lot of tension to the monologue because I think it's pretty clear that Claire does need help badly, and it's precisely the attitude of people like you that is standing in her way. What if you had a problem, and nobody wanted to help you because you were a "College Student," and that didn't seem serious enough to them.

DAN: Well, excuse me, I stand corrected. If it makes any difference, I do agree with you guys about how well-written this is.

KG: What is the playwright trying to do? How should we feel about *Group Session*, about Claire?

ALICE: I think he's trying to write a serious episode of *thirtysomething* and that it works. . . . Well, isn't that better than most TV?

CATHY: I'd call this a comic monologue with serious intent, an image of a woman trying to get her balance back.

KG: Okay, just one more monologue: *Therapy*.

## Therapy
### by Judy Woodside

*(The scene is set in an office-like room. There are two small couches stage left and right, facing each other. The pensive and listening psychiatrist (a woman, 40) is sitting on the right and the fourteen-year-old patient, Penny, is sitting left. Penny is tense and has a forced calmness. Her hands fidget in her lap. She tries to avoid looking at the woman and moves her eyes from wall to wall.)*

WOMAN

Okay, Penny. Let's try this again. Just talk and whenever you want to start, just start.

PENNY

*(nervously laughs)* I am so sick of this. There is nothing the matter with me. I can't believe my mother keeps bringing me here and keeps wasting forty-five dollars a week! It's like you all want to choke some feelings out of me that aren't there to begin with. *(sarcastic)* It's like you all are saying, "Oh, she's the child so she must be hurting incredibly. She must be confused and blaming herself for everything. She's just got to hate herself; that's the way it always must be with little girls in her place. Let's make sure she's feeling some pain and hand her over to a nagging shrink! Let's bring her down! Let's make her cry. Let's see some sobs." *(There is a pause while the psychiatrist watches Penny and Penny stares at the floor and begins to twitch her foot.)*

I told you before and I'll say it again: I just don't care! I expected their divorce. It's much better now than before. I knew what was going on all the time. I wasn't blind and deaf to their fights and yelling. I know why my dad tried to go overseas on his job so much. I've always known that my dad is a cheating asshole and my mom is a pestering witch. I understand it all. It hasn't really affected me. I'm the way I've always been. I lived with my mother while my dad was on his travels—now he just doesn't come back. There's no yelling. It's nice. It's a good deal. *(appeals directly to woman in quiet, sincere tone)* The only reason I watch a lot of TV and do lots of stuff alone is because I'm between best friends now, I want to be alone. Is that a crime? I'll get back into the social scene sooner or later. My grades haven't dropped. I do what I'm told; I get to the chores sometime or another. And I sleep a lot only because I'm tired—this year is challenging for me in school; it tires me out. And I like to stay out of my mother's way when I get home. I have a little nap before dinner. I am not depressed, okay? Don't let my parents tell you otherwise. My parents want to help me? Fine, just tell them to leave me alone and I'll be all right. Mom shouldn't threaten to take away my computer games and TV to get me out of my room—that just won't work. That would be very, very wrong of her. ← *Good*

*(again looks at walls, shifts in seat)* You all are so strange. It's like you are forcing me to have friends, do little girl stuff, and do things that I must do on my own when I want to. It's very unnatural. You see, I know a little about this stuff, too . . . And you can't force me to have emotion. *(sighs sadly)* It's like you are in need of more clients and you are telling divorcing parents that their child needs to be purged of all this great pain and suffering. Well, there are going to be times that you are wrong, lady; everyone is wrong sometimes and this is one of those times. *(looks at woman again)* Please don't make my family waste any more money. They are going to need it to put me through college one day. Just tell them I am fine. You know it's the truth. They are feeling a little bit guilty right now because they kind of forgot me during their yelling and battles. But I forgive them. They don't have to hire someone to listen to my silly talk. You really shouldn't act on their guilt—I mean, it's obvious that you're using them. You know they're feeling this way so you take them for every penny they've got. *(laughs)* Yeah, that's it.

*(Penny searches the woman's face for signs of change of thought. The woman remains pensive and emotionless.)* I mean, if this continues I will have to resort to . . . doing some things. I'll have to pretend I'm hurting and crap. I can act, you know. I can sob and foam at the mouth. If it satisfies my parents to see some tears and yelling—I can do that. I can do it very well. If they are in some weird state of mind where they need to see that they are hurting everyone around them—well . . . then they need to come and see you. Not me. Yeah. Then they are the ones with the problem, aren't they? I'm okay. But bring my parents in. That's the first thing to do. Then you'll see some sickos! They are going downhill fast . . . What a big mistake this all is.

> *Good return to previously mentioned topic*

> *Very good! It's about feeling now, not just feeling)*

WOMAN

Whenever you want to start, Penny. Any time is a good time.

There is some energy here, because there is deceit, pretense. The girl is trying to fool the shrink and she is also fooling herself. The audience sees more, sees better and watches the pretending, the acting. The audience is wondering when it will be over, wondering what would make Penny quit and be honest. Nobody who is not feeling pain sounds this strident. Even though not all the lines seem believable (I'm thinking of the ones like "yeah, that's it"), the pressure of the situation is dramatic. I especially like the fact that Penny seems right and wrong at the same time. The next step is to figure out and justify the therapist's silence. Is she sadistic, a bad therapist, or do they have some deal that she will not speak until she believes what she is hearing from Penny? The playwright can make the rules, make the situation, and then justify it in the writing.

## Workshop: Discussion of *Therapy*

KG: Is the writer trying to show a troubled girl and a wise therapist? Or a nightmare situation in which the therapist is as remote and mechanical as everything else in the girl's not very happy life?

CATHY: I wish I knew how this is supposed to make me feel. On one hand, I sort of felt like all this stuff Penny was saying was just her way of denying that she really is having problems because of her parents' divorce. But on the other hand, when the psychiatrist says "whenever you want to start" to Penny at the end, that seemed like such a cold thing to say that I wondered whether the things Penny was saying might have had some truth to them. It seemed like the psychiatrist should have tried to respond to things Penny was saying more seriously—and because she didn't, it made me think that perhaps there was some truth to Penny's accusations. But then again, I don't know that much about psychology so I don't know what actually would be the most effective thing to do if you were a psychiatrist in that kind of situation.

ALBERT: I felt similar confusion over this, but I think some of that has to do with this being basically just a monologue. I think if we could see more interaction between Penny and the psychiatrist I'm sure we could have a much better idea of what their relationship is really like. Maybe the writer is trying to be too ambitious, trying to tell too much of the story in what is a pretty limited assignment.

ALICE: Well, in any case I thought she did a good job at showing Penny's desperation. I felt a knot in my stomach while I was reading this. I know what it's like to be 14, and to be struggling to be heard. And yet, I don't really doubt that Penny belongs at the psychiatrist—at least I don't think I was as unsure about it as Cathy and Albert were. There might be a chance that Penny's complaints are based in truth, but I doubt that that is entirely the case. One interesting thing that I thought of while reading this is that all the monologues we've read for this assignment seem to have a similar theme—people who are struggling to be heard. In *Sleepover* there was Paul trying to express himself to Danny. Then in *After the Game*, Charlie was trying to get through to his son. In *The Room*, the one young woman was trying to get the other woman to talk to her. And in *Group Session*, Claire is trying to get people to take her problem seriously. And now we have another character, Penny, involved in a similar kind of struggle. I don't know how important that observation is, but I just wanted to say it.

KG: Well, I think that's a valid point, Alice. A lot of the similarity has to do with this being an assignment to write a monologue, which is an extended speech by just one character. If you had a character who was communicating well with other people, then you might not have a monologue, so maybe some of that frustration is inherent in the form.

---

**Assignment: Exercise 2**

Now write your own monologue—two people on stage, one person speaks, one person is silent. Make every effort to make us believe the speech *and* the silence. Avoid making the silent character unconscious or dead. Be aware that the monologue must move and build—must gather intensity—without straining our belief in silence.

---

**Study Questions and Exercises**

1. Critique further one of the monologue exercises.
2. Discuss the use of Levene's monologue in Act II of **Glengarry Glen Ross** when he tells about the deal he believes he closed.
3. Why is the workshop dialogue not *dramatic*? What, if anything, could make it so?

# FIVE

# Pantomime

## OVERVIEW

In this chapter are included instructions for the third writing assignment. You will write the opposite of a monologue—a scene without speech, a scene in which the other part of the activity on the stage—*pantomime,* action without dialogue—takes over and *is* the drama. If you can write a pantomime sequence, you will be better able to use pantomime activity dramatically when you want to. Normally, it is dialogue that carries the play, but sometimes, actions and gestures that are used *like dialogue* carry a small portion of the play, and in the case of something like Beckett's *Act Without Words,* a whole play is made of dialogic pantomime.

In order to prepare you for doing this assignment, I will give you some notes on pantomime scenes from various plays. Following these will be some examples of pantomime scenes written by other students, titled *Computer, Dress-Up, Laundry, Cross Stitch,* and *Silence.* Each will be followed by some commentary. I have dropped the workshop people. By now you should know them enough to let them comment (in your imagination) on these scenes. The subject of pantomime also brings up the subject of economy. The need for economy in all aspects of theatre is important. The need for economy in the *setting* is especially evident through the study of these exercises.

## OBJECTIVES

At the end of this chapter you should be able to

- Notice the patterns of movement in any play or scene you have read
- Determine situations in which extended pantomime is effective on stage

- Write your third exercise, which is to write your own pantomime sequence
- Compare your successes and problems with those of other people who have written pantomime exercises

Silence is a surprising thing in the theatre. There is almost a contract between the playwright and the audience that from the start of a play to its conclusion there will be orchestrated *sound.* And usually, from the first drum beats or overture music or chirping birds to the final line, there is not much silence. Usually. But every once in a while what replaces dialogue on stage is pantomime activity.

### Pantomime and Stage Directions

*Pantomime activity,* when used here, will mean the extended physical action without dialogue of a portion of a play. Pantomime activity requires clear stage directions. (In ordinary scene-writing, the playwright will also write stage directions for the *major physical moves* that underline the action of the whole play. Directors and actors will fill in a great deal of the blocking and stage business—who sits where, gets up, toys with an ashtray while speaking—but there are certain moves in most plays that are so crucial to the understanding of the play that the playwright must include them—either inherent in the dialogue [as Shakespeare did] or in carefully chosen stage directions.)

Under most circumstances, when you write stage directions you will be writing dialogue to accompany that activity. And the two things will have to be highly integrated. You can and should learn to both see and hear your characters. Words and actions have to be smoothly integrated on stage, partly in order to free the words. Most drama moves by the power of words, even the musicality of

54

words. Most of the time, the physical life on stage supports and enhances the words.

For *this* assignment, however, we will concentrate solely on stage directions for one extended pantomime sequence. Our goal will be to do more, however, than practice writing stage directions. Although it is the rule to keep sound going on stage, *sometimes the stage is empty of dialogue*, and a silent mini-drama takes place. You will not want to overuse this device because it is tricky and powerful. If you pick up the plays on your bookshelf, or at the library, or at the bookstore, looking for examples of extended pantomime action, you will first be struck by how *little extended* it is most of the time. Then you will notice how often other sounds within pantomimes take the place of speech.

## Pantomime within Plays

For instance, perhaps you look at *Amadeus*. There are times when Mozart is on stage and expresses himself with music. He is at the harpsichord. He gets an idea, he builds upon it, elaborates, shows off. Others react. It is an effective scene. In this case the music is like a line of dialogue— it works like a monologue, like a stream of words, on the listeners. Or Salieri, in a memory-sequence, enacts himself at a younger age. He looks at a manuscript, toys with it for a long time, then opens it. As he reads, sounds fill the air, and then he collapses. The pantomime is used to show Salieri's inner life, to show how overwhelmed he was by Mozart's genius. But again sound (music) takes the place of words.

You might come across *Educating Rita* (by Willy Russell). There are a few elaborate setups of the professor, Frank, in his school office. He doesn't do anything very dramatic, but we get the idea that he is not all that happy as a teacher. He dumps his lecture notes, his student papers, and gets on with his lunch. Through these small gestures, we learn something about him. These are symbolic acts—comfort and pleasure in the midst of what is his sloppy work world.

In Muriel Spark's *The Prime of Miss Jean Brodie*, there are a few action pantomimes—one in which the girls imitate Miss Brodie kissing Mr. Lloyd; one in which, with the girls watching, Miss Brodie feeds a picnic lunch to Gordon Lowther while her enemy, Miss Mackay, is spying from an upstairs window; and another when Lloyd is painting a nude model who is passing the time by reading. (We finally see who the model is—Sandy, who wants to be like Brodie.) So in these cases the pantomimes are like elongated gestures, showing images of "the romantic woman," an image Brodie promotes with her girls. The pantomimes are used in a stylistically consistent way in the script.

Perhaps you pick up *Hamlet*, thinking, "Boy, these guys really kept the talk going. No extended stage directions here. 'Dies,' is about all you get." But you might remember that *Hamlet*, an exception in so many things, does have a pantomime sequence known as the dumb show. A whole play is enacted in shortened, telegraphic pantomime. Some directors cut it, but I think that's a mistake. There is riveting dramatic tension in watching Gertrude and Claudius watching the play, once in pantomime, and yet again, with words. And it fits other things that happen twice over in the play—e.g., the Ghost says everything *twice*, the Ghost makes *two* appearances in the first scene, etc. Hamlet has to make *two* tries at actually killing Claudius. The dumb show is more integrated than some, at first, think.

As you browse, you might happen upon the fight scene in Neil Simon's *Barefoot in the Park*. That is one of the longest and most successful pantomime sequences in contemporary plays. Corey and Paul play out a whole argument about who gets to eat what and who gets to sleep in the bedroom, who has to sleep on the couch, all through physical actions. Physical gestures take the place of words in their fight.

## The Pantomime Assignment

Your assignment is to write a whole scene in pantomime. Make it stylistically consistent. Try to make it come to a full conclusion. Make us care about what happens, about what your character or characters do. You may want to look at *Act Without Words*, by Samuel Beckett, which is fully a pantomime play. Or you may want to browse through plays and notice their extended sequences. But in any case you will have to come up with something altogether original, something in which action, dramatic action, takes place through gesture, believably, without words. It's worth the effort, worth finding out how to make each move count.

All the gestures of a play—a regular play, not a pantomime—operate like a dance under the music that is the words of the play. The gestures may be ordinary but what they amount to isn't ordinary at all. A whole story is told by who moves where, who does what to whom, who touches what, hands over what. In fact, one of the best ways to test the physical side of a production—to test it for meaning and grace—is to have a run-through, late in the rehearsal period, all in pantomime. To do the whole play as if the sound has been shut off. Actors should even mouth the words, but produce no sound. It's like what you see on TV when you push the mute button but keep the picture on. People talk, argue, fight, kick, shoot, kiss. Do you know what's what and who's who without the words? All of the gestures of a play should tell the story of the play a second time, physically, underneath the words. Because the overall pantomime of a play is a story-telling device, every gesture is far more important than in life. Write *your* pantomime knowing that gesture takes on a magnified, dance-like quality when it is performed on stage. Notice the importance of each move.

It might help you to compare your work and your ideas with those of others. Here are some pantomime exercises written by others. Do these work? Following each scene is a brief commentary.

### Computer
*by Megan Graham*

The stage is dark.

The sound of a door opening and then closing is heard. Footsteps, then the thud of a human foot or leg coming into quick contact with an inanimate object is heard. A castered chair is moved and then there is a click followed by a low hum. The green light of a computer screen reveals the shape of a man. The shape reaches across the desk to turn on a small lamp.

Here, orchestrated sound takes the place of dialogue.

As the light comes up downstage right the shape is seen to be Howard, a man in his early thirties. He is an attractive man, but he doesn't show it. He wears glasses unbecoming to his face. He is in need of a shave. His permanent press shirt is wrinkled and his brown corduroys have lost all texture from the knees up.

This writer, who has a good deal of experience in technical theatre, is able to see clearly a lighting effect—actually a sequence of them.

She shows, too, a specificity in costuming.

Howard's living room is stark but cluttered. Downstage right is his work area: a desk with a small computer screen and large keyboard. Forming an L with the desk is a table with two printers and a great deal of paper and books on it. There is another smaller table on the other side of the desk holding a Macintosh and still more papers. A wheeled office chair is in front of it all. Stage left consists of a sofa, chair, and coffee table. Underneath the coffee table are stacks of books in an attempt to keep the table clean. The main entrance is stage left. An archway up right leads to the rest of the house.

While some of this scenic detail might be overkill in another scene, here it works as a signal for the rhythm of playing this scene. For about as long as it takes to read the description, the lights come up and reveal what the audience has time to take in before anything else happens. The stacks of books under the coffee table are a good touch because they tell something about the overwhelming chaos that's just kept at bay.

Howard pulls the chair back and sits down while reading a piece of paper. He types a few lines very quickly with two fingers.

The hum and then louder noise of a printer is heard.

Howard reaches in his shirt pocket and pulls out a box of cigarettes and a lighter. He takes one and lights it and throws the pack and lighter into the mess on the table.

Howard only types a few lines, but he remains busy—or busies himself with chair, cigarette, printer—giving the odd impression that he is doing less work than he should be doing. Is he really productive?

He pushes his chair over to the printer and looks at what is being printed.

He sits back and smokes as the printer continues.

Howard suddenly leans up and pulls the paper to see it. He grimaces and stubs out his cigarette in an ashtray which is already too full.

The style of the language suggests a rhythmic, mechanized action.

He rips the paper off the printer as the machine continues to print more pages. He wheels the chair back to the keyboard and starts to type with his right hand as he holds the paper in his left.

Notice this writer has often chosen to start new lines rather than write "pause" but the effect is somewhat similar. There is a *stop* at the ends of acts, keeping actions discrete, isolated.

Door stage left is opened. (*This goes unnoticed by Howard due to noise of printer and keyboard*)

Susan appears in the doorway carrying a bag of groceries.

Susan is an attractive woman in her late twenties. She is dressed in a skirt and blouse.

She stands and looks at Howard.

His back is towards her.

Susan crosses down to sofa, sets the bag on the table, and sits down.

Howard continues to type.

Susan slips her shoes off and puts her feet up on the table.

The printer and Howard continue.

Susan leans her head back and covers her ears with the palms of her hands.

The printer stops. Howard continues. The printer starts again.

Susan gets up, grabs bag, and exits upstage right.

The sound of radio static is heard followed by classical music.

Howard continues.

Music becomes louder.

Howard looks up. Then he takes a pen out of his shirt pocket and starts to write on the piece of paper. The printer stops. He pushes his chair to the printer and looks at the product of the printer. He takes the paper back to the keyboard and starts to draw lines and arrows on it.

Susan's head appears in the archway, looks at Howard, and disappears.

The volume of the music is turned down.

Susan enters, circles around the desk and goes up to Howard's back.

Susan puts her hands on his shoulders and lets them slip down his chest.

Howard continues to write with his right hand and holds her hand with his left.

Susan bends over, leaning her head on his.

Howard continues to write.

Susan stands up; Howard lets go of her hand.

(pause)

Susan grabs the back of his chair and spins it.

Howard looks up.

Susan takes the paper and the pen out of his hands and places them next to the keyboard. She removes his glasses and sets them on top of the paper. She grabs Howard by both hands and stands him up. They walk over to the sofa. Howard sits down, Susan cuddles up next to him.

Howard awkwardly starts to play with Susan's hair.

Susan smiles and lays her head on his lap.

Howard continues to stroke her forehead.

The stage directions, telegraphic and chopped, will suggest to actors an automaton-like movement. An experienced actress will read, "She stands and looks at Howard," and she will do just that. She will not try to embellish it. The words tell her not to. The printer and Howard are related by this stage direction: "The printer and Howard continue."

The music is Susan's "voice."

It's interesting that Howard writes by hand. We wonder what he is writing, and why he takes a break from the computer. What did he read that he hated? Why does he have more than one printer?

There is a sense of truth in this. Howard neither rejects Susan by refusing her hand nor abandons his work by concentrating on their physical contact.

Susan's objectives take over. She is trying to do something, trying to change something.

Susan closes her eyes and relaxes.

Howard looks over at his desk, continues to stroke her head.

Howard's left hand rests on a cushion.

Howard picks up the cushion.

He places his right hand under her head and lifts it slightly.

*(pause)*

Howard slides over to his right.

*(pause)*

Howard replaces himself with the pillow.

*(pause)*

Howard stands, looks back at Susan. He crosses to desk, replaces the chair and sits down. He puts his glasses on and begins to type.

Susan sits up.

Howard types.

Susan stands up, crosses up right, exits through archway. Howard types.

Music gets louder.

Howard types.

Door slams.

Howard types.

Music and lights fade.

The stage is dark.

Howard types.

The writer, in suggesting actual pauses, changes the rhythm once more. The pauses come at less mechanized moments, suggesting softness, uncertainty.

But Howard can't hold on.

And neither can Susan.

---

Some of the effect of this (part of the reason it does not need words or that it is a theatre piece without words) comes from the otherworldliness of the computer-land in which it is set. This is not logical day and night. It is almost dreamlike. The scene starts in darkness, but we learn soon enough that it is not the darkness of nighttime, but something else. Otherwise we would expect explanations for why Susan seems to be doing normal day-time things, like shopping, in the pitch black. Instead the stage seems to indicate the state of Howard's mind, darkness, in which there is only computer-light, or computer-related light.

Susan is not just another woman trying to distract yet another man from his work. Something more is suggested here. They are in trouble because he is mechanized; even when he *tries* to relate to her, he is mechanized. Howard is neither mean nor unwilling to give Susan some attention, he is just unable to stop buzzing and printing. Susan, less mechanized, is still a product of this world. She makes other sounds, more human ones maybe, but she too is reduced to signals and signs as if she is part of a computerized program.

A mechanized piece usually generates no emotion, but this one is sad. Howard is caught in a routine that makes him quietly desperate and less than human and he can't find his way out. If he could, there would be words. If he could, he might say, "Oh, Susan, I liked this yesterday, but today it sounds awful. Read it for me, will you?" Are there, in this script, characters who want something? Yes. Howard wants to write something he likes. Susan wants some attention. Do the characters try to do things, to change things? Yes, Howard tries to change what he's written, and Susan tries to distract him. What's at stake? His work. His self-esteem. Their marriage. Susan's sanity. What's wrong? Who is being hurt, and by what? In every play, someone is being hurt. In this case, the characters are hurt because they can't find comfort, nor can they give and take, enjoying ordinary life.

If this pantomime were in a full play, the play would not be realistic, but a step or two away from realism. Stylistically, a great deal has been established in this short piece.

Let us now look at *Dress-Up*.

### Dress-Up
*by Judy Woodside*

The scene takes place in a master bedroom. It is night. There is a large dresser downstage right. Attached to the dresser is an ornate mirror. There is a full-length mirror to the right of the dresser. A wardrobe is left of the bed. A window with billowy white curtains is on the back wall. An oriental rug covers center stage.

The room is dark except for the moon-like gleam from the window. Loud, tasteless rock music is playing in "another room." The door opens (*the music is louder while the door is open*) and a wide-eyed girl, Sara (*six*) enters cautiously. She takes big, calculated steps into the center of the room. Scans the room. Stands facing the dresser; looks at it with reverence. Goes over and turns on small lamp on dresser.

After a few seconds she looks over to the open door and motions for Amy (*three*) to come in. Amy runs up and grasps Sara fearfully. Sara pries her off and firmly gives her the "shush sign" (*index finger over mouth*). Sara carefully walks back to door and gently closes it (*the music fades slightly*).

Turning, Sara smiles craftily. Motions Amy to stay where she is (*points at Amy's space on rug*). Goes over and opens top drawer of dresser slowly. Pulls out lipstick. Amy lightly skips in place anxiously. Sara opens and applies lipstick—over, around, and above lips. Hands it to Amy. Amy smacks on lipstick with force as Sara finds blush in drawer. Applies blush to cheeks and nose. Gives to Amy. Amy drops stick and applies blush to cheeks, nose, forehead, and neck as Sara looks at herself in long mirror. Sara smiles and bats eyes. Amy drops blush and watches Sara. Sara opens second drawer with less caution. Pulls out silk scarf. Drapes it around neck. Finds half slip as Amy, restless, spies wardrobe and tiptoes to it. Sara secures slip over shorts as Amy tries to reach for knob of wardrobe. Sara spins around and sees Amy. Walks quickly over to Amy and points to her rug space angrily. Amy shakes her head and crosses her arms over her chest. Sara grasps Amy and drags her over to spot. Amy drops to floor and sits. Her face forms a "going-to-cry" expression (*deep frown, head down*).

Sara looks from Amy to door twice. Walks to wardrobe, opens it. Picks up a pair of high heeled shoes. Smiles and shows them to Amy. Amy reaches for them but Sara quickly holds them to her chest. Amy cries silently. Sara puts on shoes and awkwardly walks to long mirror. Waves at herself and imitates "fancy lady" in mirror. Amy sees and cries harder.

Makeup runs down face and onto her clothes.

Sara tilts her head to listen for tune of music. "Taps" on floor tiles in front of mirror. The music becomes faster and livelier and Sara dances more wildly and vigorously. She waves and jumps back and forth, furiously, getting makeup on rug.

Sara jumps with glee and often lands on sides of shoes. On her last, highest leap she lands on right side of right shoe and falls. Breathes hard. Looks down at shoes and picks up single "heel" of right shoe. Her mouth gapes. Picks up right "foot" part of shoe. Two headlights glow through the curtains of the window. Sara sees and puts her palm over her gaping mouth. Amy stops rolling and sees lights. Begins rolling with more fury. Sara takes off left shoe and examines them closely. Gets up and walks to nightstand by bed. Opens drawer and finds adhesive tape. Puts left shoe on bed and tapes heel to right shoe. Replaces tape in drawer and runs to put shoes away. The music from the other room stops. Sara quickly takes off slip and scarf. She spies her face in mirror and hurriedly wipes makeup off with scarf. A woman's voice and a teenage girl's voice can be heard. Sara hears and shuts dresser drawers. Looks at Amy on floor. Looks at scarf and slip in hand. Throws scarf and slip onto Amy. Turns out lamp. Woman's voice gets clearer as she gets closer. Sara looks around nervously. She sees the blush and lipstick, kicks them closer to Amy. She then goes to bed and gets underneath it.

Mother enters. Rushes over to Amy and picks her up. Turns on lamp. Examines mess and wipes Amy's tears. Mother, pensive, smooths Amy's hair and clothes. She then tilts head back and nods knowingly. Shifts Amy to right hip. Walks to bed and faces it. Puts left hand on left hip and glares at lower, underneath part (*what she can see while still standing*). Taps left foot impatiently and waits. Lights fade to black.

For a long time, people have warned "Keep children and animals off the stage!" Theater production demands enormous discipline and control. Even though the advice has been ignored, often to the delight of audiences, there's a reason for the caution: Small children and animals are hard to control. Perhaps in an unusually stylized play (like *The Dining Room*) in which adults play children, this scene would take on a new dimension. But as it stands, there are possible difficulties.

What is the writer trying to do? The play is about how older kids get younger kids into trouble. Just about everybody has been there. How do we make that idea, that theme, important? In other words, to ask our old question, what's at stake? Can there be significant stakes when children are the protagonists? It's difficult to manage.

There are very few plays with scenes between small children. Even in films, the children are usually a little older than these two. I think offhand of *Fanny and Alexander* and *Stand By Me*. In both films, there is a great deal at stake. In *Stand By Me*, the children come across a death that they have to deal with. In *Fanny and Alexander*, the children are being beaten and are looking for a way out of their stepfather's house. Not everything has to be that serious, but there does need to be some important consequence to the actions of the children. In *Dress-Up* there is not much at stake. What will happen to them when they're caught? How seriously will they be punished? The answer given in the play is "not very seriously."

When nothing much is at stake, one question to ask yourself as a writer is: "Are my characters fully believable?" In this case, there are some behaviors that are not very credible. Why would a three-year old stay quiet? Why *would* she? She does, but we don't see why. Amy's quiet is disturbing, because, unlike the exercise *Computer*, this scene is written realistically. This is a real world. In a real world, children whisper, giggle, squeak. Does that mean that all pantomime assignments have to be a little unreal, a little dream-like? No. While it's easier to find a line on a pantomime that is openly symbolic, it isn't impossible to write a non-speaking scene that is realistic.

## Conventions

It is a matter of *conventions*. You must have noticed that every play seems to have a set of rules that govern it, a set of rules that we understand very early on and that we expect the playwright to abide by. For instance, in *The Dining Room*, the rules are the following: 1) One dining-room table will stand for many dining-room tables, one place for many places. We will agree not to ask for distinctions, not to want to see other rooms beyond the dining room, not to look for the personal touches that make homes distinctive. 2) When one set of characters overlaps another set of characters on stage, they will all pretend they don't see or hear each other. They will ignore other characters as intensely as they ignore us, the audience. 3) Young actors will play old people and vice versa. We will not expect lines on faces, gray hair, or permanent outward characteristics to signify age.

A convention is a necessary lie agreed upon between playwright and audience for the convenience of telling the story. It is a promise that *this* story is better told *this* particular way and that if we all put aside objections, the deal will pay off. If the room does not have walls, we will get more for our money than if the room did have walls because the wall-lessness of the place will have some poetic or symbolic significance.

In *Glengarry Glen Ross*, we have no extreme conventions. We will agree not to expect waiters and Chinese food and lots of customers. We will agree to see only a corner of the restaurant. We will agree to let the characters speak in four-letter poetry without questioning whether everybody really talks that way—but we agree to that only if we see the pay-off, the meaning and force of the play.

In *Streetcar*, we agree that the playwright can show us outside and inside the apartment at the same time because we see that this story is about coming in for protection and coming into a trap instead. We agree that when the Blue Piano music plays and neon lights flash, anybody can hear the music or see the lights, but that when the memory-music, like the Varsouviana, plays, only Blanche can hear it. The playwright wants us to believe that the music is only in her mind—her memory—and we agree to that. Every play has conventions. They answer the question: "What is realistic and what is pretend?"

One of the difficulties with the children of *Dress-Up* is that they live in a realistic world, but they don't talk—which is not realistic. What if they were older? What if they had more at stake, more reason to be bad? More to gain from it? (If they were older, they might more easily keep the silence.) Or what if their action was stripped of minor details and became more theatrical?

## Making Each Gesture Count

Another difficulty with this script is that gestures that are highlighted come to nothing. Sara chooses a scarf for her neck, a half slip, and eventually high heels. But the use of each object is not particularly significant. Remember, everything on stage is magnified, everything assumes importance simply because it *is* on stage. A gesture creates expectations. Why a scarf? Why only two seconds' worth of scarf? Imagine the difference if a character searched and searched for a particular item and when she found it, did more than one thing with it. Imagine an article having significance, of something being at stake. A single well-chosen detail is worth a host of others. And one more thing. Be careful with and be kind to your actors. Every time you ask for a bottle broken on stage, a high-heeled shoe broken while dancing, a typewriter dropped on a foot (I'm not saying don't ask), you ought to have a good reason for it, a really good pay-off. Because it takes a great deal of rehearsal time to do an *effect* safely and believably. In this case the broken shoe doesn't inevitably *lead* to anything. It doesn't have consequences that make it worthwhile or effects that can't be gotten through other means.

However, before we get lost in what still needs attention, let us remember that this writer has begun to play with props and with physical actions. She has thought about entrances. There is a setup for the second entrance—bringing Amy into the room. And certainly adult actresses playing these roles could make them very funny.

The story this writer chooses to tell is the same story Shepard tells in *True West*: a story of sibling rivalry, a good child, a bad child, the making of chaos while they battle each other, the entrance of mother to witness what happens when she is gone.

One of the most effective moments is Sara's insistence that Amy stay on the rug. There are untapped possibilities here. This is theatrical, theatre within theatre. Does Sara *need* to perform for Amy? Is this the beginning of a long, long life battle between sisters? Ideally, the scene should suggest more than its literal meaning. It should mean either "Here are two lives that will continue to operate in this way," or "Here is a vision of how the passive ones always eventually get revenge," or "This is like our adult lives in such and such a way, like everyone's life." *Glengarry Glen Ross* is about everybody, not just about a salesman. It is about youth and age, and about a stake in things in the marketplace. It is possible to suggest more than the solitary situation even with a two-page pantomime.

Now let us look at *Laundry*.

## Laundry
*by Pamela McCready*

### CHARACTERS

WIFE—a woman in her mid-thirties. She is wearing sweats and tennis shoes.

HUSBAND—a man in his early forties. He is wearing a business suit and carrying a briefcase.

### SCENE

A bedroom. 11.00 p.m. There is a queensized fourposter bed flanked by nightstands. One doorway with a lightswitch beside it and a chair. A bedside lamp lights the stage.

WIFE is seated on the bed. There is an over-sized glass of white wine and a pack of cigarettes on the nightstand. There is a basket of laundry beside the bed and a pile of folded laundry on the bed.

WIFE folds a child's white undershirt and places it on the pile. She folds another and places it on the pile. She takes a small pair of blue jeans from the basket and examines them. They have a hole in the knee. She sighs, places them to the side.

She takes a cigarette from the pack, taps it on the nightstand, lights it and takes a drink of wine. She sits on the edge of the bed with one knee up. She rests her head on her knee, cigarette between her fingers. After a few moments she takes a drag from her cigarette and slowly exhales, staring at the ceiling. She takes a quick drag from her cigarette, coughs, takes a drink of wine and places the cigarette in the ashtray.

She empties the remaining contents of the laundry basket, small white socks, onto the bed. She efficiently, almost mechanically, sorts and matches them. From offstage is heard the sound of a door slamming. She does not look up.

HUSBAND enters. He turns on the overhead light, goes to her and kisses her on the cheek. She squints in the sudden glare but does not look up. He places his briefcase on the bed and removes his coat and tie, placing them on the chair. As his back is turned, WIFE looks at him, then at her watch. She takes another drink of wine and crushes out her cigarette. Husband takes pajamas from the chair and exits. WIFE places the torn jeans on her nightstand, and begins to put the folded laundry into the laundry basket.

HUSBAND re-enters wearing pajamas. He places his folded slacks onto the chair, sits on the bed and removes his watch, placing it on the nightstand. He opens his briefcase and removes a stack of blue-bound contracts and a gold pen. He turns on his bedside lamp and begins to read. WIFE toys with a lone sock and turns as if to speak to him. He begins to tap a cadence on the side of the contracts with his pen. WIFE looks back at the sock, turning it inside-out and right-side out a few times, finally putting it in the laundry basket. She takes a cigarette out of the pack and taps it on the nightstand, creating a near counterpoint. She lights her

---

The characters are not given names. This tends to make them somewhat generic. Is there a suggestion that these two repeat in many households?

Each detail tells us something: the wine, cigarettes tell us this woman needs comfort.

The undershirt tells us there is a child in the family. Is the child one of the obstacles to confront? Or is the child "What's at stake"?

The actions are very small and specific. This pantomime is realistic, if not naturalistic, and yet there is no speech. Does it seem stylistically consistent? For me, it is naturalism stretched to make a poetic statement, naturalism pushed to a limit, and it is effective.

Wife is more aware of husband than he is of her. This sets up a tension.

Husband's few gestures suggest a highly conventional, orderly man.

The lone sock is a good metaphor for the wife, who is unable to make a connection.

In the established silence, the tapping sounds would be very effective.

cigarette as he makes a note on one of the contracts. She coughs, he pauses briefly and continues to make his notes. WIFE takes a drink of wine, picks up the laundry basket and exits, holding cigarette between her lips.

WIFE re-enters, studies him for a moment and turns off the overhead light. She sits on her side of the bed and removes her tennis shoes. She stands and takes off her sweat pants, leaving them on the floor. She reaches underneath her sweat shirt to unfasten her bra and removes it by pulling first through one sleeve of her sweat shirt and then the next and drops it to the floor.

She slumps on the edge of the bed and brushes ashes from the nightstand onto the floor. HUSBAND places contracts on nightstand. He leans over, places a hand on her shoulder and kisses her on the head. She stiffens, pats his hand and nods. He rolls over, turns out his bedside lamp and lies down to go to sleep.

She examines the hem of her sweat shirt and finds a loose thread. She pulls at it until it won't pull any more. She picks up her cigarette and burns it off. She crushes out her cigarette and begins to play with the string, twisting it around her fingers. HUSBAND begins to snore softly. She balls up the string and tosses it on the floor. She opens the drawer to her nightstand and takes out a bottle of pills. She taps one into her hand, begins to re-cap the bottle, stops and takes another. She washes them down with the remainder of her wine.

She gets under the cover to go to sleep and stares at the ceiling. HUSBAND shifts slightly in his sleep, touching her under the covers. She pulls away and sits up, lights another cigarette, takes a drag and places it in the ashtray. She gets out of bed and exits. She returns carrying a small plaid blanket and a stuffed rabbit. She gets into bed, strokes the blanket against her cheek, puts out her cigarette and turns out the light. She lies in the semi-darkness, clutching the blanket and rabbit to her, staring at the ceiling.

Something almost happens here. She coughs. He pauses. What is it he almost said?
She becomes tough, carrying the basket, cigarette between her lips.

Her style of preparing for bed is completely different from her husband's.

Husband makes some effort toward wife, but it's not enough. The small moves are detached, not intimate. Here, and later, wife pulls away.

She's "unraveling." She resorts to pills. A decision: The second pill. If she tapped out two to begin with, the gesture would be less telling.

This is a sad conclusion. She has failed to change things, cannot receive the small offerings of her husband, resorts to a child-state. Even with imported comforts, she does not fall asleep easily.

---

Marital trouble breeds silence, the lesson of Exercise 3. I remember lighter views of this silence by several writers. One student had a husband and wife keep missing each other. He'd go out of the room, she'd come in and select a TV program, she'd go out, he'd change the program, he'd go out, etc. Another had a couple fight via cleaning and cooking. Some of the best pantomime fights in drama appear in comedies of marriage. In Sir Noel Coward's *Private Lives* and in Neil Simon's *Barefoot in the Park*, people use movements—entrances, exits, the handling of props—instead of words. But in both *Laundry* and *Cross Stitch*, which follows, writers have dealt with more serious marital trouble, and in both cases they've allowed interesting contradictions to give texture to the people.

Now let's look at *Cross Stitch*, which tells a long story in a short time by using a suggestion that memory sweeps over time.

## Cross Stitch
### by Kirsta Bleyle

*The stage is bare except: two identical rocking chairs side-by-side at center stage, a standing chest of drawers, a knitting basket beside each rocking chair, and an over-stuffed Lazy-boy up stage left.*

An old woman of about 70 years of age enters from down stage right. What she is wearing is not important, except that she wears a bedraggled orange cardigan sweater. She moves to the rocking chair on the right and slowly lowers herself into it. She settles herself and removes a large ball of yarn and knitting needles from the basket beside her. However, she does not start knitting, but instead turns towards the audience with a dazed look. She holds her gaze until a young couple in their twenties enters from down stage left. As they enter, she turns slowly towards them while remaining silent.

The couple is dressed as a bride and groom, and the groom is carrying the bride as he would "over the threshold" to their new home. He sets her down and she looks around, taking in her new surroundings with obvious joy. She turns to him and hugs him tightly. He, in turn, picks her up again and carries her off down stage right.

The old woman returns her attention to her knitting when the entrance of another couple in their forties (similar enough in physical appearance to the previous one that it is obvious they are the same people), enter from down stage left and take her attention away from her knitting. The man has developed quite a paunch and is balding. The woman is graying and has on a house dress. She sits in the rocking chair next to the old woman and removes a large piece of canvas from her knitting basket. There is a threaded needle hanging from it and she begins to cross stitch, using large, flowing movement. The man walks to the chest of drawers and takes out a wrapped package. He walks over to the woman and hands it to her. She sets her stitching down in her lap and opens the box. Inside is the same orange sweater the old woman has on, only it is brand new and has the tags still on it. The woman looks at the sweater with obvious distaste, nods a thanks to the man, places the sweater and box beside her chair, then continues to work at her cross stitch. Obviously angered, the man rips the cross stitch out of the woman's hands, takes it over to the chest of drawers, yanks one of the drawers open and throws it in. He then slams the drawer shut and stomps over to the woman, where she has been watching him with horror. He grabs her by the arm and pulls her out of the chair, slaps her, picks up the sweater and box with his free hand, then drags the woman off, down stage right. The old woman follows this action with her head, and as the younger woman is being dragged off, the two women make eye contact, then quickly look away. They both sob violently.

As the old woman straightens up in her chair while drying her eyes, a woman dressed in black with a black veil covering her face enters from down stage left. She walks over to the chest of drawers and opens the top one. She first takes out the orange sweater, tags still on it, and lovingly caresses it, before putting it on over her black dress. She then removes a very large picture frame from the drawer. After running her fingers over it, she places it on top of the chest of drawers so that it is standing up. In large block letters it holds a cross stitched piece of canvas that reads, "God is Love." She then turns to the old woman, who has been watching and rises from her chair. They slowly walk towards each other and embrace. Lights out.

In **Cross Stitch**, the main character relates to herself at three crucial stages in her relationship with her husband, and interestingly feels similarly about both herself and him at each stage. Because the writer does not simplify their relationship, she tells a story of acceptance—of the imperfect orange sweater, of widowhood, of self.

## Economy

Some of the things that writing a pantomime can help you do are: 1) choose actions carefully; 2) notice economy and efficiency in both choices of stage setting and props; 3) think about the large, chance-like, shape of an action; 4) conceptualize longer works by seeing the whole drama as a series of images that are major points in the action.

The writer who wrote about the TV couple discovered he had asked his characters to have a tug of war over the remote control device but there was not enough variety in the tug of war. It was just a back and forth, undisguised by lines of dialogue, and it required development. This same writer asked for silent laughter throughout, but suddenly one laugh erupted and was audible. This inconsistency brought up the whole problem of conventions. What rules govern each piece?

The writer who put two characters into a fight over housekeeping asked for clutter—books, papers, clothing, shoes, coat, dishes—and lots of furniture, including kitchen cabinets. The man re-shelves books, vacuums. There is so much going on that it is too much. Not all of the clutter is relevant; the actors can't relate to most of it. When the writer looked at the whole thing, he understood that the vacuuming would take too long and that nothing was being furthered in the script by it. He also realized that he could choose props—give the woman spices and the man books, develop those limited parts of the action, and maybe manage to suggest more, perhaps that the woman is spicy, the man bookish.

Finally, we'll look at *Silence*. In it, there are many stage areas. Yet all are used. In *Silence*, there is a good deal of repetition. Yet each instance is painfully meaningful. *Silence* is a pantomime play that dramatizes an inner state—despair—and a decision.

## Silence
*by Punnasak Sukee*

The stage is dark.

The noises begin to be heard from softly to louder and louder. It is the world's noises. The noise of traffic, horns. The noise of whispering, talking, laughing, crying, screaming and the shouting of people in anger. They are men, women and children. Old and young. The sound of someone slamming the door closed.

The world's noises stop.

The stage is very quiet.

The sound of someone turning the switch on.

The lights come up.

There is an armchair in the center of the stage. Beside the armchair is a small desk with a telephone on it. The armchair is facing towards the television and the auditorium. This is a living room.

Upstage right, a small end table with one chair. There is also a small table beside the wall. This is the dining room.

Stage left, a pillow and a blanket are on the floor. This is a bedroom. A mirror is hung on the wall.

The woman, about forty-five, stands still at the door. She has a weary look. She dresses very simply, almost cheaply and in bad taste. She gazes fixedly towards the auditorium and this is her characteristic. No facial expression at all. No one could ever tell what she really feels deep down inside. Her movement is slow, unrealistic and looks like the dead-living.

When she begins to move, the sound of a Thai percussion instrument will be heard. This percussion gives us a ritualistic, mysterious, but monotonous sound and it will keep going for the whole play. Her slow movement is according to the rhythm of this percussion.

Now, she begins to move to her bedroom. The percussion begins to be heard.

She reaches her bedroom, stops and faces the mirror. She looks at herself in the mirror. Pause.

She slowly takes her wig off. She is bald. Pause.

She begins to take her clothes off very slowly. Her eyes keep looking at the mirror. Pause. She is in her underwear. She still looks at the mirror, begins to examine her own body. Pause.

She slowly moves to the living room, sits on an armchair. Pause.

She picks up the newspaper from the floor. Pause. She begins to open it, page by page, until the last page. Pause. She puts the newspaper down on the floor. Pause.

She rises up. Pause. She moves to the television. Pause. She turns it on, goes back to the armchair, sits. Pause.

She looks at the television fixedly. No facial expression. Pause.

Then she smiles. Pause. She ceases suddenly. Pause.

Then she smiles again. Pause. She ceases suddenly. Pause.

Then she smiles again. Pause. She ceases suddenly. Pause.

She rises up. Pause. She moves to the television. Pause. She turns it off. Pause. She goes back to the armchair, sits. Pause.

She rises up again. Pause. She goes to the dining room.

A plate, a spoon, a fork, a glass of water and a bowl of rice are already on the table. She sits on a chair. Pause. Hands on her lap.

She begins to eat. Fork in her left hand. Spoon in her right hand. She eats slowly. Her movement now is still unrealistic, a little bit stylized.

Then she stops. She puts the spoon and fork down on her plate. Her hands go back to her lap. She drinks water. Pause. She rises up. She goes to a small table beside the wall and comes back with a small bottle of pepper in her hand. Pause.

She sits down. Pause. She puts the pepper in her rice. Pause. She begins to eat it again. Then she stops. She drinks the water. Pause. She begins to eat again. Her tears are rolling down on her face. She stops. Pause. She drinks the water. Pause.

She rises up. She goes to the living room. She sits on the armchair. Pause. She rises up. Pause. She goes to the television. Pause. She is about to turn it on. She changes her mind. Pause. She goes back to the armchair, sits. Pause. She looks at the telephone on a small desk beside her. Pause.

She looks at the telephone again. Pause. She reaches her hand for it, changes her mind, takes her hand back, turns her face back to the audience. Pause.

She looks at the telephone again. Pause. She reaches her hand for it, changes her mind, takes her hand back, turns her face back to the audience. Pause.

She rises up. Pause. She goes to the bedroom. She lies down, covers herself with the blanket, closes her eyes. Pause.

She opens her eyes, rises up, goes to the living room. She grasps a small bottle, placed on the television. She goes to the dining room, opens the bottle. She takes one pill out from the bottle, places the bottle down on the table. She takes that pill, drinks the water. Pause.

She goes back to her bedroom. She lies down, covers herself with the blanket, closes her eyes. Pause.

She opens her eyes. Pause. She rises up. Pause. She goes to the dining room, takes another pill, drinks the water. Pause.

She goes back to her bedroom. She lies down, covers herself with the blanket, closes her eyes. Pause.

She opens her eyes. Long pause. She rises up, moves very slowly to the dining room. She takes another pill. Pause. Then, another pill. Pause. Then, another pill. Pause. Then, she turns the bottle upside down in her hand. It is a handful of pills. She takes it all, drinks the water. Pause. The tears in her eyes. Pause. She smiles. Pause.

She moves slowly to her bedroom. She lies down, covers herself with the blanket. She closes her eyes. She smiles. Her tears roll down on her face.

The sound of the percussion still goes on, but the rhythm is slower and slower and then it stops. The stage is in complete silence for a while. Then, black out.

The world's noise is heard again louder and louder. Then it fades away very slowly as if it were going to last forever.

In *Silence*, the writer (not a native speaker of English) uses fascinating, evocative phrasing. He has suggested, without saying so, that perhaps a lighting effect reveals this life a bit at a time. Living room, dining room, bedroom. He does not specify a darkening of any area so the sudden revelation of food on the table is probably not possible. We would see it from the start, as we would the bottle of pills on the television.

The class was very taken with this piece. A few wanted to know, "Why is this woman bald?" Is it illness, the effects of chemotherapy, age, other disease? Others didn't question the reason because they felt the whole piece was at a remove from reasons. When the workshop discussion ended, and the writer was invited to speak, he said, gently, "She is just bald. I wanted the comedy of human ugliness and sadness."

One person said, "When that percussion instrument stopped, it went right to my heart." Another said, "We've all been there. That kind of loneliness." The play succeeds in being about a specific day and a whole life time, about one and all.

**Assignment: Exercise 3**

The assignment is this: write a pantomime sequence of one to three pages in which something happens, in which—preferably—words are not needed at all as the means of communication. This is your chance to investigate gesture and pantomime, to write action and interaction without dialogue. Think about an extended action, which does not *need* dialogue, or which is dramatic *because* dialogue is avoided.

**Study Questions and Exercises**

1. What is the effect of pantomime on stage?
2. What is a playwriting convention? Give examples.
3. What is the reason for economy of scenery? Economy of movement? Economy in the choice of props?

# SIX

# Dramatic Devices

## OVERVIEW

Tennessee Williams' *A Streetcar Named Desire* has, over the years, proved so powerful an influence on playwriting students and so convenient a teaching tool that I have included a discussion of it here.

Because *A Streetcar Named Desire* is beautifully physicalized, it serves as a casebook on the physical aspects of dramatic action. But I would have a hard time resisting talking about some of the other subjects it calls to mind—autobiography in playwriting, the use of devices like *dramatic irony* (superior knowledge on the part of the audience) and *peripety* (action that results in a reversal of intention).

The discussion of *Streetcar* will lead to and include a review of playwriting principles 1–15 as set forth in Chapter 1. Remember, these are not rules but tendencies in most established plays.

## OBJECTIVES

At the end of this chapter you should be able to

- Discuss the movement patterns in *Streetcar*
- Define dramatic irony and discuss its use in *Streetcar*
- Define peripety and discuss its use in *Streetcar*

**Plot Summary of *A Streetcar Named Desire*** by
*Tennessee Williams*

**Scene 1.** Exterior of New Orleans tenement, twilight, May. Women of the neighborhood sit outdoors. Stanley Kowalski announces that he's going bowling with his pals; his wife Stella follows to watch. Blanche Dubois enters and asks for Stella. She is shown indoors by Eunice as the lights fade outdoors and begin to come up indoors. Blanche steals a drink and she sits alone, horrified by the apartment. Stella rushes in and the sisters reunite, exchanging compliments and then stories. Stella tells how desperately she misses Stanley when he is traveling; Blanche reveals that she is out of work and has lost the family home, Belle Reve. Stanley enters and discovers that Blanche has come to stay for an indefinite time.

**Scene 2.** Interior, mainly, the next night. Stella will take Blanche out to dinner because it is Stanley's poker night. Stanley confronts Blanche with his suspicions that she has money and is cheating Stella of Belle Reve. He goes through her papers, but she snatches back a bundle of letters from her deceased husband, written when he was very young. Stanley reveals that Stella is pregnant.

**Scene 3.** Interior, mainly, later that night. Stanley and companions play poker and argue drunkenly. Mitch thinks he should go home because his mother is sick. Stella and Blanche return. Stanley turns off the radio moments after Blanche turns it on. Blanche and Mitch get acquainted, but Mitch's absence from the poker game (and the renewed sound of the radio) infuriate Stanley who hits Stella, breaks the radio, and lashes out at his companions. Blanche and Stella flee upstairs to Eunice's, but Stanley bellows for Stella and eventually she returns to spend the night with him.

**Scene 4.** The morning after. Blanche returns to find Stella lolling in bed, contented, and tries to talk Stella out of her relationship with Stanley. Stanley returns unseen and listens. Blanche describes him as common, like an animal, primitive. Stanley pretends he has just returned and he and Stella rush into each other's arms.

**Scene 5.** A hot summer evening. Steve and Eunice fight upstairs. Stanley lets Blanche know he's heard rumors about her seamy sexual encounters back home in Laurel.

Blanche asks Stella if she's heard the rumors and defends herself, explaining that she is not "putting out" for Mitch because she wants to make him want her. After Stanley and Stella go out, a paper boy comes to collect. Blanche talks seductively to him and kisses him before she lets him go. Suddenly brightly theatrical, she flirts with Mitch who arrives in the next moment.

**Scene 6.** Same night, two in the morning. Blanche and Mitch return from their date. Blanche apologizes for not being cheerful. She asks Mitch if they can stay in the dark and have a drink. Blanche flatters Mitch about his strength and his physique. She flirts, but pretends that she is prudish, and has prim and proper ideals. She tells him she has no money and that Stanley hates her. Mitch reveals that he's going to be very lonely when his mother dies. Blanche tells him about discovering her husband making love with another man, about the disgust she felt, and about her husband's eventual suicide. She and Mitch decide that maybe they can cure each other's loneliness.

**Scene 7.** Afternoon in mid-September. Stella prepares for Blanche's birthday celebration. Blanche sings from the bathroom where she is getting bathed and dressed. Stanley tells Stella that Blanche had many sexual encounters with strangers when she lived in a disreputable hotel called the Flamingo, that she was considered crazy by the townspeople, and that she lost her job for seducing a seventeen-year-old student. Because Stanley has told Mitch about this, Mitch will not be coming to supper as planned.

**Scene 8.** Three-quarters of an hour later. The birthday party is a disaster. Stanley sweeps dishes onto the floor. Blanche can tell that Stella knows something. Mitch doesn't come. Stanley gives Blanche a present of a one-way bus ticket back to Laurel. Blanche breaks down. Stella gets labor pains.

**Scene 9.** Later that evening. Mitch arrives. Blanche is very disturbed. Mitch wants to turn the lights on because he's never seen Blanche in the daylight or any strong light. When he switches on the light, he sees that she is older than he thought. He doesn't mind that, but he does mind the fact that she pretended to be virginal. She talks about her life in Laurel, and even earlier after the death of her husband—one man after another. Mitch wants to go to bed with her, but says he won't marry her because she's not clean enough to bring into the house with his mother. Blanche screams, "Fire," until Mitch runs out.

**Scene 10.** A few hours later that night. Blanche is very drunk and dressed in an evening gown. In her derangement, she believes someone has sent her an invitation by wire for a cruise. Stanley comes home. He has left Stella at the hospital. He brings out his silk pajamas and a bottle of champagne. Blanche is afraid of him and tries to call for help. She attacks him; he fights back; she collapses. He describes the rape that is about to occur as a date they've had from the beginning.

**Scene 11.** Weeks later. Stanley and his friends play poker. Stella and Eunice help Blanche to dress. Eunice tells Stella she must never believe Blanche's story about the rape. Stella has told Blanche they're sending her for a rest in the country. Blanche seems to think she's going on a cruise. A doctor and matron come for her. Mitch breaks down. Blanche fights the matron, but the doctor subdues her. The men play poker as Blanche leaves. Stella sobs. Stanley caresses Stella and reminds her how good life was before Blanche's arrival.

You should now read *A Streetcar Named Desire* by Tennessee Williams. There is a great deal to learn from the way this play works. And we will discuss the play at length. But do notice the stage directions, and the way the story is told in gestures as well as in lines. Notice especially some of the extended sections of pantomime in which Blanche is dreaming or in which Stanley stakes out his territory. There is a heightened quality to all the movement, an almost-dance. At first we see Blanche entering, like a moth entering a net, fluttering, about to be trapped. For our purposes here, if you imagine the first scene without the intervening dialogue, and watch Blanche's progress as far as the inside of Stella's apartment when she takes a drink of liquor and then hides the evidence, you will have an excellent example of a pantomime sequence.

Be aware too of the quality of pantomime in Scene Ten, right before the rape scene. There is not a great deal of extended pantomime without dialogue, but the dramatic dance—the physicalization of the script—is especially vivid in Scene Ten. Blanche's desperation is shown by the way she dresses herself, the way she avoids Stanley, and is echoed by the scene outside the apartment in which a prostitute rolls a drunkard.

Look at whole scenes (even when there is dialogue simultaneous with action) as a *dramatic dance*. Stella decorates a birthday cake, Stanley comes in and talks to her, he becomes more and more tense, he makes her sit down, he tells her something she doesn't want to hear. We *see* that. And then into the midst of this tense scene, Blanche comes, opening the bathroom door, going out and in again, performing. She is telling herself that everything is all right. The tension of seeing her enter brightly, towel around her head, is dramatic and promises a climactic scene. Stella goes back to decorating the cake. This is physical action showing us that she will try to deny what Stanley has just told her. When Stanley finally routs Blanche out of the bathroom, after pounding at the door and yelling, Blanche enters even more gaily, laughing. The contrast is strong and a setup for Blanche's fall—which begins with her growing recognition that she can't play the role she has cast herself in, that she can't have peace here, that something, in fact, really is wrong. If you saw the whole scene with the sound turned off, you would know a great deal about these characters. You would have seen something like a dance performed, with repetition, with significant, highlighted gestures, with pattern and meaning. It is very important that Blanche pokes her head out of the bathroom more than once and very important that Stanley turns to violence when he wants the bathroom. It is the whole play in miniature: she is protecting herself, closing herself in; Stanley seems to go along with it in a surly way, but there is real violence underneath. Finally he gets angry and repossesses his territory, routing Blanche out.

Stella starts out making a birthday celebration. Even after things are shaken up, she forces herself to continue, withdrawing into pretense herself. It is her play in miniature too! There are many such wonderful scenes of pantomimic action to study in *Streetcar*. See if you can identify them. But now, let's turn to other features of *Streetcar* that might be useful study for beginning playwrights.

## Transforming Autobiographical Materials

The preface to *A Streetcar Named Desire* ("On a Streetcar Named Success") tells something about Tennessee Williams' personality and his reaction to fame. It also provides a glimpse into the life of a playwright. Williams had become used to working in poverty when the success of *A Glass Menagerie* catapulted him to fame and to what seemed like blessed financial security. He went a bit crazy with the strangeness of the changes that came upon him. Voices didn't sound right to him, food didn't look right, and luxurious accommodations made him sick. He couldn't bear hearing compliments. He voluntarily went for an eye operation (he *wanted* to be sick, to rest), an operation that kept him in gauze bandages, removed a little from the world. This was the beginning of what he saw as a cure from being always in the public eye. The second step of the cure was to leave for Mexico where his success meant nothing. And the third was to write the first version of *A Streetcar Named Desire*. Williams tells the story to illustrate that work, not success, is the salvation of an artist, that nothing really satisfies *except* the struggle to do something artistic.

In the story of his success and his breakdown, we can see Blanche and we can see the seeds of *Streetcar*. One never knows where ideas will come from, or to what use our lowest moments may be put. But if you were meant to write, you will find yourself using your lowest moments. And in unusual ways. Williams did not write about a man losing his grip, or an artist losing his grip, but about a woman who had come to the end of the line, who was alienated from the world, a woman who searched for a secure haven and couldn't find one except in insanity. In other words, he transformed his experiences into something else.

I met Tennessee Williams when he came to Pittsburgh to give a reading. I gave the introduction.

Things were tense that evening. He arrived too late to have dinner with all of us who were gathered to greet him. Instead he had to be rushed from the airport to the theatre. He was supposed to read poetry in the first half of the evening, and drama in the second half. He had a sly, strange look and he mumbled something about manuscripts back in some hotel room in Florida. Then he asked for a coffee cup to take on stage with him and we saw his assistant pour him something other than coffee. When he got onto the stage, he drank and winked at the audience so that they would know it was not coffee in the cup. So why take a coffee cup on stage? He was playing, posing, acting all the time. He was impish, charming, and maddening. He announced to us at intermission that he was finished and that there was no second half. I can't remember how we communicated that to the audience. I do remember a feeling of chaos in the lobby. I remember that people wanted to hear him read from the *plays* for which he is world famous. (He is not known for his poetry!) Williams was self-defeating, alienated, accustomed to riding the line between being adored and despised. He was testing our affection as a child tests.

There is much of this in Blanche, also a grown-up troubled child. She is a character who has touched men and women all over the world. In South America, France, China, Japan, name it, she has come to mean the softer, more idealistic part of the human spirit, weakened and dumped into a hostile world where it will be snuffed out. Williams evoked the *feeling* of this play by having Blanche seek a home with her sister Stella and by having Stanley try to get rid of her. The story must have happened in a million real and analogous ways billions and billions of times across the whole world.

## Setting as Treasure

Let us notice some of the things Williams does. He writes long stage directions of a descriptive sort. He makes the setting a vital part of the action. There are few plays that require the lyrical setup that Williams gives this one. The amount of time the reader requires to read the passage is about how long the theatre audience needs to see and hear the New Orleans street corner he describes. The lights come up slowly. The Blue Piano plays. It is a hot spring night, moving on to summer. Twilight. Stanley brings raw meat for Stella. The women make a dirty joke about it. The people who live here seem comfortable, earthy. Blanche comes in. She doesn't fit.

Most plays have a treasure. In *Streetcar*, it is a place to stay. Blanche needs a place to stay. She needs a home. This one seems wrong for her, but she doesn't appear to have other choices. Something is wrong with her. She is desperate. Something is at stake. She must fit in even if she despises the place and the way her sister lives. We don't know what is wrong with Blanche, but we have no doubt that something is at stake.

In a fiction workshop, I heard novelist Hilma Wolitzer say to prose writers, "I want to know what's at stake and what's *the ache*." I think that is as good a question for plays as for fiction. Not only is something at stake, but somebody is hurting in a play. There is an ache. Curtain up. Something's wrong.

## Framing Entrances

Notice the setup of entrances as Williams introduces characters. It's interesting that we get a glimpse of Stanley and Stella (and even Mitch) before we meet Blanche. We see how they live, we understand the neighborhood. Blanche's entrance is certainly "set up." But so is Stella's second entrance! Williams has let us see Stella before Blanche does, so he has built tension and expectation. Stella, arriving back at the apartment, calls out to Blanche before they meet. Then they actually *see* each other and fall into an embrace.

And Stanley's second entrance is built up to by the voices of the men coming back from bowling—again pointing to the contrast between Stanley and Blanche. Blanche darts to the bedroom, looks at Stanley's picture, then hides from him before she ever meets him. Doesn't that set up an expectation of drama to come? Doesn't it predict what is to follow? The rape scene will echo this moment physically. The natural staging of the play will have a dance-like aspect.

## A Dramatic Triangle

Once Stanley is in the apartment, the triangle is complete. The moment in Scene One in which we feel the tension of the triangle—all three people in one place—is a key moment. The play will continue to work on the triangle basis in spite of the character Mitch. Blanche is like the child in a family. It's no mistake that the play will progress with Stella's pregnancy and end with the birth of a child. In one sense, Blanche and Stanley battle for Stella's attentions. But Blanche is also a threat to the marriage, an interloper who in some ways does battle with Stella over Stanley, competes for him.

## Complex Characters

When Stanley and Stella argue about Blanche, they are arguing over their own lives, their marriage. Stella can see Blanche's innocence. Stanley sees nothing but scheming. Both are true of Blanche. (She is scheming to cover over her past, to make herself a place; she does not deliberately want to hurt anyone.) As such she provides a mirror to Stanley and Stella. The triangle is loaded with tension. Everyone is desperate.

Mitch is the hope for the breaking of the triangle. But he isn't strong enough to find his own way in the world. Blanche isn't strong enough to be honest with him at the beginning of their relationship. And Stanley has the energy and motive to destroy Blanche.

And so the characters, complex, and much like real-life characters, carry their dramatic conflicts with them through all scenes. They are dramatic because they have *things they want, things they want to do*. Stella is trying to take care of her sister and to find a way to make her sister and Stanley get along. Blanche is trying to talk Stella out of Stanley, to make her remember another way of life. And Stanley is trying to separate the sisters, trying to get rid of Blanche, and get rid of "airs" once and for all in Stella.

Most important plays start a drama with people who have a history, a past. In the case of *Streetcar*, all of them are looking for ways to live with the compromises they've made: Stanley won't ever be anyone important; Stella has left elegance, art, literature behind; Blanche has slept with a lot of men in Laurel in an attempt to feel some union with another human being. They have to find a way to live with these things, which is why each of them, not just Blanche, becomes indirect, pretends, and tries to deny the truth. *Streetcar* is about pretending. It is about acting. And lying. As many plays are.

When people pretend, when they hold back what they think, it will usually come out eventually. This is the motivation for Blanche's monologue in Scene Four. She has held her tongue about Stanley. Now she believes it's safe to let her feelings out. And besides, she hopes to save her little sister. We can well imagine why Stella doesn't have a lot to say while Blanche speaks. Her silence during the monologue is motivated several ways. She understands how Blanche feels, for one thing, and she also understands how impossible it would be to stop Blanche from talking once she has begun. But maybe, too, Stella needs to hear what Blanche is saying. Blanche's voice is like an inner voice, Stella's own voice, which she won't allow herself to hear.

In Scene Four, Blanche believes she can talk Stella out of Stanley. Not only is she faced with something she can't understand in Stella's attachment to Stanley, but she tries, fails at her mission, and worse yet, is overheard by Stanley. So in addition to failing with Stella, she manages to make Stanley her determined enemy.

## *Dramatic Irony and Peripety*

Two classic dramatic devices are present in Scene Four. You will probably find yourself using them soon. The first is *dramatic irony*. Williams has Stanley enter unseen by the women and overhear Blanche call him *common* and refer to him as a beast. The audience sees Stanley and knows he hears. The audience also knows that Blanche doesn't know he hears. The expectation is that something will happen to resolve this difference between what she knows and what we know. We, the audience, will wait for Blanche to "catch up" with our level of knowledge. We will watch Stanley, knowing what he knows, but wondering how he will use it. Here is a definition of *dramatic irony*. The definition is something to refer to—for dramatic irony comes in different forms and guises. *A remark made for two audiences, one of which will hear and not understand, the other of which will hear and understand not only the remark, but also the first hearer's incomprehension.* It is important to understand that the *second audience of this definition is a theatre audience*. The first audience is somebody on stage. So the device of dramatic irony comes about when somebody on stage makes a remark that is not fully understood on stage, but is fully understood in the audience. Therefore, in this case, Blanche not only makes the remark but she and Stella become the first audience of the definition. Blanche hears herself but doesn't understand that Stanley also hears her. She doesn't understand the full implication of the remark. The theatre audience knows she doesn't know and waits for a result.

Dramatic irony is also possible when a gesture, a line, an action is made for two audiences, one on stage, which does not understand the full implications, and one—the audience—who does understand both the remark and the implications.

The reason you will want to use dramatic irony is that it is the motivator of hidden situations, hidden meanings, indirect actions—all of the things that characteristically make plays. The audience stays interested when they know something a character doesn't know. Dramatic irony is a device for giving the audience superior knowledge about the situation on stage. And there is always the pressure of a future just around the corner when the unknown thing will become known.

The second device that is common to all drama and that is used in this scene is *peripety*. *Reversal of intention*. A character intends to do one thing, takes an action, but that action results in the opposite of the intended result. Blanche tries to separate Stella from Stanley so that she will have a safer life herself, safe from Stanley whom she fears. Her attempt not only backfires, but it backfires neatly as a reversal of intention. She has made herself less safe with Stanley now. She has driven Stella and Stanley back together and she has turned Stanley resolutely against her. Reversal of intention: an action that has the opposite of the intended reaction: peripety. Plays are made of peripeties. Bert States in *Irony and Drama* says that peripety is so much what a play *is* that "We might as well say, 'Let's go to the peripety tonight.' " (Ithaca: Cornell University Press, 1971, 27)

*Streetcar* is a full-length play put together with separate scenes. This is one way to structure a play. The structure usually tells us something of importance. Ask yourself, "What is the *place* of the play? What is the *time* of the play? How is the action broken up in terms of place and time?" With these three questions you will reveal a great deal about the structure. In *Streetcar*, the place stays the same— outside and inside—womb and world. The lapse of time is seven months, spring to autumn. We watch the seasons come and go through Stella's pregnancy. In a good play, both place and time are symbolic.

The scenes are each developed so that something happens in them. In each scene you can find dramatic irony and peripety at work. The scenes are very efficient in that a great deal is accomplished in each one. The scene lengths are long enough to develop a complete action, but never so long that we find a situation over-written.

## Summary and Review of Principles

Let us just review the play, briefly, looking at most of the twenty "principles of playmaking" that I refer to often as points for discussion.

1. The characters of the play must be different from each other in order to make a dynamic of character interaction. Blanche is highly strung and nervous while Stella is quieter and calmer. Blanche puts on airs. Stella is pretty and natural looking. Blanche is the older sister, Stella the baby. Blanche is unmarried and has had a professional life. Stella is married and has no job or career. We could go on, but you get the idea. The differences are already there and they will cause tension. Stanley is different from both of them—he's a man, for one thing. And he's poor, of the working class, uneducated, aggressive, and proud. The differences are there.

2. The setting of the play is a metaphor for the action of the play. A well-chosen setting pressures the action. The setting of *Streetcar* is no exception. There is a small, cramped apartment that is charming, but awful, comfortable for two but not for three. There is an environment around it, the streets of the poor quarter of New Orleans. The play is about Blanche trying to move into her sister's apartment in order to find safety, to pull herself together, to find herself a family. There is the outside and the inside. Blanche comes in for safety. She is destroyed. She is turned out. The set works to give a place for the symbolic action to take place. Notice that Blanche tries to change the place, tries to fix it up, decorates, covers light bulbs. None of this works to protect her or to give her what she needs—a home.

3. In a play something is at stake for more than one of the characters. Action is only possible when more than one person cares about what happens. Four people have large stakes in the action of *Streetcar*. Whether Blanche stays or goes matters to her, to Stella, Mitch, and Stanley. Blanche's insanity and her removal to an institution affects not only her but Stella, Stanley, and Mitch, too.

4. Dramatic characters want something. They want to do something and to change something. Blanche's want is the greatest—which makes us see her as the protagonist. She needs a home. She wants to make a place for herself; she wants to recover herself. Stella needs her man and her marriage because they define her. She wants to keep peace between Stanley and Blanche. Stanley needs territory where he is king. He wants to get rid of Blanche who sees him as valueless. Mitch needs to break away from his mother. He wants to woo Blanche, to find love.

5. At the center of the play is a treasure of some sort. This thing of value is fought over, struggled over. It often has a financial value. In *Streetcar* it is the apartment and its comforts, meager though they are, including the bathroom, the bathwater, the bottles of liquor. Stanley points out that Blanche isn't paying for any of it. These small comforts are all Stanley and Stella have. And they are all Blanche has too. She comes without any money of her own. That's why the *seeming* treasure of her fur pieces drives Stanley crazy.

A secondary treasure is Stella. She is motherly and representative of the comforts of home made from this tiny apartment. She listens, she tries to make peace, she stays home (locates herself at home base).

6. There are always many obstacles to the pursuit of the treasure. Obstacles are necessary. We wouldn't have any play if Stanley and Stella welcomed Blanche as a member of their household. Obstacles are crucial to drama and they have to be serious obstacles. Blanche comes, not exactly

unannounced, but without *an arrangement* with Stanley and Stella. She comes without money. She is troubled and puts on airs. She sees the place she has come to as beneath her. Stella is pregnant. Blanche has a secret past. There are many obstacles to the basic arrangement. There are obstacles to the characters' goals as well. For instance, Stanley would like to get rid of Blanche, but he can't do it easily. That's what makes for drama. He can't do it because he can't find *a way* to do it without alienating Stella; he can't get around Blanche's pretend-cheerful mood; he doesn't have the goods on Blanche at first, and when he does, there is still resistance from Stella. The characters, then, become obstacles to each other.

7. Characters must try to get what they want more than once. Otherwise the playwright has written a single situation, an incident, but not drama. When you hear an idea for a play that doesn't work, it may be because the idea encompasses only *a situation* and not an ongoing action. Somebody says, "I'm going to write about a guy who tries to break up with his girlfriend but she doesn't understand him so he chickens out." That is a single incident, and unless it's developed in a unique way, not a play.

In contrast, Stanley tries more than once to talk to Stella about Blanche. Blanche has more than one encounter with Mitch. Drama consists of *multiple attempts and multiple strategies* on the parts of characters to get what they want. If every incident were similar, the drama would not progress and it would be boring. Blanche tries several things with Mitch. She flirts, she pretends to be someone she isn't, she tells him about her husband's suicide, and finally, when confronted by him, she tells him the whole truth about her past. She makes many, *varied* attempts to connect with him. Likewise, Stanley tries many strategies to get rid of Blanche. He confronts her, he teases her, he tells his wife on her, he embarrasses her at a birthday dinner, he does her out of a lover, and he rapes her.

8. Most plays are built on pretense. Theatre is about acting, lying, pretending. Blanche is performing through most of the play. She is lying about her past, about her prospects for a future, about her age, about her need for alcohol. Stanley and Stella and Mitch find themselves pretending too. Blanche even pretends that she isn't bothered by Stanley's baiting her. The atmosphere is filled, more and more, as the play progresses, with pretense until Blanche's insanity takes over and she encloses herself in a world of pretense.

What happens in a play generally happens *indirectly*. Dramatic characters do not go about their goals directly. Pretense causes much of the indirection and vice versa.

9. A play's story or action is usually accomplished by dialogue. The dialogue is the action in that characters seek to change things by words. It is with words that Blanche weaves the false fabric of her life, the *airs* that make Stanley hate her. Blanche tries to win her place in the apartment and in the lives of the other characters with words, charm, wit, a constant burbling chatter. Stella tries to mollify both Blanche and Stanley by imparting little bits of advice, by being a listener, by trying to hear them out and divert anger (notice that she doesn't talk about herself!). And Stanley, not a thinker, is nevertheless *verbal*. Even in the end, words don't desert him. He tries to control Blanche by calling her bluff, over and over again. Even when he rapes her, he puts into words what he thinks the situation is—that they've had this date for a long time. It is with words that Blanche tries to drive Stella from Stanley. And words are what Stanley uses to tear Blanche down. Notice that the dialogue is never lazy. It is always filled with one character's attempt to affect another.

10. A play also has physical action, but the physical action should accompany and underline the language. The physical pattern of a play is dance-like, patterned. We dealt with this aspect of *Streetcar* above. Blanche rushes in, hangs on, is driven out. That is the pattern of the whole play. Each scene has its pattern, too.

11. Plays are heavily dependent on the device known as *dramatic irony*. It is a device for plotting and keeps the audience engaged in the action. Blanche's taking a drink when she is alone in her sister's apartment and then hiding the glass is an example of dramatic irony. The audience sees her. Then she tells Stella she doesn't drink much. Two audiences. Stella is the audience who does not understand. And the theatre audience is the one who does understand. Dramatic irony sets up an expectation that it will be resolved. Every time Blanche protests that she doesn't drink and every time Stanley calls her on it is an example of the working of dramatic irony. When we see Blanche alone and then with the paper boy, we see how fragile she is. We know something about her. This increases the tension when Mitch arrives and also later with Stanley. We already know that Blanche is fragile enough to break. A good way to use dramatic irony is to allow your character to be on stage alone or with a character other than the main opponent for a brief time. What is revealed in this setting is often an excellent way to pressure the action when the main opponents are engaged.

12. Plays are dependent upon peripety, reversal of intention. Blanche takes up with Mitch because she thinks he can save her. His inability to forgive her for her lies drives her deeper to despair. This is a reversal of intention. Blanche goes to her sister to escape from her past. She goes looking for a home. She is plunged into her past by Stanley's bringing up the past. She is cast out. What she thought would help has harmed her. Peripety—an action intended to bring about one result, but that brings about its opposite—is at work. Reversal of intention, or peripety, is one of the pleasures of theatre.

13. The best dramatic characters are complex. The more human they are, and the more faults they have, the more interesting they are. Mitch is a coward who can't escape his mother. Stanley is cruel, even violent, and has no ability to sympathize with someone who is unfortunate. Stella is placid and cowardly, and would tell herself a lie to protect her life. These are not good qualities.

Stella creates havoc with her passivity. Can she be so

dependent on sex with Stanley that she will let her sister be treated badly, let herself be physically abused, refuse to hear about what drove Blanche crazy? Tennessee Williams describes Stella as someone walking around in narcotized tranquility. She is sex-drugged, dependent. She might as well be an addict. She can't be depended upon.

Blanche too is *filled* with faults. She is full of schemes and lies: she's selfish and desperate. She insults Stella, she tries to get Mitch interested in her even though she is not much interested in him. You wouldn't want to live with her.

But Stanley would be hard to live with too, wouldn't he? Unless you learned to look the other way, to do his bidding, never to cross him, to cater to his needs. And yet, these characters are not only fascinating, they are sympathetic too.

Complexity of character will come from giving the people you write about complex, full backgrounds, pasts, problems, things they need to do or to accomplish, obstacles in their outer worlds and in their inner worlds (inner conflicts pulling at them, too). That makes for good characters. When you model characters on people you know, get tough. If you don't make those characters complex, you will not have a very interesting play. If you can't write those characters with more faults than virtues, you'd better not use them. A common problem in the plays of novices is that the characters are too nice.

14. Style—we'll talk more about it later—is partly a matter of establishing a convention and using it more than once. In *Streetcar* movement from outside to inside the apartment is used more than once. The underlying music is used more than once. The fights of the neighbors come in more than once. The strange, dreamlike effects of neon lights, sounds of locomotives, and the Blue Piano are used more than once. Altogether the style of this play is not realistic. It is dreamlike, even nightmarish. It follows Blanche's state of mind. Style has everything to do with what is *highlighted* and what is *missing*.

15. The language of the play may or may not mimic realistic language. In itself it has to be believable and ideally it should be language that an actor would like to speak. Actors want to speak language that is interesting, language that allows them to develop character.

The language of this play is rich, partly because it is specific to character. *Characters should have a way of speaking that is consonant with their lives.* Blanche tries to prettify situations with her language just as she tries to prettify rooms with lanterns, or herself in perfumes and gauzes. Her language is perfumed and gauzed over too. She says, "I understand there's to be a little card party to which we ladies are cordially *not* invited." And "These are love letters, yellowing with antiquity." She does *not* say, "Don't worry. I get it. You don't want us around tonight while you play cards with the boys." She does *not* say, "Those don't look like much. They're letters sent to me. They're old and when I look at them I know how old I am and how long ago it all happened."

As Elia Kazan, the play's original director, points out,

Stanley caresses and sucks his beer bottles and his cigars as sensual elements, part of his nature. I think he does the same thing with words. His are primitive words and phrases, but he hangs on to them. "I have an acquaintance," is one of them. Instead of saying, "I'll take these papers to a lawyer," Stanley says, "I have a lawyer acquaintance." For some reason he needs to connect himself with people in higher positions than his own. Look at Stanley's words. *Dumb. Cut that. Rebop.* All the while he speaks, we witness him fighting his own inarticulateness. Characters have a way of speaking that *makes* them who they are and *that tells us who they are.*

Some of the remaining principles of dramatic action will be discussed in later chapters. *Streetcar* will be examined from time to time as an example of dramatic principles at work. There is a great deal to learn from this play. You may want to go back to it again and again. "Williams made eleven separate scenes of *Streetcar* hang together," I said to one class. "How did he do it? What did he do? Devices are free."

Here are some of their answers.

*He reveals something different in each scene. He reveals information not all at once, but slowly. However, he reveals enough to let you know what to look for. You know very early on that Blanche's past is a secret that will be revealed. But you don't know what all her past holds. Or why.*

*There is tension all the time.*

*Each scene has its own climax, but is linked to the other scenes because the characters progress.*

*The relationship of Blanche and Mitch keeps the play going. This thread keeps alive the possibility of a better relationship for Blanche.*

*The relationship between the characters makes the play hang together. They relate to each other always even when one or some of them are not present.*

*One thing Williams does is make many scenes out of dialogues between two people so the triangle is not always complete. In the next scene you'll get two different people. An example is that in one scene, Stella tells Stanley to compliment Blanche, but when we see Stanley with Blanche, he won't give it. This is dramatic irony.*

*This play is honest. For instance, Blanche's prudishness is masking other feelings—as so often happens in life.*

*The sisters' relationship is honest too. There is competition, but there is also a bond. That's how it is.*

*Blanche is worried that her age is a disfigurement. This is a picture of women with shaky holds on themselves, but also specific to Southern Belles of the forties.*

*Stanley's use of Mitch is consistent too. He can tell himself when he destroys Blanche that he is only doing it for the sake of his friend Mitch. Even the worst villains usually have excuses for what they do.*

*We know a lot about Blanche early on when she tells about the many deaths at the old home. The fact that she can't say the details of the deaths and that she later spits out "in bed with your Polack" tells us that she can't talk about some things. Sex and death. She is afraid of sex and death.*

The students' observations are excellent. The beauty of the workshop method is that everyone gains from the insights of others.

---

**Study Questions and Exercises**

1. Choose three entrances in **Streetcar** and describe what Williams has done to make them theatrical.
2. Choose three exits in **Streetcar** and determine what Williams has done to make them theatrical.
3. Do you notice any pattern in Mitch's language?
4. What is the pantomime pattern of the last scene?

# SEVEN

# Working on Ideas

## OVERVIEW

There are no writing assignments in this chapter except those you do naturally as you read about ways to get ideas and to begin writing plays. There are many ways to begin; this chapter gives examples of a few. Included also are examples of the writings of some well-known playwrights about their own writing. They are Ibsen (his notes for *Ghosts*) and Alan Ayckbourn (his preface to *The Norman Conquests*). Pirandello's preface to *Six Characters in Search of an Author*, too lengthy to include here, will be summarized and discussed as well.

You will be asked to read and study Ayckbourn's play *Table Manners*, part of *The Norman Conquests*, as an illustration of one way in which a playwright unifies character motivations.

## OBJECTIVES

At the end of this chapter you should be able to

- Identify the kind and source of your ideas
- Describe a work method by which you develop your ideas
- Discuss the integration of the physical action with the dialogue in Alan Ayckbourn's *Table Manners*.

Your next several assignments will be more like writing small plays. You may choose any subject you like. You may write a serious or a comic scene. You may choose to make your situation a part of a longer work that you have in mind. Or you may just experiment, just see what happens when you practice writing the materials—scene description, cast of characters, character descriptions (if applica-

ble), and dialogue. You might find yourself inspired by the monologue assignment to make one character speak more than another, or by the pantomime assignment to carve out a dramatic dance on stage, but the main focus will be to write a scene in which both dialogue and physical action are coordinated smoothly.

Thinking about what you should write and how you should begin may take up an inordinate amount of time and energy. A lot of what you are thinking of experimenting with might be better done on paper—as the actual experiment. If you are serious about writing, you know that you may have to write twenty or thirty pages before you have five that you would like to continue to work on. It is better to write than to think about writing.

### Getting Started

You may have thousands of ideas or none. You may visualize the final production before you have put a word down, or you may have no idea where you are going. People are different, writers are different, and every single writing experience is different. Some people think in terms of action and plotting, some see characters first, some get a strong sense of *feeling* that drives them to create a scene, and some hear words and voices. Plays can begin from all of these angles, so content yourself with that knowledge and go on to more important things than worrying. Get started.

Here are some of the best ways of getting started. Even if you think you have a work method down, you should try each of these on for size so that you stretch the possibilities of the ways you work with ideas.

Choose a work time that is regular and stick to it. A great majority of writers who write seriously write every day. Yes, every day. Try to find a time every day to write something. It might be before you go to bed, or just before lunch or just after dinner. But if you are like the majority of writers you will find that you like morning best, just after waking up, maybe even before breakfast. In any case, find your time of day and stick to it for a few weeks before you make any decisions about trying a different time. Get used to the schedule. Try to work at your writing every day. You have to get used to writing, and you have to get used to the fact that the first things you write will—unless you are Shakespeare reincarnated—need to be revised several times. Revision is a normal part of the process.

Clear a space that you can work in and keep that space for your writing work. It might be only half a small bookshelf, but save yourself the trouble of looking every morning or evening for your work, for the last page you did. You know where it is. You have your routine.

Do all of your thinking on paper. Whether you are using a pencil, a pen, a typewriter, a word processor, or a computer, begin to invent on paper. Maybe you'd like to write long-hand first and then do the first revision as you're typing something onto a disk. Figure out what makes you comfortable. How do you think on paper? Following are some examples of beginning work on longer plays—long one-acts or full-length plays, but the principles can work for your short exercises as well.

## When Plot Comes First

If you are a plot-oriented person and you are working out your idea for a play or a scene, you might begin with the notes for the general *movement of your action*. You might first think about what will happen and thus write something like: "Joe can't help Peter and it begins to drive him crazy. It is all he talks about at home. His wife tells him he's over the edge. But when he meets with Peter, Peter has a hold over him. Tricks him. Every time. Finally Joe catches on. Even then he is powerless. His wife leaves him. Peter starts calling him at home, which feeds his obsession. Peter gets out of the institution and breaks into Joe's house. They fight. Joe injures Peter, calls the police, makes a statement. As he makes a statement to the police he reverses roles; it is as if he becomes a patient to a therapist. He is beginning to effect his recovery. But it's just the beginning."

This playwright knows the plot. He knows that Joe is a therapist and that Peter is a troubled child. He even forgets to write it down, because the movement of the plot is so clear to him. He knows that he sees the scenes in two places, Joe's home and the institution, perhaps a consulting room. He knows what Joe will go through, how he will change. He knows what Joe wants to do, what Joe wants to change, and he knows that Peter is Joe's problem, his obstacle, his nemesis (also probably his most common scene companion). In this short note, the playwright suggests that there will be a scene at the institution, followed by one at home, followed by several at the institution, followed by a final one at home, when the institution comes to him, so to speak.

You might be thinking that this playwright seems to know everything, but maybe he doesn't. How does Joe sound? How does Peter sound? What is Peter's problem, his condition? Does Joe love his wife? And she him? There is a great deal to be worked out. He may or may not know his characters well, he may or may not know how they speak, he may or may not have the feeling of the piece. If you are like the plot-oriented playwright, fine, it is a good way to be. But be aware that you can probably still have problems getting started. It is possible—not certain—that you may have everything in mind but the play—that is, what the characters say to each other. If that happens to you, get started using one of the other means. If, on the other hand, you are full of feeling or images of character, but every time you get started your scene goes nowhere, try plotting it out in a quick synopsis like the one above.

## Henrik Ibsen's *Ghosts*

The fictional playwright above would not be working all that differently from Ibsen when he made notes for *Ghosts*. His early focus appears to be on his protagonist, Mrs. Alving. Ibsen had the basic idea of the play, he knew something about how Mrs. Alving came to be in her present situation. He had a sketch of the history of the people involved. Here is what he wrote:

## Henrik Ibsen's Notes for *Ghosts**

The play is to be like a picture of life. Belief undermined. But it does not do to say so. "The Orphanage"—for the sake of others. They are to be happy—but this too is only an appearance—Everything is ghosts.—

A leading point: She has been a believer and romantic—this is not entirely obliterated by the standpoint reached later—"Everything is ghosts."

Marriage for external reasons, even when these are religious or moral, brings a Nemesis upon the offspring.

She, the illegitimate child, can be saved by being married to—the son—but then—?

He was dissipated and his health was shattered in his youth; then she appeared, the religious enthusiast; she saved him; she was rich. He was going to marry a girl who was considered unworthy. He had a son by his wife, then he want back to the girl; a daughter.—

These women of the present day, ill-used as daughters, as sisters, as wives, not educated according to their gifts, prevented from following their inclination, deprived of their inheritance, embittered in temper—it is these who furnish the mothers of the new generation. What is the result?

The key-note is to be: The prolific growth of our intellectual life, in literature, art, etc.—and in contrast to this: the whole of mankind gone astray.

The complete human being is no longer a product of

* From *The Collected Works of Henrik Ibsen* (New York: Charles Scribner's Sons, 1911). Renewal copyright © 1936 by Frank Archer.

nature, he is an artificial product like corn, and fruit-trees, and the Creole race and thoroughbred horses and dogs, the vine, etc.—

The fault lies in that all mankind has failed. If a man claims to live and develop in a human way, it is megalomania. All mankind, and especially the Christian part of it, suffers from megalomania. Among us, monuments are erected to the *dead*, since we have a duty towards them; we allow lepers to marry; but their offspring—? The unborn—?

## From the First Act

PASTOR M.
But one has a duty towards the society in which one lives. If one has a good and beneficial vocation to work at—and such we ought all to have, Mrs. Alving—then one owes it to that vocation and to one's self to stand before the eyes of society in as irreproachable a light as possible; for if one be not irreproachable, one can make no progress with one's aims.

MRS. A.
Yes, you are perfectly right there.

PASTOR M.
To say nothing of the difficulty—I may even say the painfulness—of the position. The serious Christians of the town take a lively interest in this Orphanage. It is, of course, founded partly for the benefit of the town, as well; and it is to be hoped it will, to a considerable extent, result in lightening our Poor Rates. But now, of course, every one in the town knows that I have been your adviser, and have had the business arrangements in my hands. My parishioners might therefore so easily be led to think that I, their clergyman—

MRS. A.
Yes, it would undoubtedly be unpleasant for you.

PASTOR M.
To say nothing of the fact that I have no idea of the attitude my superiors in the church would adopt towards the question.

MRS. A.
Very well, my dear Pastor Manders; that consideration is quite decisive.

PASTOR M.
Then we do not insure?

●

PASTOR M.
That is a very disputable point, Mrs. Alving. A child's proper place is, and must be, the home.

OS.
There I think you're quite right, Pastor Manders.

PASTOR M.
Ah, you can hardly have any idea of what a home should be—

O.
Oh, but anyhow I have seen other people's homes.

PASTOR M.
I thought, however, that over there, especially in artistic circles, the life was a somewhat homeless one—

O.
Well, most of the young men are forced to live so; they have no money, and besides they don't want to give up their precious freedom—they live frugally, I can tell you, a slice of ham and a bottle of wine.

PASTOR M.
But in what company?

O.
In very pleasant company, Pastor Manders. Sometimes a few models join them and then, as likely as not, there's dancing.

PASTOR M.
Models—? What do you mean by that?

O.
We painters and sculptors require models, I suppose. Otherwise how could we reproduce the tension of the muscles and the reflected light on the skin—and all that sort of thing.

PASTOR M.
But you don't mean to say that there are women who—

O.
Who sit to us artists; yes, I can assure you there are.

PASTOR M.
And such immorality is tolerated by the authorities?

O.
The authorities tolerate worse kinds of immorality than that, Pastor, as you are doubtless not unaware—

PASTOR M.
Alas, alas, that is only too true; but as to these models, it is even worse, for it takes place openly and is spoken about—

O.
Yes, it would never occur to us to do otherwise. Oh, I can assure you, there are many fine figures among the models one doesn't often see here.

PASTOR M.
Is it in such society you have been living abroad?

O.
Sometimes too I visit my friends at their homes; one has to see what their domestic circle is like, play a little with the children.

PASTOR M.
But you said most of the artists were not married.

O.
Oh, that was a mistake—I meant wedded.

PASTOR M.
But, good heavens—

O.

But, my dear Pastor Manders, what are they to do? A poor painter, a poor girl; they can't afford to marry, it costs a great deal. What are they to do?

PASTOR M.

I will tell you, Mr. Alving; they should remain apart.

O.

That doctrine will scarcely go down with the warm-blooded young people, full of the joy of life. Oh, the glorious free life out there.

PASTOR M.

And, to make matters worse, such freedom is to be signalled as praiseworthy—

O.

Let me tell you, sir, you may visit many of these irregular homes and you will never hear an offensive word there. And let me tell you another thing: I have never come across immorality among our artists over there—but do you know where I have found it—?

PASTOR M.

No, I'm happy to say—

O.

Well, then, I'm afraid I must inform you. I have met with it in many a pattern husband and father who has come to Paris to have a look round on his own account, one of these gentlemen with a heavy gold chain outside his waistcoat; do you know what is the first thing these gentlemen do? Why, they hunt up some poor artist or other, get on familiar terms with him, ask him to supper at a smart restaurant, make the champagne flow freely—and then take his arm and propose that they shall make a night of it—and then we artists hear of places we never knew of before, and see things we never dreamed of—But these are the respectable men, Pastor Manders, and on their return you can hear their praises of the pure morals of home in contrast to the corruption abroad—oh yes—these men know what's what—they have a right to be heard.

MRS. A.

But, my dear Oswald, you mustn't get excited.

O.

No, you're right; it's bad for me—I shall go for a little turn before dinner. Excuse me, Pastor, I know you can't take my point of view; but I had to speak out for once.
(He goes out by the second door to the right.)

PASTOR M.

Then this is what he has come to!

## When Character Comes First

Let us assume that another writer puts her initial ideas on paper. This writer has a character whom she wants to write about. The character is clear and the playwright knows the character is full of drama, but doesn't know for sure what the drama is, what the scenes are, or what happens. So this person first writes: "Mona. A teacher. Very strange, very eccentric, very powerful. When she speaks, the students are mesmerized. They are very young, junior high school age. Mona is intrusive and starts to meddle in their lives. She is destructive. She is a fragile-looking, beautiful delicate woman who is very troubled. She keeps trying to recreate herself with the children."

This playwright has an interesting character, but could get stuck just thinking about character, hearing the voice of the woman, maybe even seeing her move about the classroom. So what next? There are several possibilities. Just start. Just start. It is possible that her drama will unfold if the writer makes a few decisions. She does not want to put twenty students on stage so she starts the play with the class bell and two students leaving the room and two students left behind. The two left behind clearly want Mona's attention. Mona sees this and begins to speak. In other words, the writer knows the character but isn't sure of the action in terms of scenes. She therefore writes a scene, but she doesn't have to keep it. This is what you do when you write every day. You play around with ideas. You don't write final drafts. You try things. You learn about your play and where you want it to go. One way is to try an action. Just try it. Maybe the two people who stay behind are in the first stages of love and want Mona's approval. Maybe the writer didn't know that's what they were going to say, but she does know Mona, and she knows that she is intrusive. So her situation begins to develop.

If you know that you are not sure of an action, a plot, you might want to work on what doesn't come so naturally to you. Sketch one out. Put a plot-sketch on paper and then go about writing it. For example, if you were working with Mona, the character sketched above, you might ask yourself: Where does this play take place? And you might answer yourself: In the classroom, only in the classroom. *What happens to Mona? What happens to the other characters?* They finally rebel against her and she tries to commit suicide. What does Mona want? She wants to be important to someone, special to someone. Why does she choose the children? She chooses them as a substitute for a love life. What do the children want? They want her approval. Why? She seems to be all beneficence, to give all-approving love.

How can you show this? You can have two or three sets of children with whom she sets up relationships. You can restrict all the action to a classroom. Here are some possible scenes:

1. Mona talks to a boy and girl after class. She draws them out, gets them to tell her they are in love. She tells them she will bring them some special books, some special reading.

2. Another scene with another student after class. This is a young girl. Mona gets her to tell about her abusive parents and advises her to run away from home, to cause trouble until she can find another home, another place to

live. The girl wants to live with Mona. Mona says no, but she doesn't say it very definitely. Mona begins to string the child along.

3. Scene in which young girl is hanging around and Mona has to ask her to wait in the hall while she talks to the "couple." They are disturbed by the reading, which is too advanced for them. Mona laughs, teases them, suggests that they are putting her on, gives them other books, but mostly compliments them so lavishly that they are still hooked. Mona forgets about the child who is waiting for her. The child appears just as she is putting on her coat to go.

This playwright now has a running start on the play. These few scenes will trigger others. The playwright may not keep them, but they are a good place to start because they give a clear way to develop the action of this character. All the scenes have people who want something, who want to do something, and who want to change something, and they all try to effect the changes through words. So that's to the good.

If you have become hooked on a character but don't know the drama that the character belongs in, your plight is not all that different from Pirandello's when he wrote his best-known play, *Six Characters in Search of an Author*. Pirandello had quite a struggle to come up with the right play for the characters who haunted his dreams.

## Pirandello's *Six Characters in Search of an Author*

In his preface to the printed edition of *Six Characters in Search of an Author*, the playwright discusses his struggle with his creative imagination. He found before him (served up by his imagination) a family: man, widowed woman, little girl, little boy, a brazen, sexy girl dressed in mourning, and a sober young man. They "told him" their story, quite a melodramatic story of love, adultery, incest, prostitution. And Pirandello could not find *meaning* in it, at least not the spiritual, philosophical meaning he wanted in the things he wrote. In fact he was embarrassed by their story, which he found sordid.

He concluded that he did not want to write their story. But the story, and especially the characters, would not stay locked away. They pestered him until he became obsessed with them.

Finally he hit upon a solution. He would present them *honestly* by telling the story of characters who demanded a showing and a playwright (transformed into a theatre manager in his script) who could not "buy" their story but who was fascinated by them.

The solution is brilliant—a unique play about six characters seeking an author to write their drama. In the play that resulted, there is philosophical meaning. The characters try to make something important of their sordid lives; they seek reason and meaning; they hope for understanding and deliverance.

The play Pirandello finally wrote has these ghost-like char-

acters banging into a rehearsal and trying to persuade the director to do their "drama." A brilliant play, *Six Characters* is also a brilliant and honest solution to a writer's dilemma.

The important lesson of the essay prefacing *Six Characters* is the need for the writer to struggle with an idea for as long as it takes to find the truth in it—the honest way of telling the story.

## *Strong Feelings*

Suppose you have only a feeling and you don't even know who your characters are—let alone your action. Can you start with just a feeling? You can start with anything. If the feeling is driving you, try to write about it. For example: "Angry. I am angry. I just feel like I want to tell people off. Everywhere. How can I be angry with everyone? Obviously I'm not. No, it started yesterday when those goons made all those AIDS jokes. In such bad taste. I should have said something to shock them. I should have said, "I could have AIDS." That would have flipped them. Then I could have told them they could have AIDS. They're not virgins. They could. Then I could have gone crazy while they laughed and thought they were above it all. Do I really want to write about them? No. I don't know why, I just don't. Maybe I could do a similar situation with a few old boys in a bar. The anger I have is at people who think they are safe, above it all, better than others. I could write a quiet sort of play— maybe a one-act—something that happens in a bar late at night among, say, three guys. Nothing tacky like giving one of them AIDS. More a play in which they all try to frighten off death with bravado and in which one person somehow comes to know that he isn't above it all . . ."

This one started with a feeling. A series of thoughts. A few characters are beginning to emerge. The feeling is still the strongest thing. Maybe the playwright will have his characters in a David Mamet world. Maybe the play will be excruciatingly funny. Desperation and fear of death sometimes are funny. Sometimes the rowdiest, richest-in-humor personalities are running like crazy from depression. More questions and answers will help this playwright to get started. Who are these characters? Is one of them the bartender? Is the television on? Is the radio on? Who brings up the subject of death? Diminishment? Will AIDS ever be mentioned in this play? What does each character want? What's at stake? What does each character want to change? Maybe the playwright will write: "John, Derek, and Stanton—modelled loosely on Bob, Dwayne, and Duncan, three guys I used to hang out with. I'll make them all forty-five, though. What would their lives be like if they were forty-five? And what are they doing at night in a bar? One married, two divorced? Okay. They're not in such good shape then, are they? No. Personal lives falling apart. What do they want? What do they *want*? A second chance? A second forty-five years? Okay, it's somebody's birthday and they're toasting to a second forty-five years in which they get it right. Only one of them—maybe the birthday boy has to decide whether to have surgery, maybe even minor heart surgery. He's scared of everything. He's drunk. The other guys offer their blood so he doesn't get AIDS. Okay. They focus on trying to keep the birthday boy alive, but it's really about how they all want a second chance."

Now this is getting much more specific. Maybe the first thing this writer writes as part of the play is:

*Sound of TV fading, Letterman's voice, sound of radio coming up, ball scores.*

ANNOUNCER'S VOICE

*(brings bartender out of back room. He looks at radio as if it's a television.) Pirates beat the Cubs 2 to 1 in a ten inning drama. (Bartender grunts. Noise of voices, louder and louder, until bartender turns up radio volume. Enter John who realizes that he is alone and goes back out the swinging doors to fetch Derek and Stanton who have their arms around each other and who are singing (quite well) "You picked a fine time to leave me, Lucille.")*

If all you have is a feeling and you start to write about it, you can turn it into an idea for a play.

## Undeveloped Ideas

What happens if you start out with a loose idea? Remember, you do your work, whatever it is, in writing, not by lying down to think about it. Put it on paper. You may write: "I want to write a play about a young woman who runs a package service over the Mexican border into Texas. She buys things for people in Texas on order and brings them back. She takes packages that need to be mailed in the States. Mexican mail is unreliable so this is a needed service. She goes every two weeks. The customs guys are getting to know her. She's young, stringy, and tough. She doesn't carry drugs, but somehow she gets implicated in a drug smuggling thing. I heard about a situation vaguely like this. . . . I'd like to write a play about her."

This is a situation without a plot. Notice how the stage-scenes are not clear. We might get movie-images of this young woman driving to the border but she is alone in a car full of packages. She doesn't have other people to play the scene with. It is a situation idea, not a plot idea. So the writer says, "This needs another character and a problem, fast. How about she meets a guy in her 'shop' where she takes orders. They like each other. The joke is where will she put all those packages next time because he is going with her, he's determined. Pretty soon, they're a team. First scene is in her shop, meeting him. Second scene is in her shop when he says he wants to go with her. They have been seeing each other maybe two weeks. Third scene is them in an office, the size and shape of her little shop. But it is hostile and unpleasant there, border customs. Add one officer. Scene three is about the officer questioning them and then is about whether the woman has to suspect her new boyfriend or one of her clients for the drugs found on them. The officer leaves them alone. The boyfriend asks her to pay off the cop for him. He says the officer has been primed to take a bribe.

Fourth scene. Back at the Mexican shop. Boyfriend in charge, taking orders from customer, an American who asks about the woman. He says she's staying at home a lot. It's no secret, he says, that she's pregnant. The American asks a lot of questions about the woman. Through the interview, the mailing of packages, etc., the young man comes to understand that she has been killed, that he's being *told* something rather than being *asked* something. He's being told to shut up. He's being told he could easily be next."

## Subjects that Interest You

You might start with an idea that is so loose it could be just about anything. Let us call the idea the subject. Maybe you would like to write a play about China. But China (the subject) is very big. You like China. You like the people. But where do you go from there? You may write: "I love China. I love the people, the gentleness of the people. Most Americans just see the poverty, the millions riding their bicycles, and they don't get to the real thing. You have to get past the poverty to know the people. I even thought the dormitory we stayed in was false in some way. The real feeling I got was from the people who had us to dinner. The way they treated us . . ." You might continue by asking yourself the following questions:

Where will my play take place?
Where else, but in the house of the Chinese person who invites an American to dinner?
Who will be the characters?
An American boy? (Maybe the writer is a woman and giving the story to a man will help her to invent circumstances and to get distance on it.)
And a Chinese couple of about forty and their son who is older than the boy.
What do they want? What's at stake?

If you decide to keep these characters, then you need to give them an action. You therefore continue to write: "The Chinese couple want to learn about America. . . . They want to make friends with the American boy and ask about his family. . . . They want to find their son an American family to live with and a sponsor in the States who will pay for his college education. They want to explain how brilliant their son is, how few opportunities he has in China. The American boy wants to answer their questions honestly. He has to tell them that his father is well-to-do, but that he doesn't speak to his father. His father supports him but would not be particularly interested in hearing a plea of any sort. They are estranged. The American boy has to try to make the Chinese understand this, that he cannot help their son, that he cannot help himself when it comes to living at home." Now some action is starting to come into focus. The first impressions of poverty can be handled in the details of moving through the house, the way dinner is served. The millions on the bicycles can be handled by having the woman come in on a bicycle, having bought something for their dinner, something she could clearly not easily afford. The gentleness could come through the many details of the way the family relates to each other as well as to the American boy. In other words, ideas can turn into actions if you start to write, if you ask yourself questions, and if you give characters something they want to do or want to change through words.

There are other ways to start. Maybe if you have nothing else, you can start with what plays are made of. Words. Some day sit down and begin to write, to free-associate, the first things that come into your head. Really, the first. It's seven a.m. and you don't know what to write, but you may write: "God, I'm sleepy. This getting things down without coffee is weird. What did people do before coffee? What do they do without coffee? I can't believe I'll probably have to do it myself someday—give up the bean. That's what they say. My mother is decaffed right now. And my father already popped his ticker. Maybe they'll find a cure for all heart ailments before I have to give up everything I love." Maybe at this point, you start to wake up and you think about your father who didn't care for himself or your mother's bout with caffeine withdrawal. Pretty soon you let some of what you're jotting down take the form of dialogue. You write

WOMAN
I can't. I can't change my life that much. I'd rather die, I really would.

MAN
Listen to yourself. Don't you care about anyone else?

You stop and ask yourself who these people are. Maybe you will make the woman a lot like your landlady and a little like your mother; perhaps the man will be like your brother. The landlady lives with her brother and they seem to be very close, maybe too close. But wouldn't he be terrified if she refused to take care of herself? And so a scene begins. Give the characters a place in which to play out their drama. And something they want to do and to change— each of them. And figure out who's lying and why. And then, before you decide anything more, let them talk for a while. You don't have to use every line. You might even decide that the scene you really want to write is one in which the landlady was a twenty-year-old and her brother kept her from marrying a young man she liked. When you don't know where to start, start with the words and let the words take you on a journey.

Perhaps you would like to write something now. You needn't write a whole play. A scene five to eight pages long will do. All of the ideas above are for long plays. If you can stretch yourself to see the shape of a long play, a scene, then a short play will come more easily.

## Autobiographical Materials

Two of the most frequently asked questions are, "Should my play be autobiographical?" and "Should my characters be people I know?" There is no strict rule, but most writers of all genres have found that when all is said and done their characters are usually (whether they intended it or not) based loosely on people they have known. When you think you're inventing a totally fictional character (and that's fine) you sometimes look at a script two years later and say, "Heavens, how did I miss the fact that Joe was so much like my Uncle Bob?"

How can we write and *not* use the people we've known? It's no more possible than keeping them out of our dreams. Yet when you try to write about someone as you know them, you often get stuck until you begin to invent and make that person somewhat different from the person you know. You might also be wondering how much of your life should appear on stage. Again there is no rule. The more you try to invent something new, the more distance you will have on the events of your own life, but they will creep in somewhere, somehow. That is in the nature of artistic creation. But you will always be looking for a balance between history and invention. It is freeing to invent. It is valuable to the emotional integrity of your play to be personally involved in the story you are telling. As a rule it is very hard to write about anything that is recent in your life, even when you know you are inventing a great deal of the dramatic action.

If you create characters who are similar to people you've known and partly invented, how will you know those characters? In some ways, you will have to allow yourself to let them tell you who they are. Let them behave and let them speak to each other. They may surprise you and if they do, that's good. The more they behave like real people, the more possibilities you have to develop a play.

## Casting Your Characters

However, if your characters are sitting and staring at you and if you have done what you can to understand them, if you have given them goals to pursue and obstacles to those goals, then next try casting them. In other words, take your cue from Shakespeare and Molière and Alan Ayckbourn (whom we are about to study) and use as your image *actors* who, in the theatre of your imagination, play the characters you are creating. The actors' voices, speech rhythms, appearances, and personalities will start to give life to your pale characters. Susan Harris Smith, whose plays are regularly produced by major theatre groups, told me that she always writes with specific actors in mind. Sometimes she uses local people she's seen on stage; sometimes she tosses in well-known actresses. Jessica Tandy was her model for one character. Much of the time the actors who "help out" with characterization never even know about it. But for the playwright, it's an added benefit not only to visualize a stage, but to see and hear specific actors.

## Alan Ayckbourn's *Table Manners*

In preparation for your thinking about the next writing assignment, which you will do in the next chapter (Chapter 8), you should now read Ayckbourn's *Table Manners* and then read the discussion of it that follows below. The next writing assignment will be to write a full scene of four or five pages in which a physical activity is performed and completed. Your task will be to coordinate dialogue and physical action so that they are comfortable and integral, so that characters operate both verbally and physically on stage. In *Table Manners*, as you will see, the physical activity is natural and integral to the play—it has meaning. Several meals are consumed in the play. Dishes are brought on and taken away again and again. When you write your next assignment—with as much physical action as dialogue—make sure that the physical action has something to do with the drama at hand. It shouldn't be gratuitous but should be integral to the play.

## Plot Summary for Alan Ayckbourn's *Table Manners*

**Act I, Scene i.** The dining room of a house in the country. Six p.m. Saturday. Sarah, who has just arrived, meets with Annie to learn the routine of medications for Annie's mother (Sarah's mother-in-law) whom she and her husband Reg will care for while Annie takes a holiday. Sarah tries to find out where Annie is going and if she is going with Tom, a veterinarian who spends a lot of time at the house. Annie reveals that she is going to East Grinstead with Norman, her sister's husband, and that they have already had one sexual encounter. Sarah forbids Annie to go. Sarah tries to get Annie and Tom together. When she tells Reg what's been going on, he is delighted for Annie's sake as well as surprised that she takes after their mother who had affairs when they were children. Sarah throws stale biscuits at Reg. Annie cleans up the biscuit crumbs and serves dinner (salad) to everyone except Norman who sings drunkenly from the living room.

**Scene ii.** The dining room, Sunday, 9 a.m. Norman greets Sarah and then Annie and then Reg as they come in. They don't answer him. Norman tries all kinds of tricks to get them to speak to him. He reads the cereal box, defends his almost-vacation with Annie, screams at Annie for her cowardice. Annie and Sarah run out, leaving Norman with Reg. Norman tells Reg he should have been born in a different body because he could easily satisfy three women a day except that he looks wrong. Sarah comes in to announce the arrival of Norman's wife, Ruth, whom she has summoned. Everyone runs out except Norman. Ruth, nearly blind, refuses to wear glasses so that even so simple an act as getting breakfast is filled with danger. Norman tries to talk to her about her physical as well as her emotional short-sightedness. He is so frustrated by her vanity and her self-absorption that he tells her about his intended weekend with Annie. She laughs at him.

**Act II, Scene i.** The dining room, Sunday evening, 8 p.m. Annie is preparing for dinner. Norman comes to her for comfort, but she won't have anything to do with him. Tom, having heard about the intended trip with Norman, threatens Norman to stay away from Annie. Sarah tells

Norman he's made them all homicidal. Norman convinces Sarah that they are two of a kind—both highly sensitive and emotional, not selfish like the others. He promises to change for dinner and make a nice, happy family gathering.

Sarah threatens Reg with a nervous collapse if he doesn't do everything possible toward a cozy family dinner. Annie apologizes to Ruth about Norman. Ruth waves the apology aside, saying she's missed a lot of work days because of him. Annie corners Tom and asks him not to make a fuss, just to help have a happy, quiet dinner.

Nobody can get the seating arrangements right at the table. Arguments start. Norman appears in a large suit that once belonged to his now deceased father-in-law. Reg tells jokes. Norman makes whimsical fun of Tom. Sarah and Ruth argue about whether a woman is fulfilled or not without a child. Tom misunderstands an insult directed at Ruth by Norman and, thinking Annie was insulted, punches Norman. Everyone stomps out except Sarah who shakes and Norman who comforts her.

**Scene ii.** The dining room, 8 a.m. Monday morning. Annie puts out breakfast. Norman flatters Sarah about her part in conception and childrearing, suggesting that she is tired and needs a vacation. He offers to take her. Ruth is ready to leave, but Sarah manages to let Norman know that he may give her a call sometime. Tom arrives to apologize. Annie tells him she's lonely and also that she might have to sell the house and move away. Tom doesn't pick up on the signals. Annie breaks a plate. Norman gets Tom to help start the car. Once Tom is out of the room, Norman sits with Annie and offers to take her away, to make her happy.

## About *Table Manners*

As always, we will let *Table Manners* be a review of things we have discussed and an introduction to new items as well. The play is a reminder, for one thing, that the best dramatic characters are not necessarily people we would want to live with; it's a reminder that even comic characters are often made up of complex emotions and motivations. In *Table Manners*, as in all plays, the characters must be people who want something, who want to do something, who want to change something.

## Characters' Wishes to Do Something, to Change Something

Norman *wants to* seduce all the women in the play, including his wife. But the focus—and the main action that starts and ends the play—is his wanting to take Annie on holiday. "On holiday," in this play, has a very specific meaning. It means to go away for sex, to indulge in physical pleasure. So Norman wants something. He wants to take Annie, Ruth, even Sarah with whom he hardly has a civil word, on holiday. One *could* make the argument that Norman is completely selfish and after nothing but his own pleasure, but that would be to miss some of the more interesting implications of his objective— or the thing *he wants to* do, which is to make Annie happy. He also wants to make his wife happy, so he says. He even offers to make Sarah happy. It is as if he sees his own unhappiness, his own restlessness, reflected in the three women, and his happiness, he believes, will come of changing their circumstances.

Annie *wants to* change her life. She wants a break from the routine of looking after a sick mother and of having dull evenings with Tom who refuses to see her as a woman. She wants a holiday, she wants pleasure, she wants to let Norman make her happy. And after all he's just Norman— funny, ragged, familiar Norman. It's easy for her to forget he's her sister's husband. He doesn't seem like *anyone's* husband and she's desperate with loneliness. Although the six roles are of equal length and importance in this play, Annie is the protagonist because she has the most at stake, because her attempt to change her circumstances is the catalyst for the action.

Sarah is looking for a holiday too, and so is Reg. And they are married—to each other—and both of them are lonely. Their "I wants" come of reacting to Annie's proposed holiday. Ayckbourn has focused on Annie, but given everyone a stake in what Annie does. Thus, the idea of Annie's holiday shocks Sarah, but it also intrigues her. Reg is happy for his little sister who, he hopes, will pursue sex as their mother apparently did and as he, apparently, does not. He gets a vicarious thrill out of Annie's proposed trip. A "holiday" is what everybody wants—except Ruth, who would rather be working—and what everybody except Ruth *tries to get*. It is ironic (incongruous) and *peripetous* (a reversal of their intentions) that nobody gets a holiday *except* Ruth—who also gets its analogue (in this play), lovemaking. Love comes to Ruth who doesn't value it and it escapes everyone else.

Notice how many references to needing a holiday Sarah makes. The idea of a holiday is at the center of the play. The word itself is framed, built up, highlighted. It comes up at various times with variety, and it stands for something important, something to be angled for, pursued, and lost. The play ends with a suggestion that the relationship, such as it is, between Annie and Tom, a relationship with no holiday in it, will continue. Ayckbourn has prepared us for this even though the last scene is not with Tom and he lets us know it, lets us figure it out, by giving us the circumstances of their lives and by an important early scene between Annie and Tom. A less skillful playwright would have saved this confrontation until the end of the play, but it is just right where it is. In Act I, Scene 1, Annie tries to shake Tom out of his lethargy when she asks him what he thought of her vacation plans. Surely underneath all that passivity, Tom is jealous. Surely he has longings, but he answers her vaguely, safely, expressing no hurt or anger, in fact expressing no feeling at all. We see that he is shy towards her, careful, that he initiates nothing, and that he refuses to meddle or intrude in her life. What she can't seem to tell him is *that's what lovers do*, they intrude, they change each other's

lives. With Tom, Annie has always had to take the lead, has had to ask him to treat her as a woman. That frustrates and embarrasses her. She feels as unloved as if he weren't in her life at all.

Ayckbourn writes Tom, as he does the others, with great understanding and sympathy. He is censuring neither Tom nor Annie, only investigating the possibilities for fighting loneliness when habit and unfortunate circumstances have bred a deep loneliness. He is trying to show the lack of avenues of escape, the hope that springs up, the disappointment. He treats six characters fully, but works through a focus on Annie. He sees the story of these lives as comic. Many comedies are about loneliness. *The Playboy of the Western World* is one of them and *Happy Days* is another. Norman, Reg, Ruth, and Sarah—highly comic characters— are miserable with loneliness.

## Protagonist and Antagonist

Sarah serves an important function. If Annie is the protagonist (the character whose desire we most follow and identify with), Sarah is the antagonist (the person who thwarts the protagonist). She holds the conventional values—not only holds them, but serves them up for dinner! She tries to force Annie and Tom into an acknowledgement of a relationship. She makes a phone call in the middle of the night and tries to put Norman and Ruth back together. She meddles. Her "I want to," her objective, is to make everybody's life as conventional as hers. The only trouble is, she's not happy, and the more she tries to change everyone else, the more she has to face her own unhappiness. She is against Norman and all he stands for. So it is all the more interesting that we find her as susceptible to Norman as anyone else is! One of the play's peripeties is that Sarah tries to talk everyone out of Norman only to fall for him herself. She needs romance too. She needs to let loose, to have, as Annie so unromantically says it, a good "dirty weekend . . . absolutely filthy" and, as Annie also says, to "get it off her chest."

Annie gets no holiday, partly because she has a bit of Sarah in her, a small Sarah-conscience inside her, nagging about Tom and order and responsibility. As a symbol of responsibility there is mother. "Mother," who is ill and difficult, is never seen, but her presence hovers over the play.

## The Treasure

Good titles are important. In this play, the title alerts us to food—or the lack of it. There is hardly anything to have manners for. There is only salad for supper on the first night and cereal for breakfast. Tinned soups are thrown together for supper on the second day. The lack of food stands for how little comfort there is. In *Table Manners* food is consumed on stage as a part of stage business, but it is also talked about constantly. The meals, such as they are, give the excuse for moving the characters in and out of the dining room, but the subject of food also brings out the personalities of the characters.

And, of course, food is also a stand-in for other subjects. Notice how at the end of the play, Norman teases Annie about having to eat the plates, but to make the plates tasty she'll have to pour custard and jam over them. He might as well have said, "Yes, stay with Tom, but you'll have to sugar it over to make it seem like anything." When Norman teases Annie with this image of fantasy food, she breaks down, and she tells him she wants to go to East Grinstead, which, like the poor substitutes for food, is a poor substitute for a resort. The play ends with the idea that nobody's hunger has been filled.

A man I know saw *Table Manners* and said he not only identified with all the men in it, but also with all the women. Each character is clear enough to touch a part of us.

*Table Manners* is an unusual play in that it is part of a trilogy of plays. Yet *Table Manners* stands alone, for one can produce it without the other plays and it makes a full evening. I have directed it and know it well. When it is over, the audience feels satisfied, finished.

## Other Plays by Ayckbourn

Alan Ayckbourn has been fascinated for some time by the conventions of theatre. He likes to play with those conventions in new ways and has been doing so for the last twenty years. For instance, he has written *How the Other Half Loves*, a play in which two settings are shown simultaneously on stage. Instead of one living room on stage left and the other on stage right, he asks that *both* sets use the whole stage and that both sets of characters exist on stage at once. The way the audience knows which house something is happening in is by the furniture the characters relate to—which both in arrangement and style tells what the place is.

Ayckbourn also wrote a play called *Way Upstream* that breaks other rules of the theatre (namely "refrain from putting bodies of water on stage . . ." a rule more obeyed than avoiding children and animals). In *Way Upstream*, a cabin cruiser is part of the set and it moves across real water! The play is difficult to produce well. I saw it in a production at the National Theatre in London. The sets were very complex—riverbank sections that moved to give the illusion that the boat—which also moved—was going up a river. Before the audience entered the theatre, stage hands were busy stirring up scene paint in the water—which filled the stage—to make it look more muddy.

I am not suggesting that anyone try for such effects without knowing a great deal about theatre production and without a substantial background in playwriting. It is important that there be payoffs for effects and Ayckbourn is ready to pay off. *Way Upstream* is a fascinating dark play about emotional piracy on the river. Two couples have rented a boat for a holiday. Two strangers, a man and a woman, are "the pirates." At first they seem charming, but slowly, we come to understand that they are dangerous. They prey upon the four vacationers. At first they use their money and supplies, but that is not the worst that they do;

they prey on their deepest fears and insecurities; they ridicule, embarrass, shame, and destroy their hosts.

Ayckbourn always tries out his plays in the Scarborough Theatre outside of London. He uses a company of six actors, three men and three women, actors that he knows well and whom he writes *for*. He rehearses in a theatre that he also knows well. This is a boon to him as it would be to almost any playwright. Remember Shakespeare wrote for *specific actors* and a specific theatre. Molière did too. If you haven't already tried this, let a character take shape in your mind by thinking of an actor who would play that character.

You should also work as much in theatre production in as many capacities as possible if you want to go on with playwriting. Alan Ayckbourn tries for new effects in plays but not out of naiveté. He knows what rehearsal and production are all about. His "trick," or his special idea, for the trilogy known as *The Norman Conquests* is that instead of giving us three different plays sequentially, he gives us the same play—that is the same span of time—as the six characters spend it in three different places. *Living Together* is the same situation on the same weekend as *Table Manners*, but it takes place in the living room. And *Round and Round the Garden* is the same too, but it shows the scenes in the garden. It seems at first that this wouldn't work, that it would be boring. But Ayckbourn has shown us that two more whole plays can be made of other moments, other reactions on the weekend on which Annie was supposed to go away with Norman. The fascinating thing is that each play makes sense on its own and even better sense when linked with the other two.

There is a metaphor running through the plays: the Norman Conquests of Britain. The Normans brought romantic notions, poetry, entertainers, and troubadours when they invaded Britain. It is no mistake that Norman believes in love, that he sings drunkenly in the living room while Sarah is trying to have an orderly meal, what she calls a *civilized* meal.

Ayckbourn might have gotten his idea for *The Norman Conquests* in any of the following ways: by reading something about the Norman Conquests, by thinking about the name Norman, by spending a weekend with family, by engaging in or observing a relationship like Annie's with Tom, by noticing somewhere that different parts of a "drama" took place in different rooms of a house, and more. Ideas come from all sorts of sources. They then need to be worked with and tamed, focussed and structured, put in terms of character and action, and written for actors to perform.

Ayckbourn, in his preface to the published edition of the trilogy, does not share his source of inspiration with us—except to admit that his closest friends and lovers seem hilarious to him—but he does tell us a good deal about the values of working with specific actors in a specific and limited theatre. And he gives us a glimpse of his working methods. One of the interesting disclosures is that he wrote the plays "crosswise." That means that he did all the Scene Ones, all the Scene Twos, etc. And he wrote all three plays in a several days' flurry of almost continuous writing. There are many ways to write plays. Most take a year or two to write. Ayckbourn's intense several days is the exception.

The preface follows.

## Preface to The Norman Conquests*
### by Alan Ayckbourn

In general, by an odd quirk of nature, the more fond of people I become, the more amusing I tend to find them. Love affairs in my life are matters of considerable hilarity. Necessarily, this has strictly curtailed not only my close circle of friends but my choice of female companions. Few women care to be laughed at and men not at all, except for large sums of money. All of which leads to the fact that I'm far too fond of the theatre to take it too seriously.

This preface is not intended to enlarge upon or in any way illuminate the plays contained in this volume. Despite notable exceptions, playwrights who attempt such comments are prone at best to sound faintly pretentious or (worse) untypically modest.

*The Norman Conquests* are the result of several days and nights of almost continuous writing in the spring of 1973. Already, little over a year later, it's difficult for me to remember why I chose to tackle this most ambitious and, frankly, seemingly uncommercial project. I think it was, within the context of the tiny Library Theatre-in-the-Round in Scarborough where I first stage all my plays, both a challenge and something of an adventure for the actors and for me as director. Certainly I never dreamed they would be produced elsewhere. Trilogies, I was informed by my London sources as soon as the news leaked out that I was writing one, are not Good Things for the West End. But then, when I am tackling a new play, I find it safer never to look further than Scarborough anyway. It always seems at the time quite enough of an effort to write and stage the play and achieve success there. Afterwards, when perhaps the piece is run in and seems to be working, it becomes possible to be objective and consider its chances elsewhere. In this I have always been extremely fortunate. I have written, to date, fifteen full-length plays, most of which are happily destroyed, but all without exception, even the first, guaranteed production before I set pencil to paper. In latter years, this apparent blind and some would say foolish faith that the management of Scarborough seemed to have that I would always produce the work is explained by the fact that I am also the Theatre's Artistic Director. Like most successful relationships, this one is based on implicit mutual trust. All of which, I suppose, goes a long way to explain why I continue to work there and not, as has been suggested to me, try for the "big time."

Of course, this system has its restrictions, but fortunately these too seem to work in my favour. Scarborough is a holiday town, which means that a large proportion of the potential audience changes every week of the summer. On

* From *The Norman Conquests: A Trilogy of Plays*, by Alan Ayckbourn (New York: Grove Press, Inc., 1979). Used by permission of Grove Weidenfeld and Random Century Group.

Saturdays, the roads in and out of the town are scenes of mile-long queues as visitors leave and arrive. When I first considered the trilogy, I was aware that it would be optimistic to expect an audience like this necessarily to be able to give up three nights of their precious holiday to come to our one theatre. Any suggestion that it was essential to see all three plays to appreciate any one of them would probably result in no audience at all. Similarly, were the plays clearly labelled Parts One, Two and Three, any holidaymaker determined to play Bingo on Monday would probably give up the whole idea as a bad job. The plays would therefore have to be able to stand independently—yet not so much that people's curiosity as to what was happening on the other two nights wasn't a little aroused. Second, as I have said, it should be possible to see them in any order. Third, since we could only afford six actors, they should have that number of characters. Fourth, ideally they should only have two stage entrances since that's the way our temporary Library Theatre set-up is arranged (but then this is common to all my plays). There were other minor pre-conditions peculiar to this venture. The actor I had in mind to play Norman couldn't join us for the first few days of the season—which necessitated him making a late first entrance in one of the plays (*Table Manners*) to facilitate rehearsals. If this all makes me sound like a writer who performs to order, I suppose it's true. I thrive when working under a series of pre-conditions, preferably when they are pre-conditions over which I have total control. Because ultimately, of course, all these restrictions that come as a result of operating in a converted concert room, a temporary 250-seat Theatre-in-the-Round on the first floor of a public library, tend to work in a play's favour in its later life. In these austere times most theatre managers, if not the actors, prefer small-cast plays. Owing to our scenic restrictions, they are also amenable to plays with simple sets and, in the case of the trilogy, its flexibility of presentation has naturally proved an advantage elsewhere. The traffic jams of visitors to Heathrow are no less than the ones to Scarborough.

Anyway, once I had sorted out the pre-conditions and was aware that the scheme had few precedents, the problem of how to write it arose. I'm not one of those careful methodic over-all planners. When I start a play, beyond an entirely general pattern, I have little or no idea what will become of my characters individually at the end. I generally follow their progress with a more or less benign interest and hope that the staging and construction will be taken care of by some divine subconscious automatic pilot. Since many of the actions within the plays had to cross-relate and, more important, since each character's attitude and development had to fit in with the general time structure, I decided in the case of *The Norman Conquests* to write them crosswise. That is to say, I started with Scene One of *Round And Round the Garden*, then the Scene One's of the other two plays and so on through the Scene Two's. It was an odd experience writing them, rather similar to Norman's own in fact. I found myself grappling with triplet sisters all with very different personalities. Climaxes, comic ones naturally, seemed to abound everywhere. Hardly had I finished dealing with the fury of Reg's game (*Living Together*) than I was encountering a frenzied Sarah trying to seat her guests (*Table Manners*) or Ruth beating off the advances of an uncharacteristically amorous Tom (*Round and Round the Garden*). Strangely too, each play, although dealing with the same characters and events, began to develop a distinct atmosphere of its own. *Table Manners* was the most robust and, as it proved onstage, the most overtly funny. *Round and Round the Garden*, possibly due to its exterior setting, took a more casual and (as it contains the beginning and end of the cycle) a more conventional shape. *Living Together* has a tempo far slower than anything I had written before and encouraged me, possibly because of the sheer over-all volume of writing involved, to slacken the pace in a way I had never dared to do in any comedy. This crosswise way of writing them proved very satisfactory though of course made it quite impossible for me, even today, really to judge their effectiveness downwards or indeed to assess, beyond certain limits, whether the plays stand up independently. This is not, I'm afraid, a problem that one single individual can resolve. As soon as one play is read or seen, the other two plays are automatically coloured and affected by the foreknowledge gained from the first—which may sound like some sort of warning, though, in this case I hope, a little knowledge is a pleasurable thing.

Alan Ayckbourn
*Scarborough, 1974*

---

### Study Questions and Exercises

1. Discuss **Table Manners** in terms of a repeated action, physical action that underlies the verbal action, dramatic irony, and peripety.
2. Work out an idea, just for fun, using the first thing that comes to your mind. If you are looking out the window and see a man passing and the man looks lonely to you, begin to invent a character for him. How would you put him into drama? What is his story? Where would you set it?

# EIGHT

# Writing for Actors

## OVERVIEW

When the play allows it, actors try to create a whole life for the characters they play. They undertake to make each character's thinking, moving, and speaking utterly believable. Therefore playwrights must keep in mind that they are writing for actors.

Since beginning actors and beginning playwrights often need to learn the same lessons—which include how to fill in the gaps, how to account for all the moments in an action—it is a good idea to take a basic acting class if you want to continue writing plays. Performing in scenes is good practice for writers. There are also some exercises that novice actors do *on paper* that will be useful to the playwright.

In this chapter is one of those exercises—a motivation chart. I've also included notes on timing, cueing, and the execution of stage directions. Following are examples of the fourth writing exercise with commentary on those scripts. The scripts are titled *Go Fish, Birthday, Night Repair*.

## OBJECTIVES

At the end of this chapter you should be able to

- Fill in an actor's motivation chart for characters in your scripts and in established scripts
- Write effective stage directions
- Describe what actions have been completed in each of the sample scripts
- Describe the pattern of staging for each script
- Complete Exercise 4—which is to integrate dialogue and lines in a 4–5 page script in which a "gesture" that has been begun at the beginning is completed at the end

Actors need to learn that their characters must think and feel in a continuously life-like, believable way throughout a play. They cannot just act when they have lines and stand around the rest of the time "on hold." They must act when they are listening to a scene partner as well as when they are speaking.

One of the exercises actors do is to break down a script, finding the inner life for *every moment*—the listening moments as well as the speaking moments. The sample charts that follow have several columns. Each represents a split second in the emotional life of the character as the actor sees the character.

The first column is "I think." The idea behind it is that thoughts, even fleeting ones, motivate us to do or say things. Sometimes, of course, it seems we are so much in the midst of an action that we don't have time to think—or time to *know* our thoughts. But usually, something, some stimulus, is coming in, even if it's only for a split second.

The second column is "I do." In this column belong the ordinary physical actions, like looking at someone, looking away, staring at a wall, playing with our clothing. Usually we are physically doing something when we are in interaction, even if only *standing still* in order to listen better.

(The second chart adds yet another column—"I feel." Often this is useful and the actor finds that feelings trigger the line of dialogue better than anything else does.)

Usually the third column is for the line of dialogue. The actor must come up with a whole series of purposes, whether the line is his/hers or a scene partner's. Each line of dialogue gets a place on the chart and a change of motivation. So playwrights should be aware that actors who have worked on established plays find that *every line* denotes a change of some sort.

The fourth column is for objectives, or intentions. Whether a character is speaking or not, that character wants something. Actors have to have an *intention* for each of the moments of a play. An intention is a goal, an action that the actor can play—*even* when silent. The two commonly used words for this important facet of an actor's work—*intention* and *objective*—are heard all the time in a rehearsal. It is generally believed that this is the most important part of an actor's work. So the fourth column is the most important column.

And the fifth column, "because," is the rationale for all that comes before it.

We are creatures with objectives, with thoughts, with actions, with reasons and rationalizations for what we want. The actor's chart helps to duplicate natural thought, to tie things together for the actor.

Since the objectives column—fourth or fifth—is the most important, we need to look at it more closely for a moment.

According to the principles of Constantin Stanislavsky (acting principles that most actors still rely upon), the actor must phrase objectives by saying "*I want to*" and adding an active verb. Notice I said I want *to* and not just I want. "I want peace" is *not* a playable objective. "I want to get rid of Joe so I can have some peace" is. The actor has to have an *action* to play.

The following charts are for scenes from *The Dining Room* and from *A Streetcar Named Desire.*

In *The Dining Room*, Tony has just come to visit his Aunt Harriet and to study her for an anthropology project he's doing on WASPs and how they live—or how they used to live. Chart 1.1 is from Tony's point of view and works out for the actor how to keep Aunt Harriet from minding that she is a specimen.

Chart 1.2 is from *Streetcar*, the fourth scene, after Stella has been beaten by Stanley, yet spent the night with him. The scene is from Blanche's point of view.

You've probably heard somebody say that all writers have to be actors, that story-telling is acting and that to know her characters, a writer has to *be* each of them. Tennessee Williams was Blanche, certainly, but he also had to be Stella, Stanley, and Mitch because they behave in an integrated way. The Mitch who says nothing for three scenes makes psychological sense when he does speak. Williams had to have "acted" each of them in his study or his hotel room while writing, even if he never moved a muscle.

If the actor has to act on and between the lines, if the actor has to come up with a whole life for the character, you, the writer, must help the actor. You must be aware of what each character is doing all the time. When you forget about a character—when you just leave someone hanging on stage—you make it impossible for the actor to connect what she did on page one and what she must do on page three.

It is better, of course, to be aware of each of your characters as people. If you are aware of the character all that time—even if the character doesn't speak—you will give the right cues to the actor, sometimes in what another character says or how another character speaks, just knowing that the silent character is there.

One of the first lessons for young actors, then, is learning how to fill in an inner life for the character.

A second early lesson has to do with cueing, with tightening the words and the action of a play. Actors learn, or should learn, very early in their careers to *pick up cues*. This means that a character *prepares to speak* while the other character *is* speaking so that the end of one line is followed immediately by the beginning of the next. Nothing drags a play down worse than slow cues. If and when you have your work produced you may find yourself going mad when actors pause between lines. Unless of course you have asked for a pause. And if you have asked for one, you'd better have a really good reason for it because a pause can more easily work against you than for you.

So if actors have to keep the sound going, then playwrights do too. Your characters' lines must be *complete enough* and *long enough* to cover all the physical actions they must perform.

"But what about the silences that come from actions like setting the table and other stage business—pouring wine, lighting cigarettes? Those activities cause silence, don't they?" the novice actor is likely to ask. No. . . . At least not when things are working right. Playwrights should be aware that actors should be speaking *during* the doing of tasks. An actor learns very early that the pause it takes to light a cigarette—unless there is something extraordinary going on in that pause—kills the energy of his or her performance. *The energy comes from relating to another character with words.* So, under most circumstances, the actor will soon learn to say a line during which she gets out a cigarette, say another line during which the match or lighter is readied, say another line while striking up the fire, and then light the cigarette as a punctuation to this last line. The actor works at minimizing the silence. There must be lines of dialogue through the necessary action for the actor to perform this task well.

Or—perhaps the actor must set the table. The director will help the actor to, for example, put down four plates during the speaking of one line, then fetch the silverware while listening to another character's line, then place the silverware as an aid, a series of underlines, to a longish speech of his own, then fetch the wine glasses while listening to the other character, and place the wine glasses on a line of his—or if carefully done, as a reaction-punctuation to the lines of the other character. In other words, all of this activity is orchestrated very carefully in any good production and the goal is to make it smooth as well as to use activity as a rhythmic force to underline speech and reactions. But the playwright has to have accounted for both pantomime activity and dialogue.

One of the most often-made mistakes of inexperienced playwrights is the under-writing of dialogue. Too often there is not enough to say for what there is to do. When the script is staged, we are all too aware of the gaps in which the actors must move awkwardly and quickly, trying to accomplish some physical task so they can get to the next line, which only makes sense when the task is completed.

**Actor's Chart 1.1:** *The Dining Room*

| I THINK | I DO | I SAY | I WANT TO | BECAUSE |
|---|---|---|---|---|
| "I'll have to make this enjoyable for Aunt H." | Come in from the kitchen and place tape recorder | "Would you mind setting up over here, Aunt H?" | Do the job efficiently | I'd like to write up the results and still get to the party! |
| "I'm usually a pretty charming fellow." | Call back to her and point to the spot | "I want to get you in the late afternoon light." | Flatter her | I want to get her cooperation |
| "What a nice old girl she is." | Watch her doing exactly what I've asked while I set up notebook, pen, camera | Nothing. She says, "Certainly, Tony." | Make this a pleasant experience for both of us | I'd hate to get my dad angry with me. He adores her |
| "What an ordinary-looking piece of cloth." | Make a note: Irish linen; click a pix | Nothing. She says, "Now I thought I'd use this Irish linen place mat with matching napkin, that my husband—who was what? your great uncle—inherited from his sister. They have to be washed and ironed by hand every time they're used." | Make an accurate record | Prof. says many ordinary things have special meanings |
| "*This* part is *great* material!" | Write and snap pix of "prong," "pistol-handled," and "rat-tail" | Nothing. She says, "And then of course the silver which was given to us as a wedding present by your great-grandmother. You see? Three-prong forks. Pistol-handled knives. Spoon with rat-tail back. All Williamsburg pattern. These should be polished at least every two weeks." | Operate calmly and professionally | It feels so good |
| "Bone, Steuben, Waterford." | Study each through camera eye and snap | Nothing. She says, "And then this is Staffordshire, as is the butter plate. All of this is Bone. The wine glasses are early Steuben, but the goblets and finger bowls are both Waterford. None of this goes in the dishwasher, of course. It's all far too delicate for detergents." | Make visual identification of these | It's training for more difficult field work |

**Actor's Chart 1.1:** *The Dining Room* (Continued)

| I THINK | I DO | I SAY | I WANT TO | BECAUSE |
|---|---|---|---|---|
| "Is this a finger bowl?" | Take the item in question to look at it | "Finger bowls?" | Make sure (proper identification) | It's standard practice to insist on confirmation when a doubt exists |
| "This is the part about WASPs. . . ." | Listen closely | Nothing. She says, "Oh yes. Our side of the family always used finger bowls between the salad and the dessert." | Encourage her to babble comfortably | This is the kind of supportive info I need |
| "So far she's cooperating." | Hand bowl back to her | "Would you show me how they worked?" | Get her engaged in the process | I don't want her idle and asking questions of me |
| "Her mood, manner, movements are very telling." | Snap more pix | Nothing. She says, "Certainly, dear. You see the maid would take away the salad plate—like this. And then she'd put down the finger bowls in front of us. Like this. They would be filled approximately halfway with cool water. And there might be a little rose floating in it. Or a sliver of lemon. . . . Now of course we'd have our napkins in our laps—like this. And then we'd dip our fingers into the finger bowl . . . gently, gently . . . and then we'd wiggle them and shake them out . . . and then dab them on our napkins . . . and then dab our lips . . . then, of course, the maids would take them away. . . . And in would come a nice sherbert or chocolate mousse!" | Catch her most posed moments | This is proof that her ways are vanishing |
| "That was quick good research." | Gather up notebook, pen, camera in case, tape recorder | "Thanks, Aunt H." | Formalize the meeting | She won't ask too many questions if I keep it business-like |
| "I was too formal." | Smile, stop cleaning | "That was terrific." | Loosen things up | I'm charming and nice and there's no reason she shouldn't like me |

**Actor's Chart 1.2: Blanche—Scene 4**

| I THINK | I FEEL | I DO | I SAY | I WISH/WANT TO | BECAUSE |
|---|---|---|---|---|---|
| "I'd better warn her I'm coming in." | Scared | Look through door | "Stella." | See if she is alone | He might still be with her |
| "She's hurt." | Responsible | Cry, run to her | Nothing. She says, "Hmmh." | Take care of her | She's hurt |
| "Maybe not badly hurt." | Confused | Look at her | "Baby, my baby sister." | Get the both of us away from here | Tonight might be crazy, too |
| "She's not glad to see me." | Hurt | Get up, stand up | Nothing. She says, "Blanche, what's the matter with you?" | Pull myself together | Maybe I said too much |
| "Maybe he's hidden somewhere." | Stupid | Look around | "He's left." | Find out if he's hidden | I can't talk if he's around |
| "I don't think he's here." | Better | Look back to Stella | Nothing. She says, "Stan? Yes." | Get a breath | I've got to talk fast |
| "How can she be so calm?" | Worried about both of us | Search her face | "Will he be back?" | Get her away from here | We're not safe here |
| "She's still in bed." | Angry that she's so calm | Listen | Nothing. She says, "He's gone to get the car greased. Why?" | Understand her | She's behaving oddly |
| "She's insane." | Dumbfounded | Grab her shoulders | "Why! I've been half crazy, Stella! When I found out you'd been insane enough to come back in here after what happened—I started to rush in after you!" | Shake some sense into her | She's shocked, numb |
| "She's laughing!" | Outraged | Let go of her | Nothing. She says, "I'm glad you didn't." | Slap her | She's making fun of me |
| "She's far gone." | More frightened than before | Bend down to get eye to eye with her | "What are you thinking of? Answer me. What? What?" | Make her respond to me | She's trying to avoid me |
| "She acts like I'm crazy." | Angry | Stand | Nothing. She says, "Please, Blanche, sit down and stop yelling." | Stop yelling | I'll have to get to her some other way |
| "I'm the sane one." | Calmer | Take a breath | "All right, Stella. I will repeat the question quietly now." | Show her I'm sane | She'll listen better |
| "I have to say some very intense things." | Justified | Look at her | "How could you have come back in this place last night?" | Make her listen | She's got to leave |

I'm not suggesting you pad or stretch dialogue to cover actions. Instead you will have to know your characters well, know how and why they speak, and give them a situation that causes speech, so that you will not have gaps in the action. Stage directions are for the actor. Carefully done, they indicate a great deal about the meaning of a line of dialogue. You will find that you need to say very little about the character's emotions if the line is good enough. So instead of "(*aggressively*) I don't like that," you will write, "I refuse to stand for that," or "Take that suggestion and get out!" It is very hard for an actor to be aggressive with a wimpy line.

A great deal happens in rehearsal as the director and the actor block a play. Sometimes they ignore stage directions altogether. And they are more likely to ignore them if the stage directions aren't working for them. You may find that you want to give focus to a particular prop and a particular action. If so, you should be aware that a gesture can be made before a line, during a line, or after a line, or even partway through a line. Therefore, you need to be sure when you ask for an action that you get the effect you are seeking. Where you place your stage direction and how you phrase it can change the effect of an action. The more you write, the more you work in the theatre, and the more you pay attention to stage directions, the more you will notice the distinctions.

Eventually you will become aware of the differences among

ELLEN

(*shoving the coffee cup away from her*) I think what's going to have to happen is that you leave.

ELLEN

(*shoves the coffee cup away from her*) Leave the house. That's what I want.

ELLEN

I'm going to insist on your leaving this house. (*shoves the coffee cup away from her*)

Action can happen just before a line, during a line, or just after a line if the gesture itself is brief enough to be *punctuation action*. In the first example the action happens during the line and is not a punctuation action. This is, however, the most commonly used combination. The second example makes the line more important because it is last. And the third makes the gesture of moving the cup more important (because what is last usually takes focus) with the effect of undercutting the line. If you become sensitive to the feeling your character is experiencing and the kind of movement your character is likely to make, you will find yourself phrasing the character's lines differently—according to the gesture, emotion, and so on. The ultimate aim is to get movement and lines choreographed to highlight the words and to keep the music of the words going on stage. If you call for gestures after a line or just before, they must be short enough to be punctuation gestures. Don't write, "You'll have to leave (*sets the table*)."

---

## Assignment: Exercise 4

The specific task of this assignment is to write a comfortable combination of dialogue and physical action. This assignment should average 4 or 5 typed pages. The important thing is to work on a dialogue/action combination in which "a gesture" is completed. To write your exercise, decide upon

1. a setting
2. two characters (preferably)
3. a task to be done or accomplished during the scene: something that requires movement, physicalization

Make sure your characters are different from each other and that they want something. What happens physically doesn't have to be athletic or even busy, but it should be a clear underlining to the scene, a gesture begun and completed in the course of the action. Think of the lengths of the scenes from *Streetcar* and also from *The Dining Room*. In addition, notice that in plays with longer scenes, such as *Table Manners*, the same scene lengths prevail as "actor's scenes"—that is, there is usually a sustained scene between characters that lasts for five to eight pages. And in that scene something is begun and completed. For instance, there is a scene between Annie and Sarah at the beginning in which Sarah gets information out of Annie. There is a scene in Act I, Scene Two between Norman and Ruth over breakfast. Two things happen in that scene: 1) the physical action of Ruth's eating breakfast and 2) the psychological action of Ruth and Norman arguing about their marriage. The two are connected. Norman hands Ruth food that she is unable to see because she has very bad eyesight and isn't wearing her glasses. Ruth refuses to put her glasses on and she refuses to take Norman seriously.

Following are three samples of Exercise 4. You should compare the work of these writers with your own. Have you been able to begin and end a sequence that includes both physical and psychological action?

---

## Samples of Exercise 4

### Go Fish
#### by Megan Graham

*Setting: a small living room. SR is a sofa with a missing cushion, in front of which is a small coffee table. USL is a large chair with a blanket, serving as a slipcover, thrown over it. DSL is a metal chair with a T.V. on it. The T.V. has aluminum foil as its antenna. And its cord is plugged into an extension cord which stretches across the bare floor. Bob sits in the large chair and Jim sits on the sofa with his feet up on the coffee table. The table and part of the floor around it is littered with the remains of a Sunday paper and several cans of beer.*

*Bob pulls his leg up on to the chair and begins picking at the fraying hole in the knee of his jeans. He looks at Jim every once in a while.*

*Jim smokes a cigarette; as he smokes he watches the smoke. He presses his lips together in an attempt to blow a smoke ring.*

BOB

You look like a fish.

JIM

Hummm. *(Stops trying for a smoke ring and French inhales, waits and then slowly exhales.)*

BOB

So . . . what do you want to do tonight?

JIM

What did we do last night?

BOB

*(stretching his legs out in front of him and putting his arms behind his head)* Nothing.

JIM

Hummm.

BOB

*(leans forward)* Movies?

JIM

*(puts out his cigarette)* No money.

BOB

Want to go outside?

JIM

*(crosses his arms across his chest)* Too cold.

BOB

*(looks SL)* T.V.?

JIM

*(looking up)* Broken.

BOB

Shit. *(Looks around. Lifts a section of the paper and pulls out half a deck of dog-eared cards. Lifts another section and collects the other half of the deck. He takes one card and wipes it off on his jeans. Jim continues to look up.)*

BOB

Cards? *(Jim takes his feet off the table and leans forward.)*

BOB

*(sits on the floor by the table)* Poker. *(He deals out 5 cards to Jim and himself. Jim takes his cards and leans back into the sofa as he sorts them.)*

BOB

*(after looking at his cards)* What's higher, a flush or a straight?

JIM

Flush. *(looks at his cards)* . . . no, straight.

BOB

Don't you know?

JIM

I have it written down somewhere.

BOB

Right. *(Gathers up his hand and shuffles it into the deck, he takes Jim's cards and adds them to the deck. Jim lights another cigarette. Bob deals out 7 cards per hand, and then spreads the rest of the deck on the table. Jim picks up his hand.)*

BOB

Fish. *(looks at his cards)* Got any fours?

JIM

*(smirks)* Go fish. *(Bob picks up a card, places it in his hand and looks up at Jim.)*

JIM

Do you have any nines?

BOB

Of course not.

JIM

What do you mean, "Of course not?" You are supposed to say, "Go fish."

BOB

But this deck only has two nines.

JIM

*(throws his cards on the table)* Jesus Christ, you're an idiot.

BOB

Me?

JIM

Do you see anyone else in the room?

BOB

It's not my fault if all the cards aren't here.

JIM

But what kind of asshole plays with a deck that's missing two nines?

BOB

*(collecting the cards)* And a queen.

JIM

You are so stupid.

BOB

You're just a sore loser. *(Turns his back to Jim and shuffles the cards.)*

JIM

How could I lose to someone with half a brain and half a deck? *(He puts his cigarette out.)*

BOB

*(turning his head back and sticking out his tongue)* Pbbbst.

JIM

Now there's an intelligent response from the moron in the corner.

BOB

*(turns back to Jim)* Oh . . . Oh, yeah . . .

JIM

Your rapier wit is astonishing. *(He gets up and walks behind the sofa.)*

BOB

*(stands up)* Well, excuse me, professor. *(Slumps down into the chair.)*

JIM

*(sits on the back of the sofa)* Cut the professor shit will you.

BOB

I would if you'd stop reminding me that you are a *(clears his throat)* "college graduate," and I'm just a lowly warehouse worker.

JIM

I have the same job.

BOB

*(pointing at him)* And don't you forget it, smartass.

JIM

*(turns and puts his feet on the seat of the sofa)* How can I?

BOB

What's so damn sexy about a B.A.?

JIM

*(slides down onto the sofa)* Sexy?

BOB

Jennifer must think it is.

JIM

*(runs his hand through his hair)* Whatever you say.

BOB

*(setting the cards on the table)* You always have to win don't you.

JIM

Me?

BOB

Always have to have what others have, and more.

JIM

Yeah *(looks around at the apartment, smirks)* . . . right.

BOB

You hate to see me happy. Whenever it looks like I might just get what I've always wanted, you have to take it away. Right when I'm about to sit down, you pull the chair out from under me.

JIM

That wasn't me, that was Harold, at the last company party. You were certainly trashed. I have to admit it was kind of

funny watching you come crashing down to the floor. You laughed at the time. Everyone laughed. *(Laughs)* But then, we were so drunk we would have laughed at anything.

BOB

Jennifer didn't laugh.

JIM

She was busy lusting after the new supervisor.

BOB

*(turns to Jim)* Who?

JIM

Mr. Samuel P. Wilson.

BOB

But . . . didn't you, I mean her . . . she was . . . Sam, eh? Huh. I didn't notice that.

JIM

Why anyone would want to go out with her is beyond me.

BOB

Yeah, me too. *(Jim pulls out another cigarette and lights it, he watches the smoke. Bob looks at his feet and taps them together. Jim puts his feet up on the table.)*

BOB

*(after biting a fingernail)* So . . . What do you want to do tonight?

JIM

What did we do last night?

BOB

*(leans his head on his hand)* Nothing.

What is interesting about this is that it is a physicalization of people who are trying to do something and can't. It physically shows people doing nothing, going passive, but doing it—as they have to on stage—actively. Passivity has to be active on stage. It has to be something we can witness and understand. The writer imparts the feeling of passivity by having people only talk about moving; in reality, the actors move only enough to "play" with frayed jeans, cards, and smoke.

Another thing that the writer has done here is that she has distinguished between Bob and Jim in a basic way. Bob tries to make a plan and Jim always has a quick, negative response. Jim maintains the upper hand by letting Bob do all the work, bring up all the difficult subjects, etc.

That the characters move from poker to a game of Go Fish that they can't really play is telling. They are in limbo, their lives hang on Jennifer's doings, their job offers no identity (and apparently little money), and they can't find a way to motivate themselves. The minimalist dialogue works well enough in this scene, but the playwright should be sure she can flesh out a scene when she wants to, that she can write characters who have a lot to say. The minimalist style is attractive, but limited, and many people feel it's overdone today.

## Birthday

### by Karl Hendricks

*The scene takes place in a comfortably furnished living room. Center stage is a couch, in front of which is a coffee table and to the right of which is an easy chair. Behind the couch there are two windows. The rest of the room can be decorated appropriately for someone who has a good deal of money but does not overly flaunt it.*

*As the lights come up, Mr. Price, age 70, is standing by the window on the right side, and Steven, age 20, is sitting on the couch trying to open a bottle. There are two glasses on the coffee table.*

MR. PRICE

*(looking out window)* Another birthday and no one's here. Except you. *(He turns around.)* But you kind of have to be here, don't you? Given that it's your birthday, too.

STEVEN

*(struggling with bottle)* I come here because I want to. *(He pops cork.)* Finally.

MR. PRICE

Sure you do. I bet you hate me like all the rest of them. And they do all hate me, you know. All my children hate me, your father, Elizabeth, Fred, and what's his name . . . Douglas, that's it. And all my grandchildren hate me. My nieces and nephews, too. If any of my brothers and sisters were alive, they'd hate me, too. But you, Steven, are the one person in the world who professes to love me. I think you're lying. I think you came here just because you suspect I'm going to leave you all of my money.

STEVEN

*(pouring champagne)* That's not the reason.

MR. PRICE

Good thing. Because I plan to spend it all before I die. Bought a new Cadillac last week. Don't know why. I never drive anymore.

STEVEN

Here, Grandpa, sit down, have some champagne.

MR. PRICE

*(sitting down on couch)* Indeed I will. *(He takes a glass from Steven.)* How'd you get this anyway? Aren't you a year too young?

STEVEN

I had a friend buy it.

MR. PRICE

Sneaky boy, just like I was. Well, I appreciate the trouble you went to to get it. Let me see. *(Tastes champagne.)* Not bad. Not great, but I've had worse. Hell, when I was your age I would have drunk cough medicine and liked it. Well, happy birthday, Mr. Price.

STEVEN

Same to you, Mr. Price. *(They clink glasses.)*

MR. PRICE

*(finishing glass)* Yes, that's really not too bad. More please. *(Steven pours him another glass. He takes a sip.)* Yes. Let me see. Where was I? Ah yes, everybody hates me. They haven't always hated me. One time, everybody loved me. I remember the day you were born. Happiest day of my life. Your grandmother and I . . . we . . . we had started fighting and she had found out about some of my . . . dalliances. But I woke up that morning and you know what she had done? She had made me the grandest breakfast you'd ever want to see. There were pancakes, and French toast, and eggs, and sausage and bacon. Your grandmother wasn't much for cooking you know, and here she was throwing this . . . this feast at me. And I was shocked. I said, "Christ, woman, what did you make all this food for?" And she said, "Philip, today is your fiftieth birthday, and it's about time your gallivanting about stopped. We're both getting older and pretty soon you're going to need me a lot more than you think. So this is kind of a bribe for you to give up your girlfriends and settle down." I almost did, too. I said to myself, "Philip, you've got a good woman on your hands. A sweet . . . intelligent woman. You'd better not screw this up." *(Pause.)* But I suppose in the end my . . . baser urges won out. I must have thought that if she'd taken this much she could take a little more. *(He drinks.)*

STEVEN

Have some more champagne, Grandpa. *(He pours more into both glasses.)*

MR. PRICE

Thank you, kind sir. *(He takes a sip.)* So, anyway, after breakfast I went straight to my typewriter. Seems strange. My fiftieth birthday. You'd think I'd take the day off. I think I wrote some real fine stuff that day, though. I was on a very hot streak at the time.

STEVEN

What book were you working on?

MR. PRICE

Well, when you write so many masterpieces they all sort of blur together. *(Laughs, drinks.)* Oh, let me see, at that time I believe I was working on *The Lonely Cowboy*. Hah, that book was a joke.

STEVEN

I read it. I think it's wonderful.

MR. PRICE

That's because you're young and foolish, my boy. But I guess I liked it at the time, too. *(Pause.)* So there I was typing away and I get this phone call. From your father. And he said, "Dad, you're a grandfather," and I just sat down on the floor and said, "Christ, that's terrific. That's goddamned terrific." I think I even cried. You were such a beautiful child. Your father was my favorite, you know, so I was happy he was the one to give me my first grandchild. Always wished he would have had more. He should have married a more fertile woman. Your mother's a good woman, but she doesn't seem inclined to having babies.

STEVEN

I talked to her last night and she said that you're a crotchety old bastard and that I shouldn't come out to see you because you're trying to bring down everybody else in this family along with yourself.

MR. PRICE

Did she now? All that? Well, she's smarter than I give her credit for. What did your father have to add?

STEVEN

He said that you ruined Grandma's life and that he barely escaped from your grip before you ruined his life.

MR. PRICE

And what did you say to that?

STEVEN

I told him that at least Grandpa isn't some self-pitying half-dead zombie like you are.

MR. PRICE

Ha Ha. Bet that shook him up. But you shouldn't be so hard on your father. He's a limp fish but he means well.

STEVEN

He's so self-righteous it makes me sick. He's always judging me, saying I can't do anything right. I seriously think he gets great enjoyment in picking at me, exposing my weaknesses. I told him that at least when I come here I can breathe.

MR. PRICE

You know what your problem is, Steven? You need to learn to relax, loosen up, have a little fun. You have any girlfriends?

STEVEN

I have a girlfriend.

MR. PRICE

Just one? Christ, boy, you need more than that. Sow your oats. Plant your seed. You're the only one I can trust to carry on this family. Oh well, so tell me about this girlfriend. If you're confining yourself to one, she must be marvelous.

STEVEN

I don't know. Every time I talk about her I sound so lame. Like it's some stupid high school romance or something, like we're going steady. But, you know, at the risk of sounding lame, every time I see her, I think of . . . flowers.

MR. PRICE

Ha, I know that feeling.

STEVEN

It's like I literally see flowers in my head. A field of flowers and they're all different colors. And I see birds flying around. Maybe a few deer running around in there, too. (Laughs) And it's strange, every time we're in the car, it seems like every song on the radio is about us.

MR. PRICE

Oh, my boy, you're in trouble now.

STEVEN

She's wonderful, really. Her name's Laura.

MR. PRICE

Laura. Well, that's a good name.

STEVEN

You know, I never understood why people ever got married until I met her. I think we might end up getting married.

MR. PRICE

Christ, boy, you can't be thinking about marriage yet.

STEVEN

It's funny, every time we fight—even if it's just a little fight, like I'll make some stupid remark and she'll go home a little angry—I go back to my room and cry.

MR. PRICE

You know what your problem is? You're too much like I was in college. Thought I was a sensitive poet. Used to write sappy love poems to this girl—Kathleen was her name. She was beautiful. She had long curly hair, you know, and big brown eyes, like a puppy. She broke my heart and I wised up.

STEVEN

I can't imagine Laura ever breaking my heart.

MR. PRICE

Christ, you know what you need to do? You have to stop drinking this champagne and start drinking Scotch. Put hair on your chest, my boy.

STEVEN

I don't think you understand the situation.

MR. PRICE

I don't understand? I understand all too well, my boy, all too well. I went through the same things. Pretty soon, though, you realize you're not going to get very far with those . . . romantic visions of yours. I know all about women. I've had more women than you have hairs on your head. Sometimes I think that if I write another book, it's going to be about women. All about women. Chapter one: "Stay the hell away from them."

STEVEN

I think you should.

MR. PRICE

What?

STEVEN

Write another book.

MR. PRICE

Don't get me off the subject. I'm not through with this Laura business yet.

STEVEN

I'm serious. You haven't written anything in a long time. It would do you good to get back into it.

MR. PRICE

Christ, I don't want to write anymore. I'm too old, too worn out. What would I write about?

STEVEN

Your life.

MR. PRICE

What?

STEVEN

Yes, I've been thinking about this and I think you need to write your autobiography. All the things you tell me—I don't want them to be lost.

MR. PRICE

I don't want to write my autobiography. My life's too depressing. I was either drunk or asleep two-thirds of the time and what happened in the other third isn't all that interesting. So I've written a few half-decent novels. So what? My writing career is really just a lot of failed promises, a lot of failed ideas.

STEVEN

My God, Grandpa, why do you talk like that? A lot of people read your books and love them. They're brilliant, and I know you've heard that from many, many more people than just me. People want to know about you.

MR. PRICE

What do I care what people want? Christ, the only thing that would be more depressing than living my life would be writing about it. Besides, I'm retired. I'm through with writing.

STEVEN

Then let me do it.

MR. PRICE

What?

STEVEN

Let me write your story. Let me be your biographer.

MR. PRICE

I don't think that would be wise, Steven.

STEVEN

Why not? You've read my work. You never say anything about it. Do you really read the stories I send you?

MR. PRICE

I read them.

STEVEN

Well, what do you think? I've been too scared to ask you before, but I want to know now.

MR. PRICE

You really want to know?

STEVEN

Yes.

MR. PRICE

(Stands up and walks over to window.) Steven, the truth is your writing is garbage. Totally worthless. Don't let this hurt you, I'm just being honest with you so you can avoid further pain. Your sentence structure is weak, your ideas are weak. And that would be okay, but your writing is just plain boring. I wouldn't have read past the first paragraph in most of your stories if you weren't my favorite grandson. I'm not saying you don't try, Steven, I'm just saying that you don't have any talent. Give it up and move on to something else.

STEVEN

(Stands up, facing Mr. Price.) I don't believe you're saying this.

MR. PRICE

Believe it. I'm sure other people have told you this. You're a lousy writer.

STEVEN

Actually, no one else has told me that.

MR. PRICE

Then the world has been coddling you. Steven . . . you're an intelligent, thoughtful boy. Hell, you're smarter than I was at your age. But you just don't have the ability to write.

STEVEN

(turning away) This is funny. I really hope you mean what you're saying. I really hope you do hate my writing.

MR. PRICE

(sitting down in easy chair) Of course I mean what I'm saying. Why else would I say it? (Pause.))

STEVEN

(walking over to window) You know . . . when I was eight I noticed these . . . strange books in our bookshelves. They had my Grandpa's name on them, and weird pictures on the cover. Somehow before that I didn't really know you were this famous writer, so it was kind of surprising to see your name on all these books. Pretty soon after that, I started reading them. I didn't understand them at first but I . . . I sensed something was really going on on those pages, something that was bigger than me, something that was . . . sounds corny, but something that was magic. Ever since then, I've wanted to be a writer. I've never dreamed anything else. I've never seen myself doing anything else. You're responsible for this. I admire you so much, Grandpa. So if you really believe I should drop writing, tell me, and I'll do it and we'll get back to our celebration. (Pause.) Grandpa?

MR. PRICE

"She laid her head on the pillow next to mine and I felt her hot breath against my neck. I lay there quivering, unable to move and . . ."

STEVEN

*(interrupting)* "And I didn't sleep a wink all night." That's the end of . . .

MR. PRICE

One of your stories. It was a good short story, Steven. A very nice one, indeed.

STEVEN

You son of a bitch. I can't believe you. Now I don't know if you really like it or if you just want to play with me some more. You're just like my father. You enjoy hurting people, don't you? That's what they all say. God, I should've listened. You old bastard, why do I come to see you? *(Pause.)*

MR. PRICE

My boy, I'm a very scared man. I've always been. Always been frightened someone's going to find me out. You see, the truth is I'm a lousy writer. Somehow, the drivel I threw on the page excited people. I don't know why. So I've lived in fear of some smart, brave soul stepping forward and saying, "Philip Price can't write a lick." You know, I used to do the same thing with my students I just tried to do to you. Crush them. Of course, I didn't do it with all my female students because I was trying to get half of them into bed. Lord knows why I do it. I don't know why I hurt people. You know what I used to say to your Aunt Elizabeth. I used to tell her she was ugly. I'd say, "Girl, you're ugly as sin." It'd make her cry, but I'd just laugh. *(Pause.)* The funny part is I love them all. All the people I've hurt. At least, I think I do. Christ, Steven, I can't write about my life. Cause if I looked at it long enough, I'd be sure of something that I already kind of know now. That I'm going to hell. *(Pause.)*

STEVEN

*(Slowly walks over to couch and sits.)* There's a little bit more champagne left. Do you want to finish it with me? *(Pause.)*

MR. PRICE

*(moving to couch)* A grand idea, my boy. Best idea I've heard all day. You know, Steven, I've got money, awards, nice house, couple cars, but I've realized that if you can't enjoy the little things in life, then hell, you're not living. Like this glass of champagne. I'm really enjoying it. It's the little things. They get you through. You walk down the street and pass a pretty girl and you get a whiff of her perfume. Or you read something funny in the newspaper. Or you eat a good jelly doughnut. Yes. You know what helps me the best though? It's the clouds. Just seeing the clouds on a sunny day, all puffy and white, it picks me up. Christ, I would have gone crazy a long time ago if it weren't for clouds. *(Pause.)* Right, Steven? *(Pause.)* Steven?

STEVEN

I like the clouds, too, Grandpa.

MR. PRICE

As well you should. *(Pause.)* Steven, are you angry with me? You are going to keep coming around, aren't you? This old man gets pretty lonely sometimes.

STEVEN

I get lonely, too.

MR. PRICE

What? Why are you talking like that? Only old men are supposed to get lonely. Here, this is a party, let's have some fun. Call up your friend, have him bring over some more champagne. Or better yet, Scotch. Come on, be happy, after all today is our birthday.

When this script came up in workshop, it aroused an especially lively discussion. Some people wanted more information about Steven's girlfriend because she revealed so much about the characters of Steven and Mr. Price. A question about Mr. Price's abrasiveness was raised. "Does he need to be so difficult?" one person asked. But another said, "I know who he is. He's the kind of person who alienates his family, he's the kind of person who volunteers his feelings without being asked." While one person was sure that Steven and his grandfather had different attitudes towards women, another assumed that Steven would become like his grandfather, that the issue of their birthdays and their both being writers ensured that. People were interested in Steven's blow-up and questioned whether it was more interesting that he put a lid on it so quickly or would have been more interesting if he'd held onto his anger.

When asked at the end of the notes session about Steven's abortive blow-up, the playwright said that he wanted Steven's overt anger to die down but to leave a residue of bitterness. He said he still saw many contradictions in Steven. He was not sure why Steven put up with his grandfather, but suspected that Steven sensed the old man's need for him.

When the writer causes us to speculate about what characters feel and do, he is on the way to writing complex characters. Having lived with the characters, the writer should eventually know a great deal about them. But there is mystery in people. Steven may not yet know why he puts up with his grandfather, and Steven's not knowing is, at the moment, the writer's not knowing. There might come a time in the revision process when the writer has an opinion on why—while the character may still be in the dark, unconscious of motives. And the writer can choose to leave him there.

Again, in *Birthday*, the physical action is minimal, but the gesture that is begun is completed. The two birthdays are toasted.

In general, the script works well. There is dramatic tension in it. And Steven and his grandfather have a great deal to say. They are verbal! They want to affect each other. There is a repeated move toward the window; Mr. Price makes it. We don't know what he's looking at, but we might well wonder what it is even though we understand that Price uses the window to escape from Steven or from any confrontation. At the end, he says that he looks at clouds; they lift him from his usual feeling of depression. We are getting to know this character. He thinks he's a bad person; he pushes the people he loves away from him; he refuses to admit to any of the softer emotions.

The drinking of a bottle of champagne is the major gesture of the scene. It is a simple act, but varied by the attention the writer gives to the ages and drinking experience of the characters. Steven finds and affords a bottle of champagne that pleases his grandfather. The scene is rounded out by beginning and ending with a reference to their birthdays and to their drinking the champagne toast to each other. In fact the scene is more than a scene. It is a small play. It finishes. The gestures of looking out the window and of drinking the bottle of champagne encompass the scene. The scene has a feeling of beginning, middle, and end partly because something that has begun is finished (champagne), something that is done once is repeated (window-gazing), and because Steven initiates and follows through on several changes with his grandfather.

Steven has an "I want." Several, really. He wants to write, he wants to get his grandfather's approval, he wants to show his father he is worth something, he wants to win the love of Laura. All of these "I wants" fit together. He wants to exercise his personal power as a human being to become someone. And yet to whom does he go for help? A man whose existence is spent tearing down others. The tension results from the audience's worrying that Steven won't make it, and that he's made himself too vulnerable with the wrong person. And by the end of the script we're still not sure Steven will make it, but we have hope for him: he's young and he's able to admit that he gets lonely.

And Mr. Price has several "I wants." He wants company. He wants to drive Steven away if Steven isn't strong enough to love him. He treats others meanly because he hates himself. He wants to love himself. He wants to justify his life. He wants to believe in himself. In the end, we find him as un-formed as a teenager. In the end, we see that his wants are not that different from Steven's.

Another thing that works well is the ending. Only the birthday celebration comes to an end. Mr. Price doesn't convert to a good old fellow and Stephen doesn't walk out. There are no easy solutions. Differences aren't glossed over. We suspect that Stephen will be like his grandfather in some ways and unlike him in others because that's the fate most people have when they come into the world. They are influenced for better and for worse by people they love. They try to do better than their ancestors did.

## Night Repair
### by Min-Juian Wang Chen

(The scene takes place in a bedroom. UL, a door leads to the living room. UR, a full-size bed. Next to the bed is a night-stand, on which there is a vase full of roses that have begun to wither. DR, a small dresser with a small mirror, a clock and some cosmetics on it. DL, an old closet with broken handles. All the furniture should look quite old except the sheet and the pillow cases.

When the scene begins, Su-Mei is sitting in front of the dresser, busy applying make-up to her face. She is 32 and quite attractive. She seems uneasy and discontent. On the whole she has a nice figure, though her chest is a little on the flat side. She only has a slip on and she has nothing on her feet. She is humming slowly a Chinese folksong. A few seconds later Su-Jen comes in from the UL door. She is 24, pale and slim. She is wearing an old black sweat shirt and a pair of gray sweat pants. She is not as attractive as Su-Mei, and she has a serious, haunted look on her face. It is late afternoon.)

SU-MEI

(humming) Though the sun goes down today, it will rise again tomorrow. Though the flowers wither too soon, they will come back in full bloom. And the bird of my youth flies away, it will never return. When the bird of my youth flies away, it will never return. Ta-ta-ta . . . Jesus!

SU-JEN

So, when do you have to go to work? (she sits down on the bed.)

SU-MEI

(trying to look relaxed, she looks at Su-Jen from the mirror) At six. (Pause.) But the manager likes me a lot, so I can get away with 6:10 or 6:15. (She looks at herself in the mirror.) You get to be good at this, you know. Now a lot of the ladies down in the night club ask how I do my eye shadows. (From the mirror, she catches a painful look in Su-Jen's face.) You know what, come here, let me put some eye shadows on you and let's see how it looks. Come on, don't look so serious.

SU-JEN

(almost in tears) I feel so awful seeing you like this, sis.

SU-MEI

(pretending to be in shock) Like what? In make-up? Come on, some day you'll want to use some make-up yourself. (She looks at herself in the mirror.) See, who can tell that I am thirty-two, and a mother of two children? People even send me flowers. (Pause.) That never happened in the past ten years.

SU-JEN

(as before) When did you leave that shoe factory? When? (Pause.) I should have stayed home to teach in some nearby high school. At least then . . . we could depend on each other . . .

SU-MEI

(trying to be strong) Nonsense. (She begins to put on lipstick.) I've been in the damn factory since I got divorced. (Pause.) It has been six years I worked there. Six years, and what do I get? Callosities on my hands. And they treated me like dirt. (Pause.) They treat everybody like dirt. (She turns around to face Su-Jen.) I don't have any degree . . . and you know that I couldn't save a penny from what I made in that factory. And I was told that Kwang's father doesn't even drive a taxi anymore. (Pause.) He just plays mah-jong. (She turns to face the mirror and plays with her lipstick. Pause.) I can't think about that now. (Pause. Meanwhile Su-Jen has calmed down.) Well, tonight we'll have guests from some big American computer company and the manager said that we must look sharp. Yup. Sharp. (She opens the dresser drawer and takes out several bottles of nail polish.) I'll bet that we'll get fat tips tonight. Then I want to get my babies new sneakers. *(turning to Su-Jen)* Hey, don't look so upset. Come and help me choose the right nail polish.

SU-JEN

Sis!

SU-MEI

Come on!

SU-JEN

*(jumping up from bedside, she walks toward the dresser)* That one. I don't know. The red one.

SU-MEI

*(doubtfully)* This red? *(She puts her left hand beside the bottle.)* Okay. *(Pause.)* What the heck! *(She starts to put nail polish on her fingernails.)*

SU-JEN

*(walking back to sit on the bedside)* You are going to Grandpa's grave with me tomorrow?

SU-MEI

Of course.

SU-JEN

Then don't drink too much tonight.

SU-MEI

Okay. *(Pause.)* So, how is that boyfriend of yours?

SU-JEN

*(Pause.)* He introduced me to his family last week. *(Pause.)* His mother asked me about you and what you do. *(Pause.)* She seemed to like me.

SU-MEI

Oh? *(Pause.)* So what did you tell her?

SU-JEN

I told her you work in a shoe factory.

SU-MEI

Of course. *(Pause.)*

SU-JEN

Your son will soon be twelve, you know.

SU-MEI

And I got wrinkles around my eyes. *(She looks into the mirror.)* Would you turn the light on?

SU-JEN

*(turning the light on)* You can't work in that place forever, you know.

SU-MEI

*(still looking at herself in the mirror, smiling to herself as if checking for wrinkles)* Hmm . . . you mentioned something that they have in the United States last night. What do they call it? *(She turns to Su-Jen.)* The Es- something.

SU-JEN

Estee Lauder. The "Night Repair".

SU-MEI

Where can you get that? Must be expensive.

SU-JEN

I guess. The teacher who sits next to me got one from her relatives.

SU-MEI

Oh. *(She has finished putting on the nail polish and she begins to blow on her fingernails.)* So, do you still want to go abroad and study?

SU-JEN

*(frowning, she crouches on the bed)* It depends on whether I get a scholarship or not . . .

SU-MEI

You know what? Down in the club we have a lot of customers from foreign countries, and almost all with degrees and titles, you know. Maybe I can ask them about it for you?

SU-JEN

*(bitterly, she is evidently shocked by the idea)* Don't you dare do anything like that . . . *(Pause.)* Please don't, sis.

SU-MEI

Okay, okay. *(Long pause.)*

SU-JEN

I guess you are not short of money now, are you?

SU-MEI

*(grinning)* Nope. Not at all. Save for yourself now, sis. You'll need it some day, who knows. *(Long pause.)*

SU-JEN

*(looking at the floor meditatively)* You know, last Friday I had this terrible dream. You were in it, too. And you looked so young. *(Pause.)* We were sitting right there on the living room sofa, and suddenly the wall became transparent. Then I saw Grandpa coming from the dark, having nothing on but a pair of underwear. *(Su-Mei listens attentively with growing pain in her expression.)* He didn't say anything. So we waited and waited but he just stood there. And finally he gave me a slow, sidelong glance. I shivered so badly that I couldn't move. *(Pause.)* It was like being nailed down and frozen by his glance. And then he walked away. *(Pause.)* He seemed hot and tired. *(Pause.)* There was anger, sis, *(she is now in tears)* in his glance . . . I didn't know what to do so I came home to see if we should go to his grave or something. And you gave me this. *(Su-Mei hands her paper towels.)* Why didn't you write to me or call me before you decided to work in that kind of place? And what are you going to do with . . . your kids? You can't just send them away to their grandma every evening and let them come back late at night to an empty house. And what am I going to do . . . how am I going to sleep at night, now that I know you work in that kind of place?

SU-MEI

Please don't cry.

SU-JEN

*(still in tears)* You are MY SISTER! *(Pause.)*

SU-MEI

*(handing Su-Jen more paper towels)* Pease don't cry. *(Long pause.)* I need to plan for my future, you know. Kwang's father won't give us a cent. What am I going to do with no money in my pocket? I know how little you make . . .

SU-JEN

*(She has stopped crying.)* Can't you learn something, anything?

SU-MEI

I knew that's what you were going to say. *(Pause.)* And for what? To make the same money I made from working in the factory? *(Long pause. Su-Jen looks sad and sober.)*

SU-JEN

You shouldn't have married so early.

SU-MEI

Too late, sis, too late. *(She glances at the clock.)* Gosh! *(She blows on her fingernails and walks to the closet, from which she pulls out a black dress and starts to dress herself.)* Don't be so upset, sis. It's not the end of the world. *(Pause. She says as if in contemplation)* In fact, that's what I told myself before I went down there for the interview. It's not really a bad place as you imagine, sis. *(She takes out pantyhose from the dresser drawer and begins to put it on.)* Some of the girls there are really very nice and I think I'll make some friends.

SU-JEN

Kwang told me you were probably drunk the other day.

SU-MEI

*(finishing putting on the hose, casually)* Oh, well, I guess I got really upset that day so I did it for real, you know. *(Pause.)* Kwang and her sister understood.

SU-JEN

*(sighing)* Sis! I really worry about you and the kids . . .

SU-MEI

Oh, don't worry. We'll be fine. I'll never be that foolish again. It was just one of those days, you know.

SU-JEN

You can't work in that kind of place forever.

SU-MEI

I know, I know. *(She opens the closet door and looks at herself in the big mirror behind the closet door; she holds her boobs up in her hand.)* Too small. Damn. Don't you ever feed your baby your own milk, you hear me? Remember that. Otherwise your boobs will be gone, just like that. *(Pause.)* But you don't have to worry about it, you'll find a good husband, I'm sure. *(Su-Jen smiles bitterly.)* Hmm . . . I guess I'll have to buy some new bras now. *(She walks to the dresser and gets out a wrist watch from the drawer.)* Got to hurry now. Oh, look at this watch this gentleman bought me as a gift last week. Foreign watch with Chinese numbers.

SU-JEN

*(annoyed)* Made in France.

SU-MEI

Neat, huh? *(Pause. She puts on the watch.)* Don't worry, sis. I'm not eighteen anymore, and I won't be cheated easily. *(Pause.)* Who knows, maybe I can get myself a husband there. *(seeing that Su-Jen seems to disapprove)* Well. Would you fix my hair for me? We are supposed to look sharp tonight, you know. *(Su-Jen slowly walks toward her and begins to comb Su-Mei's hair.)* I think I'll use this butterfly pin; *(she rummages in the drawer and takes out a red hair pin)* it goes with the color of my fingernails.

SU-JEN

*(giving Su-Mei's hair finishing touches)* Don't forget that we have to get up early tomorrow morning to get fresh carp from the fish market. *(Pause.)* Grandpa loved to eat carp so much.

SU-MEI

Yes. *(as if deep in thought)* Grandpa loved to eat carp. *(She looks at herself in the mirror.)* We must get fresh carp tomorrow. *(Pause.)* Hmm . . . what's that thing that could smooth out wrinkles called again?

SU-JEN

*(sadly)* Estee Lauder. The "Night Repair."

Like **Birthday**, this is a scene that is a small play because of its finished gestures. This writer introduced Su-Mei by having her hum a Chinese folksong while busily applying makeup. There is a contradiction in that, and it's a good thing. It leads us to understand the contradiction in her life and the conflict of the whole scene. Because it does all of that work, it is a very good beginning. And soon after Su-Mei has been introduced, Su-Jen is introduced. We immediately get a tension of character difference. She is dressed differently from Su-Mei and she moves in a different mood and rhythm.

The writer is from Taiwan. Her phrasing, which is formalized because English is a second language, lets us experience these characters as not Western even when the scene is performed by Western actresses (as I've seen it done in one instance).

At first we don't know what Su-Jen is doing there, but we eventually find out when she tells about the dream. The timing of this disclosure is appropriate. We don't have to know everything right away. The sense of the sisters' histories and sense of the community springs up around them as the play progresses.

It is a good idea, remember, to set up for things—jokes, entrances, mentions of important things. Notice that Estee Lauder's "Night Repair" is mentioned once fully before the last line. We have a context for it then. We know what it means. There is more than one reference to gifts from customers and the references are varied and they build tension.

And there is more than one reference to Grandfather and his grave. In this play Grandfather stands for tradition, the old ways, respectability. Su-Jen keeps bringing him up as if she is bringing him into the room to change her sister.

Both characters have "I wants." Su-Jen wants to change her sister, wants to talk her out of the night club job, wants to make her less Western, more traditional. Su-Jen wants to go back. Su-Mei wants to continue what she's been doing, she wants to make a lot of money, she wants to be attractive to Western men. She wants to change her appearance. She wants to embrace the modern world and the Western world. She wants to keep Su-Jen from suffering over the choices she has made. She doesn't try to change her little sister, but only to protect her own decision to live as she does and to pursue money. Both characters are clear. Both have motivations we can understand. Su-Mei wins this round. Su-Jen does her hair and gives her the information she wants. It's sad, touching, understandable.

The scene is also complete. One of the reasons it seems to finish is that the gesture or pantomime of getting dressed and ready for the nightclub carries the action. All the dialogue springs out of that situation. Something that is repeated several times is Su-Jen's combined quest: She wants to know how her sister got into this situation and she wants to change the situation. But the more knowledge she gets, the harder it is to change Su-Mei. Because this is ironic and because it is a peripety, too, a reversal of Su-Jen's intentions, the scene has a finished form. It is a small play-let.

---

### Study Questions and Exercises

1. Do an actor's motivation chart for Annie or Sarah in their scene with each other at the beginning of **Table Manners.**
2. What is the effect of grandfathers—a living one on stage, a deceased one mentioned throughout the other—in **Birthday** and **Night Repair**?
3. Name some ordinary actions that might carry a scene in a play. For example, a character talks while writing a letter, finishes the letter and the scene together. Or a woman scrubs the kitchen floor around her husband who sits in a chair while they decide that she will divorce him.

# NINE

# Internal and External Action

## OVERVIEW

The action in plays is both *external* and *internal*. External action is that obvious surface action that occurs on the stage—a man walks, speaks, throws a coat, or lights a cigarette. Internal action, on the other hand, is subtle and psychological. In this chapter, you will read and study two plays. The first play is *Home* by David Storey and the second is *True West* by Sam Shepard. *Home* is an example of a play in which most of the action is internal, and this chapter will discuss the internal action of *Home*. *True West* has a high degree of internal action but its external action is dominant. *Home* is a quieter play than *True West*.

This chapter will also deal with the structural points of most drama—inciting incident, crisis, climax—as they appear in *True West*. Then we will review and further explore the twenty principles, focusing on *True West* for examples.

## OBJECTIVES

At the end of this chapter, you should be able to

- Describe similarities and differences between internal action and external action
- Discuss the differences between the quiet action of *Home* and the more active, noisy action of *True West*
- Discuss the uses of irony and peripety in drama
- Explain the importance of providing preparation, execution, and follow-through in action when writing plays
- Recognize the building of tension in a play through the inciting incident, crisis, climax, and resolution

## Home *by David Storey*

You should now read David Storey's play *Home*. *Home* might seem an odd play to read at this juncture. For many people, upon first reading, it seems that nothing happens. No decisions are made, no action is taken. The characters are acted upon—by their pasts, by their society, by their craziness.

## Plot Summary of *Home* *by David Storey*

**Act I, Scene i.** A bare stage with a metalwork table and chairs. Harry, very properly attired, enters and sits formally, waiting. Eventually Jack, dressed similarly but more dandyishly, enters. They speak of Jack's recent illness, the front page story in the newspaper, the weather, other people whom they can see on the grounds, military services, relatives, marriage, their wives, women, Adam and Eve, travel. Jack does tricks with a coin and cards. They describe their jobs to each other: heating engineer and distributor of food in a wholesale store. They go for a walk.

**Scene ii.** The same. Kathleen and Marjorie enter, Kathleen limping. They argue about the weather; Kathleen complains about her painful shoes; Marjorie guesses at what will be served for lunch; they compare the place they're in with another "place." They complain about their husbands and trade stories about their own breakdowns.

Jack and Harry stroll by. The men's stories, the women note, are different from the ones they told yesterday. They all discuss some of the two thousand people who live in this place, the lack of chairs, the movie they saw last night, rumors that Harry was trying to get out. They intimate that Jack has a well-known and serious problem. Jack begins to cry. They go to the dining hall as two couples.

**Act II, Scene i.** The same. Alfred, a well-built young man, somewhat disheveled, attacks and wrestles with the metalwork table. Marjorie enters, looking for the others, whom she lost between "seconds" at lunch and remedials. She goes. Alfred struggles with one chair, then the other. He walks off with one of the chairs.

Kathleen and Harry, carrying a wicker chair, enter to find one chair missing. Kathleen sits. She challenges Harry about Jack's stories of being a doctor and a janitor and about his own lies. She points out that he uses the word "little" in every sentence. She asks Harry if it's true about Jack following little girls. Harry doesn't deny it. She tells about how Marjorie can't stop crying. Kathleen doesn't think marriage is possible. God is a bachelor, she notes. She tells Harry her husband's job makes him smell foul. Alfred comes in and leaves again. Harry begins to cry. Kathleen then tells him how she tried to commit suicide.

Jack and Marjorie enter with one wicker chair. Marjorie warns Harry that Kathleen can't resist men. Kathleen tells the men that Marjorie wets her pants. Marjorie quizzes Jack about little girls. Alfred continues to carry the chair around. Marjorie tells Alfred she's willing to fight him. Harry begins to cry and can't seem to stop. The women leave. Alfred takes the table away, then comes back for the metalwork chair. The men talk about armed services, science, finances. Alfred comes in and picks up the last metal chair. Jack shows card tricks and tries to entertain Harry, who weeps again. Alfred takes off the two wicker chairs. Jack cries too.

## About Home

The play is almost an illustration of two ways of being. One is depicted by the men who talk around things, always trying to come to a meeting of minds. The men work to squelch feelings of competitiveness, and agree silently to ignore each other's failings. The other way of being is shown by the women who say what's on their minds, insult each other, tell their histories, glory in their craziness.

Much of the action of *Home* is *internal*. What happens in the minds and spirits of the characters is the important thing. *Home* is a good play that is as quiet as a play can be. For some people it is too static and they see no movement at all in it. There *is* movement in it, but the movement is small. It is internal, psychological, and subtle. A production of this play is difficult to bring off.

The most commonly seen reaction of students to *Home* is that this play *must* be performed to be understood. However, all plays are written to be performed rather than read.

If, when you are writing, you are imagining readers rather than an audience, actors, and a stage, then you are in trouble. To write plays is to imagine them performed.

I will grant that the more experienced you are in theatre, the better able you will be to imagine a production of David Storey's *Home*. For one thing, the pauses, which are intentional, are filled with tension. The pauses are not imposed, but built into the subject matter and the conflict (which is about missed connections).

Although a few students said they felt Storey was withholding information by not writing "Institution for the Insane" as part of the scene setup, many were intrigued by the abstractness. Do you *need* to know where the characters are? Or is the play slightly dream-like, allowing the place to be no place, any place, and an institution all at the same time? One reader said she thought it was thought-provoking to think about the daily life of the insane. But this play is not really about the daily life of the insane. It's only on one level about an institution for the insane. It *is* about daily life, however. It is about people in their society, accepting routine, hiding behind social forms, looking for identity. All of the characters are in despair. The play is about that state of mind; and it is, as so many critics have pointed out, about England.

The title *Home* applies to many aspects of the play. Home is where the troubled never are, even when they are there. Home is what the lonely do not have. Home is being able to tell the truth, being at home with yourself. Home is an artificial place where people with similar problems come together. Home is peace of mind. (We use the expression that way. When someone is flaky or scattered, we say, "Nobody home.") The play is geared to showing *little* difference between the "insane" and others. So it is more appropriate not to say "Institution for the Insane" in the stage directions. The director or designer who puts a "Centercrest" sign on stage to clarify the setting is making a big mistake.

Some plays operate on the line between dreaming and waking and this is one of them. The place is a real place and not a real place. It is about "them," it is about us. Surely there is more than a table and chairs at any real place. But that's all we need in the place of this play. The setting, as always, is a metaphor for the action and the whole play is a metaphor for a lot of other actions.

The charge to make characters different from each other is upon all playwrights. And Storey does so. But in *Home* the differences are very subtle. Jack and Harry, at first, seem similar, partly because they both speak in fragments and they speak about all kinds of things. But they are different. Jack is the dandy; Harry is more conventional. They are differentiated by their dress and by ordinary behaviors. Harry is likely to be early. Jack is likely to be late. Storey tells us this with their entrances. Harry's thought patterns are slower than Jack's, who skips from one subject to another easily. Study the dialogue and you will see that Harry tries harder to stick to a subject and Jack is always looking for new and odd subjects. Harry is the heavier, more serious of the two, while Jack presents the more cheerful exterior and is the more verbally aggressive. So there is differentiation in these characters.

One way to think about the differences is in terms of "weights." *Character weights*, or *dramatic weights*, is a concept that directors use when they are casting a play. Weight is relative. The heavier character is the one who is more traditional, the one who moves less or more slowly, the one who considers things more—is more thoughtful—the one who pins the stage down. A lighter character tends to be more comic, more physically free, freer in language, the one who moves more often and more easily, the one who changes more often. When there are two men or two women with equal-sized parts, one is invariably heavier than the other. Sometimes, this takes a literal form in terms of real body weight, real pounds. However, it is possible for a chubby person to play a lightweight just as it is possible for an overweight person to be "light on his feet" as a dancer. So dramatic weights are not necessarily weights on the scale. Between the two women characters in *Home*, which is heavy? Which is light? One begins to see how the expression "a light woman" came into usage.

And between the men and the women—as character groups—the men are heavy, they weigh down the stage, while the women are the lighter force, more comic. Why is it that the men can't tolerate disagreement and the women can? What does that mean? Why do the men speak with upper-middle-class accents and the women in lower-class accents? The dialogue signifies that they do. Why the class difference? Why do the men hide their problems and the women flaunt theirs? Why do the women respond to things emotionally and the men intellectually? Both have had bad experiences, but they react differently.

Why are the men concerned with appearance and the women with comfort? This is manifested in, among other things, the preoccupation of the men with the story of the man (Saxton) who tripped and fell, or with the fiction of keeping a marriage intact when it is clearly on the rocks. The women talk about their rotten marriages, the food that will be served for lunch, and the shoes issued to Kathleen.

Why? This play is not a realistic play but a play about the conflict *inside* all people— between the polite and the natural, between the civilized and the barbaric. The playwright suggests the sadness of all people who do not know how petty and barbaric people really are. And the playwright also suggests that the conflict is England's conflict (not just a class conflict, although that is there)—a conflict between its intellectual life and its accomplishments on one side and the country's barbarism and spiritual failure on the other.

The characters do not always say what's on their minds. The men are so sad that they are given to bouts of tears. Harry feels he has disappointed God. The characters strive to fill in the gaps between people, to reach other human beings. All this is the meat of the play: people stretching and stretching to be better than they are, and failing. *Home* is a very sad play. Haunting. And also funny. It rides the line between tragedy and comedy and has a foot in both camps. It is a very difficult play to perform well. There has to be a full thought for every incomplete line and if the internal thinking of the actors is not good enough, the next response will lack sense. It is a good illustration of why an actor needs to work out a realistic thinking and feeling pattern, an inner life, to do a role.

I was fortunate to see Sir Ralph Richardson and Sir John Gielgud perform this play. The audience was literally silent at the end of the play when John Gielgud stood and cried. The effect was so overwhelming that people left the theatre without speaking. You could feel the quiet even out to the street.

The action of *Home* is as subtle and as internal as stage actions get. The important things happen *inside* Harry and Jack. Both men try to hold on to their civilization, to their lies, and both men just barely hold on. Harry breaks down, but Jack acts as a witness of and as a negator of the breakdown. Jack keeps going. He bails Harry out. This is both a blessing and a curse.

## True West *by Sam Shepard*

To make sure you understand the possible range between internal and external action in drama, next read *True West* by Sam Shepard.

### Plot Summary for *True West*

**Act I, Scene i.** The kitchen and alcove of an older home in a Southern California suburb, nighttime.

Austin, illuminated by candlelight, writes in a notebook at the kitchen table. His brother, Lee, illuminated by moonlight, stands at the kitchen counter, drinking a beer. Lee inquires how long mother will be gone and how long Austin will be able to have the place to himself. Austin tries to ignore Lee but Lee keeps talking. Austin grudgingly offers coffee, which Lee refuses, but he insists on borrowing Austin's car. Austin offers money, a place to sleep. Lee refuses.

**Scene ii.** The same morning. Austin waters plants while Lee comments on the number of locks in the house. He talks about his night travels, houses he "looks into," his time living in the desert. Austin reveals that he has a film producer coming over and he needs to see him alone. He gives Lee the car keys and tells him not to come back before six. Lee says he has some script ideas himself.

**Scene iii.** The same, afternoon. While Austin is talking with Saul Kimmer (the film producer), Lee enters carrying a stolen television set. He manages to set up a golf date with Saul for the following morning and begins to tell him about an idea he has for a Western. Austin gets very few words in. After Saul leaves, Austin asks for his car keys. Lee refuses.

**Scene iv.** Night. Austin is typing and Lee is drinking. Lee is dictating the script, which Austin questions, finding it contrived. Lee believes theft would be easier money than screenwriting, but Austin sells Lee on the idea of turning his life around. Lee has always wondered what it would be like to be Austin. Austin has always wondered about Lee's adventures.

**Act II, Scene v.** Morning. Austin washes dishes; Lee displays fancy golf clubs, which he says Saul gave him. Lee reveals that Saul will do his script and that he will drop Austin's script, but will get Austin to write Lee's play. Austin suspects that Lee beat Saul up. Austin asks for his car keys so that he can go to the desert to think. Lee refuses because he says they've got to get to writing.

**Scene vi.** Afternoon. Saul Kimmer, visiting, confirms that he is interested in Lee's story and wants Austin to write it. He doesn't bother to counter Austin's assertion that his interest in the script is connected to his losing a bet in a golf game. Lee reveals that the money is to go into a trust fund for their father, to be doled out slowly so that he doesn't drink it all up in one binge. Austin refuses to write the screenplay.

**Scene vii.** Night. Lee types. Austin sits on the floor, drunk. Lee wants him to go outside so he can concentrate, but Austin doesn't go. Lee then begs Austin to write the screenplay and promises to disappear back into the desert after they've made their money. They sit and drink. Austin tells a story about how their father tried to disappear into the desert. He tells about how their father lost all his real teeth and then his false teeth.

**Scene viii.** Very early morning. Lee smashes the typewriter with a golf club and burns pages of script in a bowl. There are stolen toasters everywhere. Austin polishes them. Lee tries to call a woman, but can't find a pencil to write down the phone number. Austin makes toast. When Austin tells Lee that he'd give up everything to go live in the desert, Lee makes him a deal: if Austin writes the screenplay and puts Lee's name on it and gives Lee all the money, he'll take him to the desert. Austin agrees.

**Scene ix.** Mid-day. The brothers are writing. Lee questions clichés and makes Austin rewrite them. Their mother enters and looks at her house, now a disaster. Lee tells his mother he'll need some of her china and silver because he's going to the desert to live. Austin tells Lee he can't give up their project and begs to go with him. Mother watches as Austin strangles Lee with a phone cord and demands his car keys back. Mother helps him get the keys and leaves to check into a motel. Lee is motionless. Austin tries to leave. Lee springs up and blocks his exit. The brothers, crouched in fighting positions, are still and watchful as the lights fade.

## About *True West*

*True West* is not without internal action, but the external physicality of the play is what strikes us first. A discussion of *True West* using the twenty principles follows.

1. The brothers are different from each other. Austin is educated and conventional, a "Yuppie" brother. Lee is unconventional, not educated, and a drifter. There is bound to be action born of this dynamic.

2. The setting is symbolic. The setting is the kitchen belonging to a very conventional woman who is their mother. It is ordinary, clean, and neat; Austin fits in. Lee's very presence is an invasion; his presence immediately begins to change the place. This is a metaphor for the ways in which Lee invades the life of his Yuppie brother.

3. Something is at stake for both brothers, and for the character of the producer and of the mother, who appears in the last scene. On a surface level, Austin wants to write a salable screenplay. Lee wants to horn in on the contact and make some money. Saul wants to buy a screenplay. But other, more important, things are at stake, too. Austin wants to express himself. Lee wants to become successful and respectable. Yet Austin, who is not particularly expressive, wants to be himself still. And so does Lee—who is hardly respectable. Their internal conflicts mirror the external conflict.

4. The characters want to do things that amount to *changing* the status quo. First of all, Austin tries to get rid of Lee. Austin wants to finish his screenplay. Lee wants to stay. Lee wants to meet a producer and to sell ideas. Austin wants to get his producer back on his side. There are enough *changes* in the works to keep this interesting.

5. At the center of the play is the salable screenplay—or the idea that will make for one. The pieces of paper, the idea, *will turn into money.* Everything that has to do with it becomes valuable—from the table on which Austin writes, to the typewriter, to the idea itself, to the peace and quiet that makes writing possible. The screenplay is the treasure.

6. There must be obstacles to the pursuit of the treasure; otherwise there is no play. Some of the obstacles are: (for Austin) lack of ideas that work, noise, Lee's presence, hangups about who he is and the life he has lived; (for Lee) illiteracy, no typewriter, no contacts.

7. Characters must try to get what they want more than once. If Austin tried to write that play once—in one scene only—the whole thing would fizzle. If Lee tried only once to tell his idea for a screenplay, the play would have no drive and no necessity. But Lee has the meeting with the producer, which "ups the ante" of the action because what he does furthers *his* attempt and also takes something away from his brother. By the second half of the play, Austin still wants to write a screenplay; Lee is still trying to sell his idea. But now he's trying to sell it to his brother. And now the screenplay Austin will try to write is both goal and obstacle.

8. Who lies? Pretends? Acts? Well, Austin does. He pretends he "has it together," that he likes his life the way it is. The producer pretends that he can betray one brother for another without any consequence. Austin pretends that he doesn't admire Lee. Lee pretends that he doesn't admire Austin.

9. The play's dialogue fulfills the two main requirements for dramatic dialogue. First, characters are differentiated by how they speak, and second, the dialogue *is* the action in

that through words, the characters attempt to affect each other and to alter the status quo. Austin's dialogue lets us know he is careful, ambitious, nervous, etc. And Lee's language is that of a man who is angry, uneducated, and aggressive. The result is quirky and comic—it's what attracts actors to the plays of Shepard—because of the way these brothers try to affect each other.

10. The physical drama of the play has a pattern that is almost dance-like. In the case of *True West* the physical drama is Lee's invasion of the house and his tracking of Austin. It imitates the story he tells about two cowboys, one chasing the other through the desert. It ends in violence— the persistent trashing of the house until the neat conventional kitchen is a landscape of broken things, dead plants, and of course, more toasters than anybody could imagine.

11. Shepard uses dramatic irony in the following ways. We know each character is lying to himself and will need to be found out. We wait for a resolution. We are satisfied when we see the brothers changing roles, becoming each other. It tells us we were right. This is a device that has to do with the superior knowledge of the audience.

12. Connected to irony is *peripety. Peripety: what is intended leads to its exact opposite.* In *True West* Austin tells about his producer friend to increase the distance between himself and his brother. But it doesn't work; his action boomerangs; he is not "one up" but "one down," for Lee is intrigued by the challenge of manipulating Saul; and the pay-off is that Saul is more interested in the rebel brother than the conventional one. He tries to humor Lee by helping him with the screenplay idea. He intends to put the wish to rest. Instead he inflames Lee to greater insistence, greater longing. Those are two reversals of intention—that is, peripety.

13. The best dramatic characters are complex and this rule *counts* even in odd, dark comedies such as this one is. The characters of *True West* are types and the play is a myth of our culture. But *still* there is character development. Austin is full of contradictions. He hates his brother and he likes him too. He hates his life and he loves it too. He wants to be free and doesn't know how to get free. He is educated, married, nervous, and serious. Actually, you see, we know a good deal about him.

14. Style is a matter of establishing a device and using it more than once. In *True West*, these things happen more than once: the action begins in the dark and the lights come up on a moment frozen in time. Most playwrights would show us the entrance, but Shepard, in not showing an entrance, suggests that Lee is a part of Austin always. The moment of intrusion is the important moment but Shepard chooses pretty consistently not to show it. He uses a late point of attack in the action of several scenes, catching the action when things are well underway.

15. Also, part of the style of this play comes from the off-center nature of its language and events—that is, one *could* say and do these things, but both words and actions are eccentric, stretched to the limits of credibility. Imagine what a big mistake Shepard would have made if he'd had Austin

steal money instead of toasters. The language makes the same strange turns.

16. Although plays should be full of surprises, the playwright must prepare for each of the surprises so that when watching we partly have a feeling of superiority ("Yes, I saw that coming"), and partly of the rightness of the surprise ("Of course!"). That means everything must be set up and framed. This includes, as we noted in the list of principles, entrances and exits as well as the use of props, even ideas. In this case one of the conventions is to do away with entrances and exits, and to start scenes right after the entrance has occurred. This is one of the things that makes this play distinctive. It isn't right for every play, certainly, because one of the joys of watching a good production of a good play is the art of entrances and exits. However, other things are framed in *True West*. It is important to see several times that the typewriter is valuable to Austin because there will be future action in which it is destroyed. It is important to establish that Lee sneaks into houses and steals whatever takes his fancy so that his challenge to Austin to steal toasters will work. It is important that the producer be mentioned before his appearance.

As important as preparation and execution is *follow-through.* Everything must have a pay-off. We hear about something, it is framed, then it happens, and it is important, and finally there is a consequence to the occurrence. The consequence is the follow-through. The toasters must pop. The thefts of appliances have to amount to something spectacular. And they do—a stage full of toasters popping is a memorable thing! The producer's role goes from promise to betrayal to promise again. Actions have three parts: preparation, execution, and follow-through.

17. *True West* is a good example of building tension— although all plays must build. (*Home* must build—and it does. It does all of what it does subtly.) A whole play from beginning to end must build. The action must accumulate tension and importance as it progresses. There must be more and more at stake and it must amount to something. When a play is building, when tension is mounting, we feel it physically. Most writers, directors, and actors have felt that human beings can't take steadily rising tension for two or three hours. That's why the graph in Figure 9.1 shows drops in tension, or *releases.* In fact, there is usually a release after each small scene as well.

For most plays there is a scene length that holds the rhythm of the *builds.* Sometimes it's three-quarters of a page, sometimes it's two pages. And these are the units by which the play moves. Stanislavsky instructed actors to find the units of a play, and he suggested that there were combinations of maybe eight smaller units in a larger unit and then combinations of larger units in still larger units. The markers for changes of unit are usually motivation changes, usually the result of one character's having affected another. The fabric of the play usually dictates the sizes of the units.

So actors learn to look for these units and to *build scenes*— or increase the dramatic tension and then release it—

accordingly. The techniques actors use to build a scene are the following: they sometimes increase in *speed*, sometimes in *volume*, sometimes in *slowness*, sometimes in the amount of *eye contact*, sometimes in the amount of *movement*. They know that whatever they start has to become more and more *something*, but there are psychological ways to build a scene as well. Actors playing a laughing, playful scene must get more and more playful until they reach the limits, actors playing at testing out each other for trust must get more and more suspicious, actors playing a fight scene must get more and more angry. One of the big rules for an actor is "don't play the end at the beginning. Conserve. Build the scene." If actors must build scenes, if actors must find an element and increase it as the scene progresses, if actors must conserve and not play the end at the beginning, it is *because drama works best that way* and because experienced playwrights give them scenes that do just that. Take for example the scene in which Lee persuades Austin to write his play for him. In that scene, Lee is wheedling, insisting on Austin's help, and Austin is humoring him, reluctantly. Lee's insistence must build and so must Austin's reluctance *and* his humoring of his brother.

Small scenes and large scenes will build, and the play will build too.

18. *True West*, like most plays, is dependent on irony. Plain irony, often defined as incongruity, is part of any play's appeal. That the unexpected and incongruous happen is germane to *True West*. When we get to the end of the play, we have the feeling that we have witnessed an incongruity, the unexpected, a wrongness, irony. It is ironic that Austin becomes a destructive thieving maniac. It is ironic that the clean, tidy, middle-class kitchen ends up like a desert junkyard. It is ironic that the brothers love and hate each other. It is ironic that they can affect each other so thoroughly. It is ironic that they are playing out Lee's screenplay.

19. Plays gather meaning and significance by the use of analogy. In many plays, it is possible to say A is like C and, therefore, A is to B as C is to D. (Formulas seem wrong, eh? But it's true! Plays often play themselves out analogically.) For instance, in *Home* the men are to the women as the middle classes are to the working classes in England (one of the meanings of *Home*). The men are to the women as the husbands (both sets) are to their wives (both sets). The institution they're in is like home, it is like England, it is like work (places of employment), and like marriage. The struggle inside the men in particular is *like* the historical struggle between primitive impulses and civilization. *Like* is an important word. Plays move by analogy.

In *True West* what happens on stage is *like* the script Lee has in mind. The brothers tracking a script idea are like the men who drive out into the desert to fight over a woman. When mother comes in we see that the brothers are like one- and two-year-olds playing in their feces. Adults are like children.

In plays we've dealt with before—the same rules hold. Regarding irony: *Streetcar* is ironic in that Blanche comes into the New Orleans apartment reluctantly and she leaves it reluctantly. It is ironic that she comes for protection and that she must leave for protection. It is ironic that the insanity that she is trying to escape is her only protection. And there are analogies. Blanche is like the child about to be raised by Stanley and Stella. Her expulsion from the apartment is like a birth. Blanche is fighting an inner war between primitive impulses and a civilized exterior. In the apartment she is fighting the same war externally, with Stanley as the "primitive" and herself as the civilized one. Insanity is *like* a death. What happens to Blanche is *like* murder. Shep Huntleigh is to the defeated Blanche as Mitch was to the still hopeful Blanche. The paper lanterns are to the harsh light as Blanche's language is to the rough truth.

20. Most plays have important structural points. They are the *inciting incident*, the *crisis*, and the *climax*. You can find them not only in most plays but in most scenes as well. The most commonly made illustration of the way to build a play or a story is a graph like Figure 9.1:

**Figure 9.1** The tension builds and releases more than once in this graph depicting a typical play.

The graph allows for releases, for drops in the tension at various points so that the tension can build up again.

*The inciting incident is the thing that makes the play happen as it does.* It is early in the play, usually before the end of the first act. It is an event that sparks the action. When you write it, you will know you have moved something. It is power-packed. In *True West* it is Lee's virtual announcement that he will take what he wants. He will stay and take Austin's car. In *Streetcar* it is Blanche's arrival. In *Glengarry* it is Levene's inability to buy leads from Williamson. In *Table Manners* it is Norman's arrival at the house, which fouls and exposes the vacation plans. The inciting incident is the event that makes everything else happen just as it does. So it carries a lot of weight.

The crisis is almost always at mid-point or just a little later. It is a mid-way decision point. As with a crisis point in an illness, something is being decided. The patient will live or die. In a play, the crisis is the point at which a decision is made. The character will do A or B. There are two choices. Of the two, one is made. In *True West* the crisis occurs when, at the end of Scene Four, Austin becomes a secretary and Lee becomes a writer. In *Streetcar* it occurs when Mitch abandons Blanche. In *Table Manners* the crisis comes at the point when Ruth laughs at Norman and Annie. And in *Glengarry* the crisis occurs when the investigation of the robbery begins. The crisis occurs when one possibility is being removed and the protagonist is gearing up to finish the action without choice.

And the third structural point is the climax—the point of highest tension—the culmination of all the tensions before. It usually comes close to the end of the play, although there is usually a resolution after it. In *True West* it is the chaotic smash-up scene. This is not only a big physical release but it is an action that brings all the previous tensions to a head. In *Glengarry* it is the "capture" of Levene. In *Streetcar* it is the rape. In *Table Manners* it is the fight at dinner. Note that after the climaxes, most plays have actions that require time to come down from the high point, and that there are varying lengths of resolution.

Each "scene" and "unit" has these points too. By "unit" I am referring to those three-quarters of a page or two-page sections of a play that have a build of their own. By "scene" I am referring to what are often—but not always—"French scenes," that is, changes in the stage population effected by an entrance or an exit, but what are certainly collections of units under a larger motivational unit. The case can be made for an inciting incident, a crisis, and a climax in each "build" or unit as well as in larger scenes. The units and builds are more unusual in Shepard than in other playwrights' works. Look at *True West*, the final third of Scene 7. Note how passing the bottle and changing of a subject are used to build and change the unit. The inciting incident is Lee's asking for help from Austin, who is drunk. The crisis or turning point is Lee's accepting a drink from Austin and accepting a change of subject (their father, the drunk). The climax is the end of the story about their father, the consummate loser.

---

### Study Questions and Exercises

1. Discuss irony in all the plays we have read thus far.
2. Discuss peripety in all the plays we have read thus far.
3. Find the inciting incident, crisis, and climax of a unit in *True West.*
4. Discuss the differences between the quiet action of *Home* and the active, noisy action of *True West.*
5. Write plot summaries of all the plays you are reading, including those from your group. What does describing action teach you?

# Dramatic Characters

## OVERVIEW

To strengthen your grasp of characterization, you should begin work on a scene in which your characters are involved in a changing relationship. You should study your characters. How do they react? What do they want? The bulk of this chapter is given to samples of students' work on Exercise 5. As you read their work, make sure you can imagine actors playing these roles. See if you can picture what the character is doing when silent. Ask yourself if you can see the characters in other situations. But first, study the exercise chart intended for actors as they work on characters. Playwrights, as well, can benefit from the exercise, which demands that you know your character in detail: how does he breathe? What is her income level? What attitudes does he have about religion? And so forth.

The scripts included here are *Disrepair*, *Initiation*, and *Passover*.

## OBJECTIVES

At the end of this chapter, you should be able to

- Discuss characterization in the work of others
- Learn to use the actor's exercise chart to help you determine aspects of your own characters
- Complete Exercise 5, which is to write a scene in which characters are caught in a changing relationship, the conflict of which tests what each wants, what each is willing to do to achieve that goal

Again, let's look at an actor's exercise that can help the writer. Let's work *backwards* from the actor to the expectation of what a playwright will provide the actor. Remember,

actors like to know a lot about their characters. Beginning actors often learn to do this by working out character biographies. One of the most useful guides to working out a stage characterization is the following chart. This one was developed by Jed Harris of Carnegie-Mellon University.

### Checklist for Character Biography

I. Intentions: What does the character do? Intentions can be explored by writing out a motivation chart for a section to see if intentions add up, if intentions take the form of actions, if there is cause and effect. For this the chart in Chapter 8 is a big help.
   a. Break part into small units (beats) of intention
   b. State intention as a strong positive verb-label in script
   c. Treat intentions in cause-and-effect manner
   d. Link intentions in larger units to discover motivating force
II. Means: How does character obtain desires?
   a. What is character willing to do to accomplish desires?
   b. What methods does character use? Violent/nonviolent, direct/indirect, honest/dishonest, tactful/blunt, etc.
   c. What obstacles does character have to overcome?
III. Dimensions of Characterization
   a. Physical
      1. sex
      2. age
      3. height and weight
      4. posture
      5. deformities
      6. health
      7. vocal quality
      8. physical and vocal rhythm and tempo

b. Sociology
   1. social class
   2. occupation
      A. frequency
      B. suitability
   3. income
   4. education
   5. home life
      A. relationship to parents/spouse/children
      B. physical surroundings
   6. religion
   7. race and nationality
   8. position in the community
   9. politics
   10. amusements
c. Psychology
   1. sex life
   2. moral attitudes
   3. temperament
   4. attitudes toward life/death

   5. complexes, phobias, neurotic-compassionate concerns
   6. inhibitions/exhibitions
IV. Character Mood Intensity—Total Nervosity
   a. Heartbeat
   b. Breathing
   c. State of perspiration
   d. Muscular tension
   e. Stomach condition
   f. Sensory condition
   g. Intelligence—kind
   h. Major disappointments/frustrations

Now if an actor needs to know *this* much about a character, where does she go to find out? To the script. To what the playwright provides in the lines of dialogue—whether the information comes directly or not. So the playwright has to know (consciously or not) this much about his characters too, because this is what the actor is trying to answer.

Next we will look at the characterization in *Disrepair*.

---

## Disrepair
*by Scott Sickles*

### CHARACTERS

MICHAEL, Early twenties. Amiable. Unkempt with hair that does what it wants, and clothes that are a bit baggy and probably don't match. He doesn't look like an explosion, but like someone who "always looks like he just woke up 10 minutes ago."

CLAIRE, Early twenties. Straightforward but polite. Always well groomed but dresses in a kind of makeshift sort of way that indicates she wore the first two articles of clothing that matched when she searched through the top of her hamper. Her hair is basically a "structured mess."

EVAN, Early twenties. Well meaning but blunt sort. Nice, short haircut. Dress is casual but neat: shirt tucked into jeans, etc.

### The Set

*A collegiate apartment. The door is in the DSL wall. At the DSR wall there is a kitchenette area (stove-sink-fridge from U to D, the fridge fitting under the counter) with a window with cute drapes above the sink. There are also cupboards. On the US wall there are three doors: two almost next to one another slightly right of the middle of the wall, and one about a third of the way in from the SL wall. At DSR there is a small round table surrounded by three chairs. At CSL there is an old sofa behind an old coffee table with cluttered papers and books. Between the two closed doors near USR there is a stereo system hooked up to two speakers which rest atop milk crates on the opposite sides of the doors (i.e., speaker-door-stereo-door-speaker). There are houseplants on top of the speakers. Between the leftmost speaker and the leftmost door on the US wall there is a shelf set with books, albums, a CD rack, and various knick-knacks. On the top of the shelves there is a tele-*

The writer has differentiated the characters, who are all the same age, by personality type. His first indication of type is done with costume. He may say more than he actually needs to, but he does have the advantage of having a clear idea of these people. Another way to give the actors and director this message is to sketch, in writing, a specific outfit meant as a clue, not a command, to costuming. Perhaps Claire wears a sequined tee-shirt and striped cotton pants.

This "playlet" is realistic in action and time scheme, so the writer has asked for a detailed set. The details specified will often be changed by a designer. But the writer has a use for some of the things he specifies—namely the doors, the CD player.

## The Play

### MICHAEL

*(A spotlight comes up on Michael who stands DSC. To the audience)* There are a great many inherent difficulties in caring about people who are mentally ill. I don't mean to sound pretentious. I mean none of the crazy people who I've cared about have actually been *diagnosed* as such. *(beat)* At least not yet. But it's kind of obvious. The sudden flashes of temper, the selective memories, the silly delusions like, for instance, the thought that God is manipulating traffic just to annoy *you* and no one else. It can be very difficult at times.

Evan is a great person; at least he can be if you're not requiring it from him at the moment. That's the problem. If it's his decision to come to the rescue, fine. But if you really need his help at the moment, and you don't even have to let him know—I think he can *sense* such expectations—he's either nowhere to be found or in such an entirely disagreeable mood you may as well face the crisis alone.

We used to be pretty close. Much closer than we are now, anyway. But that doesn't seem to say much. Whenever I used to mention one of my major flaws—all of us have them so they're okay to talk about sometimes—most people, friends that is, would say "Well, you know, you *could* do something about that." Others like Claire, my roommate, say, "Yeah, but so?" and not care about my flaws. *(Pause)* Evan denied that they even existed. He didn't think I was perfect or anything, he just thought I was taking things too seriously. So in the world according to Evan, I had no major flaws. Not that I believed it for an instant myself, but the illusion was incredibly comforting. Anymore, I wouldn't mind if he posted them in neon above my bedroom window; at least then I'd know he was paying attention.

Claire used to go out with him. When she moved back in town, she and I got a place together, and I introduced her to Evan. They broke up about a month ago. Why? Because he's nuts. I mean, he doesn't run around mutilating small animals or anything. But the sudden Jekyll-Hyde transformations aren't easy to cope with all the time.

Besides, "What the fuck do *you* want?" is not the standard answer to "Hi. What's up?" That doesn't happen often. But when it *does (beat)* I think I'd prefer being kicked in the stomach. Not that that would feel any different. But, it's better than nothing.

*(The light goes down.)*

*(After a moment, the lights come up on MICHAEL sitting on the floor between the stereo and the shelves, leaning on the door. He is nervously leafing through one of the CD stacks. He picks one, puts it in the CD player and starts it. He then takes the CD box and moves to put it back on the shelf, changes his mind, puts it on top of the stereo and runs into the leftmost rear door as Vivaldi's "The Four Seasons" begins softly. Pause. He then emerges from that room with his face and his bangs wet from splashing water on his face. He then takes the CD box over to the*

Having a character address the audience is a popular convention in today's theatre—as it was in other times. What can be gained by it? What does it replace? Does it put dramatic irony into play? When playwrights become too enamored of audience address, their plays often become unbalanced, with tiny scenes that are not really developed and very long monologues. This problem, however, does not occur here.

Is the character of Michael coming through? What do we know about him? He requires a lot of contact with people—primarily verbal contact. He is willing to talk about himself in disparaging terms to get it. He uses nonviolent means to get what he wants.

We know that he's in his early twenties and that he's male but his height and weight are open to different actors' possibilities. He should probably look imperfect—either gangly or too thin or a little overweight. This is a man whose posture is probably not so good (we get the clue from clothing and language) but who doesn't seem to have serious health problems or deformities. He probably speaks very fast, given how much he tries to fit into a sentence, but there seems to be an uneven rhythm to the fast speech. At first he's energetically assertive, then parenthetically apologetic. Speech has a slow-down, speed-up quality—like a driver going pretty fast, but not always concentrating.

The speech rhythm is borne out in the physical rhythm. Michael changes his mind mid-action. Notice he *nervously* leafs through CDs. He interrupts the action of putting the CD box away to run to the bathroom, then resumes the business with the CD box and tries to relax. We have a very clear image of how his chaotic emotional life comes through physically. The physical dimensions of characterization are handled by the playwright.

---

*phone. There can also be various posters on the wall or magazine cut out collages for atmosphere. It looks lived in.*

*shelf and puts it back. Wringing his hands, he crosses to the couch, plops down and leans back. He closes his eyes tightly and tries to get into the music. As he tries this, he starts to tap his right heel rapidly — not in time with the music. His face tenses, his fists clench, his whole leg begins to vibrate and he finally opens his eyes, lurches forward, lets out a frustrated groan and ends up holding his face between his fists. He lets out a deep breath, sits up, leans back, placing one hand in his lap and the other on the arm of the couch. As he looks around the place, his hand grips the edge of the arm and he starts tapping his heel again. He leaps to his feet and starts pacing around the room, laughing disbelievingly at times. Between laughs, there are mutterings of "Oh, God" and the like. He gets a glass from the cupboards above the kitchenette and a pitcher from the fridge and pours himself a drink. He puts the pitcher on the counter, sits down at the table, gulps down the drink, and puts the glass down on the table hard. His breathing quickens and he starts losing control of his emotions. He stands and braces himself on the table and calms down. He hears CLAIRE coming down the hall, singing something happy. He mutters something and runs into the bathroom again. (CLAIRE enters through the SL door, humming to herself.)*

CLAIRE

Michael, are you home? *(The toilet flushes.)* Guess so. *(She puts her things down on the coffee table and goes to the kitchenette. She gets a glass, pours herself a drink from the pitcher and puts the pitcher in the fridge.)* Michael, can I change the CD?

MICHAEL

*(Entering, after drying himself off)* Sure. I really wasn't in the mood for classical anyway.

CLAIRE

Great. *(As she changes the CD)* I just got back from Evan's. Which should I put in? The Chicago or the New Order?

MICHAEL

Definitely not the Chicago. *(As she puts in the New Order "Substance" CD — disc 1)* And how *was* Evan?

CLAIRE

He was in a pretty good mood I guess. What's for dinner?

MICHAEL

He was in a good mood, huh?

CLAIRE

Yeah. Why?

MICHAEL

*(Sharply)* Hm. No reason. I was thinking of ordering out Chinese or something. He was in a pretty good mood, you say?

CLAIRE

Yes. Is there any important reason he shouldn't be?

MICHAEL

How should I know? I don't have a grip on what he finds important. How was your day?

CLAIRE

Okay, I guess. How about yours?

In this case, everything is related to the character's mood intensity, nervosity. We could pretty easily answer the questions on the checklist: Heartbeat and breathing are fast. Breathing is probably shallow. This guy sweats. He has muscular tension associated with actions he tries to perform. He cannot sit still. He is unlikely, however, to have muscular *tone*. His stomach is probably over-digesting. Sensory condition? He doesn't "receive" well. He's so nervous that stimulation isn't coming in (he can't take in the music). His intelligence is quick. He's verbal. He is not street-smart. His major disappointment is being ignored. He needs much more from his friends than he's getting. He would rather be the friend, the child, the disappointed lover in a triangle, than be alone.

Do you know as much about Claire and Evan as you do about Michael? Are Claire's speech patterns similar to Michael's? Is this a good thing (their relationship) or an oversight on the part of the playwright?

Notice what Michael is willing to do to get what he wants. Does he prefer to adapt to Claire's musical tastes? Or does he really want a change of music?

The through-line of this piece is Michael's pursuit of recognition from Evan. When Evan is not on stage, Michael is smarting from the bad scene with Evan. When Claire is on stage, Michael asks about Evan. It helps to tie everything together. Begin to answer for yourself questions about the sociological and psychological dimensions of these characters. Can you make reasonable guesses about how much money they have, how often they go to class, what their politics and amusements are? See how many biographical details come through as you read on.

MICHAEL
Less than adequate.

CLAIRE
What's wrong?

MICHAEL
How long were you at Evan's?

CLAIRE
I dunno. Two—three hours. My last class was canceled today and I ran into him at—

MICHAEL
Did he mention seeing me at all?

CLAIRE
No. Not really.

MICHAEL
(Derisive laugh) In three hours of talking to you, he never mentioned me?

CLAIRE
Not that I can recall. What is it?

MICHAEL
Oh, we just spent an hour this afternoon screaming at each other, that's all. Nothing *important*, apparently.

CLAIRE
What was the fight about this time?

MICHAEL
S.O.S. I asked him to do me a favor and pick up a time schedule for me for next term since he was going that way anyway. Then he starts bitching to me about my having to start taking charge of my own life, instead of putting it on *his* shoulders. So, I reminded him of a few choice favors that I did for him and of my personal responsibilities which outweigh his considerably. So he bitched about me throwing everything in his face for about 20 minutes, and was stupid enough to ask if I agreed with him. When I didn't, he bellowed for an additional 15 minutes with no sign of stopping. I tried to interrupt him about I'd say 10 minutes into this tirade, and he tells me, *"Can I get a word in?"* At that point, I gave up.

CLAIRE
(Crosses to table) That reminds me. He did mention you. (Produces time schedule magazine) He wanted me to deliver this.

MICHAEL
(Pause, stolid) I can't believe this. Why can't he make up his mind as to whether or not he's an asshole? I mean: shit or get off the pot for Christ's sake!

CLAIRE
I guess he felt guilty.

MICHAEL
Blah! Why does he do this? Besides (goes to his room, the rightmost rear portal, returns with schedule) I went and got one myself anyway.

CLAIRE
Well. Good. I need one too, so I guess—

MICHAEL
Wait. (Switches schedules with her) Call me sentimental. (CLAIRE smiles at this.) Oh, you're supposed to call your mother.

CLAIRE
Oh? When did she call?

MICHAEL
Ummm. I think (beat) about a half hour ago.

CLAIRE
Did it sound important?

MICHAEL
I suppose. (Looks at schedule and smiles to himself) Unbelievable.

CLAIRE
(Nodding to herself) It's probably another one of my relatives dying. Shit. I'm not in the mood for this. (Goes into her room.)

MICHAEL
(Sits back down on sofa and leafs through schedule, sighs) Why do I let myself get so worked up? (Laughs quietly to himself and leafs through the pages. Then we hear an unintelligible scream from CLAIRE's room and MICHAEL jumps. He leans so as to look at her door while remaining seated. After a few seconds CLAIRE enters teary eyed.) Who kicked?

CLAIRE
Bartholomew.

MICHAEL
Bartholomew? (pauses to figure out who) Oh! Bartholomew! Oh, I'm really sorry. (She acknowledges him.) How did it happen?

CLAIRE
They're not sure. They think he was eaten.

MICHAEL
The dog next door?

CLAIRE
Probably. Who knows. I need a drink. (Goes to fridge and pours another glass of whatever's in the pitcher. As she does this, the phone on the shelves rings.) Could you get that please?

MICHAEL
(Gets the phone) Hello. (beat) Yes, she is, Evan, but she's kind of upset. (beat) The rabbit died. (Hands the phone to CLAIRE and sits at the table)

CLAIRE
(Takes phone) Hi. (beat) What? You're talking too fast. (beat) What are you talking about? (beat) No, I'm not. (beat) Yes, I'm positive. (pause) No, you silly, he was talking about Bartholomew—(beat) Bartholomew is not some guy; he's my pet bunny. Was, anyway. (tears up) Yes, he's dead. That's very astute. And if you even think of uttering the word

hossenpfeffer *(sic)* I'm putting lye in your underwear. *(beat)* Good boy. *(beat)* I just got back. I haven't had time to decide yet. *(pause)* Sure. *(beat)* Fine. I'll see you then. *(beat)* Uh-huh. Bye. *(Hangs up; sits next to MICHAEL shaking her head.)* He thought you meant I was currently with child. *(MICHAEL smiles, satisfied.)* I swear he's such a ninny sometimes.

MICHAEL

You know, he doesn't even say "Hello." He just asks, "Is Claire there?" Next time he does that, I swear I'll tell him, "Yes!" and hang up.

CLAIRE

It's not that big a deal.

MICHAEL

Well, he could at least acknowledge my presence! Watch: next time I see him, I'll thank him for the schedule and he'll brush it off.

CLAIRE

Well, your opportunity awaits you. He'll be here in an hour.

MICHAEL

Oh? Well if he said an hour then make it—

CLAIRE

He said a half hour. I know his timing.

MICHAEL

As do I.

CLAIRE

He wants to get back together.

MICHAEL

*(Freezes for a moment.)* With who?

CLAIRE

Michael.

MICHAEL

I know. I'm sorry. It's just that—it's hard enough when he's only driving one of us crazy. *(She nods)* Listen. It's up to you.

CLAIRE

I know. *(Pause)* I wish I had my rabbit.

MICHAEL

Why? *(He closes in around her.)* So you could avoid making a decision entirely by letting Barty attack Evan with his razor sharp claws and big gnashing teeth! *(She smiles at this and he hugs her from behind.)* I've gotta study. *(He stands and lets go of her. As he does this, one of her hands keeps a hold of his longer than it has to. He tousles her hair and she places her hands on the table. He crosses to the table and gets his things, while she watches him. He smiles at her and goes to his room. The lights fade, except for a spotlight on CLAIRE.)*

*(CLAIRE sits pensively for a moment and then leans back and addresses the audience)*

CLAIRE

I have this grudge with the word "just." Its two *(beat)* primary meanings, I guess you could say, are *fair* and *simply.*

My relationship with Michael has confused many of our acquaintances. Everyone assumes that since we live together there's something going on. We've been friends forever and maybe something would happen if we didn't know each other so well. But, if something like that *did* happen *(pause)*, I dunno; I think it would feel incestuous. Do you know what I mean? I dunno; it's weird.

Anyway, people always ask me when I start seeing someone, if Michael and I split up, or did Michael move out. And then I explain our situation and they say, "Oh. So you're dating so-and-so. And you and Mike are just friends. Right?" And I answer them honestly. I say, "No. Michael and I are friends. So-and-so and I are *just* dating." I honestly can't place Michael below anyone I've ever gone out with no matter how wonderful they were. Not that I've seen this myriad of Prince Charmings, God knows. But, there have been a few who could almost hold a candle to him.

At times, Evan could be one of them. The spontaneous foot massages; surprising me with heart-shaped balloons on a day that wasn't even *close* to Valentine's Day, my birthday, or any of our monthly anniversaries; and the bouquet of fifty dandelions after he helped "de-weed" his friend's uncle's lawn—it was *(pause)* the least dull ten and a half months of my life.

Unfortunately, there are only so many fights you can have when only one of you does all the yelling. So many times you can both be screaming the same side of the same argument, swearing up and down that the other person is wrong. So many times you can put a trash can next to the bed before you pour him into it. And so many times you can watch him ignore one of the people you care about the most, or ignore you to compensate for ignoring the other person.

It's just not just, if you ask me.

*(The lights fade.)*

*(The lights come back up on MICHAEL at the table, loading things into his book bag. Someone tries to open the door but it's locked, so they knock. MICHAEL looks irritated, does a quick relaxation exercise, and goes to the door. He lets EVAN in.)*

MICHAEL

Hi, Evan.

EVAN

*(Never makes direct eye contact with MICHAEL.)* Did Claire leave or something?

MICHAEL

No, she's in the bathroom. *(EVAN helps himself to the fridge)* Listen. Thanks for the schedule. I really appreciate it.

EVAN

*(EVAN pulls out a can of Pepsi)* Uh-huh.

MICHAEL

*(grimaces)* "Uh-huh." *(EVAN crosses to the couch, sits in the middle, picks up something to read off the table clutter, and puts his feet up on the coffee table. MICHAEL crosses to the table and continues stuffing his book bag.)*

EVAN

Will she be out of there anytime soon?

MICHAEL

(Pause) I don't know, really. I didn't ask what she had to evacuate exactly before she went in there, so your guess is as good as mine.

EVAN

Oh. (MICHAEL stops, nods, and goes back to organizing his stuff, looking very tense. Pause.) Mike.

MICHAEL

(Sigh) Yes?

EVAN

Sit down here for a moment, will you? (MICHAEL grabs the end of the table and pushes himself up. He crosses and sits to EVAN's right. EVAN puts his arm around MICHAEL. Can look MICHAEL in the eyes at this point) Mike, I need you to return a favor. (MIKE winces) I need to talk to Claire alone. No offense, but it's really personal. So I was hoping you'd go someplace else so we could talk—me and Claire, that is. (Squeezes MICHAEL slightly, to encourage.) Could you do that for me?

MICHAEL

I was going to the library to do some research anyway.

EVAN

(Shakes MICHAEL enthusiastically) Thanks! You're a great guy! (Removes his arm from MICHAEL's shoulder.)

MICHAEL

(Nods) I'm just so useful.

EVAN

(Considers this for a moment. Adds sincerely, as if it were a compliment.) Yeah. You really are. (Big, grateful smile. MICHAEL half smiles back. EVAN picks up what he was reading and continues to read it. MICHAEL looks at him quizzically and then leans his elbow on the right arm of the couch and his forehead on his palm. CLAIRE enters from the bathroom. She has been crying.)

CLAIRE

(Crosses and sits at EVAN's left.) Hi, there. Sorry, I took so long.

EVAN:

No problem. (Notices her eyes. Gravely serious.) What's the matter?

CLAIRE

Well, I just— (sighs) It's silly. But Barty died and when I went into my closet I found my pink, fuzzy bunny slippers and I just kinda lost it.

EVAN

Didn't your parakeet die just recently?

CLAIRE

Yeah. Two weeks ago. How sweet of you to remind me.

EVAN

Gee. Your pets are really dropping like flies, aren't they?

(MICHAEL slaps EVAN's arm slightly with the back of his left hand. EVAN takes no notice. CLAIRE just sort of looks at him funny.)

CLAIRE

(Cold, yet matter of factly.) Yes, I suppose they are.

EVAN

(Nods.) Bummer. (MICHAEL smiles and taps EVAN on the shoulder. EVAN turns around; behind him CLAIRE makes gestures indicating that she wants to strangle him, while MICHAEL whispers something in his ear. EVAN looks confused. Irritated.) What are you babbling about? (MICHAEL looks exasperated and whispers again. EVAN's face goes from confused and irritated to very amused.) Oh! I know what you're talking about! (MICHAEL slaps himself in the forehead with his palm. EVAN turns to CLAIRE, who has stopped, and tells her with enthusiasm.) Oh. This will definitely cheer you up. This is great! Bonus Dead Pet Stories!

CLAIRE

Do I want to hear this?

MICHAEL

Yes!

CLAIRE

Okay. (To MICHAEL) You, I trust. (To EVAN) Go ahead.

EVAN

(Starts off slightly confused by the trust remark.) Okay. You'll enjoy this. It even involves dead rodents, so you should be able to relate. (CLAIRE is irritated.) Trust me.

My cousin Kelly had these two gerbils, females, called Abigail and Marmalade. They were both female and she kept them in a nice clean cage and life was good. Then, one day, Abigail and Marmalade tried to mate. Yes, kiddies, we have lesbian gerbils here! So after a while of not succeeding in their efforts, Marmalade got so frustrated that she killed Abigail in a very brutal and disgusting manner that you need not hear about. It made my cousin Kelly toss her cookies, I'll tell you that much. Anyway, after the murder, Marmalade became psychotically lonely. And one day, she got into her exercise wheel and ran and ran and the wheel kept going faster and faster and then Marmalade lost her footing. She spun around the wheel a few times, ricocheting I guess, and was then hurtled out of the wheel with a force strong enough to open the door of the cage. She flew out of the cage and went SPLAT into Kelly's dresser. It was really gross.

CLAIRE

(Amused) Do tell.
    (Michael is holding his sides. EVAN gives CLAIRE a hug and nudges MICHAEL with his knee.)

MICHAEL

What? (EVAN turns around and glares.) Oh. Sorry. I gotta go.

CLAIRE

When will you be back? I need you to help me pack.

MICHAEL

Around ten.

EVAN

Where are you going?

CLAIRE

(Embarrassed.) Uh. Well, you see, it's my mother. She wants me to go home tomorrow for little Barty's funeral. We're burying him in the backyard between the canary and my little brother's python, which I never could stand anyway. But that's beside the point. You see, she won't bury him without me there. And the sooner I'm there, the less smelly the whole thing will be. My mother's weird, but I love her. And Michael has to help me pack because if I do it by myself, I'll take enough clothing for a month. And since I'm only going to be there a few hours that would be silly.
    (Everyone just sort of "is" for a moment.)

EVAN

How late will you be getting back?

CLAIRE

Considering the train time, late. Probably around 2:30 in the morning.

EVAN

Then I guess we're not going out tomorrow night.

CLAIRE

I think that's a reasonable assumption, yes.

EVAN

Oh. (Addresses MICHAEL who has gotten his schoolwork ready and is on his way out.) Mike. I'm free tomorrow night. Do you want to do something?

MICHAEL

(Exchanges glances with CLAIRE. But not about to pass up the opportunity.) Sure. Bye, all.

CLAIRE

Bye.

MICHAEL

(As he exits.) Goodbye, Evan.

EVAN

Huh? Yeah, see ya'. (The door shuts. He turns to CLAIRE and leans toward her to kiss her. She leans back to avoid it.)

CLAIRE

Evan, please. I'm not in the mood for this tonight.

EVAN

Why not? Is it the rabbit? (She nods.) Aww. Come here. (He gives her a big hug. When they let go, she's smiling. He slides over to the right end of the couch.) Lie down. (She pauses, smiles widely and does so. He begins to massage her feet.) Feeling better?

CLAIRE

(Content.) Mm. (Exhales) Evan. Have you and Michael been getting along okay?

EVAN

Yeah. I guess. We've been better; we've been worse. Why?

CLAIRE

Michael said you two had a fight today.

EVAN

Yeah. It was stupid.

CLAIRE

In what way?

EVAN

(Starts getting very tense) I dunno. I was just being an asshole. He asked me for a favor and I went off on him. It was my fault.

CLAIRE

Did you tell him that?

EVAN

I got him the schedule.

CLAIRE

I see. Don't you think, he'd prefer it—

EVAN

Have you thought about my proposal?

CLAIRE

Yes. And I don't think today is the right day to think about it. I've got too much on my mind. And it's not just Bartholomew dying. It's this and that and everything. I'm just a bit overwhelmed at the moment. I promise, though, I'll give you an answer soon.

EVAN

Stay there. (He gets up crosses to the left end of the couch. Gently tilts her body up so that he can sit beneath her. He starts massaging her temples.) How's that?

CLAIRE

Great. I'm just glad I washed my feet before you came by. (He smiles) I know you're doing this to score points with me.

EVAN

Are my motives that obvious?

CLAIRE

Naked.

EVAN

And are they working?

CLAIRE

(Opens her eyes) Give me a kiss. (He gives her a nice kiss—not too long and no slurping.) Thanks. And no, they're not working.

EVAN

Maybe I should stop.

CLAIRE

I didn't say they wouldn't work. Keep trying; nobody likes a quitter. (He continues the massage as the lights go down.)

*(The spotlight comes up on MICHAEL, as it did at the start of the play.)*

MICHAEL

Call me a nihilist, BUT . . .

I have this theory about depression. It's a very thorough disease. You see, you get depressed over something little and stupid. Then it affects your schoolwork and your job performance. Then you get even more depressed because your work and school are so bad, and you do even worse. Then, you lose your job, get kicked out of school and become so full of despair that you commit suicide. Then you probably get reincarnated as either an even more pathetic person, or you come back as a cow destined for the Golden Arches. I hope all this isn't *too* Shirley MacLaine for you all. But the reason behind all of this could be something incredibly silly. Like someone you really care about saying the wrong thing; using a rising inflection instead of a falling one. I have this tendency to be a bit overconscious about things like that. Saying things like, "Why did you look to the left when you said that?" Well, not that bad, but up there.

Evan is one of the only people who I have ever told, besides Claire of course, that I tried to kill myself once. My parents don't even know about this. What happened is that I was feeling very sick and very lonely and I swallowed a bottle of Tylenol, which most people don't know *is* lethal. Don't get any ideas out there. Anyway, I took the caplets and I lay down to die, not realizing at the time that it would take a few days to finish the job. I lay very still for about fifteen minutes. Then, all of a sudden, I got really nauseous. I ran to the bathroom and threw up everything. I was so mad at myself for being stupid enough to try this when I had been throwing up all day anyway, that I pounded my fists on the toilet seat and cursed a blue streak for I don't know how long. Then, suddenly, I stopped. I stopped because I realized I had the worst case of drymouth in history compounded by an unbearable Tylenol aftertaste. I then ransacked my room for gum, spent three days in bed, and had to make up an English Lit quiz at a later date.

I found the whole incident very embarrassing. And I knew telling Evan was a big risk. *(Pause)* He just looked me straight in the eye, listened, and when I finished, he gave me this tremendous hug. I could feel my rib cage start to buckle. It was a great moment.

We've had a few *(beat)* really great moments. *(Smiles sadly)*
  *(Light fades out)*
  *(The lights come up on EVAN standing in the bathroom doorway, his back to the audience.)*

EVAN

*(Drunkenly)* Are you okay, now?

MICHAEL

*(Off stage, drunk)* Much better.

EVAN

Okay, let me help you to the couch. *(EVAN helps MICHAEL out of the bathroom. They cross to the couch, slowly.)* Okay, you're doin' it.

MICHAEL

Evan! Evan. I just threw up, Evan.

EVAN

Yes you did.

MICHAEL

It was very pretty did you see it, Evan?

EVAN

Yes I saw it.

MICHAEL

And did you think it was pretty too?

EVAN

It was just abolooly, posilooly beautiful.

MICHAEL

Thank you, I try. *(They finally sit, resting their heads on each other's)* Did I flush?

EVAN

Several times.

MICHAEL

Good. Flushing is fun. Thanks for this, Evan. I had a really fun time.

EVAN

Sure.

MICHAEL

You said that yesterday.

EVAN

What?

MICHAEL

"Sure"—you said "sure" yesterday when I thanked you for the time schedule. *(As EVAN opens his mouth to speak)* Yes you did and you weren't being very nice at all you know sometimes you are the most impossible person to thank.

EVAN

You just called me "impossible."

MICHAEL

Did I? *(EVAN nods)* Well, then Poss Off! *(They both find this terribly amusing.)* You're much nicer when you're drunk.

EVAN

I'm a nice guy.

MICHAEL

Not always and not only when you're drunk but when you are you're a very nice person.

EVAN

I think I'm usually a pretty nice guy.

MICHAEL

I dunno. *(gulps)* Lately it's been kind of like having a beautiful, cloudless sunny day in the middle of a monsoon season. *(Their eyes meet. EVAN starts to giggle.)* You didn't get it.

EVAN

Yes, I did.

MICHAEL

No you didn't.

EVAN

*(Suddenly pissed.)* Yes I did. Goddammit! *(Pushes MICHAEL; pause)* I'm sorry.

MICHAEL

Wow, you even apologize when you're smashed too. We should definitely do this more often. I'm sorry. That was a mean thing to say.

EVAN

It's okay. I shoved you.

MICHAEL

When?

EVAN

Just now when you were being mean to me only before then when I apologized.

MICHAEL

Oh, is that what that was? I thought the room moved.

EVAN

Not to the best of my knowledge.

MICHAEL

Oh . . . Blah! *(pause; trying to summon courage.)* Blah. Blah. Blah.

EVAN

Blah?

MICHAEL

*(Nods as if to say, "pretty much.")* Blah. *(Sighs)* I'm just glad I'm drunk so I can bring myself to tell you these things.

EVAN

What things?

MICHAEL

Everything. *(Pause)* I mean we haven't been getting along swimmingly lately. *(EVAN grunts in acknowledgement)* I mean I know I could probably be a little nicer too but lately you've really been making me feel very defensive. And small. I mean I practically have to fire a cannon to get any kind of hello or goodbye from you. There are times when you make me wonder if I've vaporized at some point and just wasn't informed about it. *(EVAN pulls him up and puts an arm around him.)* It's just been really difficult.

EVAN

I'd never do anything to hurt you on purpose. You know that, don't you.

MICHAEL

Yeah, I guess. Although sometimes I have been moved to wonder if you were or not. Is he being a sadist? Or is he just being an asshole?

EVAN

Just being an asshole.

MICHAEL

I figured. *(Pause)* It's hard because I can't decide which is worse. I mean if you're doing these things on purpose, then at least I know I mean *something* to you. *(EVAN looks away)* And it's hard seeing you so often and still feeling like I miss you. I mean I miss you more now than when we went home last summer and I didn't see you at all. Do you know how awful it feels *(beat)* how it feels to miss someone while they're right in front of you?

EVAN

*(Shakes his head)* No.

MICHAEL

*(Smiles sadly)* God, I envy you.

EVAN

What can I say? I'm sorry.

MICHAEL

That's a step in the right direction. Do you mean it?

EVAN

Do I ever say anything I don't mean?

MICHAEL

Considering the things you said to me when we were fighting yesterday, you damn well better say things you don't mean!

EVAN

Well, I mean this.

MICHAEL

Good. Now I just hope you remember it in the morning.

EVAN

Mike! *(They look at each other. EVAN grabs MIKE by the face and bites his nose.)*

MICHAEL

*(Holding his nose.)* Ow!

EVAN

I would have kissed you but you just threw up.

MICHAEL

*(Nasally)* I should have sneezed in your mouth.

EVAN

*(Holds his nose; nasally)* Should you have? *(They pause and crack up. CLAIRE enters through the main door.)* Uh-oh, she's back! Pretend like nothing happened!

MICHAEL

I don't know, I think she knows.

CLAIRE

Hi, guys.

EVAN

We're not drunk!

MICHAEL

And we resent the insinuation! *(The guys crack up again.)*

CLAIRE

*(Smiles, crosses to table by kitchenette, puts her stuff on table)* Okay, I believe you. *(Goes into fridge and gets out Chinese food take-out box. Gets fork and starts eating at table.)*

MICHAEL

*(as the above is occurring)* How was the service?

CLAIRE

Oh, an arousingly large turnout for a rodent. Mostly family and friends. I did a very cruel thing and shot the dog next door with my brother's B.B. gun. It unfortunately lived. The mealy-mouthed neighbor kid confessed to ordering the assassination. So I managed to convince the 10 year old Mafia gang to do terrible things to him at school. One of those 10 year olds actually suggested hanging him upside down from the fluorescent lights naked after force feeding him Ex-Lax. Therefore, I must not have been the only negative influence on these children since I've been gone many months.

I see you guys had fun. Is everything straightened out?

MICHAEL

If he doesn't forget tomorrow morning.

EVAN

I won't forget. And if I do, you'll remind me as always.

MICHAEL

You hate it when I do that.

EVAN

I'll forgive you this time.

MICHAEL

Gee. Thanks.

EVAN

No problem. *(To CLAIRE)* Have you thought about it?

MICHAEL

Horny bastard, ain't he? I'm sorry.

EVAN

*(Covering MICHAEL's mouth)* Have you?

CLAIRE

I've thought about it.

EVAN

Good. That's all I wanted to know.

CLAIRE

I decided to say, "Yes." *(The guys clap and cheer.)* I did this of course against my better judgment, especially considering the evidence as I see it before me. But *(adds happily)* okay.

MICHAEL

There goes the neighborhood. Oh! If this is going to materialize you better fix that damn box spring because I — *(EVAN covers his mouth again.)*

CLAIRE

When am I ever *sure*? *(They just smile. She walks over and kisses them both on the top of the head, which produces a stifled "Aw" from MICHAEL.)* Good night.

EVAN *(and a stifled)* MICHAEL

Good night. *(EVAN drops his hand.)*

MICHAEL

Thank you.

EVAN

My hand was getting tired anyway.

MICHAEL

I mean for—

EVAN

I know. *(Pause. They hug. MICHAEL grunts from the pressure. They release.)* Good night.

MICHAEL

*(Nods)* I agree.
*(Lights)*

---

The class felt that the convention of the audience address was used consistently. The play framed—brought up and played with—the notions of mental illness (a strong word here for neurosis). Most of the group felt that Michael was clearly drawn as a person who nervously "picked up on everything." For various reasons, most of the class was unhappy with the rabbit joke. Some thought Claire was really pregnant and that it was a weak joke. Some thought it was a joke with unnecessary cruelty to animals. Some thought Claire would not be amused by any of the jokes about the rabbit or the gerbils. Many didn't believe that Claire would really go home for a rabbit's funeral. The joke would have to have more preparation and would have to do more work in the script to justify the writer's keeping it. It's a thin joke and a worn one, so it would be better to make it fresh, if possible.

There are other light comic moments that worked better for most people. For instance, the switching of time schedules has a ring of truth. It's an action that springs out of character.

Entrances require a build-up, or framing device. Is Evan's entrance satisfying? The longer we hear about a character before meeting that character, the more pressure is on the entrance. For instance, Molière has his characters talk about Tartuffe for two full acts before Tartuffe makes an entrance. But when Tartuffe does appear, it is well worth the wait. He both reaffirms everything we think about him and is even more horrible than we have imagined. Evan's entrance, given how much we've heard about him, could use a little more punch.

Is Claire's character consistent? She is a messy, soft sort of person. Is it easy to believe she would shoot the dog next door? The playwright reacted to this question by saying he believes people, when they're hurt, can be very vindictive. Does Claire's action work for you?

And the playwright said he wants to show that Evan "has a shallow grasp on things," which is why he releases tension with the gerbil joke. Does Evan's character come through?

Not everyone will agree on the answers to the questions I've raised. It's up to you to figure out what you think and how you would either defend the playwright's choices or suggest that he change them.

Now read *Initiation*, noticing, especially, the way the playwright has handled characterization.

### Initiation

*by Mary Hof*

*A churchyard. ROSEMARY (15) and LORI (younger) on the church steps, stage right, smoking cigarettes, a large red door behind them. The steps are curved, so that the slightly recessed doorway behind has the appearance of a small stage. Box hedges create the illusion of an enclosed room, of privacy, on the lawn.*

ROSEMARY'S MOM *(offstage left)*
*(hollers)* Rosemary!

LORI
*(looks up)* That's so gross, to holler like that.

ROSEMARY
It's embarrassing. I told her I'd be late. What's her problem?

LORI
It's the mother thing. It warps their brains.

ROSEMARY
I'll never be like that.

LORI
Wouldn't you just die if you were that old?

ROSEMARY
Being old wouldn't bother me. My grandma was so pretty, even right before she died. I remember her cutting paper dolls out of a sheet of newspaper. While she was folding the paper, she asked me, "Do you want the dolls to be boys or girls? Long hair or short? Wearing dresses or pants? Long sleeves?" And then she picked up the paper shears, big as her arm, and snipped away. When she pulled the dolls apart, there they were, all holding hands, and my grandmother holding them out. The sun came in the window behind her and through her dress. She was so tiny and thin, it seemed like she was made of paper like the dolls. She laughed, and I remember taking the dolls from her hands.

LORI
I'm going to tell Frank you play with paper dollies.

ROSEMARY
*(laughing)* Oh, no, not that.

ROSEMARY'S MOTHER *(offstage left)*
*(hollering)* Rosemary!

ROSEMARY
*(softly)* Bitch! *(hollering)* In a minute.

LORI
What's she want?

ROSEMARY
Dinner.

LORI
What are you having?

ROSEMARY
Chicken, I think.

LORI
I'm hungry. Let's go. Will she let me eat?

ROSEMARY
Go ahead, if you want. I have to wait for Frank. I have to tell him something.

LORI
Tell him what?

ROSEMARY
I can't tell you.

LORI
I won't tell anyone. What?

ROSEMARY
I'll tell you later. It's just that I have to tell him first. It wouldn't be fair to tell you first.

LORI
*(listening)* I hear a truck coming. Is that his?
*(From offstage left, the sound of the truck doors slamming, then FRANK [18] enters stage left, followed by his younger brother RAY [16].)*

FRANK
Hey, Rosemary. *(ROSEMARY smiles)*

LORI
Hi, Ray.

RAY
*(ignoring LORI)* Your Mom says come on home, she's tired of calling.

FRANK
Not yet. *(He sits behind ROSEMARY on the steps and wraps himself around her.)* I just got here.

RAY
She said come right now.

ROSEMARY
Lincoln freed the slaves. I don't have to listen.

RAY
I was just telling you.

LORI

Ray's a Mama's boy.

RAY

(throwing LORI over his shoulder) What'd you say, Weasel? (holding her upside down by the knees) What's that you said about me?

LORI

Nothing. (laughing) I didn't say nothing at all.
    (RAY puts her down on the grass. Now ROSEMARY and FRANK are left sitting on the steps alone, and it's like they are on a small stage within the stage. RAY and LORI sit on the grass and watch them. They are aware of being watched, although they don't openly acknowledge it.)

FRANK

What's the matter, honey? Why are you so down? (He plays with her hair, pulling it back.)

ROSEMARY

I don't know.

FRANK

I brought a six-pack. Ray can take Lori to the Dairy Queen while we go for a drive.

ROSEMARY

I'm pregnant.

FRANK

Don't say that. You can't be.

ROSEMARY

You know I can be.

FRANK

You were sure last time, too, remember? What makes you so sure?

ROSEMARY

I'm late.

FRANK

How late?

ROSEMARY

I'm a week behind, almost. I should have started Tuesday.

FRANK

That's only four days.

ROSEMARY'S MOTHER (offstage left)

(hollering) Rosemary!

ROSEMARY

I have to go. I'll be back in a bit. Wait for me. (She leaves stage left.)

FRANK

(puts his head down in his hands) Oh, God. Not this again.

RAY

What'll you do?

FRANK

I don't know. I don't know.

RAY

Will you marry her?

FRANK

No. I'll get some money. She can go to a doctor. Where'll I get the money?

LORI

She's not pregnant. She's late all the time. She always says she's pregnant, and then it turns out she's not.

RAY

Are you sure?

FRANK

You don't know what you're talking about. She could be. Three or four times this month, she could be.

LORI

I know she could be, but I bet she's not. Bet you twenty dollars.

RAY

Why's she say it then?

LORI

She does it for the attention. (Both boys are looking intently at LORI) Everybody acts upset and feels sorry for her for a week, and then she gets her period and everybody's happy and parties for a week. Then life gets boring again, for a while.

FRANK

That's the worst thing a girl could ever do.

RAY

It could be true this time.

FRANK

That's the worst, to lie like that. I'm just sweating.

RAY

Are you sure she's lying?

LORI

She lies like a rug. All the time.

RAY

Some friend you are.

LORI

Hey, I just don't think it's right. I'm late all the time, and I don't go around making a big deal about it, trying to scare my friends, just to get attention. I'm not that type of person.
    (Both boys laugh at this)

FRANK

(standing up) Is that so? Tell us all about it, Virgin-i-a.

RAY

Was it as good for you as it was for him? Where's Mr. Lucky hiding out right now?

*(ROSEMARY enters stage left. LORI moves over and sits on the church steps.)*

ROSEMARY
Are you leaving already?

FRANK
Honey, I have to get the truck back.

ROSEMARY
Will you come back tomorrow?

FRANK
Call me if anything happens. If it starts. *(He kisses her good-bye.)*
*(FRANK and RAY move offstage left)*

LORI
Bye, Ray. *(From offstage comes the sound of the pickup doors slamming, the engine starting, and then a horn tooting.)*

ROSEMARY
*(crying)* I miss him so much when he's gone. I wish we were married right now, so he wouldn't have to leave me.

LORI
*(lighting two cigarettes)* Here, have a smoke.

ROSEMARY
*(drying her eyes, taking the cigarette)* I hope it's a boy.

LORI
You're probably not.

ROSEMARY
I'm sure.

LORI
I'm late all the time.

ROSEMARY
This time I know. I feel it inside me. And something else.

LORI
What?

ROSEMARY
The last time we were together, Frank stayed in me a long time. He didn't, you know, finish right away. And then when he was done, he went to pull out, and I said, "Wait," because I wanted to see how it would feel, to feel him go small inside me.

LORI
That's weird. What'd it feel like?

ROSEMARY
It felt so odd, so soft and small, just for a moment. Then Frank held onto the rubber and pulled out, and I remember he said, "I can't do that. That's a good way to make a baby."

LORI
Wouldn't it be something, if it did happen that way?

ROSEMARY
Almost like it's planned that way. But it's not. I want a boy.

LORI
Would you get married before the baby's born?

ROSEMARY
We'd have to get married. Frank told me once we had to be careful, because if I got pregnant, then we'd have to get married.

LORI
What if he doesn't want to marry you?

ROSEMARY
Don't say that. Don't ever say that.

LORI
But what if? What'll you do?
*(ROSEMARY stands up and holds her cigarette out like a sword, thrusting lightly at the cigarette in LORI's hand.)*

LORI
Oh, no. *(laughing)* Not that again. Not the cigarette wars.
*(They parry back and forth, LORI mostly laughing and trying to keep from getting burned, until ROSEMARY knocks the cigarette out of her fingers. ROSEMARY stands serious, staring down at LORI, who backs as far away as possible)*

LORI
*(worried)* Don't burn me. Don't really burn me.

ROSEMARY
It doesn't hurt. I do it to myself all the time. *(She puts the cigarette to her arm; it sizzles)*

LORI
God, that's sick. How can you do that?

ROSEMARY
It doesn't hurt much if you do it to yourself.

LORI
It's so ugly.

ROSEMARY
It's like a tattoo, that's all. You want one?

LORI
No.

ROSEMARY
Sure? I can do it for you.

LORI
I'm sure.

ROSEMARY
*(sitting down again)* Ray likes you.

LORI
Nuh-uh. Who told you that? Did Frank tell you that?

ROSEMARY
*(smiling)* I don't want to say who told me. He's a little shy.

LORI
You're lying. I can always tell when you're lying.

ROSEMARY

If they come down tomorrow, want to go out in the truck with us? We can all go, like it's a double date, and drink some beer. It'll be fun.

LORI

What'll I wear?

ROSEMARY

Wear what you got on.

LORI

No, I mean really. What are you going to wear?

ROSEMARY

I never think that far ahead.

LORI

For real, Rosemary, what should I wear?

ROSEMARY

The jeans with bows and your Metallica shirt.

LORI

(examining ROSEMARY's arm) It's all puffy now.

ROSEMARY

It'll go down. Tomorrow it'll just be pink.

LORI

Give me one. (holding out her arm, closing her eyes) Will it hurt, really?

ROSEMARY

It only hurts when you hold back, just for a moment before you touch.

LORI

Oh! (ROSEMARY touches the cigarette to LORI's arm, and it sizzles)

ROSEMARY

You see?

LORI

I see what you mean.

ROSEMARY

Now we're twins. It doesn't hurt now, does it?

LORI

It kind of itches.

ROSEMARY

Scratch it, make it bleed. That way the scar will last.
    (both girls scratch their arms)

LORI

I can't wait until tomorrow. I wish it was tomorrow now.

ROSEMARY

Can't wait to guzzle that beer?

LORI

It's not that. I just want to go out in the truck. I'm tired of walking around, nothing to do.

ROSEMARY

It's not so great. It's just like walking, only you're riding, that's all. Let's take a walk down Main Street.

LORI

Let's make them drive around here before we go out in the country. I want everybody to see us. The truck is so cool.
    (They exit stage left.)

This is a rite of passage play. Even though it's a brief scene, there is something finished about it. Both Rosemary and Lori are learning about sex and sexuality; they are experimenting with rebellion, fear, excitement, and pain. Lori is jealous of Rosemary and wants to have her experiences. But she's younger. She's uncertain how to go about it. She is Rosemary's enemy and Rosemary's friend at the same time—willing to speak against her, determined to imitate her. There is a suggestion that Rosemary is in a similar but reversed relationship with her mother. There is a suggestion that both women are bound to hurt themselves.

Have you been able to answer questions posed by the characterization checklist? What is Lori willing to do to get what she wants? What is Rosemary willing to do? Are their methods direct or indirect? What do you know about the social class, home life, religion, politics of these characters and their families? What about sex life, moral attitudes? Can you extend these to attitudes about life and death? Do you believe the playwright knew enough about her characters when she wrote this?

One small technical matter: The playwright should introduce a few lines about the proximity of the church to the house and account for how Ray can bring word from Rosemary's mother and still use the truck. This is simple enough to do. All we need is a line or a speech about the landscape. (They always turn the truck around in her yard, or something like that.) Or we might actually hear mother's and Ray's voices offstage after we hear the truck.

Scripts, at this point in your writing, may not always resolve into finished small plays. If they don't, you still have a chance to explore characters, to show them in a changing relationship. In the next script, Shira and Aviva are cousins with a long history of holidays spent together and the kind of friendship that develops among family members. But as they move into their adult lives, Shira and Aviva have less in common than before.

This writer knows the characters and their sociological and psychological makeup. Has she found ways of conveying their sameness and their differences?

Next, get to know the characters in *Passover*.

## Passover
*by Sarabeth Sclove*

TIME: Passover (a Jewish holiday in the spring)

PLACE: Grandparent's house

SHIRA, 22, senior in college

AVIVA, 22, her cousin, also in college

*The living area of a house. The living room and dining room are open to each other, with the living room SL and the dining room table SR. Between them, to designate the difference, is a china cabinet against the US wall. To the right of the dining room table is a door leading to the kitchen.*

*SHIRA sits on couch in living room reading. AVIVA enters from front door offstage UL in high spirits.*

AVIVA

*(seeing SHIRA and coming to give her a hug)* Hey! When'd you get in?

SHIRA

*(rising to greet AVIVA, but not as happy as her cousin)* Just a few hours ago. Did you get in last night?

AVIVA

Yeah, my parents flew me in this year. Are your mom and Adam in yet? Are they driving too?

SHIRA

They should be here anytime. I think mom picked Adam up at school and then they headed out. Where's everyone else?

AVIVA

Mom, Dad and Jason went out to the airport to pick up Aaron and Naiomi, they'll be here soon. I came over to help Grandma. *(walking through dining room to kitchen)* Where is Grandma?

SHIRA

*(alone in living room and calling after her)* I asked her if she wanted help. She said not right now. Grandpa's at work, but he should be home soon. *(sitting back down on couch)* She didn't want any help right now.

*(AVIVA returns from the kitchen and takes a white tablecloth out of the china cabinet.)*

AVIVA

She said we should set the table. *(SHIRA joins AVIVA in getting dishes, silverware, napkins, glasses, etc. out of china cabinet)* How many are we for dinner tonight?

SHIRA

Well, there's the seven of you, Mom, Adam and I, and Grandma and Grandpa. Twelve.

AVIVA

*(flying out the table cloth and letting it float onto table)* Twelve, and soon thirteen, and fourteen . . . do you realize how big our family'll be once we all get married? *(laughs happily smoothing out and evening the tablecloth)* And how much family we'll have for Seder once we all have children? Grandma'll have to have another leaf made for the table!

SHIRA

*(annoyed)* Are you finished yet? *(AVIVA gives her a surprised look)* I'd like to get the plates down, that is if you're finished fluffing the tablecloth. *(moves around table, laying down plates)*

AVIVA

You're awfully cranky. Have a difficult drive?

SHIRA

*(still annoyed)* Yeah, I had a difficult drive. The drive is always difficult.

AVIVA

*(laying silverware around table and trying to remain chipper)* Well, you won't always have to make the drive alone. I hate flying alone. I hate having to figure out how much to tip the skycap, and if I don't tip him enough I hate worrying whether my luggage will make it on my plane or whether it'll end up in Montana or God knows where. And I hate having to figure out where my gate is, and then rushing down all those ramps, because my gate is always clear across the airport from wherever I've come in, and it's always the last gate, it's always like, gate 37C or something. *(smiling to herself)* But this time Daniel came with me. He arranged his flight so that it left after mine, and he took care of my bags, and made sure we left early enough so that I wouldn't have a canipshit rushing to the gate. He's really wonderful.

*(Both women have finished their tasks and are opposite each other at the heads of the table.)*

You haven't met Daniel, have you? It's unbelievable to me that he could be so important to me, and half of my family hasn't met him. *(in a singsong voice)* You will though, you will though, very soon.

SHIRA

Do you want to do napkins or glasses? *(AVIVA gives her a puzzled look)* Napkins or glasses?

AVIVA

Oh, napkins I guess. We're probably having salad, don't you think? And most people like an extra plate for the gefilte fish. Oh, and soup bowls! *(gets soup bowls, salad plates and fish plates out of china cabinet and begins to place around table)* You should see the matzo balls my mother made. They're big and fluffy and perfect circles. I hope someday I can make matzo balls as nice as my mother's. *(SHIRA places napkins and glasses around table)* Do you ever think about that kind of stuff? Like having your own Seder? Your own Shabbos dinner?

*(SHIRA turns away from AVIVA and fights not to cry.)*

SHIRA

*(at china cabinet)* I guess we'll need wine glasses.

AVIVA

Shira, what's wrong with you? You're all . . . you're not saying anything. Are you angry with me? *(SHIRA doesn't say anything. She moves around table, placing wine glasses.)* It's not fair for you to be angry with me and not tell me what I've done.

SHIRA

You know Aviva, you always expect things to be fair, and sometimes they just aren't.

AVIVA

What are you talking about? *(silence)* I don't know why you have to be this way. Why do you have to be all moody and everything? Everyone's going to be here soon and you're going to be a grouch. *(silence)* Fine, that's your business. If you want to talk, I'll listen, but I will not let you be a bitch to me when I haven't done anything wrong. *(surveying the table)* Now, what else do we need?

*(SHIRA stands at the table with a sorry dog expression. She looks as though she may break down, but will not allow herself to do so.)*

Oh my God, the Seder plate! Where's Grandma's Seder plate?

SHIRA

She has it in the kitchen.

AVIVA

Well then, all this table needs is a bouquet of flowers, and Grandpa will bring those, won't he? *(smiling and dreamy)* I hope Daniel will be just like Grandpa and have flowers for me and little toys for our children, and sit at the head of the table and bless everyone with words that make us feel special and . . . we'll just be happy.

SHIRA

*(giving a wry smile)* You're getting married.

AVIVA

Oh Shira, it was supposed to be a surprise. Please don't say anything. I want to surprise everyone at dinner tonight. *(goes to hug her)* But I'm glad you know, I'm glad someone knows! It was so difficult not to say anything to Mom or Dad last night. But look surprised at dinner, OK? I want everyone to be surprised. *(awkward silence while SHIRA moves away from AVIVA)* So, what are you up to? Are you seeing anyone special?

SHIRA

No, not anymore. A relationship just ended recently, a few days ago actually.

AVIVA

I'm sorry. Did it run its course or something?

SHIRA

No. No, not really, it ended on account of someone else.

AVIVA

*(happily)* So you're seeing someone else then?

SHIRA

Not quite yet.

AVIVA

But there is someone else in your life?

SHIRA

Unless I decide to terminate it.

AVIVA

Well, for goodness' sake, give it a chance. I'm going to check on Grandma. *(exiting)* Make sure we have enough chairs, will you?

*(scene ends with SHIRA alone at dining room table)*

A revised and expanded version of this script will follow in the next chapter. See if you can critique the earlier version. Ask, "What's at stake?" Are there sufficient character differences? Are characters believable? Can you identify a protagonist who is trying to *do* something? Can you watch that character trying more than once to accomplish an end, finally either succeeding or failing?

---

**Assignment: Exercise 5**

Concentrate on writing a scene in which a character acts on a decision and in which the action is completed. Knowing your characters will result in stronger characterization. In order to do this, ask yourself, "What are my characters trying to do? What are they willing to do to get what they want?" For this exercise, challenge yourself. Try an unusual setting or action, if you'd like. As you stretch yourself, try to write about people in a relationship that passes through a crisis. Make clear what circumstances change and how the relationship changes as a result.

---

**Study Questions and Exercises**

1. Make your own critical notes on your own script. What do you think should be changed? What do you intend?
2. Do a character biography for one of the brothers in **True West**. Find the reference or the quality of action in the script that has led you to discover this character.

# ELEVEN

# Revision

## OVERVIEW

There is a subject that sometimes daunts beginning writers and that is revision. Revision is the second stage of your work, and the third, fourth, fifth, etc. Ayckbourn's experience with *The Norman Conquests* is unusual. Ibsen wrote his first drafts in a few days, but he revised a play for a year or more. And Ibsen is not alone. Most first drafts should not be seen on paper, let alone on stage. Most writers need to experience the freedom of getting things down. Then they need to develop the discipline of cutting much of what they've written. In subsequent revisions, writers will change sentence structure and alter characters. It is important that you understand from the beginning that revision is *a necessary part of your work*. Your exercises will probably succeed in proportion to the number of times you re-work them. I suggest that before you show an exercise to a workshop or study group, you revise it several times.

In this chapter I will give notes on revision—that is, what to do when you revise. Your last two exercises (6 and 7) will be longer works. These are examples of both these. To help you think about revising your own works, read a revised version of *Deadlines*, with notes about the changes from the original, and *The Quality of Life*, a revision of *Passover*, which appeared in Chapter 10. You should try to critique these exercises asking, "Do scenes build?" "Do characters speak language that is interesting and filled with tension?" "Is there something at stake?" etc. You will do Exercise 6 at the end of this chapter.

## OBJECTIVES

At the end of this chapter, you should be able to

- Revise your scripts
- Point out structural properties and structural choices in plays that you read

- Complete Exercise 6, which is to either revise and expand something you have already written, or write a scene for a longer play that you have in mind for your final assignment

Certain issues come up again and again while writers are working on scripts. Here are some of the questions. Since they are typical problems to be worked through and may be helpful to you, they are included here.

## *Making Decisions*
### Technical Aspects of Theatre

**Q.** *There are so many things to know about the technical aspects of theatre—even about the parts of the stage and how doorways are used. How can I learn all that?*

**A.** It really is no accident that most playwrights who "get produced" come out of producing situations of one sort or another. Many playwrights have been actors, directors, stage managers, or people who worked on crews for a time. For instance, Ibsen stage-managed plays by Eugene Scribe. Probably the best way to get to know the materials of theatre is to work on productions. That is the *best* way. You will do more for your playwriting by becoming an assistant stage manager and by reading plays, one after another, than by reading other forms of literature or by watching films and television. Theatre is a field that you have to experience to really know.

If you want to write plays, go to every production you can get to. Then choose a theatre group and sign on for even a small crew position. At the least, ask to sit in on a few rehearsals somewhere. In some productions it won't be appropriate—maybe the actors need security and privacy to develop their roles, maybe the material is delicate—but someone somewhere will say yes. Then just absorb the process. The better the group, of course, the more you will learn. That's why it's advisable to sign on even as usher or a "gopher" just to get the experience.

## Flashbacks

**Q.** *What about using flashbacks? Isn't that a good way of getting some of the exposition across?*

**A.** At this early stage, flashbacks can get in the way of learning traditional dramatic technique. *Most* plays don't look backward. You can mention the exceptions all you want—*The Glass Menagerie, Death of a Salesman*—but you should be aware that they are exceptions. The *flashback*—going back to a previous scene before the present one or before the *narration*—is a narrative device. Every novelist and short story writer must learn to use flashbacks. But it's as unusual to tell a story for the stage in which flashbacks are dramatic (that is, in which they have an immediate impact on the present action) as it is unusual to write a novel without them.

Drama is a storytelling form with its focus, in most cases, on what *will* happen. Plays like *The Glass Menagerie*, a lyrical memory play with its main story in the past tense (something that *has* already happened) were for a long time the rare exception. More and more narration is being used today, making large scenes virtually flashbacks. Often it's difficult to give the overall play a sense of drive when so much of the action is in the past, although there are notable exceptions.

In any case it's a good idea to learn the craft of telling about the past through the present and there are ways to do it. For example: have characters fight about the past, or get nostalgic about the past. Have one character tell about a past event that is hidden from another character, or just let the characters *have pasts*. It's amazing how much of the present action we will understand without a flashback to show us the characters at younger ages. And remember, not all ideas are best realized as drama. Some ideas might make better short stories. If the story is internal, if the relationships made are internal and don't have external consequences, the story may not be right for the stage.

There is an unusual flashback sort of technique in Pinter's *Betrayal*. It's a play that goes backwards. Pinter starts at the end of the story and goes back to the beginning. The scenes show the characters at younger and younger stages of an adulterous affair. The effect is fascinating—but again it's a one-of-a-kind thing—because the adulterous and embittered middle-aged people are explained, even justified, when we see them caught almost innocently by the circumstances of attraction.

## Revealing Characters

**Q.** *I want to write a character who is an older woman who never married. Should this come through in character development or should I write "spinster" in the stage directions?*

**A.** When you include a one-word description for a character in the stage directions, you give the signal that you are drawing that character in a cartoonish way, exaggerating one aspect of the character and neglecting the others. You should also be aware that *spinster* is a little-used term these days because it carries the baggage of years of value judgments; it carries the assumption that the woman would not naturally choose this state. This is simply not true of many unmarried women, so it's a prejudicial and unspecific term. Better, if you want to draw a complex character, to let who she is come through in actions, not in labels.

**Q.** *How do characters ever become three-dimensional with only dialogue to develop them? How do I get it across?*

**A.** There are two things that help enormously with characterization: decisions and second thoughts. Dialogue—and a way of speaking—will do a great deal to tell us about characters. But more important is action. What they do, what they want, what they are willing to do to get what they want. That's how we understand character. And, certainly, face your characters with needs and wants. Give them actions. Face your characters with the need to make decisions. When characters make decisions, we know more about who they are. When characters re-do something, re-think something, when characters have second thoughts, we also know a great deal about them.

## Plot Ideas

**Q.** *Adultery and sex: why are so many plays about adultery and sex?*

**A.** In *Adultery in the Novel* (Baltimore: Johns Hopkins University Press, 1979), Tony Tanner suggests that adultery comes up often in fiction because it is a natural way to show one of the things fiction tends to be about: a contract being made, and a contract being broken. You have probably noticed by now that sexual behavior, infidelity, and adultery make their way quite often into plays as well. And for similar reasons. Plays are about situations loaded with tension. They are about pretending, lying, acting. And something at stake. The situation of infidelity, even proposed or imagined infidelity, is strong motivation for the stage.

**Q.** *I want to write a play about a girl who turns out to be a murderer. She has just opened fire on a street full of people and got away without being recognized. She's at home and she confesses to her mother. I'm having trouble with it, though.*

**A.** If this idea is for a short writing exercise, it's virtually impossible. Unless you are doing a spoof. Big subjects require big treatments. And a lot of care. For us to understand a mass murderer, we have to have some background, a context into which to put her. When events are so overly dramatic or melodramatic, we need *detail* to support them. I admit there would be a lot at stake, but the surprise is too much. And you have no time to prepare the audience to be surprised. The audience is learning along with the girl's mother a horrible, unacceptable truth. How can you tell us and help us to accept it and help us to care about what happens in five pages? Be aware of the size and complexity of the subject you are biting off. Write an earlier scene between the girl and her mother. There must be something interesting going on there.

**Q.** *Why is it so hard to write plays that work?*

**A.** In fact, it's true that very few good plays are written in any age. It's a very difficult form. You want to make the play credible in its own terms, you have to rely on dialogue to do most of the work, you want to write something significant, important without over-sentimentalizing the piece. Many novelists and short story writers and poets have come to me saying they thought they would just sit down and write a play only to find that what they wrote was dialogue that didn't tell a story or was otherwise undramatic. A play is not like a novel or a short story. Some part of the conflict has to be externalized, yet the characters must be complex enough to have internal lives.

Of course there are exceptions to everything. One student (Punnasak Sukee) wrote a fascinating short play between a man in black and a man in white. The man in black taunts the other about keeping a date with a woman he does not really like. The event, or occasion, is the night this man will meet the woman's parents. Only after a while does it become apparent that both characters are the same man with an internal struggle, because each "character" operates independently and argues interestingly. The conflict is externalized because White can't go out the door (into the rain) to meet the woman and can't call her either. Nor can he relax. Finally Black takes over, calls her, and White is able to sit down and relax.

### Finishing Scripts

**Q.** *What happens when you're facing a deadline — like for this group? I had three scripts and I hated them all.*

**A.** Choose one and finish it. You don't have to like it. You just have to do it. You should treasure your problems and your failures. I know that's hard to believe, but from those you will learn more than from your successes. If you are not trying things and seeing where they go wrong (and right), you are not working effectively. If you are going to write, you must get it out of your head that each line you put down must be good. Or each page. Or each draft. If you continue to write, you will change things many times. You may very well throw away 2,000 pages to get a good 120.

**Q.** *What if I am writing and writing — several scripts — and then none of them go anywhere?*

**A.** Give your character an action to accomplish, a goal, something that matters. When a script doesn't go anywhere, usually things are happening *to* a character and the character is inactive. Plays cannot be made out of passive charac-

ters. Even the Black and White characters described above are not passive. Black is trying to change White's mind. White is trying to talk himself into a relationship that isn't working. Both of these are actions.

### What Characters Want

**Q.** *I'm writing a confrontation scene that doesn't seem real. I don't know what's wrong. They just yell at each other.*

**A.** Maybe they're having too easy a time fighting. Most people do not want to fight. Most fights happen in spite of people's attempts to be reasonable or humorous or whatever. There is a wonderful fight between Brutus and Cassius in *Julius Caesar*. It's wonderful because we can feel it brewing while both characters, smarting with insults, try to patch things up. Then when they can't contain their anger any longer, and the fight erupts, it's believable.

There are things normal people *don't want*. They don't want to be afraid. They don't want to be mean. They don't want to be out of control. They don't want to be snide and sarcastic. When you write characters who are afraid or who lose control, make sure that those negative emotions come as a by-product of their pursuing positive emotions. Normal people want to maintain peace, make a point, show others where they're wrong, defend themselves. If the obstacles are great enough and the situation is loaded with intensity, people do things they don't want to do and feel things they don't want to feel. The things that emerge from an angry person should be the by-products of intentions, not the intentions themselves.

Once more, let's look at the issue discussed above as it relates to actors. Actors are told that to play fear they must try not to be afraid, to play drunk they must try not to be drunk. Characters, like the rest of us, don't want frightening or dangerous things to affect them. Once more, the playwright can learn from the principles of actor training.

## *Language*
### Revision

When you revise look for places in the script in which your characters speak too generally, lines on which they might be anybody, and figure out how to give them distinctive speech. Listen to people. What kinds of things do they do when they speak? Some people qualify what they're saying often, with lines like "Now, I did think about this, and you have to believe that I even asked around, but it seems that . . . " And others are abrupt, even rude. "I asked around. Believe it." And others are overly dramatic: "I asked *everywhere* and I know you're not going to believe this but—." To write dialogue with character, you have to first know your character, you have to make it a habit to listen to people and to notice the ways in which they speak. And you have to revise. Read your lines aloud. Find places that are difficult to read and make them move more fluidly.

## Cutting

A second thing to do when you revise is to cut lines. Almost everybody writes far more than is necessary for a given emotion or a given situation. (This is not the same thing as finding new actions to keep the verbal part of the play going during physical actions.) Search out repetitions. If Dad says, "I think that's a dumb idea," more than once, find out why Dad is stuck. He should say something else. Strict repetition is boring, but even general repetition without new stimulus is boring.

*Don't* pad your script. Padding does the opposite of what drama must do—and that is keep the tension going under every line. If characters go over the same ground and repeat the same sentiments without additional action and additional pressure on the script, then the drama lags.

## Larger Changes

And don't be afraid to make changes. You may write a character who laughs and teases another about some matter, maybe something serious like the health of the second. You may want to try responses that are not light-hearted at all. You say, "But that would change my character! I can't!" Of course you can. Revision also includes going back to the original idea if you find that it works better.

Another thing you may do when you revise is another kind of cutting. You may cut characters and elements of the setting as the focus of your work becomes clearer to you. You must understand that cutting does not diminish effectiveness. And there is no rule that says you can't substitute something for what you've cut, something fresh and unpredictable.

Following is a script that was done for Exercise 6. A really interesting aspect of it is that it is a story on the same themes as *Disrepair* by the same writer. And yet it's different enough to be another play altogether. In one sense, *Deadlines* is a revision of *Disrepair*.

## Using Workshop Notes to Revise

The version you see here is a second version of *Deadlines*—a revision of an earlier version, which took place at a college newspaper. The writer took notes in class and revised his script, using what made sense to him from the class's reactions. Here is what he wrote as the class spoke:

People didn't know it was a college newspaper. Kurt needs to be developed more. Rich is too egotistical to care about his flaws. References to Nicaragua and UCS are good. Also Kurt's avoiding the door works. Too much profanity.

The writer continued to make notes of his own on his work about how he wanted the characters to come across. Here are his thoughts:

The play is more about insecurity than anything else. Rick's frenzy is in his opening moves and in his speeches.

He's concerned about his inadequacies and overcompensates by being too demanding for the sake of efficiency. Kurt knows that he's important enough to Rick that he can afford to be inconsiderate sometimes. But he does feel badly about it. They have a very weird relationship and put up with each other's flaws constantly—in fact use them for entertainment. Rick's door speech is the character parodying himself. Vicky has a tumultuous and altogether confounding personal life, so she takes out her frustrations at the paper. She is instinctively attracted to men she can't have while Kurt needs to abuse women, or use them rather, when he doesn't like them. He requires forgiveness and in order to be forgiven, one must first sin. And his machismo act is clearly that, especially when Rick brings it down. Lara is a conformist who has no clue to reality. A good question is, "Why was she made Acting News Editor?" My answer: "Somebody screwed up." Re: profanity: Some people under pressure cuss a lot. . . .

Because of these notes, the playwright changed the newspaper from a college paper to a fledgling local paper. He expanded the parts of Kurt and Vicky, added a whole conversation between them to make them more believable. He improved on the first version. Here is the second version of *Deadlines*.

## Deadlines
*by Scott Sickles*

CHARACTERS: (All are in their mid to late twenties)
RICK, Patrick Crowley, the Editor in Chief of a local newspaper. He's a nondescript man. Very tense and frantic.

KURT, the Managing Editor. He is an attractive person, dressed casually for the office—nice shirt, sweater, nice jeans, Docksider shoes, no tie. Usually very laid back.

LARA, the Acting News Editor. Completely unqualified. Pretty-until-you-look-close woman wearing a ton of facial cosmetics and very big hair.

VICKY, Victoria Medoff, the Features Editor. She's an attractive, high strung, usually professional woman who's having a bad day. The only thing unprofessional about her appearance are her Reebok tennis shoes.

THE SET
*The door at SL reveals with reversed lettering on its window that this is the office of the "VILLAGE TIMES: Editor in Chief." There is a desk at DSC, the front of which is facing the audience. On the desk there is a telephone, blotter, bins of stationery supplies, and personal effects like an appointment book. Beside the desk on the right, adjacent yet perpendicular to it, there is a small work table just big enough to fit the IBM-PC and the laser printer beside it. Against the SR wall, there is a set of book shelves stacked with books, binders and random papers, and office supplies. On top of the shelves is a small, four-cup automatic drip coffee maker and a tray holding a small can of coffee, a jar of non-dairy creamer, a bowl of sugar with a spoon in it, four coffee mugs, four additional*

*teaspoons, and coffee filters. Behind the shelves USR are two filing cabinets. Between USC and USL there is a large drawing table, slanted so that the audience would not be able to see what is placed on it. There is a window at USR by the cabinets, and at USL behind the drawing table. Each window has drawn mini-blinds, open enough to let in the light of dusk.*

## THE PLAY

*(The stage is dark. The lights come up on RICK. He appears tired, flustered, and frantic as he pours himself a cup of coffee, notices a file left on top of the filing cabinet, and puts the cup down. He gets the file and starts to leaf through it to see if he still needs it. He sips his coffee and grimaces. He sets the file aside, puts sugar in his coffee, and opens the jar of creamer when he notices a pen on the floor. He picks up the pen and puts it on the desk. As he goes to put the creamer in his coffee he notices he still has the file out, so he takes the file to the second cabinet and files it. He seems perplexed as he looks into the drawer. He then mutters something under his breath, takes out a different file from this cabinet and replaces it in the first cabinet. He then, finally, goes back to the coffee cup, adds creamer, sips, and smiles. He crosses and sits at the desk. He sips, sets his cup off to the side, leans back in his chair and stretches. Still with his arms extended, RICK reaches over and grabs the opposite end of the desk, thus being face down across it. He tenses, then relaxes, and, still face down, grabs the phone. He sits up, dials, and leans back in his chair, waiting. When the party answers, he leans forward on his desk.)*

### RICK

Hi. Is this Printing? *(beat)* Good. And who is this? *(beat)* Okay, A.J., in the future please say the department so I know who I'm talking to. This is Patrick Crowley. I wanted to inform you that the Weekend Edition is going to be about 60 to 90 minutes late. Make sure everyone there knows so they're not all hanging around waiting for it. *(beat)* Thanks—I'm sorry, what was that? *(pause)* Thank you. I'm glad you enjoyed it. I had a lot of fun writing it. *(beat)* Thanks. *(beat)* Uh-huh. Goodbye.

*(Rick hangs up and collapses back on the desk for a moment. He then looks up at the phone and gives a quiet, disbelieving laugh. He turns serious again and leans back and rubs his eyes with his hands. There is a knock at the door. KURT enters, uninvited, and is carrying a portfolio.)*

### KURT

Hello, there.

### RICK

*(coldly)* Where have *you* been?

### KURT

*(apprehensively)* Well, I got in late, so I've been running around organizing ad layouts and the like and the classifieds. It's all done except news and features—

### RICK

*(with KURT)* ". . . news and features." I know. It's only most of the paper. But, I'm glad you've done the rest of it. *(As KURT is about to accept this gratitude)* You could have called

first *(KURT leans on the door, hanging his head and letting the portfolio hang from his fingertips)* or at least left a message for me *(KURT looks up)* and don't tell me you tried because my machine is fine and it would have recorded the call waiting beep if you were calling when someone else was; it has before.

### KURT

I'm sorry. It's just—*(beat)*—I made this spur of the moment date and I forgot. *(RICK looks back at him with utter disbelief.)* It was rude and insensitive of me and I should have called you, but—

### RICK

Save it. Please. *(Gets up and starts pacing around CS and SR; with disbelief)* Oh, God, a date? *(tosses hands in air, goes to shelves and pours a second cup of coffee.)* You made this spur of the moment date *(pause as he adds sugar)* and you forgot. *(Pause as he adds creamer; as he stirs angrily)* Well, just for your information *(Crossing back to desk)* I canceled a date *(sits)* and I remembered. *(puts second cup down beside first cup without noticing it.)* What are you grinning at, you pompous fool? *(KURT looks at the two cups; RICK looks at him confused for a moment and then discovers the cups for himself.)* Would you like a cup of coffee, Kurt?

### KURT

*(smirks, as he takes the portfolio behind the drawing table and starts laying out the poster-board-like contents of the portfolio)* Seriously, I'm sorry I screwed up your night. If it's any consolation, I had a lousy time.

### RICK

*(Sarcastic)* Really? Good. You know I derive such glee from your sexual dissatisfaction. I can now die in peace. What the hell difference does *that* make to me?

### KURT

Sorry. Is Vicky in to do the Features? I haven't seen her at all today.

### RICK

*(sigh)* You changed the subject, and yes she is, and she is a bitch on wheels. Some guy started checking her out in the lobby *(There is a knock at the door; RICK moves to answer it.)* and she just shot him this look and said, "Well, you're fucking subtle!" *(Opens door. It's LARA, carrying a small stack of papers.)* At long last, Lara. *(LARA holds out the papers as RICK crosses back to his desk. She is not pleased by this rebuff, but notices KURT and smiles brightly at him. KURT smiles back nervously. RICK leans on his desk and LARA crosses to him.)*

### LARA

Here are the revisions you wanted. *(KURT gets up from his stool and walks the long way around the front of the table and ends up by the door, where he was before, and shifts all the while, as the following occurs)* I took a few liberties, but I figured that I'd just use my best judgment and everything would turn out okay and it did. *(Holds out the papers to RICK.)*

RICK

*(Takes the papers)* Thank you. Good night. *(LARA gives RICK a snotty look, pivots, and crosses to the door. RICK notices LARA running her hand across KURT's chest as she exits. KURT's eyes are like saucers, and RICK looks on for a moment with disbelief.)* No. *(KURT averts his eyes.)* Last night? *(KURT looks up at the ceiling, like a trapped animal accepting the impossibility of escape. RICK getting progressively louder)* I thought I was angry before. I was mistaken. That, by comparison, was ecstatic bliss. Now. Now! I am angry! *(KURT stands in that spot by the door and stews)* You know I cannot stand her *(beat)* and that we—, *(beat)* but you just— *(temporarily at a loss)* You know, it seems that every time you stand by my door, I somehow end up being made to feel insignificant and small and even almost—almost *betrayed*—though I'm sure that's just my insecurities blowing things a bit out of proportion.

KURT

Just a tad.

RICK

SHUT UP! THAT'S IT! FROM THIS MOMENT ON YOU ARE PROHIBITED FROM STANDING NEAR MY DOOR! *(KURT goes back to the stool as RICK paces around the office frantically.)* GO BACK TO YOUR STOOL OR GO ANYWHERE IN THE FUCKING OFFICE BUT JUST STAY THE FUCK AWAY FROM MY FUCKING DOOR FROM NOW ON AND NEVER GO NEAR IT AGAIN EXCEPT WHEN ENTERING AND LEAVING! DON'T EVEN GO NEAR IT BY ACCIDENT! IS THAT CLEAR TO YOU? IS THAT UNDERSTOOD?

KURT

*(Suppressing laughter)* It's clear.

RICK

GOOD!

KURT

Feeling better?

RICK

Yeah. *(Picks up the news revisions.)* Thanks.

KURT

No problem.

RICK

I'm just very tired. *(As he starts to look over the papers)* I'm going to try to be a bit more pleasant from now—FUCK!

KURT

What? I'm nowhere near the door.

RICK

*(Absolute horror on his face as he looks over the papers)* Not you this time. It's that Mall Chick! I can't believe this. I'll be right back. *(Storms out.)*

KURT

*(Looks after RICK and just shrugs. He goes back to organizing his materials for a moment. Then he looks over at the desk. He spies*

the door. He crosses to the desk, staying clear of the door, and picks up the papers. He saunters over to the filing cabinets, back to the audience. When he turns back around and leans on one of the cabinets, his face, too, is in a complete state of shock. He flips a page and reads something and then starts to giggle.)* Oh, God. *(He crosses back to the desk, puts the papers down, and gets back to his stool just as RICK and LARA enter.)*

LARA

I fail to see what your problem is. *(To KURT)* Hi. *(Tosses hair back.)*

RICK

Kurt, could you excuse us, please. *(KURT jumps up, crosses gingerly to the door, cautiously grabs the doorknob and bolts through. RICK suppresses a wide, silly grin, and LARA just looks confused. RICK hands her her "work.")* Could you tell me what might be wrong with this?

LARA

*(Leafs through the pages quickly.)* Well, gee, they look fine to me, so I'll be going. Got a really big date tonight.

RICK

Freeze your ass! *(LARA freezes, more out of offense than respect. RICK proceeds to point out directly in front of her face the mistakes she made, and she never fails to look somewhere else or blow gum bubbles defiantly)* First of all, revisions are to be done on the computer and printed out. You made all revisions directly on the printout I gave you at 10:30 this morning and you did them in *pencil*. They were due here by 4:00, yet you delivered these to me at quarter of five without bothering to inform me that they would be late. I needed twenty lines cut and recommended thirty possibilities, and in six hours and forty five minutes you managed to cut twelve lines that were essential to stories and someone's by-line. *(Making eye contact)* They won't appreciate that. *(Resumes pointing)* And on top of this you add an extraneous five line editorial disclaimer about how the article on the drawbacks of S.D.I. does not necessarily reflect the opinions of this newspaper.

LARA

I am *for* S.D.I. and I felt that my voice as Acting News Editor should be heard loud and clear, and far and wide. After all that's what Freedom of the Press is all about!

RICK

The point is that out of a required twenty line cut, you cut a total of eight lines, one of which was a by-line, and insofar as the editorial note is concerned, current S.D.I. margins will still sacrifice at least forty major U.S. cities and cause a world-wide nuclear winter *regardless* of whether or not this newspaper thinks it's a *(reads)* "really nice idea."

LARA

Well, I just think that that's all bullshit anyway.

RICK

Well, then, I'd guess we'd better retract the whole article. *(LARA ignores him by pacing around the drawing table to look at what KURT has been doing.*) I mean who would listen to a report from the Union of Concerned Scientists if they suspected that *you* thought it was all bullshit.

LARA

*(noticing one of KURT's pages)* There's a shoe sale at K-Mart if you're interested.

RICK

Just make the revisions, so I can get them in without another delay. *(He holds the papers out to her. LARA gives him a look, ignores the papers, and crosses to the door. As she opens it)* Lara. *(She stops and looks.)* Don't come back tomorrow.

LARA

*(Gives RICK another snotty look as KURT enters; to KURT)* See you tonight. *(She exits)*

KURT

*(When the door closes, he points to it, indicating LARA)* Ba-ha. *(Goes back to his work.)* I just saw Vicky. *(RICK joins KURT behind the table and looks over the pages.)* She'll be right in just as soon as she's done bawling out half of her staff. Are they okay?

RICK

Her staff or these? *(KURT indicates the pages.)* Oh, yeah, they're great. Unfortunately, the News pages are going to take a little bit longer than anticipated.

KURT

I figured. Oh, well. Look on the bright side. I did her out of spite.

RICK

You make the male ego so respectable.

KURT

I try. *(VICKY storms into the office without knocking, carrying a printout.)* There she is!

VICKY

Hi, Kurt. Rick, I'm sorry this took so long but I've been having a few very bad days. *(She hands the printout to RICK who takes it back to the desk, looking it over.)* Everyone is turning articles in late. I tell them I have to cut a few lines and they take a shit fit. One of the recently-graduated-from-college-so-my-shit-smells-like-roses junior reporters demanded that I put ellipses everywhere I made a cut so that his readers would know his work was altered.

KURT

I never saw where you got off distorting dogma in the first place.

VICKY

I see no dogma in an article about Chuck Norris.

RICK

What about this one about real butter on popcorn?

VICKY

That's actually almost brilliant.

RICK

Isn't it written by the same guy who submitted the commentary on the historical ramifications of pantyhose on fashion, politics, and crime?

VICKY

If you put a thousand chimps behind typewriters, on a fluke, one of them can pump out Shakespeare. I think this is similar. *(RICK's phone rings. RICK reaches for it, but VICKY beats him to it. Into phone)* Victoria Medoff. *(beat)* Yes, he's right here. *(Hands phone to RICK)* It's for you.

RICK

Really? For me? *(Takes the phone)* Rick Crowley. *(beat)* Hi, Joe, what's up? *(During this, VICKY indicates to KURT that she wishes to look at the pages he's arranged for her. KURT welcomes her over and she goes behind the table. They collaborate quietly. Their conversation can slightly overlap RICK's.)* Yes, A.J. informed you correctly.

VICKY

*(Quietly, to KURT)* Heard you blew him off again. *(KURT looks irritated)* Do you treat all of your friends this way or just the ones who give a shit about you?

KURT

Look, I already discussed this with Rick and he knows I'm sorry.

RICK

Yeah, I know. And the real kicker is I miss my first deadline ever the night before a meeting with the corporate representative. You know, the people who let us exist.

VICKY

Why should you be sorry, when you know you're already forgiven. *(Before KURT can answer)* And if you're so sorry, why do you do it so often?

KURT

Listen. I don't have to justify anything to you. And I don't do this all the time. We haven't even had any time to schedule anything like this in months.

VICKY

I see. So this mini-reunion must have been an important event for the two of you.

RICK

Yeah. We will, sometime. Listen, I gotta go.

KURT

*(Accusing)* And why are we in such a lovely mood, today?

VICKY

I don't have to justify anything to you either; but I know what you're thinking and this has nothing to do with my menstrual cycle, so fuck off.

RICK

You do? Okay, I'll be right there to sign it for you. Uh-huh. Bye. *(Hangs up phone and looks over VICKY's work.)* Vicky, this looks fine. You can just prep them for the printer and get back to me later. I have to re-revise News myself.

KURT

VICKY

No problem. Why do you have to . . . *(pauses)* Oh, yeah. Her. *(Remembers)* Oh, Kurt, speaking of *her*, she was giving you raves in the Ladies' Lounge.

KURT

*(Blushing)* Thank you for letting me know this. *(pivots in his seat)* Let me just leap out the window now.

RICK

Kurt?! I'm shocked. I thought you'd be proud of something like this. *(KURT flips him a friendly finger.)* Oo. *(To VICKY)* Then I guess we won't publish it. I'll be right back. *(Grabs a pen and exits in a rush.)*

KURT

Where the hell do you get off dictating my personal life?

VICKY

Listen, when I have to put up with a lot of idiots who think sentence fragments and rampant comma placing is avant garde journalism, in addition to my own personal life doing flip flops around me, I don't need to find out that you're shitting all over Rick. Because when you do, it upsets him and when he gets upset I get even more upset. And when I see that you don't seem to give a shit either way it only pisses both of us off even more. Then we start screaming bloody murder at everyone around us. And then everybody knows not only *that* the people they work under are neurotic, but also *how* neurotic they are. It's all very political.

KURT

I'm sorry I upset everyone so much then. What's the matter?

VICKY

You keep *saying* you're sorry. Pretty soon you may as well just cry "Wolf" whenever you want to apologize for anything.

KURT

DAMMIT!! I SAID I WAS SORRY! *(Pause as they both are surprised.)* I know *(beat)* I apologize for a lot of things and there are probably a great many more things I should be sorry for that I'm not. But at least grant me this. I may not feel sorry when I say I am, but it eventually catches up with me. I mean, it may be on delay, but at least it's sincere. *(Pause)* So, what's the matter with you?

VICKY

Oh, just everything. I don't want to go into it right now.

KURT

Oh, come on. You can tell me. *(makes puppy dog faces)*

VICKY

*(Attempts to remain stolid, but in vain)* Okay, I'll let you know. I just want to tell Rick first.

KURT

No problem. Is it men trouble?

VICKY

*(Pauses, stiffening for a moment)* You could say that. *(They just nod.)* Here I am talking about *you* being self-centered, and I haven't even asked about you. How are you, Kurt?

KURT

Besides sorry? I dunno. I'm hanging in there, I suppose.

VICKY

Rick mentioned you were preparing a groundbreaking editorial series for the near future.

KURT

He didn't tell you what it's about, did he?

VICKY

Not yet. Why? Are you keeping it secret? *(KURT nods)* Why?

KURT

In case I can't finish it. Which could be likely.

VICKY

What's it about? I promise not to tell or laugh.

KURT

I can trust you?

VICKY

Hey. If you can't trust me, who can you trust?

KURT

*(Pause)* Rick.

VICKY

Ditto. And I'm sharing my personal life with both of you later. So you can tell me what your proposal is.

KURT

I'm doing the series about graffiti.

VICKY

No! That's a great idea.

KURT

Are you being sarcastic? Because I really don't need—

VICKY

No, I'm serious. I'm just sorry it's not my idea. Listen, if you need assistance, I'm willing.

KURT

How can you help me?

VICKY

*(Shrugs)* I can *(beat)* investigate the Ladies' Room stalls for you.

KURT

Good point. Are you sure you're not making fun of me?

VICKY

Kurt, please. Look at my mood lately. If I didn't like the idea, I would have told you so and given you fifty reasons why it would be trivial and petty, most of them unfair. I'm serious. If you need help, let me know? *(Extends hand.)*

KURT

*(Considers her a moment, then takes her hand.)* Okay. Deal.

VICKY

*(Shaking his hand)* I lied. I think the idea sucks. *(He looks panic stricken.)* I'm just kidding. *(He looks like he's thinking "Aren't I a chump," and she tousles his hair. He smirks in reply.)*

RICK

*(Entering)* I'm back. Any calls? *(They shake their heads. To VICKY)* Listen, since you're going back, could you deliver this memo to your lovely fashion reporter—

VICKY

*(Spastic)* OOOH! YUCK! BLAH! OOOH! BLECH! BLECH! YUCK!

RICK

*(After exchanging an astonished look with KURT)* Is that a no?

VICKY

Clearly a no! I cannot tolerate him.

KURT

Do I detect the surfacing of latent homophobia, perhaps?

VICKY

No. More like xenophobia. Anyone who smells like that and dresses like a cross between a Pizza Hut mint and Baskin and Robbin's sorbet section cannot be of this earth. *(beat)* And homophobia is the very last thing I could be accused of.

KURT

Why's that?

VICKY

Just trust me.

RICK

No.

VICKY

Yeah.

KURT

What?

RICK

*(Looks at VICKY seeking approval; she grants it. To KURT)* The last three men Vicky has tried to establish relationships with have been gay.

VICKY

Try four.

RICK and KURT

Four!?!

VICKY

Last night was numero quatro. Why do I attract gay men? Maybe I'm attracted to them, but why? They've all assured me that they were gay before they met me, so I don't have to feel as though I've converted them, but still.

KURT

And you really don't look that masculine.

RICK

Yeah, except for the Reeboks, you'd look almost entirely female—I mean feminine.

VICKY

*(genuinely upset)* Fuck you, both!

KURT

Vicky, we were just kidding.

VICKY

*(Shoots him a look)* I know. I'm sorry. I've just been really high strung lately.

RICK and KURT

Try Sanka brand! *(They both get up and high-five)*

VICKY

You two scare me sometimes. *(The phone rings; RICK answers it.)*

RICK

Rick Crowley. *(beat)* Yes she is. *(Hands phone to VICKY)* Why is it for you?

VICKY

I had my calls forwarded here. *(RICK and KURT just look at each other and nod.)* Victoria Medoff. *(beat)* What? WHAT! I don't care how it happened! Fix it! Listen, Conrad, I am on my way back and that printer better be working when I get there or I swear to God I'll make Nicaragua look like a docile nation! *(RICK and KURT just exchange glances and pace around the office, trying not to laugh.)* And tell that lobotomized mass of gleep we have for a fashion reporter that I have a memo for him from the CEO! And I want to see you in my office when we have a free moment. Goodbye! *(Hangs up)* I plan on apologizing to him and wipe those smirks off your faces. *(To RICK)* I'll see you in about half an hour. Bye, Kurt. *(KURT extends his arms and looks wounded. She rolls her eyes.)* Oh, Jesus. *(She gives him a hug.)* I'll see you. *(She leaves with some of KURT's pages and her printout.)*

RICK

*(leans on shelves, plays with sugar spoon)* I don't know how I'm gonna get all this done. In addition to revising and prepping the news section, I've got to finish the report for the Royce meeting tomorrow. I'm not going to get out of here until ten. I'm gonna end up studying the latest AP and UPI teletype dispatches until at least three. And then, I have to get up in time to be here for the corporate encounter at 9:30 and be prepared for a meeting with a potential sponsor at noon. *(with mock melodrama)* What am I gonna do!!!! *(sighs)* I seriously don't think I have the fortitude for this anymore. If I ever had it in the first place.

KURT

What are you talking about?

RICK

I think I should at least have the leadership skills to get an editor to edit.

KURT

Don't worry about her. Andrew will be back from vacation in a few days to resume his position over her. *(Sly grin)*

RICK

So *that's* why he recommended her.

KURT

Of course.

RICK

He'll be pissed when he finds out I fired her.

KURT

He won't care. The man has the morals of a snake. I'll be shocked if he doesn't bring a disease back with him. *(RICK looks amused.)* Yeah, I know who's talking, but he gives *me* room. Believe it or not.

RICK

I'll plead the fifth.

KURT

Thanks. *(beat)* And your leadership skills are fine. *(RICK doesn't believe him.)* Have you ever missed a deadline before? *(RICK shakes his head.)* There you go. *(RICK smiles.)* Listen, you just worry about the report for what's-his-name, the corporate asshole. I'll do the news. *(RICK is about to say something.)* No. I don't have plans tonight. I can stay another hour and do this.

RICK

Thank you.

KURT

It's the least I could do. I'll bring the revisions back to you before I put them on the pages.

RICK

Damn right you will. Oh, I meant to ask you: how's the series on graffiti coming?

KURT

Doing anything tomorrow night? *(RICK shakes his head.)* Come over, I'll tell you then. It'll give you time to prepare for my answer. *(RICK winces.)* Yeah. As for tonight, put on some Steely Dan. You'll feel better. *(RICK grins)* Later.

RICK

Bye. *(KURT leaves. RICK sits at his desk and turns his computer on. He takes a sip of coffee and makes an unpleasant face.)* Ugh. *(He goes back over to the shelves and pours yet a third cup.)*
   *(Lights.)*

When this version of *Deadlines*—the revision that was done after one workshop discussion and a class reading of the original script—came up in workshop again the class pointed out that there were still problems. Rick and Kurt seemed to have a clear focus—the newspaper. But when Vicky's role was expanded a second, personal, focus took over. Was everything integrated, really, they asked? Some felt the play was a well-done sit-com. But what that meant was that issues were glossed over and treated superficially. For some, the conversation in *Deadlines* was funny, but they felt it didn't ring true. The conflict and the resolution were external. The play—if it was to become a play—could use a bigger issue.

People said: there is a great deal of craft in this exercise. The writer is imaginative. The text is lively. And we can imagine it being staged. The interest in Kurt and Rick stems from the conflict set up at the beginning between two different personalities. This could have ironic implications throughout in a firmer, extended play. For instance, perhaps it's possible that Kurt, who is "laid back," is the one who gets everything done and Rick is really dependent on him. Or maybe Kurt's unethical personal life has implications for the ways he operates at the newspaper. Maybe he makes unethical power plays. Maybe he can sweet-talk Rick when it comes to assignments as well as he sweet-talks the women in his life. It is possible to steer this play-in-the-making away from the glibness of a sit-com if there are real power issues at stake, things that don't get solved by convenience or coincidence.

The playwright said he would think about all of this, should he do further work on this script. He still wanted the play to be about Rick and Kurt and about their insecurities. The insecurities of his characters attracted him most from the start. When a writer has a strong psychological interest in a story, that interest is usually the best key to working on it. It's the writer's motivation, and writers need "I want to's," as much as characters do.

A term later, we took *Deadlines* to a production workshop. The results are discussed in Chapter 15.

Here is an expansion and revision of *Passover* from the last chapter. There are several more characters. But that isn't the only change. The tone is more comic. The dialogue between Aviva and Shira is revised to be more believable. Shira emerges as both a member of the fold and an outcast, a person struggling to be heard in the face of an all-embracing family. About half of this revision appeared for Exercise 6 and then the rest for Exercise 7. Later we went on to give this material, too, a production workshop. I'll talk about that along with *Deadlines* in a later chapter.

You might become aware, as you read, of what appear to be run-on sentences. The writer acknowledges them and explained to the class that they represent the way this Jewish family phrases things. Does this work for you?

## The Quality of Life
*by Sarabeth Sclove*

TIME: Passover

PLACE: Grandparents' house
   —somewhere in the eastern midwest

CHARACTERS

ABRAHAM, grandfather, 78

ESTHER, grandmother, 76

REBECCA, eldest daughter, 54

RACHEL, younger daughter, 48

AVIVA, Rebecca's daughter, 22

SHIRA, Rachel's daughter, 22

SCENE ONE

*The living area of a house. The living room and dining room are open to each other, with the living room SL and the dining room table SR. Between them, to designate the difference, is a china cabinet against the US wall. To the right of the dining room table is a door leading to the kitchen.*

*(ESTHER, busy vacuuming living room. SHIRA enters through front door USL into living room carrying travel bag.)*

SHIRA

*(putting down bag, walks up to ESTHER)* Hello Grandma. *(ESTHER does not hear her over machine. SHIRA puts her face in Esther's path. Louder.)* Hello, Grandma.

ESTHER

*(very startled)* Oh-mi-God! *(turns off vacuum)* Shira! Well my God, Shira, you startled me! *(sits down)*

SHIRA

I'm sorry, Grandma, I really am sorry. Can I get you a glass of water or something?

ESTHER

*(getting up and hugging SHIRA)* No, no. I'm sorry, baby, I didn't mean to make you feel bad. Did you have a nice trip? *(looking out in direction of front door)* Where'd you park your car? I hope you left room for Grandpa to get his car in the garage. Have you eaten? *(heads off towards kitchen)* I've got sliced turkey, and yellow cheese, I just took them out of the freezer this morning. Come on, I'll make you a sandwich, you can help me get rid of the bread. *(exits to kitchen)*

SHIRA

*(calling)* I'm not really hungry, Grandma. I packed a sandwich for the road and some pretzels and things.

ESTHER

*(entering with tray of cheese and crackers)* Well, maybe you'll help me finish off the crackers; the turkey's not thawed yet. *(Both sit at dining room table. ESTHER unwraps cheese from freezer wrap and pours some crackers onto tray.)* Now don't feel like you have to eat, Shira. I saw one of those programs on children with eating disorders, and I said to myself, God forbid I should be one of those mothers who makes their children eat only so they'll throw it up later. *(eating)* There's no pressure here. Listen, what bread we don't eat I'm going to put in the freezer in the garage. The rabbi said it's no sense giving it to the poor, they don't take opened food any more.

SHIRA

*(eating)* Is that kosher though? To have it in the house?

ESTHER

It's not in the house. It's in the garage. If I put it in the basement freezer, then it would be in the house.

SHIRA

I always thought it had to do with being under your roof or something, nothing with yeast under your roof.

ESTHER

You want me to get rid of the bread, Shira?

SHIRA

No, Grandma, I don't care what you do with the bread. I was just telling you what they'd always taught us was traditional.

ESTHER

I know the tradition. *(eating)* Listen, I won't eat bread for eight days, but I will not throw out all my bread and crackers and cereal and noodles and muffin mixes and pancake mixes and cake mixes, and what ever else rises, no sir, I'll put them in the outside freezer.

SHIRA

I agree with you, Grandma. I think I'd do the same.

ESTHER

Well, that'll be your decision when the time comes. You never know, Shira, you never know the way you're gonna be. *(pause)* How's school? Have you heard from those graduate schools yet?

SHIRA

No, I won't till the end of the month, but I'm kind of thinking it wouldn't be all that bad not to be accepted. *(ESTHER looks as though she's going to interrupt her)* Because I wonder if I shouldn't earn some money first, in case of emergencies, because you never know what's going to come up, and I'd feel a lot better knowing I had money in the bank, because at the end of this semester I'll have used up what I saved in high school and summers and I'd like to have something behind me. It would also give me a chance to figure out what I'm doing.

ESTHER

I thought you knew what you were doing. I thought you wanted to become a teacher.

SHIRA

Yeah, I do, it's just that I could really use some time to think, Grandma.

ESTHER

You don't think you'll be accepted.

SHIRA

No, I know I'll be accepted. I'm just feeling rushed, like things are going a little too fast, and I need time to sort things out. The problem is I need the time now, and I'm talking about taking time then, so I don't know, Grandma, I really don't know what's going to happen.

ESTHER
It sounds to me like you're nervous about graduation and what that means about who you are and becoming an adult.

SHIRA
You sound like my mother.

ESTHER
Well, I'm your mother's mother.

SHIRA
No, I mean, she just said something like that to me the other day.

ESTHER
Alright, so . . . *(pause)* we're concerned about you.
*(REBECCA enters from front door carrying large pot of soup)*

REBECCA
*(sing songy voice)* Halloo? *(sees them at table. Places pot on table. SHIRA rises to give her a hug.)* I thought that might be your car in the driveway. Is your mother in yet? *(SHIRA shakes head. REBECCA hugs ESTHER)* Happy Passover, Mother.

ESTHER
*(pointing to pot)* What is that?

REBECCA
That is the matzo ball soup. I brought it over early to get it out of the way.

ESTHER
Get it out of whose way? I don't have any room for that in my refrigerator.

REBECCA
I would think there'd be room for it in one of your refrigerators, Mother.

ESTHER
*(getting up to go to kitchen)* Nope. They're all full. Besides you don't want to put fresh soup in the freezer to serve it tonight.

SHIRA
Why don't you put it in the garage?

ESTHER
*(exasperated)* The garage freezer's full of bread, Shira!

SHIRA
In the garage itself, why don't you put the soup in the garage itself?
*(REBECCA looks to ESTHER for approval)*

ESTHER
Well, it's up to you. It's probably cold enough. Just make sure you put it somewhere where Grandpa won't run into it. *(ESTHER exits to kitchen)*

REBECCA
*(sitting at table, nibbles on crackers)* How are you, Shira? When will you hear from the graduate schools?

SHIRA
Not for a few more weeks. Is Aviva in? Is she coming over?

REBECCA
I would think sometime soon. She went out to lunch with one of her high school girlfriends.

SHIRA
When will Aaron and Naiomi get in?

REBECCA
*(getting up with soup)* They won't. They are spending Easter weekend with Naiomi's parents. However, yesterday your Uncle David drove up to the University to pick up Adam, so he'll be here.

SHIRA
Well, that's nice. And it's probably nice for Aaron and Naiomi to be with her parents this one year.

REBECCA
I don't know, Shira, I'd like to be a grandmother someday and I don't know how I'd feel knowing my grandchildren celebrated Easter, or Christmas. Now Naiomi's a beautiful girl and I love her dearly, but she chose to convert to Judaism and I don't think religion is something to take lightly.

SHIRA
No, of course not, but maybe Easter is just a time of the year to get together with family.

REBECCA
Passover is more than a family get together, it's the upholding of religious remembrances and traditions. All over the world Jewish families are getting together tonight to remember their heritage, except for Aaron and Naiomi, who find it necessary to celebrate Easter with her family. But they're adults, they can make their own decisions, and I have to live with them. I only hope when there are children involved . . . , *(focuses on vacuum)* why is that vacuum in the middle of the living room?

SHIRA
*(turning to see)* Oh, Grandma . . .

REBECCA
*(calling to kitchen)* Mother? Mother, what's with this vacuum in the living room?
*(SHIRA goes to vacuum. ESTHER stands in doorway.)*

ESTHER
What's wrong with the vacuum?

SHIRA
I'll take care of it.

ESTHER
What's wrong with it?

REBECCA
Nothing's wrong with it. Are you done with it?

SHIRA
*(coiling up cord)* I'll put it away.

ESTHER

What are you doing with the soup? If you're going to put it outside, put it outside.

REBECCA

*(on way to garage through kitchen)* I didn't come over here to fight with you, Mother.

ESTHER

Of course you didn't come over here to fight with me, it's Passover. *(sees SHIRA wheeling vacuum towards front door)* Shira, where are you going with that vacuum cleaner?

SHIRA

Doesn't it belong in the front hall closet?

ESTHER

No, it belongs in the kitchen closet. Here, give it to me. *(SHIRA rolls vacuum to ESTHER)*

SHIRA

Can I help you with something else, Grandma?

ESTHER

No, no. You just relax, I can do it by myself. I'll need your help later, but right now I need to do it by myself.

REBECCA

*(entering)* Is there anything you need, Mother?

ESTHER

Where'd you put the soup?

REBECCA

Next to the freezer. I'm picking up the macaroons, do you need anything?

ESTHER

*(taking the vacuum into the kitchen)* No thank you, I have everything. I'll see you later. *(kisses her cheek)*

REBECCA

*(to SHIRA)* When's your mother getting in?

SHIRA

I don't know. Probably soon.

REBECCA

Maybe you want to move your car so she has room in the driveway. *(gives SHIRA a kiss)* It's good to see you.

ESTHER

*(entering)* Rebecca!

REBECCA

Mother, I haven't left yet.

ESTHER

I need parsley.

REBECCA

Parsley for the Seder plate. Anything else? *(ESTHER shakes her head)* Eggs you have, bitter herbs? *(ESTHER nods)* The shank bone I'm bringing, salt water, charoset?

ESTHER

Buy me a cheap bag of apples and a bag of walnuts. I'll make more for Shira and Aviva to take back to school.

REBECCA

*(exiting)* Apples, walnuts and parsley. I hope they have nice parsley.

SHIRA

My mother used broccoli one year.

ESTHER

Your mother put broccoli on her Seder plate? *(gathers up the cheese and crackers on the table)* Well, it's green, grows in the ground, I guess it could be a symbol of springtime. You want some more of this, it'll be a while until we get to dinner.

SHIRA

No thank you. Maybe I'll read in the living room, if that would be out of your way.

ESTHER

Yes, that's a good idea. Why don't you do that? *(exits)* *(SHIRA gets a paperback out of a travel bag and settles down on the living room couch. AVIVA enters from the front door carrying dress in plastic dry cleaner's bag, pumps, and is in high spirits. She waves to her mother's car from the doorway.)*

AVIVA

Hey, cuz, long time no see. *(SHIRA gets up and they hug, Aviva checks SHIRA for fat)* You look good, you look really good.

SHIRA

I'm not really, you're the one who looks good. I like your hair like that.

AVIVA

Do you? I had it done special. I treated myself to a manicure, too. *(wiggles fingers for SHIRA to see)*

SHIRA

Very nice. Very becoming.

AVIVA

*(hanging dress over back of chair and putting down pumps)* You'll have to tell me all about what's going on with you. I just got in last night myself. *(exiting to kitchen)* I came over to help Grandma. Where is Grandma?

SHIRA

*(calling after her)* I asked her if she wanted help. She said not right now. Grandpa's at work, but he should be home soon. *(sitting back down on couch)* She didn't want any help right now.
*(AVIVA returns from kitchen and takes a white tablecloth out of the china cabinet.)*

AVIVA

She said we should set the table. *(SHIRA joins AVIVA in getting dishes, silverware, napkins, glasses, etc., out of china cabinet)* How many are we for dinner tonight?

SHIRA

Well, my mother and I, you, your parents, Adam, and Grandma and Grandpa. Eight.

AVIVA

*(as if it were a secret)* Can you believe Aaron and Naiomi are spending Passover celebrating Easter with Naiomi's parents?

SHIRA

I know, your mother told me.

AVIVA

I don't know what they're thinking. *(begins pulling chairs away from table)* My father's furious and my mother's worried about what will happen when they have kids.

SHIRA

*(taking dishes, etc., off table and putting onto chairs)* I don't see what the big deal is. She converted. She chose to convert; no one told her to. When and if they have children, I'm sure they'll raise them Jewish.

AVIVA

What do you mean "when and if"? Of course they'll have children.

SHIRA

Why "of course"? Not everyone has children, Aviva.

AVIVA

I'm not talking about everyone, Shira, I'm talking about Aaron and Naiomi. They'll have children, and soon I would think, and someday you and I will get married and have children, too.

SHIRA

What makes you so sure you'll get married?

AVIVA

Because I will! And you will too, someday. Wouldn't it be wonderful if we had our children at the same time, and then we could be pregnant together, and our children would always have someone close to their age to play with, and then they'd be second cousins together.

SHIRA

They'll be second cousins together regardless of when they're born.

AVIVA

You know what I mean, they'd be like us; there'd always be someone their age to sit next to and whisper things to at synagogue, and someone to sit with at the childrens' table on holidays, and someone to help set the table. My God, Shira, can you imagine, someday we'll have children who'll have to set the table and clear the table. They'll fight over who washes and who dries and who puts away, and we'll sit in here at the table, handing them our plates and chatting to each other and our husbands.

SHIRA

Yeah, well, I don't know if that's exactly how it's going to be for me.

AVIVA

What do you mean?

SHIRA

I mean I don't know that I really want to get married.

AVIVA

Oh, Shira, you're just saying that. Of course you want to get married.

SHIRA

*(angrily)* No, not "of course." Why is everything so taken for granted with you? Why do you assume that what ever you want someone else would want? You know what works for you doesn't necessarily work for everybody else.

AVIVA

Well, excuse me, Shira! It's news to me you don't want to get married and have children.

SHIRA

I never said I didn't want to have children.

AVIVA

*(sarcastically)* Oh, so now you're not going to get married, but you're going to have children. *(realizing SHIRA'S not kidding)* For God's sake, Shira, what would make you say such a thing?

SHIRA

Aviva, you may not have thought of this, but a woman doesn't have to be married to have a child.

AVIVA

Why would a woman who was not married want to have a child? That's ludicrous. Who would take care of her?

SHIRA

I can— Why can't a woman take care of herself?

AVIVA

How many women do you know who are happily unmarried and with children?

SHIRA

My mother. My mother is happily unmarried and with a child.

AVIVA

Oh, Shira, that's different! Your mother was married when she had you. This is a silly argument. No woman in her right mind would have a child without being married. I certainly wouldn't, and neither would you. *(Flying out tablecloth and letting it float onto the table, she speaks cheerily again.)* Someday we'll both be married to wonderful men and have several beautiful children. Do you realize how big our family will be once we all get married and have children? And how much family we'll have for Seder? Grandma will have to have another leaf made for the table!

SHIRA

*(annoyed)* Are you finished yet? *(AVIVA gives her a surprised look)* I'd like to get the plates down, that is, if you're finished fluffing the tablecloth *(moves around table, laying plates down).*

AVIVA

You're awfully cranky. Have a difficult drive?

SHIRA

Yeah, I had a difficult drive. The drive is always difficult alone.

AVIVA

*(laying silverware around table and trying to remain chipper)* Well, you won't always have to make the drive alone. Maybe someday you'll have someone special to make the drive with you. I hate flying alone. I hate having to figure out how much to tip the skycap. Is it fifty cents per bag, a dollar per bag? Or just a dollar for all of it regardless how many bags you have? Grandma and Grandpa don't tip the skycaps at all, which is one way to handle it, I suppose, but then I worry about whether my luggage will make it on my plane or whether it'll end up in Montana or God knows where. And I hate having to figure out where my gate is, and then rushing through all those terminals, because my gate is always clear across the airport from wherever I've come in, and it's always the last gate, it's always like, gate 37C or something. *(smiling to herself)* But this time Daniel came with me. He arranged his flight so that it left after mine, and he took care of my bags, and made sure we left early enough so that I wouldn't have a canipshit rushing to the gate. He's really wonderful.
*(Both women have finished their tasks and are opposite each other at the heads of the table.)*
I wish Daniel were here now. I wish he could celebrate Passover with us tonight. *(in a singsong voice)* He will though, he will very soon.

SHIRA

Do you realize how incredibly, well, I mean, you're so, you know, you could learn to do things for yourself instead of relying on men to do them for you. *(AVIVA gives her a puzzled look.)* Do you want to do napkins or glasses? Napkins or glasses?

AVIVA

Oh, napkins I guess. We're probably having salad, don't you think? And most people like an extra plate for the gefilte fish. Oh, and soup bowls! *(gets soup bowls, salad plates, and fish plates out of china cabinet and begins to place around table)* You should see the matzo balls my mother made. They're big and fluffy and perfect circles. I hope someday I can make matzo balls as nice as my mother's. *(SHIRA places napkins and glasses around table)* Do you ever think about that kind of stuff? Like having your own Seder? Your own Shabbos dinner?

SHIRA

*(at china cabinet)* I guess we'll need wine glasses.

AVIVA

Shira, what's wrong with you? You're all . . . you're not saying anything. Are you angry with me? *(SHIRA doesn't say anything. She moves around the table placing wine glasses.)* It's not fair for you to be angry with me and not tell me what I've done.

SHIRA

You know, Aviva, you always expect things to be fair, and sometimes they just aren't.

AVIVA

What are you talking about? *(silence)* I don't know why you have to be this way. Why do you have to be all moody and everything? It's Passover. Everyone's going to be here soon and you're going to be a grouch. *(silence)* Fine, that's your business. If you want to talk, I'll listen, but I will not let you be nasty to me when I haven't done anything wrong. *(surveying the table)* Now, what else do we need?
*(SHIRA stands at the table with a sorry dog expression. She looks as though she may break down, but will not allow herself to do so.)* Oh my God, the Seder plate! Where's Grandma's Seder plate?

SHIRA

She has it in the kitchen.

AVIVA

Well then, all this table needs is a bouquet of flowers, and Grandpa will bring those, won't he? *(smiling and dreamy)* I hope Daniel will be just like Grandpa and have flowers for me and little toys for our children, and sit at the head of the table and bless everyone with words that make us feel special and . . . we'll just be happy.

SHIRA

You're getting married.

AVIVA

Oh, Shira, it was supposed to be a surprise. Please don't say anything. I want to surprise everyone at dinner tonight. *(goes to hug her)* But I'm glad you know, I'm glad someone knows! It was so difficult not to say anything to Mom or Daddy last night. But look surprised at dinner, OK? I want everyone to be surprised. *(awkward silence while SHIRA moves away from AVIVA)* So, what are you up to? Are you seeing anyone special?

SHIRA

No, not anymore. I just broke up with someone a few days ago actually. It wasn't a major relationship.

AVIVA

Oh, I'm sorry. Did it run its course or something?

SHIRA

No. No, not really, it ended on account of someone else.

AVIVA

*(happily)* So you're seeing someone else then?

SHIRA

Not quite yet.

AVIVA

But there is someone else in your life?

SHIRA

Unless I decide to terminate it.

AVIVA

Well for goodness sake, give it a chance! I'm going to check on Grandma. *(exiting)* Make sure we have enough chairs, will you?

*(SHIRA grips the back of one of the chairs and looks over the table. RACHEL enters from the front door and unloads bags [one large suitcase and several filled paperbags] in the living room.)*

SHIRA

*(going to her)* Mom.

RACHEL

*(hugging SHIRA)* Hello, Sweetheart. Have you been here long? Did you have a nice drive? *(taking off coat and noticing AVIVA'S clothes on chair)* Are these yours?

SHIRA

No, they're Aviva's.

RACHEL

Nice. A little dressy though, don't you think? I didn't bring anything that dressy. Are your things in your car?

SHIRA

I didn't bring very much, just that bag there.

RACHEL

Well, I have more in my car. *(rearranging contents of paper bags from one to other)* Here, this is for you, and there's a twelve pack of toilet paper in the back of my car for you, too. Do me a favor and bring me the shopping bag from the back seat driver's side. The rest can stay. Oh, and Shira, would you mind putting your car on the street? *(hands SHIRA keys to car)* I'm parked in front of the garage and Grandpa should be coming home soon.

SHIRA

I'm sorry, I meant to move it and then Aviva came over and we set the table.

RACHEL

Is something wrong with you? You look tired.

SHIRA

I just had a long drive. You don't need anything else from the car? Do you want it parked in the driveway or on the street?

AVIVA

*(enters)* Aunt Rachel! Did you just get in? *(hugs)* Grandma's in the kitchen, *(calling)* Grandma, Grandma, Aunt Rachel's

here. I'm so glad you got in. Grandma and I just heard about the storm on the radio and we were worried about you and Daddy and Adam.

ESTHER

*(entering)* You're just in time, Rebecca, I'm right now ready for the apples. Rachel! *(hugs. To AVIVA)* Where's your mother? I thought you said your mother was here.

AVIVA

I said Aunt Rachel was here.

ESTHER

How'd you get in so quickly with that storm?
*(SHIRA exits the front door)*

RACHEL

I didn't have any storm.

ESTHER

Well you should have, it came from your direction. *(sees bags)* What's all this? I just vacuumed this living room, Rachel.

AVIVA

*(getting clothes)* Excuse me, I'm going to go get dressed. *(exits to kitchen)*

RACHEL

*(rummaging through bag)* I brought you some things.

ESTHER

*(with her)* What's this? Crackers? Why would you bring me crackers at Passover?

RACHEL

Those are for Shira.

ESTHER

Well, she can't eat them now, she'll have to put them in her car.

RACHEL

*(producing box)* Here, Mother, this is for you.

ESTHER

What is it?

RACHEL

Bittersweet chocolate covered marshmallows.

ESTHER

*(peering into bag)* And your sewing.

RACHEL

Your favorite candies, Mother.

ESTHER

I'd be happy to do your sewing, Rachel.

RACHEL

Weren't they Great Grandma's favorite as well?

ESTHER

I know you know how to sew. Did you sell your machine?

RACHEL

I don't have time to sew, Mother. Would you mind fixing a few things for me?

ESTHER

I'd be happy to, Rachel, thank you for asking. I won't be able to get to anything until after Passover though.

RACHEL

Have you stopped liking bittersweet chocolate covered marshmallows?

ESTHER

(sincere) Oh no, of course not. Thank you, Rachel, thank you very much. Do you want to put those things downstairs by my machine? And why don't you put the rest of your things upstairs in the guest room. Take Shira's too.
(AVIVA enters in smart dress and pumps) Well, isn't that a nice looking dress.

RACHEL

Very nice, Aviva. (sits in living room)
(enter SHIRA and REBECCA, REBECCA with paper bag)

REBECCA

Oh, that's just stunning. Is that the dress I bought you? (sits next to RACHEL)

AVIVA

I'm not sure I like the shoes with it though. What do you think? I brought another pair.

ESTHER

I like those shoes just fine. Where are the apples? (REBECCA hands over bag and ESTHER exits to kitchen)

SHIRA

Do you need any help, Grandma?

ESTHER

I'll tell you when.

RACHEL

Shira, why don't you get dressed? And would you mind taking my things upstairs with you when you go?

SHIRA

(getting bags) I'm not wearing pantyhose tonight, is that going to bother anyone?

REBECCA

Why wouldn't you wear pantyhose?

SHIRA

Because I don't want to.

AVIVA

I brought another pair if you want them.

SHIRA

No, I'm wearing boots, I just wanted to make sure my bare knees won't offend anyone.

RACHEL

Won't offend me.

SHIRA

All right. (exits)

AVIVA

(sits across from them) She's been really weird, Aunt Rachel.

RACHEL

What kind of weird?

AVIVA

Kind of cranky.

REBECCA

I didn't think she was cranky.

AVIVA

Well, let's say more than her usual moodiness.

RACHEL

She's like that around her period. She must be having her period.

AVIVA

I don't know, but like, everything I said was dead wrong. I felt like I was talking to a Martian feminist or something.

RACHEL

Why not an Earth feminist?

AVIVA

Well, it's like there was an edge to everything she was saying. Like only she knew what she was talking about, and I just tried to end the conversation.

REBECCA

What was she talking about?

AVIVA

Ok, don't let her know I told you this, but she was talking about having a child and not being married.

RACHEL

That's nothing new. We talked about that the last time she was home.

REBECCA

Oh, Rachel, I hope you haven't been filling her head with ideas.

RACHEL

No ideas, just the honest truth that living with another person can be more difficult than it seems. I think it's natural for her to be thinking about having a baby. Don't you think about having a baby, Aviva?

AVIVA

Certainly, but not before I'm married.

RACHEL

Well, I think Shira may be a little more independent than you.
(enter ABRAHAM with flowers, soaked)

ABRAHAM

Hello, hello!

AVIVA
*(rising and going to hug him, RACHEL and REBECCA follow)*
Grandpa! You're soaked! Grandpa! You're soaked!

ABRAHAM
*(taking off coat)* Here are my girls! I am soaked, soaked through to the bone. Got out of the car to get your grandmother's flowers, and the rain came down. I said to myself, it's rain like this that's going to float me away like Noah and his ark, but I had to get your grandmother's flowers, yes sir, had to get flowers for my Queen Esther. I'll tell you something, I think that rain floated me home, floated me home and into the driveway. Now then, where is everybody?
*(SHIRA enters. She is nicely dressed, though more casual than AVIVA)* Here's my Shiraleh. How are you, Shiraleh?

SHIRA
Grandpa, you're all wet. Maybe you should change clothes.

ABRAHAM
I'll change clothes, I'll change clothes for supper. Where's all my family?

REBECCA
Aaron and Naiomi aren't coming, Daddy, and David and Adam should be here any minute.

ABRAHAM
If they're not here, I don't think they're coming, Rebecca.

REBECCA
Of course they're coming, Daddy. David left last night.

ABRAHAM
Radio says the expressways are flooded over and the eastern part of the state has sleet and snow. All I'm saying is, don't be disappointed, I'm sure they're fine, but they probably won't make it in for dinner tonight.

AVIVA
Well, they just have to make it in. It's Passover.

ESTHER
*(in doorway)* Any one want to help me in the kitchen? Abraham! Weren't you going to let me know you got home?

ABRAHAM
*(rising)* Of course I was going to let you know, I swam through stormy waters to rescue this precious treasure for my beautiful Queen Esther. *(hands ESTHER flowers)*

ESTHER
*(hugs)* Thank you, Abraham. Why are you wet? Are you all wet? How long have you been home in these wet clothes? *(Abraham kisses Esther and exits)* How much longer do you think David and Adam will be?

REBECCA
Daddy doesn't think they'll get in at all.

ESTHER
He doesn't? He said that?

RACHEL
Wouldn't they call though? They'd let us know.

REBECCA
Of course they would.

ESTHER
We should begin the service soon though, I started the brisket. I could turn it off.

REBECCA
*(rising)* No, no, they'll be here. What can I help you with? *(exits)*

ESTHER
Shira, get the Haggadahs from the china cabinet, Aviva, Rachel. *(exits, motioning them to follow)*
*(SHIRA rummages through china cabinet, enter ABRAHAM)*

ABRAHAM
What are you looking for?

SHIRA
Haggadot. Grandma said they should be here.

ABRAHAM
They're not. She thinks they're there every year, but she always forgets she puts them in the cupboard with her cookbooks. *(SHIRA pulls out prayer books)* Well, what do you know? *(sits in living room)*
*(SHIRA puts a haggadah by each plate, AVIVA enters with matzos and puts a piece on each plate. REBECCA puts vased flowers on the table. RACHEL gets the candlesticks, etc., for the table. Phone rings offstage)*

ESTHER
*(in doorway)* Well, hello, Aaron and Naiomi! *(to others)* It's Aaron and Naiomi. Yes, we're having a fine Passover so far. We haven't started the service yet, you know. No, your daddy and Adam aren't here yet. No, Grandpa doesn't think they'll make it in tonight, but we're praying. Oh, you're kidding! *(to others)* They have six inches of snow there! Oh, I can't imagine, snow for Easter weekend. Well, how's your family, Naiomi? Oh, good, yeah, we're fine. Sure, sure she's right here. They want to talk to you, Rebecca. *(sits with ABRAHAM)*

REBECCA
*(on phone in doorway)* Hello, happy Passover. We haven't heard from them yet, but, you know, we may have to start without them. I'm worried about them, but I'm sure they're fine. Yeah, everybody else is here. Oh, *(to others)* they have something to tell us. Ok. You aren't. Are you really? Oh, Naiomi . . .

ESTHER
Naiomi's pregnant.

REBECCA
Naiomi's pregnant! *(on phone)* That's wonderful! Yes, that's just wonderful!

ESTHER
*(rising)* Oh my God, I don't believe it.

ABRAHAM
You just said it.

ESTHER
Oh my God. This is why they're with her parents for Easter!

REBECCA
Oh, I wish your father were here.

AVIVA
So I'm an aunt. Aunt Aviva. Auntie Viva.

REBECCA
When'd you find out? But you wanted to be sure. Yes, I understand.

RACHEL
You're right, Mother. Of course they'd want to be with her family. Well, I'm glad I had a girl. When you're pregnant, Shira, I want to hear it to my face.

SHIRA
Wouldn't you just be happy I was pregnant?

ESTHER
Well, this really is something else. It's always a miracle, life is always a miracle.

ABRAHAM
*(rising)* I want to talk to them.

REBECCA
Grandpa wants to talk to you.
*(ESTHER, RACHEL, and AVIVA hug REBECCA. SHIRA drops back)*

ABRAHAM
I want to tell you that your grandmother and I love you both very much, and that this is truly a blessing in our lives. We are very, very proud of you and proud to be the great grandparents of your child.

REBECCA
Oh my God, I'm a grandmother.

ABRAHAM
So, here's your grandmother. *(hugs REBECCA and sits)*

ESTHER
Mazel tov! But you could have told me when I talked to you, my God! I wouldn't have said anything! No I wouldn't, I can keep a secret. Well, I think it's just as well you told your mother. No, I'm not angry. Of course you should be there to tell your parents, Naiomi. You'll be here next year for the baby's first Passover. Well, listen, we all love you very much and we're very proud of you. Ok, give our love to your parents.

AVIVA
I want to say something. *(on phone)* Congratulations, guys! I'm just absolutely thrilled! Yeah, well I've been thinking,

I'd like to be called Aunti Viva, or Aunti Vivi, what do you think? I'll let you know. Well, you guys take care, all my love, bye-bye. Oh, here's Aunt Rachel.

RACHEL
Mazel tov. How are you? This is very exciting. *(exits to kitchen with phone, REBECCA following)*

ESTHER
Shira, do you want to say something to your cousins?

SHIRA
No. I mean, congratulations, mazel tov. This is really wonderful.

ESTHER
Yes, it is really wonderful. A great grandchild. *(sitting next to ABRAHAM)* You're a great grandfather, old man.

ABRAHAM
I'm not an old man.

ESTHER
You all probably don't remember your great grandmother.

AVIVA
I remember her blessing the candles on Shabbat. I remember her standing at the dinner table in front of the candles with a black lacey veil over her face welcoming in the Sabbath as she pulled the smoke to her. But that's all I remember.

SHIRA
I remember her teaching me how to make peppermint milk by breaking the curved part off a candy cane and using the rest as a straw for the milk. I remember thinking that must be what Jewish people did with candy canes, made peppermint milk.

ESTHER
Well, I remember when Aaron was born I thought, oh my God I'm a grandmother, and then I thought, my mother's a great grandmother, and I knew someday I'd be a great grandmother, but I didn't think it'd be now.

ABRAHAM
When'd you think it'd be?

ESTHER
Well, I don't know! Just you wait, tomorrow you two will be having babies and I'll be saying, where'd the time go? And where's your father, Aviva? Who'd have thought it would snow on Passover? *(enter RACHEL and REBECCA)* Have you heard from David?

REBECCA
No, I haven't heard from David. Maybe if you'd have gotten call waiting, I'd have heard from David.

ESTHER
Well, it's a good thing you're off the phone now so he can call through.

ABRAHAM

I'll bet they pulled off the road somewhere and a nice Jewish family took them in and they're trying to get through right now to tell us they're fine and they're having Passover with their new friends.
(Phone rings, REBECCA rushes to phone.)

REBECCA

(in doorway) Hello? Oh David, where are you? Are you alright? Is Adam all right?

ESTHER

Are they going to be here for supper?

REBECCA

How far is that? Oh my God. Oh my God. Well, then stay where you are. No, no, we'll be fine. Oh David! Naiomi's pregnant. Yes. Yes, they just called. She's eleven weeks. I love you too.

ESTHER

If they're not coming I think we should get started. I'm getting hungry.

ABRAHAM

Where are they?

REBECCA

They're in a truck stop, over two hundred miles away. He says they sat on the expressway unable to move for an hour and a half. The closest thing they can find to a matzo is paper napkin. Sweetheart, why don't you and Adam get a room and come in tomorrow? We'll do a second Seder tomorrow night.

ESTHER

I'm not cooking for a second Seder tomorrow night.

REBECCA

I'm glad you're alright, honey, we were worried about you. Give my love to Adam.

AVIVA

Wait! Wait, I have to tell you something!

REBECCA

Aviva, your father's on a pay phone.

AVIVA

I didn't want to tell him this over a pay phone, but I want to tell you all this tonight. Hold the phone out so Daddy can hear.

REBECCA

Aviva has something she's dying to tell us. Hold on.

AVIVA

Mother, Father, Grandma, Grandpa, Aunt Rachel, Adam, Shira. Daniel and I are getting married. He proposed to me last Saturday night at eight fifty-seven.

ESTHER

Oh my God, I don't believe it.

ABRAHAM

Mazel tov!

REBECCA

Did you hear her? She said she's engaged. Your father wants to know if he gave you a ring.

AVIVA

He's getting it at home this weekend.

REBECCA

(on phone) You didn't have a ring for me.

RACHEL

Walter had a ring for me.

ESTHER

Some difference that made.

ABRAHAM

(standing) Mazel tov, mazel tov! Come here and give Grandpa a hug. Daniel is a very nice boy, your grandmother and I like him very much. We wish you all the happiness in the world and we give you our blessing.
(Esther hugs Aviva)

REBECCA

Your father and I love you very much, and we're so happy you've chosen Daniel. (Aviva hugs Rebecca) Your father wants to talk to you.
(Aviva exits to kitchen. Rachel hugs Shira)

SHIRA

Why are you hugging me?

RACHEL

Because I love you.

SHIRA

I'm not the one getting married.

RACHEL

You're the one who's being you.

ESTHER

What's going on with you, Shiraleh? You're so quiet there.

SHIRA

I'm just tired, Grandma.

ESTHER

Tired, I'm tired. And I'm hungry.

REBECCA

(sits in living room) I feel so old.

ESTHER

You'll get used to it.

RACHEL

You're not old. This is the natural progression of things.

ESTHER

The natural progression of things is to get started with the Seder. (exits to the kitchen)

ABRAHAM

Well, who would have thought? Who would have thought two miracles in one day? I'll tell you girls, I'm a lucky man. I'm a lucky man to have such a beautiful family. I always wanted to have a large family, and here it is. Except not everybody's here. Well, they're here in our hearts.

(enter ESTHER carrying Seder plate, followed by REBECCA)

ESTHER

Alright, everyone come to the table. Come on, come on, let's get started.

(ESTHER and ABRAHAM sit at heads, RACHEL, REBECCA, SHIRA and AVIVA on sides. There are open spaces for the obviously missing four family members and the women try to take up the space to make up for it.)

ESTHER

Is this it? Where is everybody?

REBECCA

It'll be better tomorrow night when David and Adam are home.

AVIVA

And next year Daniel will be here, and Aaron and Naiomi, and the baby.

RACHEL

Maybe I'll have someone special to bring.

ESTHER

That would be nice.

(pause)

ABRAHAM

Dear God, we thank you for keeping us healthy and safe in the past year, for all the happiness you have given us, for the pain that has kept us human, and we thank you especially for the blessings you have bestowed upon us tonight. Although much of our family is not with us this Passover eve, they are here in our good thoughts and within our hearts. I want you all to know, those seated around this table and those who could not be with us, that you all are truly a blessing in my life, and I love you very much. Let's turn to page three of our haggadahs.

(as lights fade to near darkness)

"Long ago, at this season, a people—our people—set out on a journey. On such a night as this, Israel went forth from degradation to joy. We give thanks for the liberations of days gone by. And we pray for all who are still bound, still denied their human rights." Everyone sits in near darkness for a moment, and then ESTHER rises, taking some things off the table, REBECCA rises, taking some things off the table, RACHEL rises, AVIVA, SHIRA, until the table is cleared. Only at the end does ABRAHAM rise and exit with the women.)

SCENE TWO

(Lights up, no one on stage. Enter ESTHER with five shoe boxes filled with goodies [cans of nuts, soup mix, jello, soap, toothpaste, small bottles of shampoo, boxes of pasedic (kosher for Passover) matzo tea crackers, and sandwich baggies]. She dumps everything out of boxes and rearranges in piles to put back into boxes.)

(Shira walks through from kitchen to living room)

ESTHER

What are you up to, Shiraleh?

SHIRA

I'm just getting my book, Grandma.

ESTHER

Why don't you help me here?

SHIRA

(coming over to her) That's a lot of stuff for two care packages.

ESTHER

(putting matzo crackers into baggies so that each box gets some) Five care packages. Just because Aaron and Naiomi and Adam aren't here doesn't mean they don't get care packages. Reach me that far box there, would you?

SHIRA

(arranging the contents in even piles) You're sending two to Aaron and Naiomi? Won't her parents give them an Easter basket or something?

ESTHER

I'm making one for your mother. She deserves something nice. (eyeing SHIRA) It's difficult being a mother.

SHIRA

I can imagine.

ESTHER

(packing care packages slowly) It can mean sacrificing a lot. Sometimes losing a good deal of your independence. Putting your child before yourself.

SHIRA

Please don't put any jello in mine.

ESTHER

I always put jello in the care packages.

SHIRA

I know but, I don't really like jello.

ESTHER

Jello is a good thing to have. You can get your Aunt Rebecca's sour cream recipe, or add sliced pears. You never know when you're going to need jello. It's the emergency dessert. I always kept a jello mold in the refrigerator. You kids may not have always liked it, but you ate it. What color do you want? I've got yellow, green, and orange.

SHIRA

Green, I guess.

ESTHER

You see jello is the one thing you can always count on to be there. No matter what happens, there's always jello on the shelf. And you don't need a fancy mold or anything, a regular mixing bowl is fine. I just love jello after it's been chilling in the ice box a few hours. Cool and smooth, and it's not fattening you know, so you don't have to give me any of that nonsense. Should I give you another box?

SHIRA

*(smiling)* No, thank you Grandma, one will be fine.

ESTHER

*(taking SHIRA'S face in her hands)* There's that smile. I knew it was hiding somewhere. *(kisses her)* Where has it been? You want to tell me, Shiraleh? Something you want to tell me? *(At lack of response from SHIRA she resumes boxing; SHIRA makes upside down pyramid with bars of soap.)*
So, I don't know, do you like cashews or mixed nuts?

SHIRA

Mixed. I'm sorry, Grandma. I'm not myself lately.

ESTHER

Who could be themselves? What with Aviva announcing her engagement, and Aaron and Naiomi announcing their pregnancy . . .

SHIRA

I guess I'm just nervous about graduation.

ESTHER

Of course.
*(Shira places a tube of toothpaste across the top layer of her inverted pyramid and it topples.)* Have you decided what to do about your pregnancy? *(SHIRA looks wide eyed at her grandmother and ESTHER looks wide eyed back)* Have you told your mother? Don't you lie to me now.

SHIRA

I haven't told anyone. How do you know?

ESTHER

*(continuing to stuff boxes)* It was a hunch, but I know you. I know you better than you know yourself. Your mother was the same way when she carried you. Thought she could hide her pregnancy until she was ready to tell me, but I knew. *(stops stuffing)* He doesn't want to marry you, does he?

SHIRA

Grandma, he doesn't want to talk to me.

ESTHER

Good. You're better off. *(stuffing again)* Do you know what you want to do?

SHIRA

Well, no. I've been so wrapped up in not talking to anyone about it, it's been the main thing on my mind not to say anything when I've needed to say something to someone so badly and I thought you'd all look at me like I was some kind of, some kind of mistake, like I'd made this great big mistake and I was this swirling mass of idiocy because I mean, no one gets pregnant anymore, everyone uses birth control, and I swear to you, Grandma, I use birth control, I always use birth control, I just don't know how this thing happened and I didn't do it purposely. That's what he said to me, he said I did it purposely, to trap him or something. Like I want to spend the rest of my life with that shit head. Oh, excuse me, I'm so sorry. It's just that I don't want to have this baby. I mean it's his baby and I don't want any part of him, but, you know, it's just been occurring to me that it's my baby too. You know, when I first found out and I sat there with that stupid nurse practitioner who kept holding my hand and asking me if there was anyone she could phone for me I thought, forget this, I'm going to abort this. I don't have room for this in my life. And I asked the nurse what kind of information she could give me on abortion clinics and she dropped my hand and stared at me like I'd told her I planned to have the baby so I could eat it. They're not allowed to issue that kind of information. I'll tell you Grandma, I'm ashamed to say this now, but I went back to my apartment and looked at that closet of hangers and thought of trying to get rid of an unwanted pregnancy . . .

ESTHER

There are safer ways to do it.

SHIRA

Whatever. Grandma, I don't want to have an abortion. I think I want to keep this baby.

ESTHER

*(begins stuffing)* Let me tell you something. When I was your age I was married and already carrying your mother. I didn't have any choice as to whether I wanted to get married and have children. That's what you did. It's what everyone did. Now of course I love your grandfather and wanted to get married, and of course I love your mother and aunt and wanted them too, but I'll tell you, Shira, I'm not so sure I wanted it all right then. I was so young, and you're so young. I couldn't admit it to myself at the time, but I wasn't as happy as I thought I should be as a wife and mother. And I think a lot of other women felt the same way, but we didn't know how to put it into words, and no one would have thought to live any differently. You just couldn't then, but you can now. You don't have to burden yourself with children or a marriage this young, take this time to figure out who you are and who the people are around you, sometime later you'll be ready for a husband and children. Sometime later you'll want a husband and children.

SHIRA

What are you saying, Grandma?

ESTHER

I'm saying have the abortion, and thank God you can while they're safe and legal.

SHIRA

How can you say this to me? I'm pregnant! I'm pregnant with your great grandchild! Where are the blessings and praise like for Aaron and Naiomi's kid? How is my baby so different from theirs?

ESTHER
Your baby is so different from theirs because it is your baby.
Who's going to take care of it? Who's going to take care of
you?
*(enter RACHEL from kitchen)*

RACHEL
Shira, what are you shouting about, Grandpa and I could
hear your voice clear through to the basement?!
*(silence)*

ESTHER
Shira's pregnant. *(SHIRA stares at ESTHER, RACHEL stares
at SHIRA)* And she wants to keep the baby.

RACHEL
You can't be serious.

SHIRA
Yes, Mother, I am very serious. *(RACHEL takes seat, ESTHER
takes seat)*
What is going on here? I would have thought you'd be
thrilled I wanted to keep it instead of killing it.

RACHEL
I'm supposed to be happy you're killing yourself?

SHIRA
What are you saying, Mother, motherhood is suicide?

RACHEL
I didn't raise you to get pregnant and ruin your life.

SHIRA
Since when is bringing new life into the world such a terrible thing? I don't hear anyone telling Naiomi to terminate
her pregnancy.

RACHEL
Aaron and Naiomi are a completely different story, Shira.

SHIRA
So I've heard. You know, if we were orthodox you'd both be
beside yourselves with joy and treating me like a queen.

RACHEL
If we were orthodox you'd be married and your head
would be shaved.

ESTHER
Don't talk about the orthodox. Let it be their job to populate
the world, you've got time yet.

SHIRA
*(ignoring her grandmother)* Oh, I should be married? And being married solves everything does it, Mother? Being married means living in a strong brick house with glowing
windows behind a white picket fence protected by some
ignoramus man with two blue suits and six white starched
shirts?
*(enter ABRAHAM from kitchen)*

ABRAHAM
What's this about ignoramus men? I don't own a blue suit
anymore, do I, Esther?

RACHEL
Come have a seat, Daddy, Shira's pregnant.

SHIRA
Why is it that either people tell me I'm pregnant or they tell
other people I'm pregnant? It's my pregnancy and I want to
tell people about it!

RACHEL
You've been telling about it.

ABRAHAM
What did you say? I missed it.

ESTHER
*(getting up)* Well, I'm going to make some decaf. Would
anybody else care for some decaf? *(ABRAHAM and
RACHEL raise their hands)* Shira?

SHIRA
I can't believe this. I'm pregnant and you're making coffee.

ESTHER
I'm making decaf, do you want any?

RACHEL
I don't think the chemicals are good for the baby.
*(ESTHER exits)*

SHIRA
Oh, so now we're concerned with the baby's health?

ABRAHAM
When weren't we concerned with the baby's health?

SHIRA
They want me to have an abortion.
*(ABRAHAM looks at RACHEL inquisitively)*

RACHEL
I never said that. I haven't decided.

SHIRA
Why is it your decision?

ABRAHAM
*(calling)* Esther!

ESTHER
*(from kitchen)* What?

ABRAHAM
Come in here.

ESTHER
Decaf's not ready.

ABRAHAM
I don't care about the decaf.
*(ESTHER stands in doorway)*
What's this about an abortion?

ESTHER
There's no reason for her to have a baby now, she's too
young. Now is for herself, she can have babies later.
*(silence)*

ABRAHAM

There will be no abortion.

RACHEL

Daddy . . .
(*ABRAHAM shakes head*)

ABRAHAM

There will be no abortion.
(*SHIRA sits down. RACHEL begins eating the package of nuts from the table.*)
(*loosely quoting from bible*) "and God said to Abraham, 'Your children shall be as many as the stars in the sky.' " (*slowly*) " '. . . as many as the stars in the sky.' "
(*long pause*)

ESTHER

Rachel, those are for the care packages! (*rolls up uneaten portion and places in a box*) Fine, those nuts will be yours then.

REBECCA

(*enters*) Who's eating nuts? You can't eat nuts on Passover.

ESTHER

What do you mean you can't eat nuts on Passover?

REBECCA

I mean you can't eat nuts. Nuts are legumes, and you can't eat legumes on Passover.

RACHEL

Why are they here?

ESTHER

How was I supposed to know nuts were legumes? I never knew nuts were legumes. Rebecca, are you sure?

REBECCA

Of course I'm sure. Nuts are part of the legume family as are peas, beans, and whatever else that expands when you cook it.

ESTHER

Well . . .

ABRAHAM

Listen here, I think it's up to the individual's discretion as to whether or not he or she decides to eat legumes, and as to whether or not he or she considers nuts to be part of the legume family. Now we don't eat bread because the Israelites didn't have time to let it rise and take it with them, however, they didn't have legumes in that part of the country then, and so it wasn't an issue as to whether they had time to take it with them or not. Therefore, I believe it should be up to the individual as to what they decide to do for Passover. Now then, as a family I think we should get back to the issue of Shira's pregnancy.

REBECCA

What pregnancy?

RACHEL

Shira's pregnancy. Shira's pregnant.

SHIRA

Good God, Mother, why don't we just hang a banner on the house?

REBECCA

Shira, why didn't you tell me?

RACHEL

Why didn't she tell you? Your children tell you everything, I had to hear it from my mother.

SHIRA

Mother, I just found out about this myself!

RACHEL

And you told your grandmother.

ESTHER

No, no. I told her.

RACHEL

And you gave her the same "I told you so" speech you gave me?

ESTHER

I gave you that speech when you filed for divorce. I suggested to Shira she should get an abortion.

REBECCA

Mother!

ABRAHAM

Esther, why would you say that?

ESTHER

Because, she's too young to be clouding her life with children now. She can do anything. If she has children now she'll just put off figuring out who she is and who she wants to be.

REBECCA

She can give it up for adoption if she doesn't want to keep it.

RACHEL

I don't think adoption's always the answer. There are too many people in this world who have no business being parents, God only knows who the baby might be adopted by.

SHIRA

If I carry this baby full term, I'm keeping it.

RACHEL

Don't be impetuous, Shira.

REBECCA

If she hadn't been impetuous she wouldn't have gotten herself into this mess.

RACHEL

This is not a mess, this is something we will figure out! (*pause*) Who is the father? Is it that guy you've been seeing? He didn't sound like much. (*pause*) There's no chance of him marrying you I suppose.

SHIRA

Mother! Do you hear what you're saying? You want me to end up like your marriage did? You want me to marry a total jerk just because I'm pregnant?

RACHEL

If he's such a total jerk what were you doing with him?

SHIRA

Oh God!

RACHEL

And I didn't marry your father because I was pregnant. I married your father because I had a temporary lapse of reason.

ESTHER

A temporary lapse of reason that lasted twelve years.

ABRAHAM

Shira's not getting married.

AVIVA

(entering) I'm getting married.

REBECCA

Sit down, honey.

SHIRA

Wait! (to AVIVA) I'm pregnant. I, Shira, your cousin, am pregnant. I am pregnant!

AVIVA

But you're not married.

RACHEL

And you're not getting married. You're right. I don't know what we're going to do, but you shouldn't get married unless you're in love. And unless he's a decent person. And preferably if he has money. Shira, why did you do this? This isn't at all what I had in mind for you.

SHIRA

I don't think it's what I had in mind for myself, Mom, but here it is, and I have to deal with it.

ABRAHAM

Shira, it comes down to this: It's the quality of life. There's a certain quality of life that we all want for ourselves, and as parents or grandparents, there's a quality of life we want for you. We want you to be happy, we want you to reach your potential, we want you to enrich yourself and your life so that you live the best possible existence, but you have to decide what that best possible existence is for you. Now, you have to think, what's important to you, how do you want to live your life, and what do you need in your life to insure this lifestyle, or, what would hinder this lifestyle? What does it mean to you, the quality of life, what does it mean for you?

SHIRA

I'm not sure I know right now, Grandpa. Even without the pregnancy, I'm not sure I know.

ABRAHAM

Well, these are things to think about. And you're welcome to think about them here, for as long as you like. We love you, Shira, and we're proud of who you are. You're a blessing to us too.

ESTHER

(hugs SHIRA) That's the truth. Ain't that the truth! (hugs everyone) Well, I'm hungry again. What's there to eat? What can we eat? (exits)

RACHEL

(hugging SHIRA) I love you, too. I just want the world for you, that's all. And you can still have it, with or without the baby. If you want to, I know you'll find a way to make it happen.

ESTHER

(entering to living room) This is what I've got: I've got matzo crackers, I've got pasedic rolls, I've got bittersweet chocolate covered marshmallows, I've got nuts.
(everyone heads to living room)

AVIVA

Are nuts kosher for Passover?

REBECCA

They are if you want them to be.

AVIVA

So, does this mean you won't want to be a bridesmaid?

SHIRA

I don't know, Aviva, can we play it by ear?

AVIVA

Oh sure, but let me know, you know, because I'll have to ask someone else.

ABRAHAM

"Next year in Jerusalem!"
(lights begin to fade)

REBECCA

Next year with David and Adam.

AVIVA

And with Daniel, and Aaron and Naiomi, and the baby.

RACHEL

And maybe Shira's baby.

SHIRA

All of us. Next year, it'll be all of us. (lights out)

The class was enthusiastic about *The Quality of Life* and felt the writer had forged a strong bond with her material. Some felt the grandparents were sentimentalized, too sweet, and others thought the point of the play was that Shira and her mother would always be outcasts in a subtle

---

*(The prayer on p. 146 is an excerpt from* Gates of Freedom: A Passover Haggadah *by Chaim Stern.)*

way in spite of the seemingly all-embracing nature of this family. Some found Shira too self-pitying, others very sympathetic. While we recognized that realism is only one kind of play and only one way of getting at characters, everybody agreed that these characters were coming alive. The playwright knew how they would react, how they breathed, walked, spoke, what level of education each had.

But do we need punctuation omissions to capture their speech? After several test-readings, the class determined that, for the most part, the minimal punctuation reflected speech patterns. But is it necessary? Good actors will capture the speech rhythms. There's always the possibility that any script will be overlooked by a potential producer because the script reader assumes a lack of attention to mechanics. (You need to give your script every advantage when you send it out.) So, my own advice is to correct the run-ons.

The playwright talked about her need to focus the script more but wasn't certain yet what she wanted to do with it. We hoped, at this point, that we could find actors to do it. In practical terms, this play is more difficult to rehearse than plays with fewer characters. And several of the actors would have to play characters much older than themselves. On the other hand, actors gravitate toward realistic characters. Playwrights have an easier time attracting actors to scripts with sustained scenes and realistic characterization. Many people despair about this: "What is to become of theatre? Are we daring enough?" Much of the time, I think we're not. But I'm reporting a fact. Actors like to play characters they can get hold of in terms of psychology, mood, manner.

---

**Assignment: Exercise 6**

This assignment is to revise or greatly expand something you've begun before (making it substantially different and adding some seven or eight pages) or to write a scene for a longer play that you have in mind for your final assignment. Make sure you know your characters well enough that you can imagine them in another situation. Test yourself by looking at the character biography chart. Do you know how your characters breathe, how they feel about sex and death? How they live? What they do for entertainment? How much money they have?

---

**Study Questions and Exercises**

1. Why are flashbacks more common in fiction than in plays?
2. Make suggestions for the revision of **Deadlines**. What elements would give the play a pressure? What action would give the play an end result that is ironic?
3. Make suggestions for the revision of **The Quality of Life.**

# TWELVE

# Scene, Act, One-Act, Full-Length

## OVERVIEW

This chapter will cover subjects like: how do playwrights begin to think about structure? What is the best length for a scene? When is a scene finished? What makes a scene satisfying? Which kinds of ideas end up as one-acts, and which as full-length plays? How do you know, when you're starting out, which length you're aiming for?

In this chapter are notes on scene construction and a few pointers on structure and length. Practical matters that affect structure—like costume changes and scene changes—are discussed.

To some extent, the materials in this chapter are a review of issues you've probably been thinking about but that we haven't stopped to discuss earlier. I prefer to let people try things first and then begin to reflect about form. One of your exercises may already have led to a one-act without your thinking about what a one-act is. As you develop, you'll probably begin to make decisions about form at earlier stages than before.

## OBJECTIVES

At the end of this chapter you should be able to

- Make preliminary decisions on the shape and length of your final exercise
- Be able to sketch out a structure for the other scripts you would like to write

By now, you are probably walking around with so many ideas in your head that you wonder which to develop. And

how to develop them. You get on the bus and hear a snatch of conversation. You think, "I could use that." You find yourself dreaming while you eat lunch; you have the beginnings of a scene in your head. What do you do with this scene idea? *Is* it a scene? What other scenes would belong with it? Will it make a one-act play? Or is it too big an idea for a one-act?

### Scenes

#### The Actor's Scene Unit

Let's stop for a moment to discuss the scene, the basic building block of drama. When actors in a class look for a scene to perform, they usually choose something not marked or labelled from the center of a script. The more actors develop, the more likely they are to be able to identify a scene unit quickly.

The early playwriting exercises are intended to give you a sense of scene as directors and actors think of the word—a chunk or unit of action. In fact, many scenes in plays are actually built around 1) two characters and some physical object that that scene is about, 2) a physical action or gesture that is completed in a scene, or 3) a changing character relationship. In fact, it's possible for all three characteristics above to appear in a single scene. For example, Anna and Mary (two characters) meet to go through their deceased mother's papers (object). They need to pay bills and handle correspondence before they consider themselves finished (the scene covers these tasks). The bill-paying and correspondence bring out their relationship, which goes through a conflict and resolves itself (changed relationship, either to each other or to the memory of mother).

A scene, the unit or building block of drama, might be as

short as two pages or as long as twenty. It might last for thirty seconds in performance or twenty minutes. We can often *feel* when a scene is complete, satisfying. What is likely to make it so? Obviously it isn't simply a question of length. It's more that something is begun and that something is concluded in a scene. Directors sometimes say, "Something is accomplished." Or "Something happens." In our sample case, it is not just that the bills get paid (not interesting on its own), but that whatever emotional/psychological action goes along with the bill-paying comes to resolution. Perhaps it's that Mary and Anna get to know their mother in a new and fresh way, or that Mary and Anna say goodbye to their mother more completely, or that Mary and Anna find that they cannot agree on their mother's life and what it meant and they separate emotionally from each other, or that Mary and Anna come to understand each other and end the scene more together than when they arrived.

*What is dramatic action?* A dramatic question is asked and answered. It has to do with who will succeed at a task to be accomplished. Will the property be sold?, etc.

Something happens. It can be a small thing. Perhaps the most satisfying aspect of the happening is, for the audience, being allowed to participate in it. If you guide the audience to see what the scene is about from the beginning, the progress of the scene is easier to follow.

## Dramatic Questions

Theorists often talk about a play's major dramatic question—its "what will happen?" In almost every play is a question that keeps the audience watching until the final moments when the question is completely answered. When a play's ending seems to drag out, the cause may be that all the questions, including the major dramatic question, have been answered. There is nothing more to wonder about. One way to think about the sense of momentum in a play— also the ideas of change, action, event—is to see momentum as a product of question. What is true of the whole play is true of scenes—those smaller units of action that make up the whole. Just as most scenes have an inciting incident, a crisis, and a climax, most operate on a question. Will John leave home? How will Robert feel about his wife's infidelity? Will Mary persuade Anna to sell the property? In the scene the question is answered—for a time at least. There is a battle between two forces—not necessarily the two characters—two possible ways of feeling, two ethical positions, etc. One will win. One will lose. On to the next scene and a new, related question with a tension between two forces—two possibilities, two decisions, two outcomes.

If the audience has a question to go on, the scene is more likely to succeed.

## Basic Possibilities for Scenes

If you start with a small task—scene construction—you are likely to be able to find a way to put many scenes together to make a play. *The fascinating thing is, there are* only a few things that can happen in a scene. In the following list, A and B stand for characters or clusters of characters whose effect is singular for a time. On the playwright's game board are nouns (people, places, things) and verbs (actions). What are the few things that can happen in a scene? People do things to other people, places, things, and they usually do those things in dialogue. Think of even words and ideas as things to be handed over, handled, manipulated. So:

1. A can try to get B to accept something (physical or verbal: a thing or an idea or another person).
2. A can try to get B to give up something (physical or verbal: a thing or an idea or another person).
3. A can try to join B—move in with, marry, become partners with, seduce.
4. A can try to separate from B—move away from, divorce, break a partnership, end a relationship, kill.
5. A can try to get B to leave the place. (A can try to *separate* B and the place.)
6. A can try to get B to stay in the place. (A can try to *join* B to the place.)
7. A can try to get B to take some action.
8. A can try to stop B from pursuing some action.

*All of these possibilities imply movement of some sort.*

### The First Two Scenes of Hamlet

Shakespeare is good at making something happen in each scene. He frames events so that the audience knows what the dramatic questions are. Will Cassius be able to persuade Brutus to the cause? Will Brutus accept the letters thrown in at his window? Will Petruchio be able to get Kate to marry him? Shakespeare sets up the question and lets you watch for the answer.

Let's take the first two scenes of Hamlet as examples. The sentinels of the guard try to "give the ghost" to Horatio. Horatio resists their story. The ghost appears. They succeed. They get him to accept the ghost. At the end of the scene they all decide on the action for the next scene. They will give the ghost to Hamlet (in words).

The second scene, which takes place in the throne room, has two performance scenes (basic units of action) within it. First Claudius takes the throne. By making speeches, announcing his marriage, acting publicly as king, Claudius takes the throne, or joins himself with place. Who will win? Claudius with his subtle insistence that he belongs there or Hamlet who tries to shake him with subversive comments? Claudius wins this round. He leaves the stage. Horatio and the guards come in and they give Hamlet the information about the ghost. They give something to Hamlet. He takes it. The basic dramatic question is: will he take it? Yes, is the answer. A scene is a push and pull of forces pressing an idea, an object, or an action on each other. Will the attempt succeed? The scene tells us yes or no.

Of course, it's crucial that whatever the question, the answer is not easy to come by. There is a struggle. What each character attempts to do is not easy to do.

## French Scenes

You should know the term *French scene*. Because classical French plays were so clearly divided into acting scenes based on a change of stage population, the term *French scene* came into use. It means that at least one character exits or enters and a new unit begins. Most playwrights find themselves structuring things by French scene. When Sarah and Annie are interrupted by Tom in **Table Manners**, one French scene ends and another begins. After a while Sarah hurries out, leaving Annie and Tom together, and a third French scene begins. Exits and entrances key the changes. Actors and directors work by the concept in rehearsals. Playwrights often handle setting up of dramatic irony and cluing the audience into dramatic questions by these shifts in the stage population. Within each French scene, something must happen.

## Cross Purposes

A good reminder of the bare bones of scene construction— enough background, given circumstances, and obstacles to make the task difficult to accomplish—is the *cross-purposes improvisation*. In this exercise for the actor, the "playwright" must come up with a set of circumstances and a goal for each character. The information each character gets is not identical. The way this kind of improvisation should be done is by giving each actor the situation separately, out of hearing of the other. Each actor is told to go into the scene acting on the set of information he or she has, to accomplish the task of the improvisation. Here is a sample, an improvisation that has worked well many times.

## An Improvisation

A. MAN or Character One: You are a graphic artist for an advertising firm. You have worked for this advertising firm for twelve years. And you are the best in the firm. Your years there have been happy, pretty much, until lately, when WOMAN or Character Two came to work at the firm. Here's how it happened. You ran into her on the street. (You knew her in college.) She was jobless at the time. You pretty much extended yourself to get her a job—put in a word for her, etc. Ever since then, things have been awful. Your colleagues used to be your friends, now they avoid you. When you take a coffee break, they leave the room. Yet she's always with them. She must be talking against you. Worse things have happened, too. She's been stealing your ideas. She pretends to want to visit, just to chat, and the next thing you know your ideas are on her sketch pad! You're not stupid. You can see how successful she is lately. And at your expense. You can also see her staying late, leaving with the boss, sitting with him over at the bar across the street. You're not stupid. You know what's going on. The next time she asks to visit you, you are going to tell her what a whore, in every sense of the word, she is. The time arrives. She calls and asks you if she can come to see you. Task: to tell her off.

B. WOMAN, or Character Two: You have been hired by an advertising firm where you are very happy and very successful. The only trouble is, there is an old acquaintance of yours working there and he is a real pain in the ass. He acts as if he got you the job—all he did was tell you the firm was hiring. You got the job on your own qualifications. Nobody there likes him. He is really an egomaniac. He thinks his ideas are better than anyone's. You've tried to befriend him, tried to have friendly talks with him. But he's so suspicious and strange. Nobody can stand his fits, his egomania. Especially the boss.

Some new things have happened. You have just been told there is to be a merger with another firm and some cutbacks. The boss says your work is the best he's seen in decades. You are really good. So he's just promoted you. He is also firing MAN. But since nobody can talk to him, he's sent you, as the new second-in-command, to do the firing. Your task: Tell him you've been promoted and must fire him. Tell him he must be out of the office immediately. The scene starts when you enter his office. You have called him and asked him if you can come to visit.

This improvisation has the characteristics of a scene. At the end of the scene something will have happened— something will be accomplished. There is a major dramatic question. How will MAN react when he is fired? There is movement. (One of the scene possibilities is that A tries to get B to leave a place. That is the drive of this particular scene.) Scenes, put together, make plays.

## Decisions about Place

A reminder: a story idea that demands *few, if any, changes of place and time* is easier to work with if you are new to playwriting. With experience you can manipulate this factor, but it is easier to make a play work if you put characters in a place and don't move them, or change the scene, or let a lot of time go by. In fact, a way to counteract this temptation toward multiple changes is to choose a place that you would really *like to evoke* (not necessarily realistically), a place that interests you—even if that place is the inner world or mind of your main character (as you will see in the two samples of Exercise 7).

## Event or Occasion

And it helps to choose a limited time: in terms of story structure, we call this the *event* or the *occasion*. What is the event? It can be a Fourth of July party. The baptism of a child. Thanksgiving—the family coming home. Passover, as it was in **The Quality of Life**. It doesn't have to be a holiday. Perhaps it's the day a man loses his job. Or the day a woman decides to terminate a marriage. Or the day a woman makes a decision to change jobs from something secure to something risky. Or as in Lanford Wilson's **Burn This**, Act One, the day Pale comes to pick up the effects of his dead brother, and Act Two, the New Year's Eve on which Anna tries to cement her relationship with Burton. Ask yourself—to find an *event* or *occasion*—how is this day different from any other day? What is special about this day?

## One-Act Plays

*What is the difference between full-length and one-act plays?* Plays come in all different lengths, but we pretty much talk about them as full-length plays and one-act plays. A one-act play means simply that the thing is written to be played without intermission. It has one act. A one-act play may last for ten minutes or one hour. There are even a few one-act plays that run a bit over an hour. In the past, it was less usual to see a one-act play with more than one scene in it. A classic one-act, then, was a play under an hour long that took place in one place at one time. Synge's **Riders to the Sea**, Albee's **The Zoo Story**, Sartre's **No Exit**, Strindberg's **The Stronger**, Stoppard's **The Real Inspector Hound.**

If anything changes in a standard one-act, it's likely to be time rather than place: i.e., characters stay in one place, but there is more than one scene, e.g., Kate's bedroom before the wedding, Kate's bedroom after the wedding. Or there might be three scenes between mother and daughter in a living room over a matter of weeks. If the play is realistic, the characters will probably need to look different from scene to scene. In this case, the playwright must account for time for costume changes. In a recent Pittsburgh New Works One-Act Festival, one playwright set three scenes between mother and daughter in a living room. The audience could hear the actors rushing to make costume changes during the fifteen-second blackouts between scenes. It was distracting.

There is an absolutely practical part of structuring a play. You must ask yourself what physical changes in the characters and settings are going to be necessary and if you've given the actor and crew time enough to make those changes. If you have two characters on stage all the time in all three scenes, you are not allowing for off-stage time in which to do a complex costume change. If you want the house to be cleaned between Scene 1 and Scene 2 you should be sure the stage dirt and clutter are cleanable in a few seconds. Why not let the audience wait a couple of minutes? you ask. It breaks the illusion, ruins the flow, kills the momentum.

For the most part, in a standard one-act, a character does not age thirty years, nor do we move from Joe's living room to a park unless we're doing without complex scenery. A one-act—whether ten minutes long or an hour long—will have a flow, an uninterrupted quality, in the telling of the story. It will have momentum.

If you are writing a one-act in which twenty years go by, you will almost certainly have to make sure that you are not requiring a literal rendering (that aging and makeup changes are not needed) and multiple, detailed scenes are not needed. If you know the materials and limits of the stage well, you can probably figure out ways to tell a story with a huge time lapse and many places shown within an hour. (Perhaps you use locations, like a medieval stage, and specify no makeup changes, only acting changes to simulate aging. Or, if you feel really inventive, the make-up change could happen right on stage during a scene, etc. In this latter case, you will be coming up with theatrical means to do something unusual.) I want to say, "Don't let things stand in your way. Write what you want." And I want to say, "Learn to draw the nude before you paint the abstract painting." Both pieces of advice are valid. One allows you to explore. One teaches the discipline of the craft. In any case, make sure that scene breaks do not interrupt the flow, that there is no need for long changes of scenery, that there is no hold-up while actors change costume and makeup.

A one-act is an hour long or less. Whether or not it is divided into scenes (time and place changes), it will have units of action that are actor's scenes. There might be one unit in a play twenty minutes long or three units in a play fifteen minutes long, or ten units in a play an hour long. A unit, or actor's scene, can be quite long or quite short, depending on the kind of story being told.

## Full-Length Plays

A full-length play usually lasts between an hour and a half (the shortest ones) and three hours. Two hours in the contemporary theatre is the standard, but more and more plays are running closer to an hour and a half. And it usually has one or more intermissions. One is the standard in the contemporary theatre. The major units of a full-length play are acts. They are usually between thirty minutes and ninety minutes long. An act encompasses a large part of the story. For instance, Act I might be Christmas of 1981, Act II Christmas of 1991. Or Act I is a morning in June, Act II is an afternoon in July, Act III is an evening in August in a story about a family's coming together for a summer and disintegrating. The breaks or the intermissions are part of the effect of the play. They contribute to the whole story.

How many scenes can be in an act? One, two, ten, twenty, depending on the kind of story. For instance, in **Sexual Perversity in Chicago** or **The Dining Room**, there are a dozen scenes to an act. In other words, the big story is told through small scenes that are connected by plot or theme.

To review: an act is a unit of stage time with a great deal happening within it. There are one-act plays, two-act plays, three- and four- and five-act plays. An act may have scene changes within it. An act may be thirty minutes to ninety minutes long. A scene may be two minutes to sixty minutes long, depending on the story to be told and the breakup of time.

The playwright's decision about structure is often a way of outlining a story. **Glengarry Glen Ross**: before the robbery, after the robbery. *Speed the Plow*: not just morning, night, morning, but before the date with Karen, the date with Karen, after the date with Karen. I think it helps to frame imaginary stories in terms of acts and scenes, e.g., I i & ii: Morning and evening before the property is sold. II: Morning, ten years after the property is sold. Or I: Charlie's 40th birthday, II: Charlie's 41st birthday, III: Charlie's 42nd birthday. Or I i: Party preparations, I ii: the party, II: after the party.

Try at this point outlining some of your story ideas.

## Two-Act Plays

Notice how many contemporary full-length plays are two-act plays. *The Dining Room, Old Times, Glengarry Glen Ross, Happy Days, Home, True West, Table Manners* are all two-act plays. Forty years ago, the three-act play was more common. The two-act structure has effects on mood, tone, and meaning. It is an ironic form. We'll discuss this further in the next chapter.

## Other Concerns

A major structural decision has to do with where you begin your play. Where does the story begin?

In Chapter 9, we discussed how the inciting incident, crisis, climax, appear in each play's overall structure and in each scene as well. You should be getting adept at finding these points in the scripts you read. Meanwhile there are other issues relating to structure that we should begin to take notice of. What is the difference between the structure of *Streetcar* and of *Glengarry Glen Ross*? And of *Home* and *The Dining Room*? The first thing you might notice is that all of *Streetcar* takes place in the same setting, but over a period of several months. The structure is episodic, but contained by the limits of place. (Some episodic plays change the setting as well as the time, but *Streetcar*'s story is a story about what happens between spring and autumn after Blanche enters the home of her sister. There are eleven separate scenes, each one the length of a short one-act play—ten or fifteen minutes long.)

It is important in *all* plays to keep the flow going, to not stop the action for long scene changes. So be aware of the ways entrances and exits are written to allow for a minimal change of scene before the next one starts.

*The Dining Room* takes place on the same set (although it represents different places) and the time (even the decade) changes with the characters. The unusual thing about *The Dining Room* is that the scenes overlap. Notice too that *The Dining Room* is divided into *two acts*. The modern two-act structuring device is so widely used that it has affected even Shakespeare production! Twenty years ago directors of Shakespeare plays typically chose two points in a production for two intermission breaks. In other words, a director turned Shakespeare's five-act structure into a three-act structure. Now, more often than not, Shakespeare's plays are

divided in two. The two-act structure is now the modern classic.

Likewise, you might notice that often the acts are divided into scenes that show a change of time while the place stays the same, but a scene change is often necessary *after* the first act. This is true of *Glengarry, Old Times*, and *Happy Days*.

When plays have a two-act structure, the first act is usually an exploration of what is wrong in the character's world. The second act shows things having gotten worse. (If it's drama, things get worse!) The landscape is more barren, the character's problems have increased, the world is less hospitable. Something we thought was bad is now worse.

There are practical reasons to notice these tendencies in structuring a play. For one thing, it would be self-defeating to ask for a lot of scene changes in one act. The time it takes to change the stage is the time you lose the audience and destroy the tension you are building.

And drastic passages of time can also be a problem. If you jump from a character's being eighteen years old in Act I, Scene i to sixty-eight years old in Act I, Scene ii, in addition to all the other problems you've caused yourself, you have given the actor no time to do a costume and makeup change. But usually (you could choose to use two different actors if your story will benefit from such a choice), unless your whole play, and all your conventions of presentation, are stylized, as they are in *The Dining Room*, you probably can't jump a great number of years in one act. So some of the structural decisions you make will come of practicalities.

## Point of Attack

Other structural decisions have to do with the telling of the story. Where does the story begin? Where does the drama begin? These two points may not be the same at all. In fact they probably aren't. Most dramas begin with what is known as a late point of attack. *A late point of attack is starting the drama at an advanced place in the story*—starting the drama when a great deal of tension has accumulated and something is about to happen. Sometimes this is described as starting the drama near the crisis. So, instead of starting *Streetcar* back at Belle Reve when Blanche first started to lose her grip on things, rather than starting it with a short exploratory visit to New Orleans, rather than starting with the beginning of Stella's relationship to Stanley, Williams starts the drama with Blanche already in trouble, coming to the place where she will have more trouble. Stella is not only *with* Stanley, she is married to him and pregnant. The long years of trouble that Blanche has seen are shown in their last few months.

Oedipus puts in half a lifetime before the start of the drama of *Oedipus Rex*. The drama begins on the day that he will find out who he is, on the very day that he will find out he is the murderer of his father, on the day that he will have to banish himself from his kingdom. *Glengarry Glen Ross* doesn't start back with the first inklings of trouble or the first failures of Levene or the first successes of Roma, but it begins on the eve of the robbery, when everything is pressured and more is at stake than ever, when Levene is defeated and Roma is at the top of his game. Notice how much more pressure there is when the play starts late in the story, right before something big happens. *Home* doesn't start with admission to the home; it doesn't even start with a first meeting between the men and the women. They have met before; they have had these conversations before. And *Table Manners* doesn't begin with Christmas, when Norman first seduced Annie, but later when they have one sexual encounter already behind them and another planned. The late point of attack—later in some plays than in others— pressures the action.

So you must figure out what your whole story is but then figure out where to begin the drama. Your drama must be tight. The changes of time, changes of scene, and changes of place must be carefully chosen to mean something.

In *Streetcar*, notice the way time moves through the hot months, through Stella's pregnancy. Notice that each scene in *Table Manners* is a meal. Notice that the three scenes in the Chinese restaurant in *Glengarry Glen Ross* are moving the action forward, showing us more than one kind of theft, more than one example of a person preying on another. The first scene shows us management and worker, a person in power and a person who is powerless. The second scene shows the guys in the middle, hanging on, looking for a way out. And the third scene shows how one succeeds—by turning the aggression outside the club, by selling.

Every story has an ideal structure for how it should be told. Find the place. Find the major incident that is *about to happen*. Change to a new time and a new place *only when necessary*. Be aware that the best scene changes are simple ones.

In summary, structure is important. You'll decide where your story starts, how you will show it in terms of time and place, how often you'll need to break up the story with a change of time or place, and what happens in the whole play, what happens in each act, in each dramatic scene, and in each acting unit or scene. However, for your one-act you will probably have few if any changes of place. Remember also, it will help to frame each unit (actor's scene) in terms of a dramatic question that the audience can follow and that the scene answers.

---

### Study Questions and Exercises

1. Describe a story idea in a paragraph. Decide how you would divide it into acts and scenes.
2. Describe the outline, or structure, of **Home**.
3. Make a list of plays and decide where the playwright might have begun the action and compare it with where the playwright did begin the action. Can you see reasons for the decisions?

# THIRTEEN

# Contemporary Classics

## OVERVIEW

Polonius refers to the players' repertoire in *Hamlet* as containing many kinds of plays—tragical-historical, historical-pastoral, pastoral-comical, and so forth. And there *are* actually many kinds of plays. But contemporary commercial plays, both full-length and one-acts, are likely to be among the following: ironic comedies, dark comedies, or tragicomedies. This chapter includes a brief discussion of contemporary forms, including some notice of the prevalence of the two-act structure. You will read Harold Pinter's *Old Times* and Samuel Beckett's *Happy Days* in this chapter. Both are dark comedies pressing toward the tragic.

## OBJECTIVES

At the end of this chapter, you should be able to

- Distinguish tendencies toward the types of drama listed in the overview
- Critique Harold Pinter's *Old Times*, seeing if most of the twenty principles are in operation here
- Critique *Happy Days* in the same way

Whether you are writing a light comedy of the sort Neil Simon writes, a highly verbal comedy of manners of the sort Sir Noel Coward wrote, a poetic tragedy in Tennessee Williams' style, or a dark comedy like *Glengarry Glen Ross*, you will need to have characters who are engaged in an action, characters who are different from each other, something at stake, language that is action-filled and that suits the story, and characters about whom there is a good deal to know. You will need to have an inciting incident, a crisis, and a climax. Otherwise you will have a dialogue that may

be play-like, but that is not dramatic, and that does not have enough tension. It will, without the basic structural ingredients, not *feel* like a play. Witness, in fact, the simulated workshop sessions. They are play-like, but they do not have enough at stake, an action being performed through dialogue, or the structural ingredients of an inciting incident, crisis, and climax, which could make them dramatic.

You may have noticed that you have a tendency to write either serious or humorous scenes. You may be naturally better at one than the other. Molière wasn't very good at writing tragedies although he wanted very much to be a tragic playwright. But he was a glorious comic playwright. Sir Noel Coward didn't do so well with his serious dramas, but his comedies are bright, witty, and well put together. Chekhov's works fall almost invariably on the line of dark comedy, sometimes of tragicomedy. Most of contemporary drama is both comic and serious at the same time, ironic in tone. Don't limit yourself as you write. Instead explore the possibilities of seriousness and humor in all you do.

### Tragedy Today

Some people believe that we cannot write *tragedies* today, that the belief in the power of human beings (and their importance) is not part of our world. Many believe that *A Streetcar Named Desire* is not and cannot be considered a tragedy for the following reasons: Blanche is not noble enough to be a tragic heroine, Blanche's fall is not significant enough to a community of people, and Blanche doesn't have a "recognition" at the end, that is, she does not come to grips with what has happened to her and transcend it. The following characteristics have belonged to many if not all the tragedies of the past: a character who has some sort of power and who matters to a community, a character whose decisions come out of a high level of consciousness, a character who is destroyed by her own attempts to take control of her world, a character who at the end of the play (often the end of the character's life as well) has a spiritual recognition of the frailty of human beings and the brevity of happiness. Most tragic characters die at the end, leaving the stage to mourners who put the tragic experience into perspective. There are exceptions, though, as there are exceptions to everything. Oedipus doesn't die physically. Nor does Mrs. Alving. Their hell is that they must go on living, having lost all they struggled for. But Hamlet dies, and Lear dies, and Othello, too. The Duchess of Malfi dies. Hedda Gabler dies. And so does Strindberg's Captain in *The Father*. At the end of a tragedy, what has been sought is lost. The battle is over and the protagonist has lost the earthly battle, won only the spiritual one. Instead of physically dying, Blanche loses her mind, dies mentally and emotionally. Since she does, she cannot have the fully meant, conscious "putting together" that many tragic protagonists do. So *Streetcar*, for some people, is not fully tragic. How do you feel about it?

## Two-Act Structure

Most important contemporary plays are both comic and dark—and are most often called *dark comedy* or *tragicomedy*. For one thing, the two-act structure almost predetermines the ironic-tragicomic tone. The two-act structure is negative. It fits the following kinds of stories: Act I: X is in a bad way. X tries to do A but B is in the way. Act II: X is in a worse way. X does A in spite of B and then finds it necessary to face C. X spins his wheels, self-destructs, comes to rest defeated by the problem.

The more old-fashioned three-act structure fits this kind of story: Act I: X tries to do A, but B is in the way so X does C. Act II: X finds that C was a bad choice and tries to undo it, only making it worse with D. Act III: X goes back and conquers A and B, which has either favorable (comic) consequences or unfavorable (tragic) consequences. The three-act structure (and likewise the five-act structure) allow for more conscious, effective protagonists, partly because they divide up the action with more than two major attempts to pursue the objective, whatever it is. Two attempts often seems like "quitting early," or "giving in to bad luck," or just wearing out. Think of *Home, Old Times, Glengarry Glen Ross*. None of the protagonists pick up and try *yet* again (if only to fail), as they do in *Hay Fever, The Father, Ghosts, Private Lives, All My Sons, Arms and the Man*, and *Cat on a Hot Tin Roof*.

## Dark Comedies

Ironic comedy is a term that refers to plays that move as comedies—many releases of tension, many reversals, protagonists who survive in spite of their problems, protagonists who compromise in order to survive—but that focus on the incongruity of survival, the chance and happenstance of successes and the near certainty of failure. They are often plays in which what is pursued and what is accomplished have little value to begin with and in which the attempts to control "the treasure" are virtually devoid of meaning. One way of identifying these plays is to see the main gesture being performed (selling real estate, sitting on ironwork chairs) as empty. A lot of effort is expended for something that is hardly worth it in itself and the gesture toward which is empty.

Ironic comedy bears resemblances to tragicomedy. The differences, for those who want to make distinctions, come in the level of consciousness of the protagonist. Sometimes protagonists in what would otherwise be ironic comedies come close to having tragic recognitions. Sometimes they graze the boundaries of tragedy. When they do, and when the action settles enough to feel the feelings of loss, the play is tragic-comic. Beckett's *Waiting for Godot* is called a tragicomedy for just these reasons. And *Happy Days*, by Beckett, contains tragic feeling as well.

Often we simply hear the term "dark comedy" used to describe contemporary plays. Whatever happens in the plays, the resolution is full of compromise—and a suggestion of continued tension. We have probably laughed. We have seen flawed human beings stuck in those flaws. In the mirror that is theatre, we have seen our faults. I think *Old Times* is a dark comedy. One can easily argue that *True West* is a dark comedy. Dark comedies can be fascinating, but the human race doesn't come out so well in them. Two-act and four-act structures often lead quite naturally to dark comedies.

## Ending Plays

How do you know when to end a play? When you've got on the right train for telling your story, you will not have to search for an ending. The ending will be a part of it from the start. In fact the ending is usually inherent in the beginning. The amazing thing about drama is that it can hold us spellbound, feeling that we don't know where it's going, and it can complete itself, letting us feel that we knew all along where it was going. Not all plays come full circle, but many do. Notice for example that Harry and Jack are alone, minus a table and chairs, at the end of *Home*. Notice that Norman, having just told Sarah he's available for her, ends the play promising a holiday to Annie. Blanche leaves the apartment in the care of a doctor at the end of *Streetcar*. *The Dining Room* begins and ends with a dream of the past. Winnie is still working for a happy day. Roma is taking Levene's leads—the very subject of the first conversation of *Glengarry*. The brothers have trashed their mother's kitchen in *True West*. And she is there to see it. The plays end with characters at least a step worse off than they were at the beginning.

Coincidence is the *worst* way to end a play. The critical term for ending a play by means extrinsic to the plot is *deus ex machina*. The term comes from the Greek theater and means literally "god from the machine" because sometimes plays were concluded by the lowering of gods whose decrees solved human dilemmas. But whether you are tempted by gods or last-minute conversions, by a neighbor who just happened to know what was going on, or by a misunderstanding suddenly cleared up (Bob was not gay, he just moved effeminately, etc.), you would do well to examine your initial idea and find what is steady in it, what will *not* be solved by sheer coincidence.

## Old Times *by Harold Pinter*

You should now read the play *Old Times* by Harold Pinter, and then read *Happy Days* by Samuel Beckett, two classics of the contemporary theatre.

## Plot Summary of *Old Times* *by Harold Pinter*

This play has several unusual features, but most of them can be categorized by its comic dream-like nature. Characters always appear to mean more than they are saying or to be speaking in two dimensions—existing in the past and present at the same time or treating metaphors as actual events. Furniture arrangements are spare and precise. Properties are few and are used symbolically.

**Act I.** A converted farmhouse. Autumn, night. Two sofas and an armchair. Deeley, Kate, and Anna are seen when the lights come up, but Anna remains still in the dim light.

Deeley quizzes Kate and she answers. The questions are about a friend of Kate's youth who is coming that night. Kate describes her as her *only* friend at the time, but she appears to remember little except that this woman used to steal her underwear and that this woman had many friends. Anna turns from the window and joins the action, revealing herself as a woman who lived with Kate when they were young women excited by London life.

Deeley and Anna compare the Kate of the old London days with the Kate of the present time, in a place remote from London. They describe her as a dreamer, a woman who takes long walks. They sing about her and to her with snatches of lines from old romantic songs, ending with parts of "These Foolish Things (Remind Me of You)."

Deeley tells a long story about going to see the film *Odd Man Out* at a run-down movie theatre in which one usherette tried to seduce another. At the end of the film he picked up Kate by talking about Robert Newton's performance. Anna, who has seen the film, says that she knows how sometimes one remembers things that never happened and that as one remembers them they occur. She then tells about a man sobbing in their bedroom, "crumpled in the armchair" while Kate sat on the bed. When he approached *her*, she would have nothing to do with him, but later she woke to find him in bed with Kate. Kate complains that they talk about her as if she is dead, but they protest and go on to discuss their feelings about her, specifically about the decision to marry. Anna asks Kate to remember how they went to see *Odd Man Out* together at a run-down theatre.

Deeley describes his work as necessitating travel all over the globe. Anna answers his questions about her villa in Sicily and her husband. Kate begins to ask questions of Anna. Then Anna talks to Kate as if they are young girls in London living together. They plan their evening at home—washing hair, calling a friend over. Anna offers to run Kate's bath. Kate says she will do it herself.

**Act II.** A bedroom. Two divans and an armchair in an arrangement reversed from Act I.

Deeley and Anna only, dim light. Deeley brings Anna coffee and tells her he remembers her from the Wayfarer's Tavern where she used to go, wearing black, where men always bought her drinks. Anna, at first, denies it. Deeley persists in telling the story of how, at the Wayfarer's one night, he looked up her skirt and up the skirt of another woman who came in and joined her until men who wanted to talk politics surrounded him. When he got free of the men, the women were gone.

The length of time Kate takes in the bath is the next subject they turn to. They agree she luxuriates. Deeley describes her as thorough in her self-cleaning, Anna as someone who floats out of a bath. Deeley complains that Kate doesn't dry herself properly and Anna challenges him to dry her. He agrees to do it with Anna supervising, but he quietly explodes that Anna is now forty years old and that he'd not recognize her in the Wayfarer's these days.

Kate emerges from her bath, smiling. Deeley and Anna sing alternate lines of "They Can't Take That Away from Me." When Anna tells Kate she looks beautiful, Kate begins to speak about how she likes the softer lines and non-definition of the country, the sea, but not London except when rain blurs things. She'd like to live in the East where it's hot and you breathe slowly.

Briefly Anna and Kate drift into their "young women of an evening in London" routine but are brought into the present by Deeley who quizzes Kate about whether she's fully dry. Anna goes back to the "young women" routine, asking which male friend they should invite over. They discuss McCabe. Deeley interrupts, saying McCabe is out of town. Anna tells a different story about the stolen underwear. She says she borrowed it from Kate to go out, after which she would come back and tell Kate anything of interest about her evening. Then he and Anna argue more forcefully about Kate and who knows her passion best. Deeley makes it clear that Anna is not particularly welcome. Kate tells him if he doesn't like it he can go.

Deeley reveals to Kate that he met Anna before at the Wayfarer's when he was pretending to be Kate. Kate explains that Anna found his face very vulnerable at that time and wanted to comfort him. Kate tells Anna she remembers her dead, lying in bed with dirt on her face. It felt good, she says, to bring a male body into the room. She tells Deeley that she tried to do something different one night—put dirt on his face—but he resisted and proposed instead.

Anna walks to the door and stands looking away from them. Deeley sobs. Anna comes back. Deeley goes to her, but she is still. He goes to Kate and lies across her but she does not react. He sits in the armchair; each of the women sit in divans. All three are alone.

## About Old Times

I asked one class, what is the main feeling of this play? And one fellow said "sex." He found the whole play an experience in frustrated sex. That's pretty good for a gut reaction to *Old Times*.

In fact, others in the class pointed out that most plays seemed to have a lot to do with sex and they wondered why. Are playwrights sex-obsessed? Well, yes, I think they often are. If you are writing domestic scenes, stylistically realistic or not, you are likely to write about sex. Because plays are most often about people relating to people (not to memories, not to self, but to each other), when you write about relationships, a good deal of the time sex is the major issue. It is, after all, a significant way of relating. And as we noted when discussing *Table Manners*, adultery and infidelity are common themes in plays because they are a way to deal with a contract broken. They are themes that mean trouble between people; they are themes in which pretense, lying, acting, are natural; they are themes of problem-solving by indirect means. Infidelity and adultery *are* dramatic.

The sexuality that the student felt in *Old Times* is less clear-cut. There does not seem to be an affair going on. Instead, there is sexual tension in all legs of the triangle. Nobody is satisfied. And Anna and Deeley are in some kind of battle over Kate. Yet *Old Times* does not operate in the head-above-water conscious way that realistic plays do. This play is not realistic. It is about two steps away from realism. It is dreamlike, actually more nightmare-like than dreamlike. Something is wrong, but as in a dream, it slips by before anyone can get to it. This is classic Pinter. He has written other plays that ride the line of the dream, plays that are large, mythic, and symbolic. There is *Betrayal*, which moves backwards; there is *The Caretaker*, which is haunted by strangeness; *The Birthday Party*, with its rituals of cruelty; *The Homecoming,* in which a man's family behaves to him in hostile, threatening, and incestuous ways. And *A Slight Ache*, made up almost entirely of monologues to a silent matchseller who looks like he arrived from the Middle Ages.

In *Old Times*, there are three people and three pieces of furniture (and like the three people on three pieces of furniture in *No Exit*, they are in hell, they can't get out). The hell of *Old Times* is a psychological one: the people are entwined. It's tempting to want to put the play together, to understand it in a realistic context. But it yields less that way than if one just lets it happen, just experiences it.

I was fortunate to see the original production in London. It was very funny, illogical, dreamlike, threatening, with a constant suggestion of sexuality. Effective productions since have maintained those qualities—although American directors are less likely to see the humor in the play than British directors are. Under British guidance, the play is extremely funny, as dark comic plays often are.

An American director I know interpreted the play in production as a dream in which Anna was really Kate, an unrealized part of Kate, a hidden part that might bring some life to Kate and to the marriage, if she were expressed. This director saw Deeley as wanting to bring Anna back because he could not get to Kate in any other way. In his interpretation, Deeley was the protagonist in a failing marriage. This reading of the play helps to explain why Kate and Anna share the same past. If they are indeed the same person, then their pasts would be one.

The puzzle of the play does not *have* to resolve in an answer like the one above to be effective in production. Even if Kate and Anna are literally friends rather than parts of a self, there are dynamics in the action that move it. For one thing, there is a search going on. The thing sought is a memory—a more abstract treasure than in most plays—a memory of Kate alive and lively. However, interestingly, the divan of Act I and the bed of Act II become operative as treasure. Both are large enough for two, but Kate occupies double-space alone. Therefore, the on-stage Kate is a symbol of the treasure and an obstacle to it at the same time. All of Deeley's and Anna's lines have, as the action, the ultimate control, possession, management of Kate. Notice Kate's silence. She is an object of mystery throughout. When she speaks at the end, the result is that her memory, her self-identification, defeats Deeley and quiets Anna. They want her; she remains untouched.

Notice that the setting is highly stylized, symbolic too. The stage directions for Act I will tell you that there are two sofas and an armchair. In the bedroom are two divans and an armchair. Most designers find ways to show that the sets mirror each other. The set is evocative because the furniture invites some (minimal) togetherness, with two divans, two beds, but the characters constantly miss their opportunities. The set is often white and ultra-modern. Each character is alone.

The original production of this play (in London) emphasized the aloneness of the characters, partly through use of the set for blocking choices and partly through the magic of small gestures. The audience hardly cared what logic the play held. It was like watching a dance unfold, a dramatic dance, one with Suzanne Langer's description of drama manifest—the feeling of impending futurity. Every time a character poured coffee or handed out glasses of brandy, the gestures were large, important, carved in space. And they each had meaning: the ways pairs of characters felt about each other was apparent from the handing and receiving of a cup. The gestures were in line with the spareness of life Pinter describes in this place—this half-awake, half-asleep land where there is no clutter, where things are wrong and every tiny move counts.

## Happy Days *by Samuel Beckett*

You should now read Samuel Beckett's *Happy Days* and then read the discussion that follows.

## Plot Summary of *Happy Days*

This play has both an unconventional plot and unusual characters. The staging is stylized, the gestures and dialogue symbolic. The world of the characters is spare, with only a few items of daily life to keep them going.

**Act I.** A low mound of burned grass. Winnie is buried up to above her waist in the mound's center. Winnie awakens to the sound of a bell and immediately begins praying. She brushes her teeth, turns to spit, and sees Willie sleeping behind her on the other side of the mound. She inspects her toothbrush, her teeth, her brush again. She says that Willie has no interest in life. She polishes her spectacles, claims she would not miss sleeping. She wishes that like Willie she had the ability to sleep through anything. She claims to have much to be thankful for in spite of migraines. She repeats several times the inscription on the toothbrush: "fully guaranteed . . . genuine pure." She tries to wake Willie with a parasol.

Winnie asks Willie if he will please not leave her again, as she may need him. She takes an elixir that supposedly aids the dispirited, those without appetites, etc. Willie's head appears, he puts on a boater, and we see him open a newspaper. Willie reads a succession of snippets from the paper, each of which elicits a flood of memories from Winnie. He says that a Dr. Hunter was found dead in a bathtub; Winnie was apparently acquainted with him. She remembers her first ball in response to another item.

She resumes her routine, examining her toothbrush, finally saying that if one takes pains, one can add to one's knowledge every day. And when one can no longer take pains, "just close the eyes and wait for the day to come," the day when human flesh begins to melt at a certain temperature. This thought gives her solace. She examines with disgust a postcard that Willie has been reading. Winnie wishes that she could bear to be alone, even though Willie does not answer her and she basically talks to herself most of the time. She claims she would sit in silence if he were not there. She forgets whether she has brushed and combed her hair. She remembers Willie calling her hair golden a long time ago, and then her words fail. She says one must occupy oneself with trivial tasks until they come back.

Winnie tells Willie to crawl back into his hole. He does so and moves to where he apparently cannot see her. She claims it is because the earth is tight today or perhaps because of the heat within. Winnie sees an emmet carrying a white ball that Willie says are eggs. They laugh and although she feels guilty, Winnie concludes there's no better way to honor God than to laugh at His jokes.

She asks if Willie ever loved her, and as he doesn't answer, she assumes he did not. Thinking of her loaded bag sparks Winnie to speak about thinking about the future rather than the past and so she resolves not to care about the bag. She does however reach inside, pulling out a revolver. Saying she is tired of it, she sets it aside. Gravity not being "what it was," Winnie says that if she were not held down, she would float up into the sky, and she thinks the earth may someday let her go. She says that sometimes she feels the fear of running out of things to do or say before the day is over. Running out of things to do before it is time for sleep is the danger to be avoided. She says she is tired of holding up her umbrella but she cannot let it down; she says a change in the world must take place first. The parasol catches fire and she hurls it downward, calling the earth an "old extinguisher." Winnie takes a music box out of her bag and listens to a waltz from *The Merry Widow*. Willie sings something unidentifiable in response. Winnie tells the story of a man (named Cooker or Shower) and woman who stopped by her mound and were puzzled as to her presence. They talked about digging her out, then disappeared. Winnie begins putting the objects around her into her bag. She is momentarily distracted by Willie's moving and calls mobility a curse. Winnie says she dreams that Willie would move to a spot in front of her head so she wouldn't have to crane her neck to see him. But she knows he can't. She asks what a hog is, Willie answers her, and she manifests a happy expression, says this will be a happy day.

**Act II.** Same scene. Winnie is now embedded further, up to her neck, and she cannot move her head. A bell rings and she opens her eyes. She tries to speak to Willie but there is no answer. She closes her eyes and a bell rings loudly. She asks Willie if he thinks the earth has lost its atmosphere. She says days are happy when she hears sounds. She says that things (e.g., a looking-glass) have a life of their own and so do not need her. She says she has often wanted to ignore the bell and open and close her eyes as she pleased, but she cannot. Winnie begins telling the story of her life, particularly about an incident with a doll she had been given around the age of five. She undressed the doll at night in the nursery, scolding her, and saw a mouse.

Winnie calls out to Willie and when he does not answer, she wonders if he is in distress, if he has been crying out and she has not heard him. She talks about when the proper time to sing would be, how many times the bell sounds before one has had time to sing. She mentions the sadness after singing, and also the approach of Mr. Shower (or Cooker) again.

She returns to the doll story, says that the mouse ran up her thigh and she screamed until the entire family awoke.

Willie appears crawling, dressed in suit clothes. He comes out from behind the mound. Winnie sees him, makes fun of his clothes, and ridicules him for not answering her earlier. She reminds him of how attractive she was to him once. He approaches the mound. After she berates him for not speaking, Willie finally and quietly utters "Win." Winnie reacts with happiness, saying this has been another happy day. She begins singing a tune about a love communicated through dances and gestures, and not through words. She closes her eyes, opens her eyes. She and Willie stare at each other.

## About Happy Days

Sometimes *Happy Days* is staged to suggest the aftermath of a nuclear holocaust. The earth itself is scorched and barren. Nothing grows. The look of the place in which Winnie exists is deadening, depressing, and stark. But did Beckett intend the play to be so specific? Did he have in mind reasons for the barrenness of the earth? Could the play be done—one student wanted to know—so that we felt we were seeing ordinary mainstream busy society? Or should a director add details to suggest that Winnie is crippled?

The play has been performed many times, many ways. And it stands up to the re-interpretations of actors, designers, and directors. When a playwright asks for scorched earth and a woman half buried in the scorched earth, when the lines of the play suggest no concerns with real life—like the needs for food and elimination—he strongly suggests that we are in an other-than-physically-realistic world. Yet within the context of this strange barren limbo in which the characters find themselves, the playwright has made some moments very detailed, some aspects of the characters' existence very real.

An MFA directing student who loved this play directed it as a final project. His love of the play came through. He said *Happy Days* appealed to him because it was a love story. His production was funny and touching and not the least bit sentimental. He had found the humanity in the play by seeing it as a love story about a married couple who had everything against them. He saw them as two people near death and aware of the question, "Who will go first? Who will be alone?"

Another student who was less in love with the play thought the whole play was a joke—a study of the way stage directions could dictate an overwhelming number of facial expressions.

In fact, Beckett *is* playing with theatre conventions. He is interested in exploring the *limits* of theatre and expanding the *possibilities*. The sum of his work tells us that; for instance, in *End Game*, two characters remain in ashcans for the whole of the play. In *Act Without Words*, a single character adjusts to a malevolent world that tantalizes him with sustenance.

In another of his plays, *Krapp's Last Tape*, Beckett puts an old man and a tape recorder on stage. No other characters. But the play is a drama and not a long monologue because Krapp relates to the tape recorder as if it were another character. The tapes that he plays are of himself at younger ages—so that he is really in a dialogue with himself as a younger self, a different man in some ways, and very much the same man in others.

In all of Beckett's plays there is some kind of *reduction* that is central to the meaning. For instance, in Act I of *Waiting for Godot*, two destitute tramps meet two travellers, Pozzo and Lucky. In Act I, Pozzo and Lucky can eat, speak, walk, and see. In Act II, the tramps, with no more hope, no food, no prospects, meet Pozzo and Lucky again. Now the *travellers* have no food. They drag along together: Lucky is dumb; Pozzo is blind. In a Beckett play, things are taken away from people. Their world is reduced as the play progresses.

*Happy Days* is no exception. Winnie can move from the waist up in Act I. In Act II she is buried to the neck and can only move her face. That is one of her losses. The gun, which is within reach in Act I and is her solace, is out of range in Act II. She cannot use it, no matter how bad things get. Another loss. And Willie talks little enough, and shows himself to Winnie only briefly in Act I. Until the last moments of Act II, she must do without seeing or hearing Willie altogether. Loss. Beckett's habit as a playwright is to give his characters too little in Act I and less in Act II.

The ending of *Happy Days* is ambiguous. Some people believe that Willie is going to leave Winnie, that he will abandon her. Some think he will shoot her to put her out of her misery. Some think he has dressed to the nines to amuse her, to give her another happy day. Beckett certainly didn't answer the question for us. He left the ending ambiguous. When an experienced playwright stops a play before a decisive action, the playwright usually means, "Look at the options. All are unbearable." There is no hope for Winnie, except what she finds inside herself, built out of practically nothing.

Why does Winnie speak almost interminably and Willie hardly at all? Why does Willie preserve the capacity to move, although at a reduced level, while Winnie is less and less able to move? Sometimes the dependence of people upon each other suggests itself to Beckett as if the two people are divided parts of one self. I had a friend who was legally blind and she married an almost completely deaf man. She used to say, "We're like a Beckett play." Perhaps one of the answers to why Winnie speaks and Willie does not is that she can, and he can't.

Some readers and some directors ignore the fact that Winnie is about fifty and see the play as one about old age. Does age really matter at all? Or does the play manage to touch a chord about relationships, no matter what the age? The woman wants love and reassurance. She has a million analogous ways of asking, "Do you love me?" The man thinks it's enough to say "Yes," once because why go over and over a thing? One of the comic aspects of this play is that these relationship dynamics exist in the lives of many men and women, and Beckett hits home. Winnie needs and wants so much more than she has, but she works at being happy in spite of the meager support for her needs. "Meagerness" does not only describe the time Willie gives her but describes as well the few possessions she uses in Act I—the toothbrush, the lipstick, etc. Everything is worn, dying. Is her body dying? Is the earth gradually swallowing her up?

There are some unusual stage directions in this piece. An actor quickly sees that the pantomime activity with the toothbrush and the lipstick is very important and that it takes the place of what in another play would be larger moves. In fact, Beckett is so careful with stage directions, he even goes so far as to write, "Pause. Do." Does he think the typical actor will cut those pauses too short without the "Do"? One can't read, "Pause. Do," without taking the pause seriously. As one actor pointed out, just reading the "Do" adds an extra beat to the pause. The actor is forced to hold back for just another brief second before moving on.

Even though Winnie can't move, she has *intentions, motivations, objectives,* and like all characters she wants something. Her actions are not largely physical actions but they are dramatic actions. Nonetheless, what does Winnie want to do? One student answered, "I want to get from one bell to the next." Another said, "I want to live." Another said, "I want to get control of my life." Another said, "I want to find happiness." Yet another said, "I want to find a way to go on." All of these are true, all of them are playable. The ones that emphasize her need to not only live, but to find joy in life, are closest to the play's meaning. Her resilience in a bleak landscape is both pathetic and admirable, both irritating and inspiring, both ordinary and amazing. The end result of plays is *irony*. Irony comes of our witnessing *incongruity*. It is incongruous, therefore ironic, that Winnie finds happiness.

*Old Times* and *Happy Days* are both stories about reduction, loss. All ages have the experience of loss. Two-act plays of the last half-century are less likely to show the possibility of rebuilding after loss. Can you think of reasons for this?

---

### Study Questions and Exercises

1. Decide on an objective for each of the characters in **Old Times**. There are different possibilities for phrasing the objectives and a range of possibilities for the objectives. For instance, this is only one set: Deeley wants to make Kate notice him; Kate wants to preserve her aloneness; Anna wants to take ownership of Kate.
2. Critique **Old Times**, using the twenty principles. Do you find dramatic irony, analogy, pursuit of objectives, etc.? Are the characters different from each other? Is there rising tension? Is the place important, metaphoric?
3. Critique **Happy Days** in the same way.

# FOURTEEN

# Exploring Form

## OVERVIEW

In this chapter are three scripts that were written by students in a first workshop and turned in for Exercise 7. The assignment is to write a one-act play complete in itself to be performed without intermission—a substantial piece of a full-length play. In each case the writers experimented with theatrical form. The first piece is a long section of Act I (Scene 1, a little more than one-half the act) of *The Etiquette of Mourning*. In this script the writer is exploring the challenges and limits of absolutely traditional dramatic form. The other scripts, the one-acts, *Double Entendre* and *Death in G-Flat*, are experimentations with non-traditional form.

## OBJECTIVES

At the end of this chapter, you should be able to

- Critique these scripts, determining whether you find rising tension, characters pursuing objectives, etc.
- Write your own Exercise 7, a one-act or a major part of a longer play

### Traditional Form

Because Scene 1 of *The Etiquette of Mourning* is long, I'm going to interrupt it at the beginnings and ends of French scenes to suggest things worth noticing about the way the playwright is working with traditional materials.

## The Etiquette of Mourning
### *by Stan Denman*

CHARACTERS

BETTY, age 49

SHIRLEY, 38

LINDA, 35

DIXIE, 27

LELA, their mother, 68

SIDNEY, their father

MR. POSS, 66

MRS. POSS, 62

PLACE: A town in Texas

TIME: The present

ACT ONE

SCENE ONE

*(The play takes place in the living room/den of a middle class home. UC is a sliding glass door leading out into a patio and yard. UR is a china cabinet. SR a hallway leading to the rest of the house. DL is a couch and a coffee table. Just L of C is a dining table. SL is an exterior door and UL is a swinging door leading to the kitchen. To the extreme R of the stage is the bedroom, partitioned off from the rest of the set. It contains a double bed, a dresser, and a door leading to a closet.*

*The lights come up and Mrs. Poss is seen sitting on the living room couch, dressed casually [perhaps in one of those floral print, polyester double knit pants/blouse combinations that some older women still wear] and snapping beans. After a moment, the telephone rings. Mrs. Poss looks to the phone and at her work [the bowl, beans, paper sack, etc.] in a dilemma. She begins to set the bowl aside and struggle out of the couch, but shows visible relief as a voice calls from the kitchen after several rings.)*

---

Notice the pace at which the playwright introduces characters. A voice from off stage prepares us for (frames the entrance of) Shirley. Meanwhile we get to know Mrs. Poss for a few seconds before we have to concentrate on Mr. Poss. The Posses exist here for two purposes. They set the scene up: they speak the exposition, letting us know that there has been a death in the family, that the sisters are gathering, that there is trouble with one of them (Linda) and that another (Shirley) always does the right thing. They set up a great deal that is factual. They also let us in on the demographics, the kind of community this is, who lives in it, what its expectations are. They are like the scenery outside the room.

When Shirley enters, we've been prepared by a second call from off stage. She enters doing something characteristic—taking care of someone, politely bringing water. Her entry starts a new French scene in literal terms, but the whole unit, in rehearsal terms, is the scene up to and including Lela's entrance. Shirley's coming and going affords the playwright opportunity to let the audience in on information that would be impossible to convey if she were on stage the whole time. The whole unit is one of exposition and preparation for the family gathering. When the Posses leave, a new unit begins: the family. Having strangers, servants, outsiders begin a scene to set it up is an old device. Does it work for you here? Does it seem old-fashioned? Do you need the information you get from it?

---

VOICE

*(Calling from offstage)* I'll get it!

*(As Mrs. Poss continues her work, Mr. Poss enters the front door, SL. He is wearing a dirty old pair of work overalls, a straw hat, and is wiping the sweat from his brow with a red shop cloth.)*

MRS. POSS

Well, did that do it?

MR. POSS

Yea, that'll do her, for a couple a weeks at least.

MRS. POSS

Good then. You've done your deed for the day. I'm almost finished myself.

MR. POSS

It's as hot as the devil out there.

MRS. POSS

Nearly half a bushel.

MR. POSS

A hundred and ten in the shade.

MRS. POSS

Make'r about six quarts.

MR. POSS

Enough to make a pig sweat.

MRS. POSS

Well, she needed the place lookin' nice.

MR. POSS

That Bermuda was nearly this high.

MRS. POSS

I wouldn't doubt it. She hadn't had time to tend to a thing. You know what she told me?

MR. POSS

What?

MRS. POSS

She said one a the older neighbor boys come by a couple a days ago and said he knew Mr. Davis was sick so he come by to cut the grass for her. She told him how nice that was of him and how much she appreciated it and turned to go back inside the house. And that boy stood right there in that yard and told her that he'd only charge her twenty dollars! Can you imagine! And her with all these doctor bills and not knowin' what Medicare'll pay. Why, if I was his Daddy, I'd wear his hide out with a cane switch.

MR. POSS

Hm. If that don't beat all. That's today's kids for ya.

MRS. POSS

Well, if it is you can have 'em. I'll tell you right now. What are neighbors for if not to help out when needed. Knowin' she needs us and we can help, that's payment enough. That's what neighbors are for. *(Pause)* Did you make sure and put the mower back in the shed?

MR. POSS

Yeah. Needs a little oil, but I couldn't find where he keeps it. *(Pause)* I guess we'll just have to hunt for it.

MRS. POSS

Oh, Ray, it's a cryin shame. You couldn't find a better man if you tried.

VOICE

*(Calling from off stage, in the kitchen, UL)* Mr. Poss, you want some ice water?

MR. POSS

Believe I would, Shirley! Thank you!

MRS. POSS

Isn't that sweet. That's just like her Daddy. Always a goin' and a blowin'. She hadn't stopped since she came in that door. Walked straight to the kitchen and started fixin' supper.

MR. POSS
That girl is a blessing to her parents.

MRS. POSS
Always has been. Just can't do enough.

MR. POSS
She not bring the family?

MRS. POSS
No. She and Betty just went home long enough to gather a few things and check on the family.

SHIRLEY
(Entering from the kitchen, UL. She is 45) Here you go, Mr. Poss. Have a seat. You didn't get too hot, did you?

MR. POSS
Naw. (She hands him the glass) Thank you, Shirley.

SHIRLEY
Well, that was Linda. She's on her way over. I wasn't sure if she was gonna come. I was kinda holdin' my breath, but it looks like she is. (Silence) Mrs. Poss, are you sure I can't get you anything?

MRS. POSS
No, Shirley, I'm just fine. As soon as we water the work horse here, we've got to be gettin' along.

SHIRLEY
So soon?

MRS. POSS
Yes. Ya'll have got enough to worry about without havin' us under foot.

SHIRLEY
Can't you stay, just til Mother gets back? I know she'd like to thank you for doing the yard . . . and these beans . . .

MRS. POSS
Now those aren't finished.

SHIRLEY
Oh, I know. I can put em up tonight after . . .

MRS. POSS
No, now tell ya what, you just run some cold water over em and stick em in the ice box and they'll keep. 'Cause after everything quietens down and everybody goes home, I imagine Lela will be lookin for something to do.

SHIRLEY
All right, but are you sure you won't stay for supper? It'll probably be just Mother, Linda and me.

MR. POSS
No. No. I think we'd better . . . (He is interrupted by a buzzer from the kitchen.)

SHIRLEY
Oh, that's the corn bread. Wait just a minute. I'll take this out, put some more in. I'll be just a minute. (She exits into the kitchen. After a few seconds the buzzer stops.)

MR. POSS
Now, Ellen, don't start gettin' that look. I know what you're thinkin.

MRS. POSS
Oh, you don't know any such thing! Besides, how's a person supposed to look! (Glances back toward the kitchen.) All that time. All that time, her own father sittin' up there fightin' for his life and she never even darkened the door step. It's a cryin' shame. And now she calls up and says, "I'm comin' home," when it's too late!
(The front door opens and Lela enters. She is dressed very nicely, wearing a conservative, long sleeve navy blue dress. She is weary, but does not forget her Southern hospitality.)

MR. POSS
Ellen.

MRS. POSS
Wha? . . . oh . . . Well, here she is!

LELA
You're still here! I didn't see your car.

MRS. POSS
We walked up. Does us good, so they tell me.

MR. POSS
Yeah, the doctor tells me it'll keep my ticker tickin'.

MRS. POSS
Yeah, well I'll tell him you were tickin' away when you dropped cold on the pavement. (Slight pause.)

LELA
Yes, it is hot isn't it? (Crosses to the table and sets her purse down.) The yard looks so nice.

MR. POSS
Just finished her up.

LELA
I saw. For a minute there I thought I was pullin' up to the wrong house.

MR. POSS
Well, it ought to do you for a couple of weeks, at least.

LELA
Oh, thank you. It'll look so pretty for all the visitors.

MR. POSS                              MRS. POSS
It's no trouble at all.          That's what neighbors are for.

LELA
Any how, I thank you. You gonna stay for supper?

MRS. POSS
No. We gotta be goin'.

SHIRLEY
(Entering from the kitchen with a bag full of trash.) I just thought I'd get this while I was . . . (Sees her mother.) Oh, you're back.

LELA
Yeah. When did you get here?

SHIRLEY
About an hour ago. (Sets the bag down, goes to her mother, and gives her a hug.) How do you feel?

LELA
Oh, I've had better days, but I'm all right. I'm just not kickin' too high.

SHIRLEY
Were you all right last night? I don't think I . . .

LELA
Whatcha got there? You cleanin' up?

SHIRLEY
Oh, no. I was just taking out the kitchen garbage. . . .

MR. POSS
Here, Shirley, let me help you with that.

SHIRLEY
No, no, I've got it. Mother, I'll be right back. (Takes the garbage bag and exits through the patio door, UC.)

MRS. POSS
Come on, Ray. We need to make ourselves scarce. Lela (kisses her on the cheek), you take it slow and easy and let us know if you need anything.

LELA
All right. (Noticing the things on the table.) Wait a minute. You're forgettin' somethin'.

MRS. POSS
No, those are some snaps for you. You just keep em cold and after the weekend we'll get busy on em. Just the two of us.

LELA
Well, thank you. I'd like that. I'd like that a lot.

MR. POSS
Now, Mrs. Davis, you just call and we'll be here.

LELA
I know you will and I thank you again. Havin' folks like you makes all this a little easier.

MRS. POSS
We'll be talkin' to you tomorrow . . .

MR. POSS
And we'll see you Saturday, if not before.

LELA
Alright. Bye, bye.
(They exit out the front door and she closes the door after them, turns around and looks at the empty room, and crosses to sit in the rocking chair, R of C. Shirley enters through the patio door UC.)

There is a rhythm change after the Posses leave. The stage becomes quieter, slower. There is still an insistence on showing Shirley as someone who keeps doing, keeps working. This will be important later. It's Shirley's contribution to the family, her virtue, and also her fault. We learn both how strong and how fragile Lela is through concrete details like the way she imagined Sidney patting her on the leg at night and the fact that she has her shoes on the wrong feet. We also get more expository information about the sisters, leading us to expect their entrances. This is a help to the audience—is an outlining of what will happen in the whole scene.

What happens in this unit? Shirley takes charge of all arrangements, gives Lela plans and ideas about how to proceed. Lela tries to hold onto herself.

SHIRLEY
Mr. and Mrs. Poss leave?

LELA
Just now.

SHIRLEY
The yard looks nice.

LELA
Uh huh.

SHIRLEY
Mother, do you remember the last time you watered your potted plants?

LELA
Oh, Shirley, I . . . I couldn't tell you.

SHIRLEY
That's all right. They were really dried out, so I watered them pretty good. One of them was already dead though and I'm not sure the others are going to make it. We'll just have to wait and see.

LELA
Oh, dear.

SHIRLEY
Don't worry about it. Those things happen. (Kisses her mother on the cheek. Pause.) All I could do last night was to lay awake and think of you in this house all by yourself.

LELA
I was fine.

SHIRLEY
But, Mother, Betty and I both wanted to stay.

LELA
I know, but I didn't want you to. I just needed some time by myself to think is all. I know you wanted to stay. I practically had to shove you out the door.

SHIRLEY

But it just didn't seem right. Leavin' you alone . . . so soon and all. I couldn't sleep a wink.

LELA

That makes two of us. (*Pause.*) Every time I started to doze off I could feel him stroke my hair or pattin' me on the leg. I'd try to roll over and shake the feelin' and then I'd feel him spoonin' up to me. . . . Warm. I don't know when I've ever been so glad to see daylight.

SHIRLEY

Oh, Mother, one of us should have been here.

LELA

No. It . . . wasn't bad, not like it sounds. It was nice . . . almost . . . comforting. The only bad part of it was when I went to touch him back or whisper a thought that popped into my head and I would suddenly realize he wasn't there. That bed always seemed so small with the two of us in it, but last night it seemed twice as big.

SHIRLEY

Oh, Mother . . .

LELA

No, no, I'm fine. I . . . just stop and think now and then and get it out of my system, then I can move on. Sometimes I feel like I'm holdin' myself together with pins and needles, but I'm holdin' together and that's somethin'. Isn't it?

SHIRLEY

Yes, ma'am. It is.

LELA

Has anyone called? I'm gettin' kinda worried.

SHIRLEY

Betty called about a half hour ago and said she was runnin' late, and Linda just called to say she's in town but had to run by the store before she came over. She should be here anytime.

LELA

And Dixie?

SHIRLEY

Still the same, but I left another message anyway.

LELA

Well, I'm gonna go wash up and change before they get here. I think I'll feel better if I do. This dress is just too hot.

SHIRLEY

Alright.

LELA

You know, I haven't done that much today, but I'm just bone weary. Not like I just didn't sleep good last night, but I just ache. My feet and legs. Seems like I've just run a marathon.

SHIRLEY

You have every right to be tired. Now, you just go on and change and when you're . . . (*Looks at Lela's feet.*) Mother?

LELA

Huh?

SHIRLEY

Are you . . . ?

LELA

What's that?

SHIRLEY

Are your shoes on the wrong feet?

LELA

What? (*Looks at her feet and begins to laugh.*) Now, would you look at that! I knew there was something wrong with me today! (*They both laugh.*) The director at the funeral home must have thought, "That poor lady can't even dress herself."

SHIRLEY

Oh, he probably didn't even notice.

LELA

I wondered why I kept having the urge to walk around corners all day! Just look! If Sidney saw that he'd never let me forget it! (*They both stop laughing. Lela takes the shoes off. Pause.*) I guess my mind just hasn't been on doin' my business.

SHIRLEY

Oh, that's all right. You've just had a lot to think about. Who knows, you may have even started a fad. (*Pause.*) Did you get the clothes there okay?

LELA

Yea. (*Pause.*) He'll look real nice. (*Pause. Fighting back the tears.*) Only I forgot the . . . (*She is interrupted by the buzzer from the kitchen.*)

SHIRLEY

Oh . . .

LELA

Are you cooking something?

SHIRLEY

Supper. (*Running to the kitchen.*) Just a second . . . (*After she exits the buzzer stops. Lela dries her eyes and regains control. After only a few seconds, Shirley reenters.*) I just had to take the cornbread out of the oven.

LELA

Cornbread?

SHIRLEY

Yes, ma'am, and fresh purple hull peas, and corn from the garden, and candied sweet potatoes.

LELA

Great land a Goshen! After all that hospital food, that sounds so good. I can smell it, now that you mention it.

SHIRLEY

I thought we'd just have vegetables tonight, if that's all right.

LELA

Oh, it's fine, fine. I just didn't realize how hungry I was until I smelled somethin' cookin'. I think I forgot to eat lunch.

SHIRLEY

All right, you go change then, I'll set the table, and we'll make it an early supper. *(They both begin to exit, Shirley to the kitchen and Lela down the hallway, SR.)*

LELA

Are you sure you don't need any help?

SHIRLEY

Yes, I'm sure. Now, go. *(They both exit.)*
*(After a beat the front door slowly opens and Linda steps in. She is dressed in tight, faded blue jeans and sweatshirt decorated with sequins or feathers—a cheap attempt at a designer look. She quietly creeps in the room looking to see if the coast is clear. She crosses to the dining table. Just as she reaches for Lela's purse, Shirley enters from the kitchen carrying dinner plates and silverware. Linda jerks back and Shirley doesn't see.)*

---

The entrance of Linda is very well handled. The writer allows the stage to go empty and quiet before Linda enters. Her entrance is sneaky. She tries to and almost manages to steal money from her mother. Dramatic irony is in motion. We know Linda tried to take money from her mother's purse. Shirley and Lela don't know. It gives us the edge on information and makes us watch Linda with interest.

Notice that we get a scene unit between Shirley and Linda before Lela returns. Again, this allows the playwright to get across bits of information that would be off-limits if all three were on stage. We learn about Linda's private life (Danny) and just how low on cash they are. We learn Linda has been drinking. We see Shirley, again, taking the controlling role, trying to protect her mother from Linda. Even short scene units have the characteristics of scenes, e.g., Shirley brings a cup of coffee to Linda who didn't ask for it and she tries to get her to take it. This is a metaphor for her giving Linda advice and censure.

We get a set up about Dixie's life—a hint that things are not right there. This should lead us to want to know more and to expect Dixie's entrance.

Finally the civility between the sisters cracks enough that we get the first round of major resentments. Linda has been absent at all the difficult times. Shirley has been there facing things. Each resents the other.

How do you feel about the lengths of scenes? Do you have long enough with each character? Too long? Have you noticed that Lela is the sought-after character? Everyone wants to please her. She is the parent the sisters still have—in some ways a substitute for father. In a later scene, there is a struggle over some of Sidney's things—who will possess them. Is the theme of trying to earn a parent's love and recognition coming through?

---

SHIRLEY

Hi! I didn't hear you come in! *(She crosses to the table and sets the dishes down.)*

LINDA

Yeah. I just kinda snuck in on you, didn't I?

SHIRLEY

Well, come here! *(They hug.)*

LINDA

Is Mother here?

SHIRLEY

Yeah, she's just in the back room changing.

LINDA

Oh.

SHIRLEY

I know she just can't wait to see you.

LINDA

Is she okay?

SHIRLEY

I think so . . . She just tries to keep busy . . . keep her mind occupied. She's holding up as good or better than any of us . . .

LINDA

I mean . . . about me.

SHIRLEY

Oh. Well . . . maybe a little disappointed.

LINDA

So what else is new?

SHIRLEY

Well . . . She does have cause. *(Pause.)* Oh, let's not talk about that. There's plenty of time for that.

LINDA

Hmm.

SHIRLEY

*(Leading her over to the couch.)* What I want to know is what have you been up to? You cut your hair! Turn around and let me see. It looks so good!

LINDA

*(Nervous and impatient.)* Shirley, I . . .

SHIRLEY

I always said your hair looked better, up and away from your face. Why do you want to keep colorin' it though?

LINDA

I don't have . . . *(She is interrupted by a car horn which blows several times.)*

SHIRLEY

*(Gets up quickly and moves to the door.)* That must be Betty.

LINDA

*(Following her.)* No . . .

SHIRLEY

She called to say she was running late, but she didn't say why.

LINDA

It's not Betty . . .

SHIRLEY

I was starting to get kind of worried when she didn't say, but I surely didn't expect her this soon after she called. *(Opens the front door and looks out.)* Why that's not . . .

LINDA

No. It's Danny. He brought me.

SHIRLEY

*(Pause.)* Did Mother know he was coming?

LINDA

He's not staying. He just brought me over.

SHIRLEY

What's he waiting for?

LINDA

He needs money for gas. *(She makes a show of checking her pockets.)* Do you have ten dollars I can borrow? *(Shirley looks at her for a moment, then crosses to her purse, on the china cabinet, UR, and takes out some money, giving it to Linda. The horn is heard again.)* Thanks. I'll write this down so I won't forget to get it back to you.

SHIRLEY

*(Not looking at her.)* That's all right.

LINDA

No, really I want to pay you back.

SHIRLEY

Don't worry about it.

LINDA

No. I will. I'll . . . *(The horn again.)*

SHIRLEY

Just take the money!
*(Linda exits. Shirley waits a beat and then crosses into the kitchen. She comes back with a cup of coffee and sets it on the dining table. She looks out the door, then begins to set the table. Linda reenters, carrying an overnight bag. There is a long silence while Linda puts the bag on the couch.)*

LINDA

Thanks. *(Pause.)*

SHIRLEY

Here's some coffee for you.

LINDA

No, thanks. I'm really not . . .

SHIRLEY

Go ahead. It's yours.

LINDA

No, I . . .

SHIRLEY

Linda, drink the coffee. *(Pause.)*

LINDA

Listen, it's not what you think.

SHIRLEY

I know . . .

LINDA

Really. It was just one drink.

SHIRLEY

I know. I just don't want Mother to smell it. It might upset her.

LINDA

Okay. *(Pause.)*

SHIRLEY

Everyone was pretty worried, you know.

LINDA

Everyone?

SHIRLEY

Yes. Mother, Betty, me . . .

LINDA

Daddy? *(Pause.)*

SHIRLEY

I think so, yes.

LINDA

Hm. *(Pause.)* Did he ask for me?

SHIRLEY

He was very weak. He couldn't say much.

LINDA

Was he alert?

SHIRLEY

Fairly, until later Tuesday night, then he drifted in and out.

LINDA

Did he know I wasn't there?

SHIRLEY

*(Pause.)* I don't know. Maybe.

LINDA

But he didn't call for me.

SHIRLEY

He really didn't call for anyone. He just called out names and words. . . . He rambled.

LINDA

Who?

SHIRLEY
What?

LINDA
Whose names?

SHIRLEY
I don't really remember. So much was going on then. *(Pause.)*

LINDA
I see.

SHIRLEY
I'm sorry, Linda. I tried calling you, but there was no answer. I tried all night after he began to get worse, and then I had one of the nurses try while we stayed with him.

LINDA
It's all right. Looks like I wasn't needed anyway.

SHIRLEY
Oh, don't say that. Don't feel that way . . .

LINDA
And Mother?

SHIRLEY
She's alright. She understands. She wanted you and Dixie both to be there, but she knew . . .

LINDA
Wait a minute. Dixie wasn't there?

SHIRLEY
No. She's still out of town. I thought you knew. We haven't been able to get in touch with her to tell her what happened. I've left at least half a dozen messages on her answering machine.

LINDA
You didn't tell her on the machine, did you?

SHIRLEY
Of course not.

LINDA
Then she doesn't know?

SHIRLEY
We've got to tell her when she gets here.

LINDA
Oh, great.

SHIRLEY
Mother thought she said she had to go to Houston, but we're not sure. Something to do with this new research job of hers.

LINDA
Oh, really?

SHIRLEY
Yea. I thought for sure she would have told you. She didn't say anything to you about this job?

LINDA
No. She didn't say anything about any job.

SHIRLEY
Houston sounds right doesn't it?

LINDA
Hm? Oh, yeah. Houston sounds right.

SHIRLEY
She did call though. Tuesday night. Right before he began to get worse. We held the phone to Daddy's ear. Sounded just like she was next door, but I don't think he could understand her. His mind just wasn't right. If she sticks to her pattern, she'll call sometime tonight. *(Pause.)*

LINDA
When exactly did he go?

SHIRLEY
The death certificate says Wednesday morning at 6:36, but I think it was earlier than that. It wasn't even light outside. It took a while to get someone from downstairs to confirm it officially. *(Long pause.)* So, what did you do with the girls?

LINDA
Hm? What?

SHIRLEY
The girls, where are they?

LINDA
Oh. With Billy.

SHIRLEY
Linda! How could . . . !

LINDA
It's a court order. There's nothing I can do about it.

SHIRLEY
I don't see . . .

LINDA
It's just every other weekend.

SHIRLEY
But still . . .

LINDA
Shirley!

SHIRLEY
I'm sorry . . . it's just . . . I'm sorry. (Silence.) So, how long are you going to be able to stay?

LINDA
I told my boss I'd be back on Monday.

SHIRLEY
The whole weekend?

LINDA
Surprised? *(Shirley doesn't answer.)* Me too.

SHIRLEY

Oh . . . well . . . anyway . . . That's good. It'll be nice to have you here. We need this time together and it will help Mother to get along a little easier. I think she had a rough time of it last night. Dealing with an empty house.

LINDA

Weren't you and Betty here?

SHIRLEY

No. Mother wanted to be alone.

LINDA

And you agreed? You just left her here by herself?

SHIRLEY

She insisted. It was what she wanted.

LINDA

That's what she said, but I can't believe you actually left her the night after . . .

SHIRLEY

Linda . . . we were here when it counted.

LINDA

(Pause.) Well . . . there's not a whole lot I can say to that, is there?

SHIRLEY

She's fine now. We just need to be supportive. Take some of the burden off.

LINDA

All right.

---

The tension rises when Lela and Linda are on stage together—not only because they have a history of hurting each other, but because that history makes them more concerned with each other than with Shirley. Shirley suffers rejection when Lela re-enters. Notice how Shirley continues to attempt to control everything—from directions about where the butter is kept to information about Linda's plans for a long stay. Lela and Linda relate with Shirley between them.

When Lela tells stories about herself and Sidney, she symbolically reclaims him and declares her separateness from her daughters.

Bringing food to the table and sitting down to supper is an action that makes characters move naturally and focuses the scene.

Does this scene have enough tension?

---

(Lela enters wearing casual pants, a cotton blouse, and comfortable shoes. She stops just outside the room.)

LELA

I thought I heard somebody a honkin'!

LINDA

Mother?

LELA

Linda. (Pause.) What's this? You'd better get over here and hug my neck. (Linda immediately crosses to her Mother, hugs her and begins to cry.) Now, now, none of that.

LINDA

Mother . . .

LELA

Shhhh.

LINDA

. . . I . . .

LELA

Quiet now. It's all right.

LINDA

But, I . . . I'm sorry . . .

LELA

I know. I understand.

LINDA

I'm so sorry. I didn't mean to hurt you . . .

LELA

Shhhh. You didn't . . .

LINDA

. . . I didn't . . .

LELA

You didn't.

LINDA

I just couldn't. I couldn't come.

LELA

And I didn't ask you to.

LINDA

I couldn't. Please don't be angry with me . . . please . . .

LELA

Shhhhh. That's enough now.

LINDA

I couldn't come! He wouldn't . . .

LELA

Shhhh. Linda, quiet.

LINDA

He didn't want me there! He didn't want me! . . .

LELA

(Firmly.) That's enough! (Pause.) Didn't want you? You have no idea what he wanted. (Pause.) Here now, let's not drag all that up. It won't do any of us a bit a good. Just pouring salt on old wounds. Now, come on. It's getting late. Let's go ahead and eat. Betty can warm up a plate when she gets here. (Exits into the kitchen.)

SHIRLEY

It's all right. You're both upset now. It will pass. She's just worried that Daddy may have . . .

LINDA

I don't care about Daddy! I just didn't want Mother to be angry.

(*Linda exits down the hall, SR, and Shirley is left in the center of the room. After a moment Lela reenters from the kitchen with a bowl of peas and a bowl of corn and places them on the dining table.*)

LELA

Shirley, is that tea sweet or unsweet?

SHIRLEY

It's sweet, but I'll get it Mother.

(*Shirley exits into the kitchen as Lela removes her purse from the table and sets it on the china cabinet. She crosses back to the table and moves the bowls to the center as Linda reenters from the hall with Kleenex in hand. They look at each other for an instant.*)

LELA

You best come on before it gets cold. (*Lela exits to the kitchen. Linda crosses to the table and looks on as Shirley reenters with four glasses of iced tea. She holds the door for Lela who follows with the sweet potatoes and cornbread.*)

SHIRLEY

I just went ahead and fixed Betty's glass. I bet she'll be here before the ice melts.

(*Shirley sets the glasses at the four places and they all sit at the table. Linda begins to serve her plate. The following action is not a "big moment," but a simple ritual that has become second nature.*)

LELA

Shirley, you want to offer thanks?

SHIRLEY

You can, Mother.

LELA

(*The two women bow their heads. As the prayer begins, Linda puts down the bowl in her hands and bows her head.*) Our Father in Heaven, we thank you for this day that you have given us, and for the food we are about to receive. (*During the prayer, both Shirley and Linda look up and find themselves looking at one another. After a beat, they bow their heads and close their eyes until the prayer is over.*) We ask that you bless it to the nourishment of our bodies and bless the hands that prepared it. Be with us as we go through our daily lives . . . and please . . . be with those who are no longer among us. It's in your Son's name we pray, Amen.

(*There is a short pause as the three women take in the end of the prayer, then Lela begins to help her plate and the others follow.*)

LELA

These fresh peas smell so good.

SHIRLEY

This corn too. (*To Linda.*) It's from our garden.

(*Silence. Linda gets up and begins to cross to the kitchen.*)

SHIRLEY

What do you need, Linda?

LINDA

Butter, for the cornbread.

SHIRLEY

Oh. I did forget that, didn't I? You sit down. I'll get it.

LINDA

No, I'll get it. I'm already up. Mother, where do you keep . . .

SHIRLEY

It's on the second shelf of the refrigerator. Right hand side. (*Linda exits into the kitchen.*)

SHIRLEY

Linda! You might bring the salt and pepper too! It's on the stove! Mother, did Linda tell you that she got the whole weekend off, so she'll be able to stay with us?

LELA

Oh, well that's good. (*Pause. Linda reenters with butter, salt and pepper, and sits.*) When do you have to be back?

LINDA

Monday. I can't afford to stay away any longer. Billy still isn't sending the alimony checks.

SHIRLEY

You are kidding?

LINDA

No. Seventh month in a row.

SHIRLEY

But he still gets to see the girls.

LELA

You don't mean it.

SHIRLEY

Yes, ma'am, I do. I tell you, I'd be on the phone to my lawyer.

LELA

Is there anything they can do about that?

SHIRLEY

Of course, there's something they can do.

LINDA

Yes, but that takes time too—more red tape—and I can't afford to wait around for red tape. I've got to buy groceries. Anyway, now he's filed for Chapter 13.

SHIRLEY

Oh, no.

LINDA

Oh, yes. And I know he did it just to spite me.

SHIRLEY

Linda, how are you going to pay rent? That job at the convenience store is not going to do it. You're going to have to find another job.

LINDA

Well, that's easier said than done. Besides, I'm doing okay. I scrape by. The rent's not that bad. Just two hundred a month.

SHIRLEY

Only two hundred?

LINDA

Uh huh. I also have the . . .

SHIRLEY

You only pay two hundred for that apartment?

LINDA

Well, that's my half . . . I . . . I split it with a friend. *(Long silence.)*

SHIRLEY

Mother, did you tell Linda about your shoes?

LELA

I don't believe so.

SHIRLEY

Oh, you've got to tell her.

LINDA

What?

SHIRLEY

Mother and I thought it was so funny.

LINDA

What?

LELA

Well, I was just wearing the wrong shoes . . .

SHIRLEY

. . . On the wrong feet! *(They all begin to loosen up and smile.)* Her feet looked just like this. *(She demonstrates with her hands.)*

LINDA

When?

| LELA | SHIRLEY |
|------|---------|
| This morning. | This afternoon. |

LELA

Well, really I walked around all day like that.

LINDA

Oh, no!

LELA

Yeah. I did. I told Shirley I just ached all over from running in circles all day. *(They all laugh.)*

SHIRLEY

She did. She walked just like this. *(She demonstrates again with her hands. They laugh again.)*

LELA

Well, I'll tell ya, there's one thing I can say about myself. I have certainly never been boring to live with. I could always

make your Daddy laugh about something. Of course, most of the time it wasn't intentional. It was just pulling dumb stunts like today.

SHIRLEY

Like what?

LELA

Well . . . I . . . I remember once . . . I don't think I've ever told you this. You know how your Daddy felt about talking about sex or any off-color remarks . . . anyway, it was the year that Martin Luther King led the big civil rights march on Washington, D.C. . . . uh . . . nineteen sixty-three?

SHIRLEY

Sixty-four.

LINDA

Uh uh. Sixty-three.

LELA

Sixty . . . anyway, Sidney and I were over at the Poss's having dinner and they were showing off their new television set. Well, the news was on and they were showing this march. You know, how the white people on the side of the road were spitting at the marchers, and cursing, and acting so ugly. So, the longer I watched it, the madder I got. And then, I remember, it showed a group of young white and black people, standing on the side of the road, who wanted to march, but were afraid to. Well, that was it. I was so mad, I stood up right there and shouted, "That is wrong! *Everyone* ought to stand up and menstruate!" *(Shirley and Linda react.)* I thought your Daddy was going to die of embarrassment. His face turned every shade of red and I could see him just sinking into the floor. But no one laughed. Then Ray Poss leaned forward and looked up at me with a straight face and said, "Demonstrate, Lela?" And then Ellen began to snicker *(Shirley and Linda begin to laugh.),* then Ray. Well, I couldn't hold it any longer either and Sidney wound up laughing harder than any of us. *(They all laugh.)*

SHIRLEY

Daddy?

LELA

Uh huh.

LINDA

I can't believe that.

LELA

Oh, yes. There I was in my Sunday best, standing in the Poss's living room, on Ellen's brand new carpet, trying to get everyone to "stand up and menstruate for civil rights!" *(More laughter.)* I think the closest your Daddy ever got to a dirty joke was later that year when I was going through "the change." He said, "Good. You may have a few hot flashes now and then, but at least you won't have to demonstrate anymore." *(Laughter again.)*

SHIRLEY
Daddy said that?

LELA
Mm hmm.

LINDA
I can't believe it. I sure never saw that side of him.

LELA
(Smiling.) You never looked for it.

SHIRLEY
Did you hear a car door?

LELA
Maybe so.

---

We end another French scene and begin a new one with the entry of Betty. Will she vie for mother's attention, too? The answer is yes.

Betty's entrance has been prepared for by the references to it in earlier scenes.

Betty is drawn by: how she comes in the door, what she brings, what she says.

Shirley is likely to exclude Betty. Lela is the one who includes her. Lela accepts the offering of chicken, says the meal needed it. A decision on stage even so small as that is significant. Lela is changing a plan made by Shirley who prides herself on ordering and deciding things.

Is Linda included in the dinner table conversation? Why? What does this set up?

How do Shirley and Lela react to the story Betty tells? Can you see how their reactions are different and reflect attitudes towards other things, including death, by suggesting who needs to re-define, who is accepting?

Linda and Betty have both been outcasts in different ways in this family. How do they cope with each other? Can you feel the tension rising between them?

The hymn-singing segment is comic and is meant to be so. Does it work? Can you sense Lela's getting lost in all the hubbub around her?

What is the treasure? What is being fought over? The materials of mourning. The things that symbolize the grieving process. The food served. The funeral service. There is even a scene later in the play when Shirley inadvertently takes something away from her mother. She does the laundry and puts it away. Lela is furious because she can no longer smell her husband in his clothing. That was part of her grieving process.

Once Betty is on stage, the scene that includes all of them is longer than anything that came before. Does this seem right? Appropriate? Rhythmically satisfying?

---

(The sound of the screen door opening is heard followed by the low thumping of someone kicking the door.)

BETTY
(Yelling through the closed door.) Mother? Shirley?

SHIRLEY
There's that Betty. (She gets up and opens the front door. Lela follows. Linda at a distance.) There you are! We were beginning to get worried about you.
(Betty enters. She is weighted down with a hanging bag of clothes, a suitcase, a paper sack, and a plate of food wrapped in aluminum foil.)

BETTY
Take something quick.

SHIRLEY
(Shirley takes the plate and the suitcase.) Good grief!

BETTY
I didn't think I was going to make it.

LELA
(Taking the plate from Shirley.) What's this?

BETTY
I thought I was going to drop it all.

SHIRLEY
(Setting the suitcase down by the door and relieving Betty of the paper sack and hanging bag.) Well, come on in.

LELA
(Peeking under the foil.) Chicken!

SHIRLEY
We'll just set this over here with Linda's. (Crosses to the couch and puts the things there.)

BETTY
With wh . . . ? (She sees Linda for the first time and stops.)

LINDA
Hi.

BETTY
(Slight pause.) Shirley, you better hold that sack under the bottom. It might split . . .

LELA
Look, ya'll, chicken.

SHIRLEY
Oh, good.

BETTY
I fried it up before I left, cause I knew you wouldn't feel like cookin'. (Linda returns to the table.)

LELA
Well, that was nice.

BETTY
Mother, how do you feel? (They hug.) I thought about you the whole time I was gone.

LELA

Well, you've only been gone since yesterday evening.

BETTY

I know, but . . . Oh, Mother. What are we gonna do? *(Pulls her close and hugs her tight again.)* What in heaven's name are we gonna do? *(Begins to cry.)* I just thought and thought about the . . .

LELA

Here now, let's not start that cryin' again. There's plenty a time for that on Saturday. You girls would have me cried out. *(Pause.)* Now, come on to the table. Let's eat some of this chicken.

SHIRLEY

Well, Mother, we've got enough. Why don't we just save that for tomorrow?

BETTY

Oh, you're already eating?

LELA

Yeah, but we didn't have any meat so this'll work out just fine. Come on.

SHIRLEY

Are you sure you . . .

BETTY

You don't have any meat? You've got to have meat. It's protein.

SHIRLEY

Well, I thought . . .

LELA

Will you two sit down before I eat mine and yours both?

BETTY

Well, all right. Is this my place?

SHIRLEY

No, you're next to Linda, over there.

BETTY

Oh . . . all right.

SHIRLEY

*(Pause. Everyone sits.)* I'm so glad you made it all right. When you just said that you were going to be late and didn't say why, I got kinda worried.

LELA

You didn't tell me that.

SHIRLEY

I didn't want you to worry. So what happened?

BETTY

Ah. You wouldn't believe.

LELA

What?

BETTY

Those grandkids of ours can get into more trouble. My own kids were never such a handful.

LELA

Are you and Gene just now figurin' that out?

SHIRLEY

Are they all right?

BETTY

Yes. The reason I didn't say anything over the phone is that little Josh was there and he would have died of embarrassment.

SHIRLEY

What?

BETTY

Well, he was playin' outside in the garden while his granddaddy was hoeing the peas and I was cookin' in the kitchen and watchin' out the window. Then all of a sudden, Gene and I heard this screamin' and hollerin' and looked up and saw Josh dancin' around like crazy, because a . . . *(begins to laugh.)* . . . a bee had flown up his britches leg.

LELA

Oh, no.

BETTY

Stung him three times.

SHIRLEY

Betty, that must have hurt.

BETTY

I know. I don't mean to be laughing, but his little legs were just goin' lickedy split.

LELA

Well, is he all right?

BETTY

Oh, he's fine. I put a baking soda paste on it and by the time I left he was laughing about it too.

SHIRLEY

Well, I'll be.

BETTY

I told him we were going to have to enter him into a cha-cha contest. *(They all laugh. Linda smiles.)*

LINDA

Pass the cornbread, please.

LELA

Tell him he's gonna have to tie a string around his britches leg to keep the bugs out.

BETTY

He's a mess, I'll tell you.

SHIRLEY

So, are you going to be able to stay the whole weekend?

BETTY
Yes, Gene and I got a transfer carrier from Crockette to take my place.

LELA
You didn't have to do that.

BETTY
I know that.

SHIRLEY
Linda is gonna get to stay too.

BETTY
Really?

LINDA
Uh huh.

BETTY
How long?

SHIRLEY
The whole weekend.

BETTY
Really? *(Slight pause.)* I tell you, it's just too much for Gene to try and do it all by himself. And we both couldn't take off.

SHIRLEY
Why, it's no wonder. I don't see how you run that post office with just the two of you.

BETTY
Well, Bivens isn't that big of a route, but the mail around April fifteenth does get awful heavy.

SHIRLEY
Don't I know it. Harold is just swamped with tax returns. He's got so many extensions to file . . . Oh, but he'll be there for the funeral, Mother. He wouldn't miss that.

BETTY
And you know Gene will be there.

LELA
I understand. Life goes on. Those men have to make a livin'. The bill collector don't wait for nobody.

BETTY
Well, Gene's gonna have some real nice things to say.

SHIRLEY
What?

BETTY
I've asked Gene to say a few words at Daddy's funeral.

LINDA
Why?

BETTY
Well, it's only natural. He was like a son to Daddy. *(Shirley and Linda look at each other.)* Anyway, I think he'll do a real nice job. He's going to tie together several scriptures about

fathers. You know, "honor your father and mother" and "a father hath compassion on his children," things like that. Won't that be nice?

SHIRLEY
Mm hm.

BETTY
*(To Lela.)* I thought you'd appreciate that. *(Lela smiles. To Shirley.)* Actually . . . it was my idea.

LINDA
I'm sure it was.

BETTY
But don't tell Gene I told you.

SHIRLEY
I thought Brother Nelson was going to do the service. I mean, he is the minister.

BETTY
Well, yes he is, but . . .

SHIRLEY
Mother?

LELA
*(Looking down, slowly eating.)* I think Betty thought Gene might do a nice service.

LINDA
But is that what you want?

BETTY
Of course that's what she wants.

SHIRLEY
Mother?

LELA
Yes, it's fine.

BETTY
I asked Brother Nelson to say the prayer. *(Shirley and Linda look at each other again.)*

LINDA
Well, why don't you just do it yourself?

BETTY
What? . . . uh . . . oh, you're joking. Don't be so silly.

SHIRLEY
Betty, we should . . .

BETTY
Oh, that reminds me. *(Getting up from the table, she crosses to the paper sack that sits by the door. She reaches into the sack and pulls out five or six hymnals, paper, and a pen, and brings them back to the table.)* I told Brother Nelson we'd pick out the hymns for the service.

SHIRLEY
We'd pick them out?

BETTY

Yes.

SHIRLEY

But I thought he usually took care of all of that.

BETTY

Well, he usually does. But ... Brother Nelson just isn't family. I thought this would make it all a little more special.

SHIRLEY

(Shirley and Linda, another look.) All right, but don't you think this could wait until after we eat?

BETTY

Oh, it won't bother us. Besides a little music will probably help our digestion.

LINDA

Then why don't we turn on the radio?

BETTY

Don't be silly. That old thing hasn't worked in years. Besides, we need to pick out hymns. That's the whole point.

LINDA

Really?

BETTY

Mm hmm.
(Betty passes the books out to the others at the table. She immediately begins flipping through hers while eating. Lela slowly turns the pages. Linda does not touch her book, but stares at her plate while eating. Shirley neither eats nor looks at the book, but watches each of the others, trying to decide what to do. All is quiet except for the light humming of Betty going from song to song. Then.)

BETTY

Oh, this would be perfect. Number four. Listen. (She sings.)

> "Asleep in Jesus. Blessed sleep.
> From which none ever wakes to weep
> A calm and undisturbed repose.
> Unbroken by the last of foes."

Isn't that pretty?

LINDA

I think it's horrible.

BETTY

(Offended.) Why?

LINDA

This is a funeral, not a slumber party.

BETTY

That's not what it means.

LINDA

I know what it means. I just ... If you're going to pick the songs, why don't you pick something a little more cheerful, huh?

SHIRLEY

That might not be a bad idea. (Shirley begins to tentatively look through her book. After a moment, Lela closes her book and pushes it away.) Mother, are you all right?

LELA

Yeah. Yeah, I just don't have my reading glasses is all. I'll get the headache.

LINDA

Are you sure?

LELA

Yeah.

BETTY

What about this one? (She sings.)

> "The sands of time are sinking ..."

SHIRLEY

What number?

BETTY

(Still singing.)

> "The dawn" —five twenty-one—"of heaven breaks,
> The summer morn I've sighed for,"

(Shirley joins in, singing alto. During the singing, Linda exits to the kitchen. She brings back a pitcher of tea and a bottle of aspirin, fills her own glass, and takes some of the pills.)

SHIRLEY and BETTY

(Singing.)

> "The fair, sweet morn awakes.
> Dark, dark hath been the midnight,
> But dayspring is at hand ..."

LELA

(Interrupting.) I don't ... I don't believe Sydney knew that one.

BETTY

Oh, but, Mother, isn't it pretty?

SHIRLEY

No, Betty. I think she's right. It is pretty, but we need to pick songs that meant somethin' to Daddy.

BETTY

Well, I know he would have liked it if he'd heard it.

SHIRLEY

Mother, did Daddy ever mention any songs that he would like sung, maybe some of the older ones?

LELA

Well ...

BETTY

Oh, there's that one that they used to sing all the time. Uh ...

SHIRLEY
Maybe it's in the index.

BETTY
No, it was in the old song book. This one doesn't have it. Uh . . . *(She closes her eyes and hums a few notes.)* Ah, that's it. *(She sings.)*

> "All along the road to the soul's true abode,
> There's an Eye watching you.
> Ev'ry step that you take this great Eye is awake,
> There's an all-seeing Eye watching you.
> Watching you, watching you,
> Ev'ryday mind the course you pursue . . ."

LINDA
*(Containing her laughter.)* That's enough. Write that one down. That's Daddy to a "T." *(Shirley is caught off guard by Linda's comment and fights to control her own laughter. Even Lela smiles.)*

BETTY
And what is that supposed to mean?

SHIRLEY
Maybe that wouldn't be the best song to choose.

BETTY
Well, I don't see why not . . .

SHIRLEY
Mother, have you thought of any?

LELA
Well, I was trying to name one . . . but . . . the title just escapes me . . . *(She sings.)*

> ". . . Free from all care,
> Happy and bright,
> Jesus is there,
> He is the light . . ."

SHIRLEY
Home . . . ?

BETTY
Home of the Soul. *(From memory.)* Number one ninety-one. *(Shirley flips to the song. Betty begins to sing from memory, writing down the number.)*

> "If for the prize we have striven,
> After our labors are o'er . . ."

*(Betty continues to sing aloud while flipping through the book for other songs. She sings while the others continue to speak. The song lasts until Linda's line "Christ Betty!")*

> "Rest to our souls will be given
> On the eternal shore.
> Home of the soul,
> Blessed kingdom of light,

> Free from all care,
> And where falleth no night.
> Oft, in the storm,
> We are sighing for Thee,
> *(Building to the big finish.)*
> Beautiful home of the ransomed,
> Beside the crystal . . ."

LELA
Yes, that's it. He liked that one.

SHIRLEY
Well, can you think of any others?

LELA
There were some he used to sing. I . . . It's . . . kinda hard to remember right now.

LINDA
Betty, Mother is . . .

LELA
I just can't think . . . There was . . . Oh, yes, uh, "Paradise Valley." He liked that one too.

SHIRLEY
Okay, "Paradise Va . . ." Betty . . . *(Unable to get her attention, Shirley grabs the paper and pen and writes down the title herself.)* All right, "Paradise Valley." Wha . . .

LINDA
Christ, Betty! If you can just wait until Saturday, we'll give you a solo! *(Pause.)*

BETTY
I'm sorry. I didn't realize my singing was disturbing anyone. *(Pause.)*

SHIRLEY
Does this have to be done right now?

BETTY
Yes, I told Brother Nelson I'd call him this evening. We only need . . . How many do we have?

SHIRLEY
Two. "Home of the Soul" and "Paradise Valley."

BETTY
When did we get that one?

SHIRLEY
Just a minute ago.

BETTY
Well, I didn't hear it.

SHIRLEY
You were busy.

BETTY
Oh.

LINDA
Geez, you should've just let the preacher do it.

BETTY
I wanted this to be a more personal experience.

LINDA
It's our father for God's sake! How much more personal can you get!

SHIRLEY
Linda.

BETTY
I . . .

SHIRLEY
Betty. I think we need to get along with one another . . . especially now.

BETTY
I'm sorry. You're right.

LINDA
Okay.

SHIRLEY
Now, how many more do we need?

BETTY
Five or six.

SHIRLEY
All right. Mother, can you . . .

LELA
"Beyond the Sunset."

SHIRLEY
Okay . . . (She writes.) We need four more.

LELA
I . . . I can't . . .

SHIRLEY
Would it help if we read the index? It might jog your memory.

LELA
Okay.

SHIRLEY
(She reads.) "A Beautiful Life," "A Beautiful Prayer," "A Blessing in Prayer," "A Charge to Keep I Have," "A Mighty Fortress," (Linda begins to smile and then giggle and it grows in waves with each title.) "A New Creature," "A Soul Winner for Jesus," "A Wonderful Savior" . . . Linda, what is so funny?

LINDA
Nothing. (Laughs harder.)

BETTY
It would be nice of you to let us in on what you find so humorous.

LINDA
(Tries to regain her composure.) Oh, it's . . . it's really not that funny. It's really kinda stupid. I . . . I just hadn't thought of it in years.

SHIRLEY
What?

LINDA
You . . . You remember when we were kids and we would get bored in church? We'd read the song titles out of the book and follow them with "in the bathtub" or "between the sheets." You remember that? (Shirley and Linda both smile at the memory. Betty does not.)

SHIRLEY
Oh, I remember.

LINDA
(Taking the book from Shirley, she goes down the list.) Listen. A mighty fortress in the bathtub. A new creature in the bathtub. (Linda makes a mock scream and laughs. Shirley laughs with her and Lela chuckles to herself. Betty gets up and crosses away from the table.) A soul winner for Jesus in the bathtub. A wonderful savior between the sheets. Abide . . .

BETTY
That's enough! I see absolutely nothing humorous about that! I never did that.

SHIRLEY
Betty, I think you were . . .

LINDA
Oh, right, right. You never did it because it isn't proper.

BETTY
It certainly isn't. And Shirley, I'm surprised at you.

SHIRLEY
Why? Betty, you have to understand, we were children . . .

BETTY
I can never understand why . . .

LINDA
She can never understand because "some of us" were never children. Sob. Sob. Sob.

SHIRLEY
Linda.

LINDA
(Mocking.) We were older. We had to sacrifice. We were neglected.

BETTY
You have no . . .

LELA

I believe . . . I'll go to my room and lie down. (She crosses to the hallway and stops.) I think it'll be a little quieter in there. Don't you? (She exits.)

SHIRLEY

(Following her to the hallway. Pause.) Three days. That's all she asks. And the two of you can't even get along for thirty minutes. (Pause.) Please. Please try. She needs our support and right now we're only upsetting her. If . . . If . . . I'll go check on Mother. (She exits. Silence.)

---

Does Shirley's characterization, as it's been set up, motivate her following her mother out of the room? The playwright wanted to get Betty and Linda on stage alone together for the argument that ends the scene. Has he done so believably, taking into account what characters are willing to do and not willing to do to accomplish objectives?

The confrontation between Betty and Linda pits the two misfits against each other—the good child and the bad child, neither of whom feels she belongs. Linda's drinking is the subject of focus—the specific thing they fight over.

---

BETTY

Well, we only got three songs. I suppose we'll have to finish the list tomorrow. Just four or five more.

LINDA

What? Does your commission double if we get eight songs, triple if we get ten?

BETTY

What are you talking about?

LINDA

You. You're treating this whole thing like it's your own personal event, like you're going to get something out of it.

BETTY

I am doing this because I love Daddy.

LINDA

Right.

BETTY

Daddy appreciated those of us who did things for him. (Pause.) Those of us who were around.

LINDA

Ah, so that's it. That's the reason that I got the ice treatment at the front door.

BETTY

That, as well as everything else.

LINDA

And what is everything else, Betty?

BETTY

Oh, stop acting so innocent! It's sickening. It didn't become you as a young girl and it certainly doesn't become you now. I think your behavior since your divorce has been absolutely disgusting. I would think that by now you would have grown tired of bar-hopping and whoring from bed to bed.

LINDA

Well, you certainly don't mince words, do you?

BETTY

No, I don't. But I don't see why this should come as any surprise. I've told you my feelings before.

LINDA

Yes, but not in such flattering terms.

BETTY

It seems that some people don't get the message until they see the handwriting on the wall.

LINDA

For your information, my "whoring" days, as you so delicately put it, are over. I'm seeing one man and only one.

BETTY

Adultery is the same, whether it's with one or with twenty.

LINDA

I am not married any longer and neither is he.

BETTY

Fornication then! The penalty's the same. I'm surprised you haven't caught some disease already.

LINDA

Well, that would certainly get me out of the way, wouldn't it?

BETTY

Yes, it would. (Catches herself. Pause.)

LINDA

You hate me that much?

BETTY

I don't hate anyone.

LINDA

Oh, so you love me that much then.

BETTY

I simply find your behavior appalling . . .

LINDA

And you resent me.

BETTY

Yes. Yes, I do. Are you satisfied?

LINDA

Well, at least I know where I stand.

BETTY

You broke his heart! He lost a daughter, a son-in-law, and two grandchildren because of your selfishness.

LINDA

I guess the fifteen years of hell I went through don't matter.

BETTY

Oh, Linda, you're so melodramatic.

LINDA

So, I'm lying, and picked up and left just for the hell of it?

BETTY

Yes! I don't doubt that some unpleasant things did happen, but I also know that you exaggerate and most likely brought them on yourself.

LINDA

Oh, God!

BETTY

You should have worked it out. You should have stayed with him. We are never given trials that we cannot overcome.

LINDA

Don't start quoting that crap to me! I don't want to hear it!

BETTY

You don't want to hear it because you know in your heart that you threw your life away along with your husband and children. And all because "mommy" was bored and wanted to go out and have a good time!

LINDA

That is not what happened! I left because I got tired of running into doors and falling down steps.

BETTY

Then, why didn't you take your children?

LINDA

I . . . I couldn't. Not then.

BETTY

No, you had to get this thing out of your system.

LINDA

I've got them now. That's all that matters.

BETTY

Then, where are they?

LINDA

They . . . I . . .

BETTY

That's what I thought.

LINDA

They're my children! It's none of . . .

BETTY

You shirk your responsibilities with your family just like you did with Daddy! He was on his deathbed and you never even came to see him.

LINDA

You know, as well as I do, he didn't want me there.

BETTY

No, not like this! But you could have changed. You could have gone to him and asked his forgiveness and started all over again. Turned over a new leaf.

LINDA

(Mockingly.) With Jesus Christ as my personal savior!

BETTY

Yes!

LINDA

Oh, God! I can't handle this. (Crossing to the china cabinet.)

BETTY

Linda, don't walk away from me!

LINDA

I need a drink. (Silence. Linda searches through the drawers of the cabinet.)

BETTY

You won't find any liquor in this house.

LINDA

Oh, really?

BETTY

You won't.

LINDA

I know, good and well, that Daddy used to keep a flask of whiskey in one of these drawers. Even he needed a belt now and then.

BETTY

That was for medicinal purposes.

LINDA

You believe that?

BETTY

I most certainly do. What else would it be for? You won't find it.

LINDA

It's here somewhere.

BETTY

No, it isn't. I poured it out.

LINDA

(Pause.) You what?

BETTY

I poured it out.

LINDA

When?

BETTY

The last time we took Daddy to the hospital.

LINDA

Why?

BETTY

He didn't need it. He . . . he had . . . other medicines. And . . . it . . .

LINDA

Right. Right. Probably drank it yourself.

BETTY

I did not!

LINDA

Jesus Christ! You are so uptight!

BETTY

Where are you going?

LINDA

The kitchen. I'll take cooking wine, sherry, whatever she's got.

BETTY

There's none of that either.

LINDA

Wait. Let me guess.

BETTY

(Pause.) I knew you'd be coming. Sooner . . . or later. We all need a little help now and then . . .

LINDA

So like the fine "sister" you are, you decided to "help" me. Well, gee thanks. Another star in your crown.

BETTY

I . . .

LINDA

Thanks for helping the poor lost soul not get carried away.

BETTY

Linda . . . !

LINDA

Jesus Christ!

BETTY

There's a bottle of turpentine in the closet!

LINDA

(Surprised.) Ouch. (Pause.) Very good. Very good. You know, I didn't realize until today that you had all this in you. Yeah. Very good. Spoken like a true bitch.

BETTY

Do not use . . . !

LINDA

Sorry! Sorry. (Pause.) What would you call it then, huh, righteous indignation?

BETTY

(Pause.) Why did you even come back?

LINDA

Mother needs me.

BETTY

Like a hole in the head.

LINDA

Listen! Mother doesn't need to worry about me. She just needs to look out for those high and mighty vultures who are circling, waiting to pick her to pieces.

BETTY

And who would they be? (Linda looks at her in silence.) Don't you dare! Don't you dare criticize me! I don't deserve that! I've worked hard! I've tried! I was with my father when he died. Where were you? I've kept my husband and children together. Where are yours?

LINDA

(Pause.) Ouch, again. They teach you well in that Sunday school of yours. You cast the first stone very nicely. Nice aim. Yes, ma'am. (Pause.) You are more judgmental than Jesus Christ himself. Just like Daddy. I guess you thought if you acted like him, you could be Daddy's little girl. But, what happened Betty? Where'd you go wrong? (Betty begins to cry.) Oh, don't cry. Let's see, I think I can remember one little verse of comfort, maybe . . . something about "faith, hope, and love, but the greatest of these is love." (Pause.) Hm. Too bad, isn't it? Too bad there wasn't enough love to go around, hm? (Pause. Betty is crushed.) I'll be outside taking a smoke if anybody needs me. (She exits SL through the front door.)

---

Does this play have a focus? Do you want to know what happens next? Do you care about the characters?

Most of the class was very interested in these people. A few found them too ordinary and their concerns ordinary too, but the majority got involved in the struggle of each to find and feel love from the now departed Sidney. As Linda says, there wasn't enough love to go around, and the characters are still vying for it.

The assessment of the dialogue in this play was that it was easy to read, easy to speak. It is not dialogue that intrudes and calls attention to itself, but is instead closely observed (or heard) dialogue. The writer wanted it to be credible, realistic. People might talk just this way. In fact, he wanted the whole situation to follow this model. When a patriarch dies and the women in his life come together, what happens?

Some decisions the playwright made along the way (he re-wrote many, many times) involved: how to motivate having only the sisters come home without their husbands or mates; when to start the story (before the death, after the death, after the funeral); and where to place it (hospital room, funeral home, family home, back yard). He decided the story was about Sidney's effect on these women, even after he was dead. He felt that the story started a long time ago, when the girls were little, but that the play began during their advanced adult years. He chose the crisis of a death in the family to bring out the thoughts and memories that fueled these women. He decided to make Act I just after the death and before the funeral, Act II just after the funeral.

Among the ways he chose to establish character are these: what they wear, what decisions they make, what they carry, what they say when first greeting someone, what they do when they are alone.

At this point in Act I it's not clear who is the major character or protagonist. All the women? Can you answer whose play this is? Whose experience?

The writer continued to work on this play in the second term and we took it to the audience in a production workshop.

## Non-Traditional Form

Both of the following scripts, one-acts, deal with characters' inner lives. In *Double Entendre*, a woman struggles with images of herself as a sexual being. In *Death in G-Flat*, a man fights death and then embraces it. Both writers explored the conventions and materials of theatre in their scripts. Both one-acts work with strong feelings and try for difficult, sometimes risky, effects.

### Double Entendre
*by Erin Flynn*

CHARACTERS

FE

MAN #1

MAN #2

OLD WOMAN

MIDDLE-AGED WOMAN

(*The stage is black. A slow instrumental piano piece is heard — the choice is up to the director, but it should be both beautiful and haunting. Another melody begins to overlap and echo, filling the stage with rougher music, hardcore and violent. A light shines DC on a fold-up chair; one that is found in city clinics, church functions. Sitting with her legs firmly on the floor, hands hiding underneath the back of her thighs, Fe stares straight ahead with an expressionless face. She is wearing an oversized white t-shirt that comes to her knees. It is a V-neck, clean and free of wrinkles. She has long, thick blond hair*).

(*The music continues for thirty more seconds followed by a sharp silence.*)

#### FE

No one listens. No one cares. I can talk and talk. No one is listening. They just watch my lips move. They never hear what I say. They just stare at these full lips that stand for sex. . . . I love you means nothing.

(*Fe remains sitting, still pressing her hands into the chair underneath her legs. Man #1 enters from UC, walking right up behind her. His hands are behind his back. He is holding something.*)

#### MAN #1

I hate girls like you.

#### FE

They ask me about my hair. They say oh, how beautiful, your hair falls around your shoulders and isn't that beautiful. They say I love women with long hair. They say that I am the ideal beauty. And blond too! I could be like Marilyn Monroe, couldn't I? With blond hair like this, I could be like any movie star they want. Without even trying, I can look like their dreams. Without even trying.

#### MAN #1

I hate girls like you.
(*Man #1 lowers a brandy snifter filled with brandy in front of her face.*)
Let's have a drink.
(*Fe lifts her hands up and takes the snifter with both hands. She never makes eye contact with the man.*)
Good girl.
(*He exits UC covering his face with his hands.*)

#### FE

Brandy. Brandy is such a wild thing to pour down your throat. It is hot . . . burns going down. It reminds me of cough syrup. (*She sips often.*) It's so thick and spicy. As if I could wash down anything with it. And the warmth of it . . . it rests in the cradle of my hand and I just swirl it round and round. . . . They love girls that drink. Liquor is a part of foreplay. (*She finishes the brandy and keeps the glass in her hands — sharing it between all her fingers. She slowly begins to move her legs — shuffling them on the floor beneath her.*) Being touched is an illusion. Sex is a dream. You know, I had a dream once that I was walking through a backroad; through these deep woods. I heard this noise and I couldn't figure out where it was coming from and then I heard it again. There was this screeching coming from somewhere and I could tell that I was really close to it but I was too busy looking up at the trees. Then I finally looked down and I saw an animal sprawled on the ground. He had been hit by a car I guess. . . . He was lying on his back crying, and howling. He arched his back; there was blood everywhere. This poor animal was helpless. I was about to turn around and run to the main road when I noticed I couldn't move. I mean, my feet wouldn't lift up. I was forced to stare at this dying animal.

(*Man #2 also enters UC and walks around the chair before also standing behind her, slowly reaching for her breast.*)

#### MAN #2

I love you, baby.

#### FE

I love you means nothing.

MAN #2

I know how to make you feel good.

FE

*(Pushing his hand away.)* Don't touch me. *(Man #2 exits the same way he entered. When he is gone, Fe stands up and goes to imaginary mirror placed in front of her. She still faces DS, standing to the right of her chair.)* I thought it was good to be pretty. I have a big mirror in my bathroom, right above an old white sink. I look at myself with my mouth open. I try to see what they see. I made the mistake of being born with a pretty face. A mistake. All I am is trouble. I don't deserve anything.

*(An old woman enters UL and stands with her arms folded. She is wearing a flowered house dress. She is smoking a cigarette.)*

OLD WOMAN

You deserve everything you get.

*(Fe runs over to her, and stands SR of her. Old Woman keeps her arms crossed and faces SL. Fe starts to extend her arms out, as if pleading.)*

FE

Tell me. Talk to me please. Tell me what I did! My stomach hurts! My arms are sore! I think I'm bleeding!

OLD WOMAN

Do you want a cigarette? *(She reaches for cigarettes out of her dress pocket when Man #1 enters UC.)*

MAN #1

Go ahead. *(Exits.)*

FE

*(Taking a cigarette and lighting it with old woman's lighter.)* I'm in trouble. My body isn't mine anymore and I need to know why. What happened to me?! *(She grabs the woman's arm but is shrugged off.)*

OLD WOMAN

I hate women like you.

FE

I'm not a woman.

OLD WOMAN

Look at the snow. Look at how white it is. *(They both look out an imaginary window DL.)*

FE

Snow. I love the way the ground looks after lots of snow has fallen. It looks like it's higher than it really is. When you step in it, you're never sure when you'll hit the bottom.

OLD WOMAN

Winter is a very deceiving thing. Snow seems so soft . . .

FE

I always feel like such a little child when I'm around snow. And when I'm near water—the sea—then I become a woman.

OLD WOMAN

I hate women like you.

FE

You aren't very sexy. Your hair is short and old-fashioned.

OLD WOMAN

I like it that way.

*(Fe looks the old woman up and down—observing the line of her body and the shape of it. She looks at her hair. She studies her face. The woman doesn't seem to notice that she is being watched.)*

FE

Does it bother you that you don't attract men?

OLD WOMAN

I don't, nor do I want to. But you, my dear, you attract the men. You attract them and you love it.

FE

No! I hate that they look at me!

OLD WOMAN

You encourage it! Otherwise you wouldn't have that face. You wouldn't have that mouth—or that body.

FE

You aren't very sexy. Your hair is short and old-fashioned.

*(The woman exits UL and Fe returns to the chair.)* Everything I touch is ruined. I'm filthy. *(She continues to smoke her cigarette and sits with her body comfortably on the chair.)* I am sick because men watch me when I walk down the street. They watch and then they want me. I keep my eyes looking at the sidewalk, observing the cracks, but it doesn't help. I can tell when I am being watched. I can feel their eyes on me like hot coins that have been lying in the sun too long. Pressed up against my body—burning through my clothes onto my skin. I want to turn around and scream, "What are you looking at? Who gave you permission to put your eyes upon me?" but I don't. I'm not in the position to defend myself. Women aren't supposed to defend themselves. They're supposed to be scared and afraid and vulnerable and . . . Oh, I hurt! Please don't hurt me . . . oh, please. Don't touch me . . . leave me alone . . . someone help me . . . I'm bleeding!!!

*(Man #1 enters UC and comes up behind her.)*

MAN #1

You deserve this.

FE

My body is not my own. I am not a woman. I am still a little girl. I am a slut. Daddy? Daddy!

MAN #1

Just close your eyes. If it's inevitable, lie back and enjoy it.

FE

I am pushed down to the floor screaming but it is muted out. Is this why women become whores? I cannot be heard. I am making my throat raw. I need some brandy. Yes. That will make it feel better.

MAN #1

Yes, that will make it feel much better. *(Exits UC.)*

#### FE
*(Takes a series of quick short breaths.)* Go away! Leave me alone! I hurt . . . I hurt . . . That hurts . . .

#### MAN #2
*(Enters UC and walks up to her behind the chair.)* I love you, baby, I know how to make you feel good. I want to make you feel good. *(Reaching for her chest — quicker than last time.)*

#### FE
I love you means nothing. *(Letting his hand remain for a moment before pushing it away.)* Don't touch me . . . I can't . . . what is daddy going to think of me.

#### MAN #2
*(Exiting UC.)* He doesn't even have to know.

#### FE
*(Standing on chair now.)* Here he comes. He comes straight for me. I seem to sit here waiting for him. Why does he want me? Why does he look at me on the sidewalk? Why do I have to be pretty?

*(Enter UL a middle-aged woman wearing glasses. She crosses to the SR of the chair. She carries a notebook and pencil.)*

#### MIDDLE-AGED WOMAN
So, do you feel that you provoked this?

#### FE
No.

#### WOMAN
What were you wearing?

#### FE
I can't remember.

#### WOMAN
Sure you do.

#### FE
I really don't remember. I'm sorry.

#### WOMAN
Well, it must have been low-cut or something. Surely it was a short skirt, was it not?

#### FE
I'm sorry.

#### WOMAN
Yes, me too. Had you ever had sex before?

*(Fe, still standing on the chair, starts to dance in a sultry style. She runs her hands around her waist.)*

#### WOMAN
Had you ever had sex before?

#### FE
*(Getting down off chair and facing the woman. Man #2 enters UC and now fully embraces Fe.)* Please leave me alone. *(Middle-aged woman exits, face flustered. Fe looks at Man #2.)* Please leave me alone.

#### MAN #2
You don't want to be alone.

#### FE
You don't know what I want.

*(Man #2 exits and sees Man #1 in the corner of UR.)*

#### MAN #1
But, you know what you want.

#### FE
Yes, I know.

#### MAN #1
Do you want me to go?

#### FE
You have to.

*(Man #1 exits UL. Fe turns DS and stands behind her chair.)*

#### FE
I always knew I was beautiful. Daddy used to tell me that he loved to watch me ride my bicycle up the street. With my little ponytails. And my "colt-like legs" he called them. I guess all little girls have long hair, don't they? . . . I think it's time to cut it all off. I could look like a boy. I could act like a boy. No one would look at me. Their heads would be turned in the opposite direction . . . *(She bends down as if hiding behind the chair. She is still visible.)* They won't see me . . . They won't recognize me. *(Fe rocks back and forth and peers from side to side of the chair.)* I couldn't run away! I had to stand there and stare at this dying animal! Oh, why couldn't my feet move! Damn! All I wanted to do was to move my feet. That's all I wanted to do! I couldn't even bend down to help. I was powerless! I started to scream hoping that someone would help me move my feet so that we could both help the animal . . . and the louder I screamed, the louder the animal whined and wailed. And then the most horrible thing happened. I looked down closely at the animal, into his eyes, and realized that it was me! And I was powerless! God damn it, I couldn't move!

*(Fe is an emotional wreck at this point. Screaming, crying, terrified. Man #2 enters from UC and lifts her up from the kneeling position.)*

#### MAN #2
I love girls like you.

*(He starts to run his fingers through her long hair and she touches his hand, encouraging it.)*

#### FE
I love you means nothing.

#### MAN #2
You really are beautiful. *(He exits UC, running his fingers through his own hair.)*

#### FE
I'm sorry.

*(Fe now sits down on the chair, which is faced backwards. She loosely wraps her arms around the chair, resting them. She straddles the chair, her legs open.)* I dream about him. I dress for him—thinking that I'll run into him, terrified that I might. He has made me beautiful. He has made me a

whore. I live in constant shame; and yet I cling to him . . . my rapist.

*(The rough yet melodic music begins immediately. It should be intense and harsh. Fe begins to tug at the bottom of her white t-shirt, folding the edges in her hands; blackout).*

The class had strong reactions to **Double Entendre**. Why is the main character named Fe? What does her name mean—female or iron or something else? Why are the other women so mean to her? Who is she talking to in the monologues? Is she a rape victim or does she use the references to mean something else?

Every interesting play leaves some questions unanswered. We wouldn't be asking still, "How much did Gertrude really know about the murder of the elder Hamlet?" or "Will Stella go back to the same relationship with Stanley?" if we were told clearly by the playwright. We wonder at the end of **Burn This** if the newly forged relationship between Pale and Anna can really work.

So the issue is really whether the unanswered questions get in the way of pleasure in the piece or not. And understanding. Did the questions get in the way in **Double Entendre**? The class, for the most part, thought not. "Why does Fe call Daddy? Is he the rapist?" they asked. But if so, why aren't there more references? When the playwright finally spoke, after she listened to comments, she said she hadn't intended to suggest Daddy was the abuser, but that Fe was calling to him for help. She thought she should write those lines more carefully so there was less confusion. To the question, "Was Fe raped?" she answered that she wanted that to be a matter of interpretation. This kind of answer can be a cop-out, but in this case, I thought it was appropriate that the answer be difficult to arrive at.

Overall, the class was intrigued, caught by something in Fe's lines to keep reading and listening. This willingness to keep reading, or listening (we were doing both in the workshop)—or, in the theatre, to keep watching with interest—is the bottom line. Do we want to know what happens? Is there rising tension (which usually is built of dramatic questions unanswered)?

I interpret this play—and this is one possible reading of it—as not so much about rape as about the paradoxical quality of sexual feeling. For me, the play moves on questions of Fe's trying to find sex without victimization and yet having strong sexual feelings as a result of victimization. We see that her relationship with Man 1 makes her reject Man 2 and we can see that Man 2 is less sadistic than Man 1. Is he otherwise better?

Does this play operate like more traditional plays? The sense of pursuit of an objective is here. Fe is not only talking—she is talking to search out and discover a truth about her feelings. Is she talking to herself? To a therapist? To the audience? To the audience in the person of a therapist? All of this must be decided in production. Are there obstacles to Fe's coming to terms with herself as a sexual creature? The other characters, men and women both, act as obstacles.

Is it producible? Yes, it's quite physical. Fe is almost imprisoned on the fold-up chair. She can't move herself easily. People come to her—like memories—but she is stuck. When she finally moves toward them, she is unsafe. The physical pattern of the play reflects the subject. It is a metaphor for the subject of her sexuality. She is beautiful. People look at her. She does not want to be an object, but she both hates and loves the fact of her beauty.

We decided to take this play to the next step—production workshop.

## Death in G-Flat
*by Gary Landis*

### CHARACTERS
G, middle aged; white hospital gown

BOY, 10 yrs. old; red shorts and t-shirt; barefoot

YOUNG MAN, 20 yrs. old; blue jeans and black sweater

DR., 40 yrs. old; black suit and tie

MAN #1, green hospital gown

MAN #2, green hospital gown

DANCER, long, black formal evening gown, black lace veil

POET, black turtle neck and pants

2 STAGEHANDS, blue overalls

### SETTING
*(Black and white checkered tile floor. Window frame hanging from ceiling, UL. Unmade hospital bed, DL.)*

*(Blackness. A spotlight comes up on Dancer, C. Her initial movements are without music. She sways simply, back and forth, lifting her feet off the ground. Gradually, the faint sound of music can be heard. It has a heavy, weighted down feeling to it. It builds in volume. Suddenly, a soft light from behind the UL window illuminates Boy, who is crouched on the DL bed watching Dancer. Her moves become increasingly seductive as the music builds. Boy continues to stare in awe. The music and Dancer climax, then stop abruptly. Silence. Dancer exits, L. Boy remains motionless. Stagehands enter, L, and carry off hospital bed with Boy, R. Stagehands reenter with an old home movie projector which they begin to set up DC. G enters, R, with movie screen and sets it up C. G looks nervously at the audience, then slowly walks DR. Stagehands turn on projector. It is a film of a hospital bed, the same one that has already been seen, but without Boy. Stagehands exit L.)*

### G
*(Clears throat. Watches the film for a moment, then squints out at the audience.)* Uh, . . . hi. My name is . . . , well it's G. *(Clears throat again. Scratches elbow.)* I'm . . . uhm . . . I'm dying. *(Points at the screen.)* I guess that's why, I mean, that's what this is all about. I wouldn't be particularly attracted to this kind of stuff otherwise. Talking, I mean, to people. Isn't something I normally do. Not one to burden myself on others. *(Looks at film again. Clears throat.)* So, you see, I'm

dying and all. Got this disease. *(Winces.)* And now ... I guess I'm seeing things.

*(Lights dim. G exits R, carrying off screen. Stagehands enter L, carrying a cardboard box in which Boy is standing. They place it UC, with Boy facing away from the audience. Stagehands exit R.*

*Dancer enters L and crosses up to Boy. She proceeds to slowly drape him in white yarn, wrapping it loosely around him as he remains motionless. She stops every now and then to make a fine adjustment. While this is going on, Young Man enters R with a cassette player. He crosses downstage of box and sits, placing the cassette player on the ground in front of him.)*

YOUNG MAN

What was I like when I was young? *(Presses play.)*

VOICE

You were a bright young boy. *(Presses pause.)*

YOUNG MAN

Did I play a lot? *(Presses play.)*

VOICE

You were an industrious young boy. *(Presses pause. Smiles.)*

YOUNG MAN

Sometimes I would lie in the grass and pretend that the sky was my head and that the clouds were my hair. And then the planes would come and I would pretend that they were massaging my scalp, just like white flying finger nails. *(Dancer massages Boy's head. Young Man presses play.)*

VOICE

You were a unique young boy. *(Presses pause.)*

YOUNG MAN

I used to lie. Did you know that? Like that time coming back from the youth group camping trip. All the other kids were bragging and telling stories, so I said that I once found a hundred dollar bill just lying on the sidewalk. But they didn't believe me. They just laughed, even the group leaders. *(Presses play.)*

VOICE

You were a sensitive young boy. *(Presses pause. Smiles.)*

YOUNG MAN

I used to build model airplanes. *(Presses play and lets it continue to end.)*

VOICE

You were a loving young boy.

YOUNG MAN

I used to draw war pictures.

VOICE

You were a generous young boy.

YOUNG MAN

I used to see scary faces in my closet at night.

VOICE

You were a steady young boy.

YOUNG MAN

But I always loved you, Mom.

VOICE

You were a brave young boy. Mommy loved you, too. *(Presses stop. Rewinds to beginning and presses play.)* You were a bright young boy. You were an industrious young boy. You were a unique young boy. You were a sensitive young boy. You were a loving young boy. You were a generous young boy. You were a steady young boy. You were a brave young boy. Mommy loved you, too. *(Presses stop.)*

*(Young Man stands up and exits L with cassette player. Dancer exits L, leaving Boy tied up in white yarn. G enters R carrying a chair, a piece of wood, and a carving knife. He places chair DR, sits, and begins to whittle. Stagehands enter and turn projector on. Since there is no screen on stage, the film is projected onto the back of Boy in box. The film is of jet plane launching off of an aircraft carrier. Stagehands exit L. Man #1 enters R, sucking hard on a Lucky Strike and staring hostilely at the audience. He spits on the stage.)*

G

You see, it's more like a dream than a memory. I'm sure I've never seen these people before. *(Stops whittling.)* And I never made model airplanes. *(Man #2 enters L and swaggers up to Man #1. They square off. Man #1 blows smoke into Man #2's face. Man #2 shoves him. They stand still. G looks around nervously.)* I'm not so sure I like all this. *(Man #1 and #2 begins to circle each other like animals.)* Nothing is familiar, yet ... *(Man #1 swings at Man #2. Man #2 tackles Man #1 and begins to wrestle and bite his neck and shoulders. They roll around the stage, loudly. G throws down the piece of wood, angrily.)* It would be nice, though, if it had something to do with me! I mean, if someone's having a life flash before their eyes in the ... when they're dying, don't you think it would be nice if it were their own! *(Man #1 and #2 stop fighting and glare towards G. They freeze. Poet enters L, with a folder full of papers and a tall, thin podium. He places the podium DR and begins arranging his papers. G looks out into the audience.)* I think my family is here. In this room. Yes, I'm sure they are here. *(Stagehands enter L and turn off projector. They exit R.)*

POET

*(Reading.)* My skin is fire ... the moon makes me circle ... *(Man #2 exits R.)* ... if you were to kiss my skin you would be so thirsty. *(Dr. enters R carrying a briefcase and a large, folding lawn chair. He sets the chair down next to Man #1. Man #1 crawls on to chair, pulls another cigarette out and lights it, taking a long, slow drag.)*

DR.

*(Sitting down beside him, on the edge of the lawn chair.)* This was a good suggestion ... to come out here today. *(No response. Pause.)* It's very pretty out here, isn't it?

MAN #1

Yep.

DR.

I think this is a wonderful sign of how far you've come

along. A wonderful sign. You've been making some very positive strides lately.

MAN #1

Yep.

DR.

Like group, for instance. I've been seeing some very positive changes in group.

POET

The wounds I have get bigger . . .

DR.

And once you build up momentum it gets easier, doesn't it? Getting to group, being in group gets a hell of a lot easier, doesn't it?

MAN #1

Easy.

POET

Bigger than my tongue.

DR.

Because now the whole picture is clear. We know what it is you have to do. To grow, to cope.

MAN #1

Grow.

POET

And my tongue is already so big.

DR.

And as soon as you are willing to take action, you can be back home, in no time.

POET

As big as a missile silo.

MAN #1

*(Sitting up abruptly.)* Now, what the hell does that mean!? In no time?

DR.

As soon as you are willing to make it.

MAN #1

*(Confronting Dr.)* And what the hell is that supposed to mean!? Willing to make it?

DR.

It means that the time you have left is completely determined by your attitude.

MAN #1

*(Softly.)* And is my attitude good now?

DR.

Well . . . yes.

MAN #1

*(Exploding.)* Then how come the only thing that I am getting here is a blowjob!? *(Spits.)* You give lousy head, Dr.

POET

I love to put things into my mouth.

DR.

Now, let's think about where this anger is coming from.

MAN #1

It's goddamn coming from fucking me, man!!! *(Jumps up on chair.)* Inmate me! And it's going out to all you fucking idiots who run this here cage! Especially to you, you shithole!

G

*(Standing. Taking a few steps forward.)* Someone is touching my hand.

DR.

I think we'd better look at where all this hostility is going to take you.

G

My wife.

MAN #1

Take me!? Take me !?? I'm as here as I can get, Doc! I've already been taken! I'VE ALREADY BEEN TAKEN!!! *(Man #1 storms off L. Dr. slowly stands up, folds chair, and exits after him.)*

G

*(Crosses to C.)* She's crying . . . she's probably crying.

POET

I found an old recipe today.

G

But, I can't be sure.

POET

For papier mâché.

G

The room is filled with flowers. This I'm sure of . . .

POET

I used to make masks.

G

Fat, white lilies. They cover up the stink.

POET

Without eyes.

G

The clean stink.

POET

I used to make masks without eyes and wear them all day.

G

My father died in a hospital.

POET

And I'd bump into things.

G

But no one brought any flowers.

POET

And I'd cry, but no one could tell. *(Long pause. Dancer enters L, to the sounds of goofy cabaret stripper music. She bops and shimmies across the stage, making jerky movements. Angrily, Poet exits L with papers and podium. G crosses back to chair and sits. Stagehands enter L, carrying buckets of paper confetti and an electric fan. They set the fan down, turn it on, and point it at Dancer. They then start throwing handfuls of confetti at fan, which in turn, blow all around Dancer. Young Man enters L, with a pink telephone receiver. He stops DR.)*

YOUNG MAN

*(Over music.)* Respect you? I don't even know what the word means . . . All right, so a couple of people get close . . . all right, intimate, physically intimate. I don't see where respect comes into play. *(Pause. Listens.)* You're obviously not listening to me. All right, what I'm saying is that when two people care about one another . . . yes, like you and me . . . then there is no such thing as respect or disrespect. *(Music stops. Dancer stops. Stagehands continue blowing confetti.)* You see, to me, you are beautiful, and everything you do . . . yes, including last night . . . is beautiful. See? *(Pause. Listens.)* Really? *(Pause. Smiles.)* Well me too.

*(Stagehands turn off fan and throw it into the box where Boy is standing. They then pick up box and Boy, and exit R. Young Man follows them out, speaking inaudibly into the receiver. Dancer remains motionless. Poet peeks his head out from L wing and cautiously surveys the stage. Silence. Poet reenters with folder of papers and the podium. He places it back in the same spot. G stands up, exits L, and then returns with the projector screen, setting it up directly downstage of Dancer. Man #2 enters L with a wooden chair and exits. G sits in chair directly in front of the screen. Stagehands enter and turn on the projector. It is a film of an arm receiving a tattoo.)*

POET

If I could, I would write your name all over my body. . . . *(G stares at arm; worried.)* I would press hard with dark black ink. I would press the pen hard, so that it would all flow inside of me. . . .

G

*(Staring out at the audience.)* My daughter plays the flute in her junior high school band. She has a pet snake in a box in her room. My wife says . . . said that she fantasizes about having a penis. I don't know if that's true. I never asked her.

POET

If I could, I'd make the ink mix with me, so your name would be forever in my veins.

G

She had lovers . . . my wife.

POET

In my brain.

G

Two. But only after she found out about mine.

POET

In my lungs.

G

I think that . . . I think that that's all right.

POET

In my heart.

G

Last year, for about a month, she'd just cry.

POET

In my eyes.

G

She would cry in the car, at the movies, with the children . . .

POET

In my testicles.

G

. . . in bed she'd cry. So, I would ask her, I kept on asking her, "what's wrong?" And she would say, say over and over, "I don't know."

POET

In my legs.

G

So, after a month of this I start thinking, maybe she'd better get some help . . . a therapist or something. I was scared, see? So right then, on the night I was thinking this, she comes into bed with this red flannel nighty on, instead of that sheer little thing I like, and she says, "I think I've got it all figured out."

POET

And your name would be in my bones. . . .

G

"I just never bargained for this."

POET

. . . forever. *(Stagehands enter. Turn off projector, grab screen, then exit. G stands and stares at his arm. Silence. G looks up at audience.)*

G

*(Remembering.)* I never was one for being alone much. Not really. I don't know, I just thought of that . . . being here and all. I guess you'd have to say that I like people. That's probably it. I just figure, you learn more about yourself through others. I'm a watcher. I like to examine. I think that's probably it. I've always been sensitive. I can pick up a lot about a person on a first impression, like I had E.S.P. or something. I don't know. I like women more than I like men. They're easier to talk to, on the whole. They're more sensitive, more perceptive than men, most men. They must make better use of the right side of their brain. Probably draw better too.

POET

(*Reading.*) The main reason I like my dog so much is that he is my dog.

G

That probably has a lot to do with why I married who I did. Magic, or the innate ability to perceive magic, the ability to see magic in everyday life. To me, it was just another full moon over the ocean. To my wife though, it was a moon that gazed at her silver self, splintering the mirror into a thousand shards of light. Magic. I wish she had wrote that down.

POET

He's a quite capable fellow. I've taught him a number of tricks. And when he rolls over or begs for food, I get the satisfaction of knowing that, if it weren't for me, he would not be able to perform so well. The dog, on the other hand, gets the satisfaction of a Milk Bone dog biscuit. And each of us gets the satisfaction of knowing that we alone are the one getting the better deal. (*Pause. G scratches head.*)

(*A single bell is heard ringing rhythmically off-stage. Stage-hands enter pushing Boy in a wheelchair. Boy is the one ringing the bell. They begin to circle around Dancer, who has been standing motionless UR. Stagehands pull similar bells out of their overalls and begin ringing them, still circling. More bells are heard off-stage. Enter Man #1, Man #2, Young Man, and Dr., one by one, joining in the circle and ringing bells. The volume grows and becomes more hostile. Poet pulls a bell out of his pocket and joins in with the rest.*

*Dancer remains motionless. The group begins to augment the bells with grunts and chants, stomping their feet as the speed of the circle becomes faster and faster. G stands and acts as though he is being pulled into the spiral. Fighting the pull, he stumbles DR, falling face first onto the stage. His fingers turn to claws as he scratches the floor, searching for something to hold onto. The pull increases. Suddenly, he makes a desperate lunge for Poet's po-dium, wrapping himself around it, both arms and legs. He plugs his ears with his hands and screams.*)

G

GOD!!! . . . STOP!! . . . I'M LISTENING!!! (*The sound of the bells and of the pounding feet decreases, but continues.*) I'm not getting it! I don't know! Maybe if it were clear . . . more clear. It's just not right, not right yet. Maybe if it were more clear. IT'S NOT RIGHT YET!! (*Sounds decrease more. G whispers.*) But I'll listen now. I'm listening. I'm watching everything. (*The circle becomes silent.*) I just don't know. Maybe if it were more clear. (*Circle stops.*) I'll try. I'm trying. I'm listening. (*Silence. G explodes.*) TALK TO ME!!!

(*The circle slowly dissipates, all exiting in different directions. G is alone. He stands still for a moment, then begins to meander about the stage, mumbling to himself and glancing off-stage in fear. Man #1, Man #2, and Young Man enter from audience carrying bar stools, bottles of whiskey, and glasses. They set everything up DC and begin to fill their glasses. They sit on the stools facing the audience, drunk and sloppy. G slowly circles, scrutinizing them as they talk.*)

MAN #2

(*Downs a shot.*) I think I'm shit-faced. (*Attempts standing. Stumbles.*) Yes, indeed, I'm shit-faced.

MAN #1

(*Downs a shot.*) Boy, you're smart.

MAN #2

What'd you say?

MAN #1

I said, that's sure some smart shit you're coming up with.

MAN #2

Oh, thanks.

MAN #1

You must have learned that smart shit in the army, didn't you?

MAN #2

Marines.

MAN #1

Same shit. Learn a lot, did you?

MAN #2

I learned how to stay fucking alive, if that's what you mean.

MAN #1

The army taught you that, did it?

MAN #2

Marines!

YOUNG MAN

(*Interrupting.*) Have either of you been to the mountains? (*Pause.*) The mountains are a very special place. Do you like the mountains?

MAN #2

Depends what mountains you're talking about. Some of them I like, others I don't. Like the ones here for instance.

MAN #1

(*Looks around the stage.*) Here?

MAN #2

I like green ones, like up north . . . Oregon maybe. Wet trees, real tall with moss . . .

YOUNG MAN

Have you ever been to Yosemite?

MAN #1

No.

YOUNG MAN

The first time I ever came close to a wild animal was in Yosemite. It was a baby deer, a doe.

MAN #2

I used to hunt deer with my family.

YOUNG MAN

It had big blue eyes—scared eyes, like in the movies. I

wanted to talk to it. I wanted it to talk. I was young. I kept thinking that it should talk. But, it was frozen.

MAN #2

Best time to nab it, you know. Right then was the best time. When it was frozen.

YOUNG MAN

I could see its little heart beating out of its skin. It was so afraid. I wanted it to talk, to tell me what was wrong, to tell me what it was feeling. I didn't want to hurt it. If it would just trust me enough to talk . . . we could be friends maybe. And once we were friends I couldn't hurt it, could I?

MAN #2

I guess not.

MAN #1

But deer don't talk.

YOUNG MAN

I know.

*(They stand, pick up everything, exit. Dancer enters with a tambourine that is tied to the end of a long pole. She crosses to C and stands motionless. Poet enters and crosses down to podium, searching through his papers and clearing his throat. When an \* appears at the end of a line, the Poet's words will be punctuated by Dancer slamming the tambourine down to the ground, ceremoniously.)*

POET

My cancer
    it hides*
    in lakes
    it hides*
    in sleeping streams
    it hides*
    with plenty of food
    it hides*
    with books to read and a new T.V. set . . . with a yacht and snifters of brandy . . . with a yearly subscription to the Sunday Times
    it hides*
    I wake up
    it hides*
    I sing in church
    it hides*
    I live a content and happy life
    it hides*
    listen to me . . . watch my feet and hands . . . it knows where I am . . . it has tiny maps and a very good sense of direction
    it hides*
    and waits.

*(G watches Dancer intently. After a moment of silence, she exits suddenly, leaving G standing alone, awkward.)*

G

*(Shivers as if it were cold.)* Something's coming . . . it's close. *(Falls slowly to his knees.)* Oh, God it's cold. What's happening to me? Somebody help me. Somebody please.

*(Enter Dr. carrying briefcase and lawn chair, followed by Man #1 who is puffing on another Lucky Strike. Dr. sets the chair down L and sits while Man #1 remains standing, pacing. G moves DS to observe.)*

DR.

Let's say, for the sake of speculation, that I had the capability of granting you one wish.

MAN #1

*(Mimicking.)* Let's say you had.

DR.

One wish before you die, what would that wish be?

MAN #1

No big think on that one. I'd wish to be free, to be out of here. *(Sings.)* Free-ee-ee-dom. *(Laughs.)*

DR.

*(Laughs with him.)* You've been here a long time, haven't you?

MAN #1

Too long.

DR.

And it's hard to forget why you are here? Why you were brought here to begin with?

MAN #1

Hell yeah it's hard. But I think that's the scam you got going here. I think that making it so I can't forget is what you get paid for. Because if I ever did forget what's inside me, if I ever did forget the reality of the situation, then maybe, just maybe it wouldn't be real. Maybe it would just go away.

DR.

Now don't get yourself carried away, relax.

MAN #1

I don't want to fucking relax. And what the fuck does that mean, "carried away?" No one's going to carry me away, you hear me?

DR.

Calm down. Now listen, the reason I asked about your wish . . .

MAN #1

My wish? My wish is to prove all you motherfuckers wrong! My wish is to shove all this shit inside me down your motherfucking throat and see how you "cope" with it. I refuse to die. I am not going to die.

DR.

And your condition is good.

MAN #1

Fuck yeah, it's good.

DR.

You've been sharing in meetings.

MAN #1

And I've been cleaning my room . . . folding my laundry . . .

DR.

That's right.

MAN #1

Working out. Here, feel this muscle. And I've been eating right, and I haven't mouthed off to the Techs in a long time.

DR.

You've been much calmer, I must admit.

MAN #1

And I've been talking in meetings. Or did I already say that?

DR.

Awhile ago, we were talking about you going home, remember?

MAN #1

Remember? It's all I've talked about since I got here.

DR.

And we talked about what needed to happen in order for you to do that?

MAN #1

Yeah?

DR.

Well, I brought you up in our staff meeting the other day, your stable condition, your strong desire to go home, and well, the feedback was extremely positive.

MAN #1

No shit?! Sweet mother of Jesus! (Lets out a loud roar.) You're not shitting me, are you? I can't believe it, there really is a God. (Grabs Dr. and kisses him on the mouth.) You know, I was beginning to give up hope. I really was. I was even starting to give in to all this death shit. I could feel it.

DR.

I know how hard it's been.

MAN #1

Shit yeah. But now it's all over. I'm going home.

DR.

Now, it's just a slight remission, remember, you could have a relapse at any time.

MAN #1

How soon?

DR.

Any time.

MAN #1

No, goddamn it, how soon can I go home?!

DR.

Soon. We just have to run a few more tests and then . . .

MAN #1

SOON!! THE DODGERS WILL BE MOVING TO ICELAND SOON!! JESUS IS GOING TO MAKING HIS FUCKING REAPPEARANCE SOON!!

DR.

Don't start this! You have to wait until . . .

MAN #1

All right. All right. You want me to wait. I'll wait. I'll wait. Hell, I've got all the time in the world. I've got . . . I've got . . . (Man #1 lunges at Dr., throwing him violently to the ground. Pause. Dr. remains motionless.) Get the fuck up! Get up Dr. man! Get up so I can knock you down again! (Kicks him repeatedly.) Get up!! Get up!!! Get up!!!! (He stops kicking him. He stands over him, hunched over and panting. He slowly begins to whimper, mumble, and shake. He falls to his knees and begins to cradle Dr.'s head in his arms.) Hey, I'm sorry. I'm so sorry. I didn't want to hurt you. (Man #1 slowly rocks Dr. back and forth.) Talk to me.

POET

(Reading.) There is a pond I see
    I go and see
    a restless pond
    moving
    it's always dark when I go
    it's always night
    and so my heart hurts
    and so my eyes hurt
    and I know what I'm going to see
    but I don't think I want to see
    but I know I'm going to see
    so I close my eyes and think about sex
    I try hard to remember the lyrics to a Bruce Springsteen
    song but I know what I'm going to see
    and I'm afraid
    but I don't cry
    I know I'm going to see
    and then
    I see.

(Stagehands enter with projection screen, place it UC, then exit. They reenter carrying Boy on hospital bed, which they place DL. They then cross down to projector and turn it on. It is the film of the hospital bed. They exit. G, jittery and biting his fingernails, paces back and forth, examining the action on stage. Suddenly, he remembers the audience.)

G

I'm sorry. I'm sorry I dragged you into all of this. It's something you have no reason to deal with, right? I mean, you don't know me from Adam. I guess I just needed someone else to see this. I don't know. Listen, I'm sorry if I wasted your time. (Poet exits. G follows him to the edge of the stage. Calling after him.) But I can assure you that it's been helpful to me, having you here. (Stagehands, Poet, Young Man, and Man #2 enter carrying Dancer, who is tightly wrapped in white sheets. They put her down just right of the film screen and circle around her. G turns to face the audience.) So, all I want to say is, thanks. Thanks a lot.

(A slow drumming sound comes up. The four characters in the circle watch intently as Dancer starts to wiggle, making increasingly stronger attempts to free herself. The drumming builds.

*Dancer pushes her arm through the sheets. Stagehands, Poet, Young Man, and Man #2 exit quickly in fear. The drumming builds. Dancer wrenches her head free into the air. Boy watches in awe. Completely shredding the sheets from her body, Dancer stands still for a moment, panting. She is still dressed in her black gown. G begins to shake. Dancer begins to move. Slowly, seductively she dances down to G. The dance of death. G falls to his knees, arms outstretched. Drumming crescendos to its peak, then stops. Dancer stops, standing over G. She lifts up her veil, places her hands on G's head, then smiles warmly. G reaches for her arms and slowly wraps them around his body. He looks up.)*

G

Talk to me.
*(BLACK OUT)*

In *Death in G-Flat*, the playwright has explored the drama of what happens within a man in a few last seconds of life. Some of the images make logical sense, some leave logic aside. It's easy to see why a man would argue with a doctor, not so clear why poeticizing about a dog or papier mâché come into the last few moments of life.

The class had mixed reactions to the script. A few were frustrated and couldn't follow it. Others were impressed by the power of the theatrical images. Some thought it was about AIDS, but others thought there would be more specific references to AIDS if this were the case. Some asked why the film of the hospital bed was necessary. Others said, if the writer wants it, he should have it.

For me, the play is immensely powerful. It has an action: G is trying not to die. He is trying to hold onto life—through memory, physical contact, looking—and he is trying to understand, to put his life in perspective. Throughout it all, he comes back to the idea of making contact with someone, whether it is mother on the tape, his wife holding his hand, the doctor to whom he tries to express himself, or the dancer, Death, whom he asks to *talk.*

The questions this play raises—and there are many—include, "Are Man #1 and Man #2 always parts of G, or are they sometimes different people (as in the bar scene in which Man #1 doesn't seem to know which branch of the service Man #2 was in)? Are all three men in the bar scene parts of G or is only Young Man a part of G? Why is there so much back and forth, in and out of characters, not to mention equipment?"

Could these questions be answered in production? Are they open to interpretation?

The busy quality of the suggested staging occurs to me as right for this play. Death is busy. The body of G is busy fighting off death. His mind is busy and the images change constantly. If I were to direct *Death in G-Flat*, I would see the whole stage as the body of G, a collision of memory and medicine, thought and mechanical struggle.

It might be interesting to developing playwrights to know that even with great effort, I have not yet managed to get this play to a production workshop. Why is this less easily produced than *Double Entendre, Deadlines, The*

*Quality of Life?* Here is one reason: it requires six men—really eight, counting stagehands. The only woman required is the dancer. In a busy production year, it is difficult to find six or eight men who are not already working on other roles. It is always easier, in universities and in community theatres, if not in New York and Hollywood, to find actresses than actors.

Which leads to the subject of cross-gender casting. Why not have women play these roles? It's done all the time, and that would help get the play produced. I am willing to do that.

But there are other difficulties. The playwright feels very strongly that, even in lab production, he wants to see the projector and the specified films. That level of production is greater than in most lab productions of new plays; so it requires more funding, more time, more of a crew. Each of these requirements—several men in the cast, the use of film, a reasonably long rehearsal time in which to get very detailed staging accomplished, small roles for most characters except G—unfortunately stand in the way of easily gathering a volunteer production team.

*Unfortunately.* Because this writer has done something it isn't so easy to do. He's dramatized an experience in a unique way. The play is about a serious subject, death from cancer, and yet it's rich with inventive humor. G is creative, even in the last moments. The truth of the play, for me, is in the balance and mix of elements. G exhibits anger, whimsy, struggle, and humility in the face of death. The play is emotional. I feel the feelings of G every time I read it. Perhaps because G remains simple, an everyman.

---

### Assignment: Exercise 7

You should now write your own one-act play, or part of a longer play. If you write part of a longer play, add two pages' synopsis of the whole. Even if you are unsure about something, write your synopsis of one version of the whole. As you actually write the rest of the play, things can change. Things probably will change.

---

### Study Questions and Exercises

1. Would you cut the first scene of **The Etiquette of Mourning**? How would you let the audience know what the community around Lela is like? Are the other scenes of sufficient intensity to keep you interested? If not, how would you change them?

2. Are there places in which you think sustained scenes would be more effective in **Double Entendre** and **Death in G-Flat**?

3. Do you find analogy operating in the plays studied here? That is, do the pleasures of noticing A is to B as C is to D occur to you?

# FIFTEEN

# Workshop Production, and More

## OVERVIEW

In this chapter we'll cover the different levels of production of a new script. I've included brief reports on *Deadlines, The Quality of Life, Double Entendre*, and *The Etiquette of Mourning* when they went before a production workshop audience.

## OBJECTIVES

At the end of this chapter, you should be able to

• Determine what level of production is possible and appropriate for different scripts
• Make plans for productions of your own

If you were not part of a workshop when you began this book, you have hopefully gathered a like group of people and started one. If you have, you have been reading scripts aloud to each other. When plays—yours or others'—are read aloud, you can probably hear lines that don't work well or that need to be cut because they're too repetitive. Often you get a bigger sense of whether scenes are working or not. Sometimes a well-written scene simply doesn't do anything for the momentum of the piece—doesn't contribute anything that hasn't already been said—and that scene, in the reading, palpably drags. If you are the writer, you are faced with the (not happy or easy) challenge of altering the scene or cutting it. Sometimes you just hope nobody else notices how it drags. But if your group is any good, the members will catch it and tell you.

When your group gives feedback, and you remain silent for the whole session, you have a glimpse into what it might be like to put the script before an audience. If you stay silent, and don't defend yourself, you can better evaluate the comments and decide what changes to make.

But when a script is playable and you aren't sure in which direction to take revisions, or when it's as good as you can make it and it is a finished draft, the next level of feedback is desirable—that is, feedback from an audience. There are a couple of ways to get this feedback. If you have associated yourself with a production group, you will proceed with one of the following kinds of production. If you haven't found a group that is interested in new works, your playwrights' group may become the production company. If the playwrights don't want to perform, you might be able to locate actors and directors who are unoccupied (there are always some actors and directors looking for the opportunity to practice their skills) and you can try to interest them in your script. If you are writing seriously, you will have the energy it takes to find yourself production opportunities.

### Short Scripts

How and when can you put short scripts before an audience? You might want to string several together for an evening of one-acts. But you should know there are other possibilities. Some theatres are willing to offer new works as extras before or after a regular evening. (It helps if it's free.) I've discovered that lunchtime is excellent for plays under an hour long. Lunchtime theatre is very popular. Advertise it as a brown bag affair. Allow the audience to bring in food and drink; tell them they must carry out all the remains. In our theatre, we've never had a problem with this. It's a refreshing way to spend lunchtime. And many theatres are more available for an hour at lunchtime than at any other time. Simply agree to work around or on the existing scenery and to use the existing lighting plot, and you've got a space to perform new works.

## Longer Works

Longer works require an evening or matinee slot. Monday nights are popular for showing new works because most theatres are dark then. Small theatres are often dark on Tuesdays and Wednesdays as well and are willing to produce or host new works then. When a theatre can't be found, look for a stage at a coffee house or a jazz club. They have off-nights, too, when they'd rather fill the place than not.

## *Levels of Production Workshop*

Here are four levels of production workshop for new plays: the public reading, the staged reading, the laboratory production, the full workshop production. To all of these, an audience comes. To the extent that the audience is unconnected with you, a group of strangers or at least not completely made up of your best friends, the experience will be what you require.

## Reading

For a *public reading* the actors usually rehearse several times with a director who chooses a method of staging the reading that is appropriate to the script. Most readings are done on chairs or stools in a semicircle facing the audience. In performance, the director can read stage directions (skipping the unnecessary ones like "to Tim" or "angrily"). If the situation of the play warrants it, the reading might be done with actors sitting on a series of platforms or some alternative visual setup that gives the right feeling for the play. Or chairs or stools can be placed in something other than a line. But you don't have to stretch yourself to come up with fancy arrangements. For a long time, the semicircle of seats has served playwrights well.

Scripts should be uniform, either bound or otherwise securely fastened. In most cases, a simple lighting cue brings performers on stage and takes them off at the end. Costumes should be chosen to make a statement—e.g., either everybody in jeans and black tops, or everybody in black, or everybody in something the character might actually wear, or everybody in just a suggestion of character clothing.

The curtain call is something simple—actors stand and acknowledge the audience. In addition to staging the reading, the director will work on clarifying intentions with the actors so that scenes play well. A reading can be very effective.

## Staged Reading

A staged reading takes longer to rehearse and is the next step up. The director and actors block the play and do the usual work on motivations. They know the lines well enough that they can look at each other when the scene requires or do stage business like lighting cigarettes, bringing food to the table, etc. They will pantomime opening doors when necessary. On stage will be the necessities: furniture, a few platforms, props like tape recorders or cameras that are used by actors. What the audience will see is like rehearsal one third to halfway through the rehearsal period. Again lights can be simple, but actors should enter and exit as the script demands, and they should take a curtain call.

In a good staged reading, the audience forgets that the actors have scripts in hand. Really experienced actors use the scripts for punctuation, as an extension of the body. There is no need, of course, to read most stage directions. Costumes will probably be selected to give an impression of character and style. A playwright can tell a great deal about a play in a staged reading.

## Laboratory Production

If you have the means—the people, the place, the time—and if you believe the script is developed enough to warrant it, you can give a play a laboratory production. This is a simple step up from a staged reading. There are no scripts in hand. The actors have been well rehearsed. There are properties and costumes—which, if not designed for the production, have been carefully selected to give an impression of what the play might be like under full production. The producing group doesn't spend much, if any, money on a laboratory production. If there's an absolutely necessary prop or if a character simply must be wearing chain mail, these budget exceptions are made.

## Workshop Production

Workshop productions can be a little more elaborate than those described above. In some cases, more elaborate lighting effects or full costumes or scenery (rocks, window units, stairways) may be necessary to see if something about the play is working. In truth, I almost never find that plays do any better before an audience when all of this is present than they do in lab conditions. In fact they often do worse because the expectations are greater when so much has been provided. However, if you choose to take a play to full workshop production, it should be a script you feel secure about. Probably it will have been through some or all of the other stages of production.

## *Actors and Directors*

The best actors to get are the best actors. It's hard enough to put a new play before an audience, but the playwright will not want to make the audience try to see through performances to what was intended. The more experienced actors are, the less they have to prove, the better a performance you are likely to get. In any case, you don't want people who are fumbling just to handle props. Experience is a valuable asset here.

Directors who are experienced are preferable too, of course. It's important for a director to be able to put aside ego and just do the play as the playwright wrote it. When the director fixes it too well with the tricks of the trade or masquerades its flaws with flashy staging, the playwright doesn't get to see the simple strengths and weaknesses of the piece. Remember, the production workshop is primarily for the playwright. It's to bring the play forward—simply.

## The Audience

Getting the audience in is crucial. Local newspapers are usually willing to list readings and other workshop productions. Make sure you get the word out in enough time. Many people are, thankfully, interested in new works. At the University of Pittsburgh where I teach, we draw regular lunchtime and evening audiences for new one-acts. Across the street, at Carnegie Mellon University, there is a summer series of new works (full-length) in production—and the ticket price is kept low. The three-hundred-seat theatre is always full to bursting. Several theatre groups in town do new works on a regular basis. And then there is a one-act competition known as the Pittsburgh New Works Festival. The winners are given productions somewhere between lab and workshop levels. The organizers get ten local theatre groups to commit to producing one new winning play each. Over three weeks, all the groups come together to perform in one space. One of the advantages of this method is that playwrights and actors alike become aware of each other and there is cross-fertilization as a result.

There is an audience for new works. With effort, you can establish traditions—where and when you go to see new work performed.

## Feedback from Director and Actors

Directors and actors will usually want to do their best for you. And in my experience they are extremely polite to the playwright. But they are such a valuable source of information that you should encourage them to be honest with you. Where are they having difficulty speaking lines? Where is it difficult to motivate movement? Do they understand what the character is doing? Do they have as much information about the character as they want? Try to strike a balance in rehearsal of being neither intrusive nor self-effacing. Allow the director and actors to do their work, but communicate regularly about what you're seeing and hearing. Rewrite as much as you need to, short of damaging the actor's ability to learn and perform new bits.

## Hearing from the Audience

You can tell something of the audience's reaction simply by watching the audience. There's nothing wrong with stopping there. But I find that letting the audience talk is really helpful to the playwright. Talkback sessions can be held after the performance. It's a good idea for playwright, actors, and director to all be available then. Gather on stage and invite the audience to make comments and ask questions. Relax and ask for an open exchange. It can be very fulfilling as well as informative. The audience, if freed to respond in a talkback session, can offer insights to everyone involved.

With any play, it seems that on some issues, just about everyone agrees: a secondary character is fascinating, for instance; or sympathy generally runs high for the main character; or almost nobody understands what you were getting at in Scene Two. Clear signals. On many issues, there will be no consistency of response, but the way the audience talks about these issues—e.g., whether the relationship being portrayed is a good thing or not, the artificial style of the language, the broadness of the comedy—can help you to make decisions. After a day or two, after the comments sift, you will be able to sense which voices matter and which don't.

## Effect on the Playwright

To give you an idea of the kinds of things that might happen as a result of production workshops with talkback sessions, I'll tell you what did happen in a few specific cases.

(With the exception of *Double Entendre*, which was produced in the first semester, the one in which it was written, these first productions happened in the second term. So in most cases, a month or two went by between writing and seeing.)

Scott Sickles' *Deadlines* went into rehearsal for a laboratory production. The playwright got to as many rehearsals as possible, but his work schedule kept him from being there all the time. When I visited rehearsal, the director told me, "I'm having trouble with how negative Rick is about Kurt's affairs. Why does he care? There has to be a reason for all this bite in his language. I'm wondering if Rick isn't sexually interested in Kurt. Can we play it that way?" I told the director to ask the playwright. He did and the playwright said, "Oh, that's interesting. Try that. It's okay with me." The production went up with an edge of suggestion about a relationship between Rick and Kurt, but without lines to support it.

We talked to the audience about this issue. What did they see as the socio-sexual politics of this office? Some thought it made sense that Rick was interested in Kurt. Others said they *got it* in production, but not from the lines. Most found it made Rick more sympathetic. Was Kurt interested in Rick? That was less clear. Some figured he wasn't at all. As to the question of a past relationship between the two, the script would need references to make that clear.

The playwright was full of energy after the workshop production. He went back to the script and doubled its length. In the later version, he keeps the same characters and adds one more. The play covers two very harried workdays—the second with odd instances of violence erupting in the city and questions of who will report the stories. The playwright makes it clear that Rick and Kurt are former lovers by giving Rick a speech early on to Kurt. Rick recites all the insulting things Kurt has said as he semi-denies the significance of the affair. And then Rick tries to separate himself from Kurt—to fall out of love and just get back to work. Kurt is maddeningly undecided about everything. He has affairs with both men and women, we learn. He has trouble sticking to one plan for any one night. He lets Rick go, but tries to hold onto him too.

In the second scene, Vicky, confused and angry, reports major moves Kurt made on her. Kurt is emotionally dangerous to everyone: he's just helpful and charming enough to keep people from staying angry with him; he's just seductive enough that they always see a possibility in him. But he's confused, too. None of the messages he sends out amount to "No."

The revised version of the play is tougher. There is more at stake. One wonders how Rick can continue to work in a place where he is constantly teased. The ending of the new version shows Rick getting control of himself—as he gets control of other incredible events on that harried workday—and then, he goes home. Kurt comes into his office, assuming he's still there. Kurt sits at his desk and waits for him. We understand there will be more deadlines, once more, tomorrow.

*Double Entendre* by Erin Flynn went before an audience as part of a laboratory production that included several works. The performers were good, especially and importantly the actress who played Fe. This actress is one who has natural appeal in everything I've seen her do. She generally communicates both playfulness and vulnerability. So the audience was very sympathetic to Fe. They made comments more often than they asked questions. Some said, "She is a rape victim." Some said, "None of the men in this script are worth much." And, "I assumed she was talking to a psychiatrist or some kind of therapist. She's in trouble." And, "No, she's everywoman." Nobody suggested changes, but the writer went home to rewrite—mostly to expand this play to include more characters and scenes. The new scenes are extremely effective but, for me, they don't add a new tension to the whole. I prefer the script without them, well-written as they are.

*The Quality of Life* got a laboratory production. It drew large audiences and long discussions. The audience encouraged the writer to expand the play. Their interest in the play was challenging. "Why does Shira have to be pregnant? Why can't she just be troubled? Then you don't have to get into all the abortion arguments." "Isn't she an outsider in her own family? I'd like to see more of her with her mother." "The mother is clear to me. I want to see more of the aunt—Aviva's mother. There's something more going on there." "This family is so Jewish." "Oh, I don't know. It's a lot like my family. We're WASPs." "Get rid of the line about the coat hanger. It's too corny and manipulative." "Couldn't you find a way to bring the boyfriend in and make the whole rejection take place on stage?" And so on.

The end result was that the writer determined she wanted the main focus to remain the keeping and breaking of Jewish traditions as a representation of how Jewish values affect life decisions. She told the audience, "I don't know where this play is going to go. I just know I'm going to work on it. It's going to change a lot and be different from what it is now, but it will still be about Shira's loneliness. She's stuck."

The whole first act of Stan Denman's *The Etiquette of Mourning* (this included a good deal more material than is printed in Chapter 14) went up as a reading—a long one in the lunchtime slot. We used a line of chairs curved slightly for the actors. Bound scripts. Costuming to suggest character. The audience wanted to know when they could see a second act. "Next week?" they joked. "What happens next?" they asked the writer. We took this eagerness to know more as a good sign, especially since the play is not about big doings, but small and subtle changes within a family. People asked many questions about characters and talked openly about their identification with those characters. The playwright talked about how he'd based the people in the play on his family but explained that the characters grew and changed as he wrote—were transformed by the necessities of the story-telling. The audience understood this principle and relieved him of the worry that people would see these as literal copies of real people. He told them about his impetus to write the play. It came of love for—really idolatry for—his grandfather, who was a fascinating, strong, and difficult man. As a child, the writer felt fierce love for this person he grew up to see as human, and flawed. He was intrigued by how this man could be so many things. So upright. So strong. Yet so hard on his daughters. Etc. The audience talked about the universality of funerals and grief, of family dynamics, of families coming together. (In fact, similar dynamics are played out in television series, when there are four or five women from one family as the cast of characters, and in another play about the death of a patriarch, *Daddy's Dyin' (Who's Got the Will?)* by Del Shores. But *The Etiquette of Mourning* came by these relationship dynamics naturally; the motivations are carefully worked out and characters are individualized.)

The writer already had Act II outlined, but he told only part of it to the audience. He went away from the reading fueled with conviction, if not altered ideas.

It's possible to go away from a workshop production clear-headed about changes or uncertain. Sometimes writers wait for another six months before putting things into effect. Anything can happen. But there's no substitute for seeing a play before an audience. That's who it's intended for from the beginning.

## Next Steps

It you're serious enough to write full drafts and put your work before an audience, you probably won't want to stop doing so. In that case, there are a few things you should start to do.

## Formatting Your Scripts

If you plan to send scripts out, you will want to format them as theatres want them and as a major publisher of scripts, Samuel French, Inc., requests. The simplest thing is to write to Samuel French and ask for their "Guidelines on Formatting." The cost is a few dollars. The address is:

> Samuel French, Inc.
> 45 West 25th Street
> New York, NY 10010
> (212) 206–8990

Some of the basic advice is this: put your manuscript— well-typed and clean—in a binder that actually holds it together. Make sure your name, address, and telephone number are on the title page. If you've copyrighted the material, put a "c" circled and the copyright year on the bottom of the title page.

Otherwise, the basics of formatting include: character names in caps, centered. Scene setups are placed halfway across the page, lined up with speaker names. Stage directions are about a quarter of the way across the page, are in parentheses, and are the only thing on the line. If you have lots of stage directions, your script will be expensive to copy.

After the title page and a page of dramatis personae, your script might look like this:

### ACT I

### Scene 1

SETTING: The backyard of a
          house in a working
          class neighborhood
          of Pittsburgh.

TIME:     Midnight on a
          Sunday in June, 1929.

AMY
*(Pacing, muttering to herself)*
Damn. Who does he think he is? Never again. . . .
*(Kicks a trash can. STELLA enters from the house.)*
Shut up. Don't say anything.

STELLA
*(whispering)*
Shhhh. You'll wake the kids.

And so on. You can find similar formatting instructions for screenplays.

Should you copyright your script? Many people do. They feel more comfortable. To get the correct form (Form PA), write to

The Copyright Office
Library of Congress
Washington, DC 20559

But don't rush yourself to send your play anywhere until you've learned more about the field. Gather information about your local theatres and local contests. Getting produced is the first goal. Try your play out before you send it out.

There is sound information on submitting scripts in Louis E. Catron's *Playwriting*. My goal has been to get you started writing and thinking about plays. But if you've discovered you want to go on, you will want to do a number of things; one is continuing to meet with your workshop group. Another is continuing to learn. You will want to read other books on playwriting. You will certainly want to read many plays.

Think of your reading as a way of getting to know other playwrights. Often people ask me to recommend plays. Here is a small, partial list of recent plays by American playwrights. It's just a start.

| | |
|---|---|
| Baitz, Jon Robin | *The Substance of Fire* |
| Blessing, Lee | *A Walk in the Woods* |
| Durang, Christopher | *Sister Mary Ignatius Explains It All for You* |
| Fornes, Maria Irene | *Abingdon Square* |
| | *Fefu and Her Friends* |
| Fuller, Charles | *A Soldier's Play* |
| Guare, John | *House of Blue Leaves* |
| | *Six Degrees of Separation* |
| | *Four Baboons Adoring the Sun* |
| Gurney, A.R. | *The Perfect Party* |
| | *The Cocktail Hour* |
| | *Love Letters* |
| Henley, Beth | *Crimes of the Heart* |
| | *Abundance* |
| Hoffman, William | *As Is* |
| Howe, Tina | *Painting Churches* |
| | *Coastal Disturbances* |
| | *One Shoe Off* |
| Hwang, David | *M. Butterfly* |
| Kramer, Larry | *The Normal Heart* |
| Kushner, Tony | *Angels in America* |
| Lucas, Craig | *Blue Window* |
| | *Prelude to a Kiss* |
| | *Reckless* |
| Mastrosimone, William | *Extremities* |
| McNally, Terence | *Lisbon Traviata* |
| | *Lips Together, Teeth Apart* |
| | *Frankie and Johnny in the Clair de Lune* |
| McPherson, Scott | *Marvin's Room* |
| Mamet, David | *Speed the Plow* |
| | *Oleanna* |
| | *American Buffalo* |
| | *Sexual Perversity in Chicago* |

| | |
|---|---|
| Mann, Emily | *Execution of Justice* |
| Nelson, Richard | *Principia Scriptoria* |
| | *Between East and West* |
| Norman, Marsha | *'Night Mother* |
| Rabe, David | *Hurlyburly* |
| Rudnick, Paul | *I Hate Hamlet* |
| | *Jeffrey* |
| Schenkkan, Robert | *The Kentucky Cycle* |
| Shawn, Wallace | *Aunt Dan and Lemon* |
| Shepard, Sam | *A Lie of the Mind* |
| | *Fool for Love* |
| | *Curse of the Starving Class* |
| | *Tooth of Crime* |
| | *Buried Child* |
| Sherman, Martin | *Bent* |
| Shue, Larry | *The Foreigner* |
| Wasserstein, Wendy | *The Heidi Chronicles* |
| | *The Sisters Rosensweig* |
| Williams, Samm-Art | *Home* |
| Wilson, August | *Ma Rainey's Black Bottom* |
| | *The Piano Lesson* |
| | *Jo Turner's Come and Gone* |
| | *Two Trains Running* |
| | *Fences* |
| Wilson, Lanford | *Talley's Folley* |
| | *Fifth of July* |
| | *Burn This* |
| Wolfe, George C. | *The Colored Museum* |
| | *Spunk* |

I had a class read most of these plays last year and they like the collection.

And go to the theatre. Often. You will no doubt want to order two books, which list contests and theatres. They are

*Dramatists Sourcebook*. Edited by N. Elizabeth Osborn. New York: Theatre Communications Group, 1992–93

*The Playwright's Companion: A Submission Guide to Theatres and Contests in the USA*. Mollie A. Meserve. New York: Feedback Theatrebooks, 1992

You should set up an account with The Drama Book Shop in New York. They carry just about everything you will want to order. They can be reached as follows:

The Drama Book Shop
723 Seventh Ave.
Second Floor
New York, NY
(212) 944–0595

The single most important thing you can do for yourself is to join the Dramatists Guild. The requirement for membership is your having written a play. You will receive monthly newsletters with valuable information about contests and theatres seeking scripts. You will also receive a quarterly journal that not only updates lists of producing organizations, but prints articles of interest as well.

The Dramatists Guild can be reached by mail or phone:

The Dramatists Guild
234 W. 44th Street
New York, NY 10036
(212) 398–9366

### Finding Your Voice

Many theatre practitioners today believe we must do away with "the plodding character psychologies of realism." (Jill Dolan, "Peeling Away the Tropes of Visibility: Lesbian Sexuality and Materialist Performance Practice," *Theatre Topics* [March 1992]: 42) I don't believe we need to throw out realism altogether to get at the challenges of theatre in our time. But I do recognize the call to write about what is significant in fresh and arresting ways. As Strindberg argued in "The Preface to *A Dream Play*," perhaps our waking life is not nearly so real or interesting as the life of imagination, or dream—or in today's terms, possibility.

As you continue to write, you should consider this growing unrest about theatre as it has been. One argument might sound like this: aren't there more important things to write about than ordinary people with their ordinary lives? Aren't there political agendas to take up, injustices to right?

There are. And so the argument continues that theatre must be responsible in addressing the mistakes and evils and false visions of society.

To some extent, the current press toward politically motivated plays (which will hopefully further the rights of women, African Americans, ethnic minorities, gays) comes of society's growing awareness of these issues. Certainly the issues were not a forgotten part of the rhetoric of the 1992 presidential campaign. To some extent, boredom with Broadway, the musical, television, and other commercial ventures that primarily entertain (and often avoid or deny the problems of an ailing society) has made theatre practitioners look for new ways to awaken and disturb people. We live in a multicultural society. There are experiences other than those of the ruling majority. The voices of those experiences must be heard.

The alternative theatre movement of the last quarter century has included ethnic theatre groups—black, Chicano, Puerto Rican; feminist theatre groups; and others. Some groups have come and gone, some remain strong over decades—e.g., La Mama, the Negro Ensemble Company, The Omaha Magic Theatre. Writers of alternative styles have gained, over the years, a wider and wider audience for their works (e.g., Maria Irene Fornes). Even when *groups* have been difficult to sustain (largely for economic reasons), new groups spring up. And when no group is available, solo performers write with great power about their own experiences. (John Leguizamo writes one-person shows [*Mambo Mouth* and *Spic-O-Rama*] about Puerto Rican Americans; Anna Deveare Smith wrote and performed 26 characters, primarily African-American and Jewish, from a Brooklyn neighborhood in *Fires in the Mirror*.)

The possibilities are numerous. If you know you must write for the stage, you will eventually make a decision about what you want to write and whom you want to write for. If you choose to devote yourself to alternative theatre, try to find a group or several groups that share your concerns. Or start a group.

If neither mainstream theatre nor experimental theatre appeals to you, continue to explore. (One former student told me he went on to write formula melodramas for companies that produce them. He is enjoying himself, and there's something to be said for that. Another, years later, began to write children's plays, and he is getting them produced regularly.) If you write consistently and aim for truth to yourself, you will find the right venue, the right audience.

I hope this book has given you a start in finding your voice—so that you will be able to write with energy, passion, and commitment about what matters to you most.